Paleonutrition

PALEONUTRITION

Mark Q. Sutton,

Kristin D. Sobolik,

and Jill K. Gardner

The University of Arizona Press   Tucson

The University of Arizona Press
© 2010 The Arizona Board of Regents
All rights reserved

www.uapress.arizona.edu

Library of Congress Cataloging-in-Publication Data

Sutton, Mark Q.
    Paleonutrition / Mark Q. Sutton, Kristin D. Sobolik, and Jill K. Gardner.
        p.   cm.
    Includes bibliographical references and index.
    ISBN 978-0-8165-2794-6 (cloth : alk. paper)
    1. Prehistoric peoples—Food.   2. Human remains (Archaeology).
3. Nutritional anthropology.   I. Sobolik, Kristin D. (Kristin Dee)
II. Gardner, Jill K.   III. Title.
    GN799.F6S88   2010
    306.4'613—dc22   2009034555

Manufactured in the United States of America on acid-free, archival-
quality paper containing a minimum of 30% postconsumer waste and
processed chlorine free.

15   14   13   12   11   10   6   5   4   3   2   1

Contents

Illustrations

Figures

Tables

Acknowledgments

This book was first undertaken more than a decade ago and evolved through what seems to be a common process of fits and starts. In finally completing it, we owe gratitude to the prodding and contributions of many of our colleagues, particularly Dena F. Dincauze, Linda Scott Cummings, Rebecca S. Orfila, and Jerry Schaefer. The work on this book done by MQS was supported by a sabbatical and a University Research Council grant from California State University, Bakersfield (CSUB). The work done by KDS was supported by a sabbatical and a Summer Faculty Grant from the University of Maine.

We also greatly appreciate the contributions of a number of other people who were instrumental in the completion of this book. These include Linda Scott Cummings of PaleoResearch Laboratory, Golden Colorado; Lee Cronk at Rutgers University for providing an excellent research project on the Mukogodo "back in the day"; Clark Spencer Larsen at Ohio State University and Robert M. Yohe II at CSUB for photograph permissions; Dr. Jerry Woolf and Dr. Oscar W. Rico for graciously assisting with the X-rays in figures 2.1 and 2.4; Gina Bahr and Janet Gonzales at the CSUB Walter Stiern Library, who were invaluable in obtaining the many books and articles we ordered through interlibrary loan; and Matthew Des Lauriers (now a professor at CSU, Northridge), who assisted with some of the references.

Statistical Research, Inc., generously supported the production of this book through a grant to the University of Arizona Press. We are very grateful for their trust in the product.

Finally, we thank Allyson Carter of the University of Arizona Press for her support of this project and the anonymous reviewers for their much-appreciated comments and suggestions. These comments made the book much better; however, we retain responsibility for any errors and omissions.

Paleonutrition

CHAPTER 1

Introduction

PALEONUTRITION IS THE ANALYSIS of human prehistoric diet and the interpretation of dietary intake in relation to health and nutrition. In essence, paleonutrition assesses prehistoric diets to determine the biological and cultural implications for individuals as well as the population as a whole, placing archaeological interpretations into an anthropological context (Sobolik 1994a). Although food is obtained through diverse and innovative means from society to society, the acquisition of food is one of the fundamental biological needs of humans and is the driving force of human evolution. It is this very diversity that interests anthropologists as we try to understand and explain our past so that we can predict and focus on our future. This latter goal is important as "much of our future survival may depend on our ability to recognize the limits of human responses and coping mechanisms, especially in adverse and extreme conditions of environmental catastrophe, malnutrition and famine, and rapidly changing ecological, political, and economic conditions" (Martin et al. 1991:1).

Culture is constantly in flux due to various internal and external stimuli, including environmental and climatic shifts, population aggregation and dispersal, and political and economic turmoil and change (Sobolik 1994a; Gardner 2007; Sutton and Anderson 2010). Changes in the distribution and availability of food resources, whether due to environmental changes, surpluses or famine, reallocation or redistribution of resources, and/or political or economic changes, can cause stressful and potentially unstable times for humans. Understanding how humans respond biologically and culturally to these changes is of critical importance. Thus, the study of paleonutrition is an integral component of the analysis of food acquisition and its role in past human adaptation. Without a firm understanding of paleonutrition, human response to changes in food resources in diverse societies and environments through space and time cannot be fully discerned.

The goals of this book are to describe the nature of paleonutrition studies, review the history of paleonutrition research, discuss methodological issues on the reconstruction of prehistoric diet, review theoretical frameworks frequently used in paleonutrition research, and showcase comprehensive examples in which paleonutritional analyses have been successfully conducted on prehistoric individuals, groups, and/or populations. It is hoped that this book will help the reader to understand the past and future of paleonutrition research, as well as to recognize the importance of an integrative framework with regard to anthropological diet, health, and nutritional assessments. While focused on the study of prehistoric populations, paleonutrition research can also benefit from the study of contemporary populations, as archaeology does, in general, from ethnoarchaeological studies (see Case Study 2 in chap. 6).

The first book specifically addressing paleonutrition was written by Elizabeth Wing and Antoinette Brown in 1979 (Wing and Brown 1979) and arose from the interest generated by a symposium entitled "Paleonutrition: The Reconstruction of Diet from Archaeological Evidence" at the 1976 annual meeting of the Society for American Archaeology. Although they did not precisely define paleonutrition, Wing and Brown observed that the most important component of understanding and analyzing prehistoric lifeways was ascertaining the most basic aspect of paleonutrition, that being diet and subsistence. They discussed the importance of an interdisciplinary approach to dietary research, in which a number of disciplines, techniques, and theories from other sciences are used. The purpose of their book was to present "diverse research techniques that may provide insight into prehistoric foodways" (Wing and Brown 1979:1) wherein an integrative approach between faunal, botanical, and human remains, as well as cultural data, was advocated for a coordinated understanding of prehistoric lifeways. Wing and Brown focused on the nutritional requirements necessary for a healthy existence and applied those requirements to the analysis of archaeologically recovered food remains. Diverse food procurement patterns observed prehistorically were illustrated and the importance of understanding cultural attitudes to subsistence was discussed, with the realization that ascertaining cultural food values from archaeological contexts is limited.

The Wing and Brown volume is actually a synthesis of nutritional anthropology and paleonutrition, in which the importance of cultural ideology surrounding food and the importance of protein metabolism, nutritional requirements, amino acid intake, and metabolic disturbances were discussed and given as much importance as the recovery, identification, analysis, and interpretation of food remains from archaeological sites. Their book only briefly touched upon problems in the identification and interpretation of cultural ideological and nutritionally based analyses in a prehistoric context. Further, while Wing and Brown discussed the identification and analysis of modern cultural subgroups within a larger population context, they did not describe how to accomplish that with archaeological remains.

The quest for small-group and individual diet, as opposed to an overly simplified dietary analysis of an entire population, is a more recent goal of paleonutritional research. In fact, in a later discussion, Wing (1994:315) stated that "to truly approach issues of paleonutrition . . . we must address many of the details of diet and health that we take for granted in our daily lives; how food is distributed among members of a family and within the community and whether differential access to food is related to status, gender, or age differences." A goal of the current volume is to showcase examples in which paleonutritional assessments of small groups have been attempted.

After Wing and Brown (1979), the next two books on paleonutrition were edited volumes in which various authors reviewed their research on paleonutrition in general (Gilbert and Mielke 1985; Sobolik 1994c). The first book (Gilbert and Mielke 1985) included discussions on a number of issues, encompassing various archaeological techniques used to reconstruct prehistoric diet, ranging from the preservation and interpretation of archaeologically derived plant and animal remains and paleofeces to the importance of ethnographic modeling for dietary reconstruction and concluding with information gained from human skeletal material through paleopathology, demography, and developmental disturbances. Gilbert and Mielke (1985:xiv) stated that their volume provided archaeologists and students with "a ready reference in which [to] find suggestions and possible solutions to problems encountered in the reconstruction of the dietary patterns of prehistoric people." They succeeded in their goal; the book is an excellent reference base for researchers looking at alternative ways to analyze dietary materials. The most applicable research tools to analyze prehistoric diet and health were discussed, offering the reader a good overview of the subject and ways in which researchers in the field analyze dietary and health remains from a prehistoric context.

In 1993, Southern Illinois University sponsored a conference on paleonutrition, led by Kristin Sobolik. At that conference, a number of researchers presented their paleonutrition studies within specific disciplines, including paleoethnobotany, zooarchaeology, bioarchaeology, and paleofecal (or coprolite) analysis. The papers presented at that conference were published (Sobolik 1994c), providing an important update on paleonutritional studies. Within that volume, Sobolik (1994a) discussed the importance of understanding the taphonomy of biological assemblages. Paleoethnobotanical and zooarchaeological assemblages were labeled "indirect" sources of dietary information (Sutton 1994), as botanical and faunal remains from archaeological sites can be deposited through a number of processes and potential nonhuman agents. It was made clear that some of the remains recovered from archaeological sites are most likely human dietary debris, but also that some remains may be debris from other human activities, such as the manufacture of clothing, the use of firewood, the construction of shelter, and the manufacture and use of tools. It was further noted that some remains may be the result of nonhuman activity, such as rodents and carnivores. Bioarchaeological and paleofecal studies were labeled "direct" indicators of dietary intake because human skeletal remains represent a lifetime accumulation of dietary information and paleofeces represent the undigested remains of purposeful consumption. Emphasis was placed on the positive aspects and limitations of each data set to paleonutritional research and how, through the integration of a variety of disciplinary analyses, a more complete picture of the paleonutrition of a population or group of people could be ascertained.

While the series of articles in that volume (Sobolik 1994c) emphasized the importance of integrative research, the relevance of dietary assessments using singular data sets was also incorporated. Most of the authors attempted to integrate two or more dietary data sets for a more comprehensive paleonutritional assessment; however, many of these analyses revealed the analytical problems inherent in such an integration, as each discipline developed as a separate field and has diverse methods of analysis. For example, Crane and Carr (1994) analyzed botanical and faunal remains from Cerros, a Preclassic Maya site in Belize. In their attempt to integrate diverse data sets into a more comprehensive analysis, they realized that only the measure of ubiquity could be used to quantify the dietary data base, as each data set and associated discipline used different quantitative methods of analysis. The ubiquity measure of quantification inherently results in a loss of information, but it was the only comparative method available at that time to coordinate the analysis.

The conclusions of the 1993 conference and of the volume (Sobolik 1994c) revolved around the need for archaeologists to attempt to reconstruct paleonutrition at an individual or small-group level, in addition to the population level, as prehistoric populations were made up of many smaller groups and individuals who most likely had differential access to food resources that affected their health and nutrition. The problematic aspects of obtaining dietary information at the individual and small-group level from archaeological contexts are numerous; therefore, paleonutritional reconstructions at the population level continue to be more frequent.

The purpose of the present volume is to take reviews of paleonutritional analyses and interpretations one step further. Even given the current limitations in our ability to reconstruct individual and small-group behaviors, a number of paleonutrition studies have been successful at such interpretations and several are showcased herein. The most recent and innovative methods and techniques used to reconstruct prehistoric diet are discussed and assessed, as well as the basic ways in which paleonutrition data are recovered, analyzed, and interpreted. Of particular importance is the role that taphonomy plays in the recovery and analysis of dietary remains. Recent studies on taphonomy are discussed to illustrate the primary importance of site formation processes on dietary remains, as well as to demonstrate taphonomic reconstructions that can be conducted in any site environment to help understand specific site formation processes on a more local scale. Many of the discussions about the history of the field and about taphonomy in general are taken from the recent book on archaeobiology by Sobolik (2003).

History of Research

Interdisciplinary archaeological research is not a recent phenomenon. Early on, a few archaeologists conducted such integrative research in the quest for a better understanding of the patterns of human lifeways.

For example, Rafael Pumpelly (1908) conducted archaeological research in the Middle East that involved a number of scientists from diverse disciplines (zoology, chemistry, human paleontology, botany, and geomorphology), and Robert Braidwood led what was undoubtedly the first specifically integrative, long-term archaeological project on the origins of food production in the Near East (Braidwood and Braidwood 1950; Braidwood 1952). Working in Tamaulipas and the Tehuacan Valley of Mexico, Richard MacNeish (1958, 1964, 1967) directed interdisciplinary teams of geomorphologists, geneticists, botanists, biologists, and zoologists, also on the origins of agriculture. Additional large-scale, integrative research was conducted in Peru as well (Izumi and Sono 1963; Izumi and Terada 1972). Such integrative, interdisciplinary research was being carried out by only a few archaeologists, and the incorporation of dietary analysis into a more comprehensive statement of prehistoric diet, health, and nutrition was not routinely performed.

The most significant aspect in the development of paleonutrition was the concept of the "new archaeology" (Binford 1962, 1968) and the methodological and theoretical changes it engendered. Tenets of the new archaeology included a cultural evolutionary perspective, systemic theory as it applied to culture and society, and hypothesis testing using deductive reasoning. Ideas related to the new archaeology had previously been proposed as the conjunctive approach (Taylor 1948), an approach that included the same basic ideas and issues as the new archaeology but did not propose a cultural evolutionary perspective.

Later, Flannery (1968) and Clarke (1968) focused on the importance of systems theory to the interpretation of archaeological remains, from which the concept of cultural ecology, as defined by Steward (1955), emerged. Understanding the cultural ecology of prehistoric populations and how humans, as biological organisms, fit into the ecological scheme of nature and the environment became an important step for paleonutritional research. Archaeologists began to systematically recover biological remains from archaeological sites, as questions revolving around diet, paleoenvironment, and ecology developed. Along with an increase in the recovery of biological remains, due in part to methodological advances such as fine-screening and flotation, came an increase in the quality of analyses. This made it possible to integrate analyses of biological remains at an intersite or regional level.

Although cultural ecology and the analysis of biological remains first became a focus for archaeologists when the age of new archaeology was dawning, some excellent earlier studies of human cultural patterns evidenced through biological remains set the stage for later systemic analyses. With a few exceptions, as discussed above, these earlier studies were not integrated with the data provided by other assemblages and were mainly conducted by specialists. Using assemblages from archaeological sites, paleoethnobotanists or botanists analyzed the plant remains, zooarchaeologists or zoologists examined the animal remains, and bioarchaeologists, biologists, or human anatomists evaluated human skeletal remains. These earlier analyses were usually not integrated into a cohesive whole, as is prevalent in paleonutrition studies conducted today.

A major goal in contemporary paleonutrition research is to integrate data sets from a diversity of disciplines for overall analysis and interpretation, although this is less common than it should be. A history of each discipline related to paleonutrition is discussed separately below, including paleoethnobotanical, zooarchaeological, bioarchaeological, and paleofecal analyses. The historical aspects of such studies are reviewed here, with the understanding that many subdisciplines important for paleonutrition research have developed from these main disciplines and that most recent research involves an integration and/or evolution of these disciplines.

Paleoethnobotany

Paleoethnobotany is the study of the interaction of humans and plants in their environment or, as defined by Renfrew (1973), the study of plants used and/or cultivated by prehistoric humans that have survived in archaeological contexts. Another frequently used term is *archaeobotany*, defined by Ford (1979) as the collection and identification of botanical remains from archaeological sites. Old World archaeologists commonly use the term *archaeobotany* (van Zeist et al. 1991; Miller 1995), whereas New World archaeologists generally use the term *paleoethnobotany*, which entails the collection, identification, analysis, and interpretation of plant materials recovered from prehistoric sites (Hastorf 1999). The inherent difference in these two definitions is that archaeobotany refers purely to the technical side of such research whereas paleoethnobotany refers to the scientific and interpretive arena (Ford 1979).

Prior to the twentieth century, the few paleoethnobotanical studies conducted were written mainly by botanists or people interested in natural history. For example, Kunth (1826) analyzed desiccated plant remains found in ancient Egyptian tombs, Heer (1872) studied plant remains from middens and houses of waterlogged villages in Switzerland, Saffray (1876) analyzed botanical remains from the stomach contents of a Peruvian mummy, and a number of researchers focused on the origin of Old World cultivated plants (de Candolle 1884; Buschan 1895; Neuweiler 1905).

An initial advance in paleoethnobotanical work occurred at the World's Fair in Chicago in 1893. Part of the exhibit at the World's Fair focused on the lifestyles of North American Indians. Many exhibits showed different segments of Indian life, including their use of plants native to the New World. It was this event that led Harshberger (1896) to examine some dried plant materials from caves in Colorado so that the materials could be placed on display. Through that study, he developed the idea of using the term *ethnobotany* for this type of research. After the Chicago World's Fair, there was renewed interest in ethnobotany, which was then being conducted mainly by museums, governmental agencies (e.g., the U.S. National Herbarium and the U.S. Department of Agriculture), and universities. The first Ph.D. in ethnobotany was awarded by the University of Chicago to David P. Barrows (1900) for his work on the ethnobotany of the Cahuilla Indians of southern California. Barrows stressed that ethnobotanical studies must go beyond the applied or economic value of plants and focus also on the role plants play in the social, religious, and folklore practices of particular groups.

Questions surrounding the origin of cultivated plants in the Old World pushed paleoethnobotanical research in that area of the world (Schiemann 1951; Helbaek 1960; Renfrew 1969; van Zeist 1988; Hillman and Davies 1990; Zeder et al. 2006), while research on Native American plant use was the stimulus for North American studies. In the early 1900s, the new and emerging field of anthropology began training ethnologists to work with Native Americans on reservations and to record the information that was still available about their past culture and lifeways. When early botanists studied North American Indians, their approach was mostly utilitarian; they wanted to record information about plants and how those plants could be used in the modern world. On the other hand, early ethnologists collected different types of ethnobotanical data from the people they studied, focusing on their point of view about the plants they used and how these plants fit into their view of the universe.

In his study of plant use by the Plains and Prairie Indian tribes, Gilmore (1919) was the first to note that even though most of these tribes were hunter-gatherers, their use of wild plants led to considerable modification of the environment. For example, he noted that groups often introduced plants from one region to another, eliminated certain weedy plants through burning, and encouraged certain plants to grow by increasing the available quantity of plant products (e.g., seeds and tubers).

The 1930s marked a change for the future of ethnobotany; a series of events occurred at some important universities that recognized it as a worthy field of study. From 1930 to the 1950s, Edward Castetter established a graduate program in ethnobotany within the Department of Biology at the University of New Mexico. This was an important event because Castetter and his students began to record the ethnobotany of the Indians still living in the Southwest. In the late 1930s, R. E. Schultes established a program in modern ethnobotany at Harvard University, with the main emphasis on the search for new plants with medicinal merit. These efforts by Schultes and his students tended to focus mainly on recording the ethnobotany of Indians living in Central and South America.

In the early 1930s, the University of Michigan created the Ethnobotanical Laboratory as part of the Museum of Anthropology. Melvin Gilmore, and later Volney Jones, headed these programs, which focused mainly on plant remains from archaeological sites. In a lecture at the meeting of the American Association for the Advancement of Science in 1931, Gilmore (1932) detailed the many aspects of his research and provided some important clues regarding how he planned to analyze plant remains. He also requested that people save plant remains from archaeological sites and send them to him for analysis. Once the word of Gilmore's request spread, material from all over North America began to arrive at his lab for analysis. In most cases, he was permitted to keep the materials, greatly expanding the paleoethnobotanical holdings of the museum. He firmly believed that the geographical influences and physical environment encompassing human life in a given region must profoundly impact human habits and inherited tendencies in the mental and material cultures of human groups. Unless the physical environment within which a complex of cultural traits derives could be visualized, it could never be understood how and why that complex resulted in a particular pattern.

Despite Gilmore's contributions, however, it is Volney Jones who is considered to be the father of modern ethnobotany. Jones, who was Gilmore's successor in the Ethnobotanical Laboratory, headed the lab for more than twenty-five years and analyzed a large number of botanical debris from sites in the eastern and midwestern United States during the 1940s and 1950s. The first major ethnobotanical study was from the Newt Kash Hollow site in Kentucky (Jones 1936). In this research, Jones dealt with the remains of an early Woodland (ca. 700 B.C.) culture and reported at least eight plants that were native to North America and that he felt were cultivated or semicultivated. He was the first to report the physical evidence of tobacco use in a prehistoric site from the early Woodland period, and he set the standard for explaining early eastern woodland subsistence patterns for years to come.

Other important questions regarding paleoethnobotany have revolved around the origins of agriculture, which plants were domesticated, descriptions of paleoenvironments, and how humans used the landscape. With the advent of the new archaeology, it became increasingly important to recover and save plant remains from archaeological sites due to their importance as a data set for testing hypotheses. Other significant areas of research revolved around methodological issues: how various plant parts should be recovered from sites, how recovered materials should be quantified, and how diverse data sets should be compared. Paleoethnobotanists dealt with numerous issues, from the technical aspects of recovery to the identification and interpretation of plant remains, including their importance in answering broad-scale questions (Hastorf 1999).

Today, paleoethnobotany encompasses many subfields, divided into two basic groups: analyses of macrobotanical remains (i.e., seeds, nuts, fruits, fiber, wood, and charcoal) and analyses of microbotanical remains (i.e., pollen, phytoliths, and microscopic fiber particles). The interpretation of macrobotanical remains from archaeological sites provides information on a number of issues, including the dietary practices of a prehistoric population. If such remains are preserved at a site and consistent sampling of all levels and areas is provided, a wide array of dietary information can be ascertained. The information can then be compared with other botanical data from nearby sites to reveal the entire botanical diet of a population, changes in dietary practices through time, possible differences in status areas of a site or a region, and differential environmental selection procedures of a population in a specific area. The analysis of seed, nut, fruit, and fiber remains can also determine dietary plant selectivity, seasonality of site occupation, and possible storage practices that could influence nutrition during seasons that provide little plant variety to the diet.

Information from flotation samples can be employed to determine dietary practices that would not otherwise be revealed, as flotation can be used to recover tiny seeds, bones, and charcoal. Flotation is particularly useful at archaeological sites in which botanical remains are infrequent or not well preserved. Flotation samples can be taken at every level and area of a site, as well as from features, pits, and/or hearth fill. Such samples may assist in determining botanical storage practices, special uses of botanical materials, or the differential use of cooking practices of indoor and outdoor fires. While the analysis of charcoal does not directly indicate diet and nutrition, such analyses may indicate resource selectivity of specific areas (but see Wright 2003).

The analysis of pollen microremains from archaeological sites began around the time that paleoethnobotanical studies were being initiated, although the analysis of phytolith and calcium oxalate microremains has only recently been emphasized (Piperno 1988, 2006a; Pearsall 1988). These microremains can determine aspects of prehistoric diet and nutrition that are not obtainable from analyses of macroremains, as they represent different parts of a plant that may be differentially used or preserved. Pollen and phytolith analyses can also complement each other; in many situations, phytoliths preserve where pollen does not, and phytoliths can identify some plants to a higher taxonomic level than pollen, such as the Poaceae (grass) family (Piperno 1988).

Paleoethnobotanical remains are a significant aspect in determining paleonutrition, particularly because plants often represent the dietary staples for some populations, as humans are "completely dependent on plants either directly or indirectly" (Smith 1985:97). As such, the analysis of botanical remains from archaeological sites is necessary to recognize the importance of plants to the diet and nutrition of a given population.

Zooarchaeology

Zooarchaeology is the study and interpretation of animal remains from archaeological sites. Robison (1978) divided the history of the discipline of zooarchaeology into three main time periods: Formative, Systematization, and Integration. The Formative period lasted from approximately 1880 to 1950 and encompassed a time when archaeologists were not systematically collecting faunal material from sites. Any analysis performed on such remains tended to be conducted by zoologists who were interested in the material for biological and environmental reconstruction, rather than for archaeological purposes. Thus, zooarchaeological research tended to be reported in biological publications, whereas archaeologists—when interested—tended to focus on one or two species, modified bone tools, or remains associated with human burials. Early studies were primarily descriptive in nature, although some studies foreshadowed the types of questions and directions of study zooarchaeologists would take in the future. Such early work includes the analysis of vertebrates and invertebrates from a Maine shell midden site that included dietary hypotheses on the importance of different species based on their abundance (Loomis and Young 1912) and research on marine shells from Arizona pueblos to determine trade routes (Fewkes 1896).

In the Systematization period (ca. 1950 to 1960), archaeologists started looking at faunal remains as a means toward obtaining information on cultural behavior and adaptations, although methodological and theoretical techniques were just beginning to be implemented. In fact, the most frequently cited article in zooarchaeological literature during this time (White 1953) introduced the quantitative concept of minimum number of individuals (MNI). In addition, Lawrence (1957) urged analysts to augment their focus on identification to include interpretation so that meaningful and stimulating information could be obtained from faunal remains. During this period, the results of early long-term, large-scale, integrative archaeological studies were being realized (i.e., Izumi and Sono 1963; Braidwood and Braidwood 1982) and the importance of faunal remains to archaeological interpretations was recognized by the scientific community, resulting in regular collection of faunal remains from most deposits.

During this time, zooarchaeology specialists started collecting and analyzing samples. These early specialists included T. H. White, John

Guilday, and Paul Parmalee (University of Tennessee), Elizabeth Wing (Florida Museum of Natural History), and Stanley Olsen (University of Arizona), who began to train students as zooarchaeologists. These specialists significantly advanced zooarchaeological studies and allowed archaeologists to realize the amount of information that could be gained through the analysis of faunal material. The collections of faunal remains from excavations began to increase and analyses started to appear in archaeological reports, although mainly as appendices. Zooarchaeology eventually became a recognized and important field within archaeology.

All of these ideas came together during the Integration period, from the 1960s to the present, as the concept of the new archaeology was being touted. Cultural ecology and environmental anthropology are the main themes of many analyses conducted today as zooarchaeologists integrate their research with other disciplines within archaeology. The analysis of the faunal remains from a number of sites of the Riverton Culture (Winters 1969) has been cited as the first significant zooarchaeological analysis of the new archaeology era. Another important analysis was conducted by Smith (1975) on the adaptation to the Mississippi area. He analyzed the remains from different site types—including uplands, lowlands, and swamps—and observed that the prehistoric peoples in this region tended to have base camps located on the ecotone between different microenvironmental areas. They would then exploit different environments, depending upon season and abundance of resources that each area could provide.

Today, a number of key issues are addressed by zooarchaeologists. The first issue is taphonomy, which encompasses site formation processes, middle-range research, preservation and modification of site artifacts and ecofacts, and determination of cultural and noncultural site components. Next is methodology, encompassing quantification, recovery, identification, and sampling. Third is anthropology, encompassing the relationship between humans and the environment, domestication of animals (which also has a strong biological component), subsistence strategies, human evolution, and human cultural lifeways. Lastly, biology encompasses paleoenvironmental reconstruction and the ecology and morphology of various animal species (Reitz and Wing 1999).

As with paleoethnobotany, zooarchaeology covers a wide variety of subfields and many analysts become skilled in the identification of particular faunal categories (i.e., invertebrates, fish, birds, or domesticated animals). Although gaining skill in faunal identification is one important aspect of zooarchaeology, researchers have become increasingly concerned with understanding and controlling problems inherent in faunal analyses.

Depending upon excavation procedures, zooarchaeological materials can provide the same basic types of information as can paleoethnobotanical remains. In many archaeological sites, faunal materials are often better preserved than botanical remains, reducing problems of recovery. Distribution of faunal remains can be used to determine changes in dietary practices through time, geographical differences in animal utilization, and possible status differences in the people consuming the animals. Faunal remains also indicate major types of hunting practices used and primary habitats exploited, both of which affect nutritional intake.

Bioarchaeology

Bioarchaeology, the analysis of human skeletal remains, is a subdivision of physical (or biological) anthropology. Johann Blumenbach is considered the father of biological anthropology, mainly for his work on cranial morphological variation to determine various races of modern humans. Earnest Hooton and Aleš Hrdlička are considered the two main originators of American biological anthropology (Brace 1982). Hooton was a professor and researcher at Harvard University for over four decades and educated most of the biological anthropologists that were hired by universities and colleges in the middle part of the twentieth century. Most biological anthropologists practicing in America today can trace their academic lineage back to Hooton. Hrdlička created the *American Journal of Physical Anthropology*, the premier journal for biological anthropologists, and founded the American Association of Physical Anthropologists. Of interest, however, is that Hrdlička, a renowned Francophile, considered Paul Broca to be the principal founder of biological anthropology and France to be the mother country of that science (Brace 1982; Buikstra and Beck 2006).

As a form of scientific inquiry, bioarchaeology arose out of early interest in understanding and quantifying morphological variation in modern human populations or racial groups, and in understanding the position of modern humans in relationship to early fossil forms, such as *Homo erectus* and Neanderthals, and to other primates (Armelagos et al. 1982). Bioarchaeologists today are concerned with elucidating processual interpretations for understanding morphological variations in humans and human ancestors, in lieu of more historically oriented typological models that tend to focus purely on description rather than attempting to understand and explain the process (Armelagos et al. 1982).

Recording and describing human morphological variation in an attempt to discern discrete biological units (i.e., racial groups) within human populations was the intent of the earliest bioarchaeological studies from the late eighteenth century through the present. Much of this work has a strong element of biological determinism. A great deal of effort was also expended in an attempt to discern and standardize morphological measurements (anthropometry) that would be the most useful for the analysis of biological affinity in human populations. Hrdlička was a proponent of standardizing anthropometric measurements (Stewart 1947), with particular emphasis on craniometry, measurements of the crania, and the cranial index to determine biological affinity, measurement devices that are still used today.

Blumenbach (1969) used his collection of 82 crania to describe his earliest views on racial classification and human variation. In his analysis of prehistoric human skeletal material, Broca (1871, 1875) developed techniques of anthropometric craniometry still used today. Other early studies include the work by Hooton (1930) on skeletal analyses of 1,254 individuals excavated from Pecos Pueblo in the southwestern United States. Hooton (1930) believed that the Pecos Pueblo individuals could be racially typed and the racial history of the population understood through analysis of the individuals.

Using the cephalic index of Jewish and Sicilian immigrants in the United States and comparing the results to populations in their homeland, Boas (1912) argued against the use of craniometry to determine and describe racial differences due to the instability of the cephalic index for such determinations. Virchow (1896) also argued against the use of cranial measurements to determine racial affinity. Both arguments were either ignored or attacked by earlier biological anthropologists (Radosavljevich 1911; Shapiro 1959).

Other bioarchaeologists, however, started to become interested in a more holistic approach to skeletal morphological measurements and began looking at functional craniology in which it was believed that there were significant environmental and developmental processes that affect bone and cranial growth, processes other than pure racial identity or grouping (Moss and Young 1960; Moss 1972; Hylander 1975; Carlson and Van Gerven 1979). This biocultural approach was used with increasing frequency by bioarchaeologists, such as Angel (1969) on morphological and morbidity changes in populations from classical Greece, Buikstra (1977) on prehistoric populations in the lower Illinois River Valley, and Martin et al. (1991) on populations from Black Mesa in the American Southwest.

Paleopathology

Paleopathology is the analysis of disease that manifests itself on bone (Ubelaker 1982). Much of the information obtained by paleonutritionists from human remains is derived through the study of paleopathology. This is due to the fact that many pathologies are caused by dietary stress or inadequacies and health problems, a core data set for paleonutritional analyses. The most frequently used paleopathological assessments for paleonutritional analyses involve growth-arrest lines, such as linear enamel hypoplasia and Harris lines on long bones; evidence of anemia through porotic hyperostosis and cribra orbitalia; and evidence of infections through periostitis and osteomyelitis.

The earliest paleopathological reports were of nonhuman animal remains, such as the pathology of a femur from an extinct cave bear in France (Esper 1774), healed trauma from a fossil hyena occipital (Goldfuss 1810), pathologies from various vertebrate species found in caves in Belgium (Schmerling 1835), and a summary of pathological conditions observed on fossil vertebrate species (Mayer 1854). Observations of human paleopathology did not begin in earnest until late in the nineteenth century since bioarchaeologists were focused on morphological measurements, rather than pathological assessments, which would have required discussions of function and causes of such stress indicators. One of the earliest studies was by Meigs (1857:45) on two Hindu crania, one exhibiting syphilitic ulcers and the other displaying "cicatrized fracture and depression of the right frontal malar and superior maxillary bones." Wyman (1868) observed periosteal lesions and dental anomalies in Polynesian skulls. The first discussion on prehistoric human disease was presented by Jones (1876) on archaeological human remains from the eastern United States. Interest in paleopathology increased with studies of the origin of diseases, such as syphilis (Langdon 1881; Putnam 1884; Whitney 1886); other "anomalies" (Hrdlička 1910, 1927, 1941); and paleopathology syntheses (Williams 1929; Moodie 1931).

Paleopathology today involves scientific research to increase accuracy in disease diagnosis and to place disease within a biocultural context (Ubelaker 1982). For example, the etiology of porotic hyperostosis was not well understood by past researchers. Hooton (1930:316) termed the porotic hyperostosis he observed on crania from Pecos Pueblo as "symmetrical osteoporosis" and a "mysterious disease." More recent research by paleopathologists, however, indicates that porotic hyperostosis is caused by a number of biocultural processes, the central of which is iron-deficiency anemia (El-Najjar et al. 1976; Mensforth et al. 1978; Walker 1985). Porotic hyperostosis is exhibited by expansion of the diploe (the central layer of the bones of the skull) and cranial lesions and pitting on the surface of frontal, parietal, and occipital bones as well as in the eye orbits (called cribra orbitalia). The etiologies of cribra orbitalia and porotic hyperostosis are the same, so some researchers do not record these pathologies as separate abnormalities, although cribra orbitalia seems to be an early expression of anemia and porotic hyperostosis a more severe reflection (Lallo et al. 1977) (see further discussion of porotic hyperostosis and cribra orbitalia in chap. 2).

Paleofecal Studies

Paleofeces are the fecal remains of prehistoric humans. In some instances, paleofeces have been referred to as coprolites, an often misapplied term. Coprolites, Greek for *copros* (dung) and *lithos* (stones), technically refer to fossilized fecal material, usually from prehistoric or extinct animals. Paleofeces, however, refer to desiccated prehistoric fecal remains that are not fossilized. All of the human feces analyzed to date have technically been paleofeces, not coprolites, although the term coprolite is prevalent in the literature.

In the past, paleofecal studies have been considered a subdivision of paleoethnobotany. However, paleofeces contain a wide variety of dietary constituents, including seeds, fiber, hulls, pollen, phytoliths, parasites, feathers, fur, bones, scales, insect remains, and chemical constituents. Therefore, paleofecal analyses involve expertise in a number of disciplines and should not be placed under the heading of a single discipline.

Paleofeces are a unique resource for analyzing paleonutrition because they offer direct insight into prehistoric diet and, in some cases, health. The constituents of paleofeces are mostly the remains of intentionally consumed food items, with the possible exception of wind-blown pollen contaminants and feces-thriving insects. Parasites are also found in paleofeces and reflect the parasitic load of the individual, and potentially the load of the population, therefore providing direct health data rather than dietary data. Proteins and DNA have also been identified from paleofeces, providing a broader range of ingested plants and animals as well as providing direct evidence of the depositor (Sutton et al. 1996; Poinar et al. 2001), as intestinal luminal cells are sloughed off during fecal processing.

The potential of human paleofeces as dietary indicators was initially realized by Harshberger (1896). The first analysis of paleofecal material, however, was not conducted until after the beginning of the twentieth century. These initial studies were conducted by Smith and Jones (1910a,b), who examined the dried fecal remains from Nubian mummies, and by Young (1910) and Loud and Harrington (1929) on North American cave material. Early paleofecal analyses were also performed on samples from Danger Cave (Jennings 1957), sites in Tamaulipas, Mexico (MacNeish 1958), caves in eastern Kentucky (Webb and Baby 1957), and stomach and colon contents from a mummy (Saffray 1876; Wakefield and Dellinger 1936). The processing techniques for these early analyses consisted of either cutting open the dry samples and observing large, visible contents or grinding the samples through screens, a process that resulted in much damage to the constituents.

Improved techniques for analyzing paleofeces were developed by Callen and Cameron (1960), refining a technique developed by Benninghoff (1947) for rehydrating herbarium specimens and van Cleave and Ross (1947) for rehydrating zoological specimens. These techniques involved rehydrating the paleofecal sample in a solution of trisodium phosphate, a mild detergent, to gently break apart the materials for ease in screening. These techniques, which are still used today, revolutionized the science of paleofecal analysis.

Using these improved techniques, early macroanalyses conducted on paleofeces included works by Eric O. Callen, who is considered the father of paleofecal studies. Callen analyzed what he termed "coprolites" from the early 1950s until his death in Ayacucho, Peru, in 1970. He conducted research on a number of paleofecal samples from around the world, including samples from Peru (Callen and Cameron 1960), Tamaulipas, Mexico (Callen 1965, 1967a), Tehuacan, Mexico (Callen 1967b), and Glen Canyon in Utah (Callen and Martin 1969). His extensive collection, which includes thousands of microscope slides of reference and coprolite material, as well as numerous seeds, bones, fibers, and residues from coprolites, is now housed and maintained at the Laboratory of Anthropology at Texas A&M University (Bryant 1974a).

Other early analyses were conducted by Bryant and Williams-Dean (1975), Heizer and Napton (1969), Heizer (1970), Napton (1969, 1970), and Marquardt (1974). Bryant and Williams-Dean (1975) were the first to examine human paleofeces from the Archaic period in regions of the arid Chihuahuan Desert of west Texas. Napton (1969) and Heizer and Napton (1969) studied paleofecal materials from Lovelock Cave, Nevada, as a result of which they proposed a lacustrine adaptation in this part of the Great Basin. Marquardt (1974) conducted a statistical analysis of two groups of coprolites from Mammoth Cave, Kentucky, arguing that the populations had similar subsistence strategies.

The Callen and Cameron (1960) rehydration technique was especially useful for parasitological analyses, permitting the recovery of fragile ova. Early parasitological analyses of paleofeces were primarily from the Great Basin in Utah. These studies include works by Fry and Moore (1969), Fry (1970a,b, 1976), Hall (1972), and Reinhard et al. (1985). Other parasitological analyses were conducted by Hall (1977) on paleofecal material from Oregon, by Patrucco et al. (1983) on samples from Peru, by Fount (1981) on pre-Columbian mummies representing diverse populations, and by Williams (1985) on the analysis of pelvic soil from a Plains burial.

Parasites found in paleofeces can help provide information on prehistoric health. For example, differences have been noted between the prevalence of parasitic disease in hunter-gatherers and agriculturalists (Hall 1972; Reinhard 1985; Confalonieri et al. 1991). A number of debilitating and possibly life-threatening parasites have been identified from agriculturally based paleofeces from the southwestern United States (whipworm, giant intestinal roundworm, threadworms, beef tapeworms, dwarf tapeworms, and pinworm), whereas only the pinworm (*Enterobius vermicularis*) has been identified from hunter-gatherer paleofeces (Reinhard et al. 1985). Agriculturalists and hunter-gatherers have very different subsistence bases and lifeways, which seem to influence the types of diseases found in each group and the types of parasites that infect them. These studies indicate that increased sedentism (Nelson 1967), increased population size, poor sanitation methods (Walker 1985), and close proximity to crops and domesticated animals (Dunn 1968; Fenner 1970) may all have led to increased parasitic load in prehistoric populations.

Using samples from Glen Canyon, Utah, Martin and Sharrock (1964) were the first to conduct direct pollen analyses on paleofeces, and Callen and Martin (1969) documented the prehistoric ingestion of beeweed (*Cleome*) from samples in the same area. Their microscopic analysis of this pollen represented the first evidence of the use of this plant as food by humans. Later, Bryant (1974b) conducted pollen analyses on paleofeces from Mammoth Cave, reconstructing diet and possible seasonality of occupation, and Williams-Dean and Bryant (1975) analyzed samples from Antelope House, Arizona. The importance of beeweed to Anasazi diet, as well as cultivated corn, beans, and squash, was indicated in an early pollen analysis of Hoy House paleofeces (Scott 1979).

Avenues of more recent paleofecal research are very broad. One arena focuses on pollen analysis, including the interpretation of pollen concentration values in paleofeces (Sobolik 1988a,b) and the identification of medicinal plant use (Reinhard et al. 1991; Sobolik and Gerick 1992). Pollen concentration values help determine which pollen types were intentionally ingested and how long pollen resides in the digestive tract before deposition. These data are also useful for determining which pollen types were ingested medicinally rather than strictly through diet. Studies of modern feces have shown that, in general, the more recently a pollen type was ingested, the higher its concentration value in the sample (Kelso 1976; Williams-Dean 1978). As the number of hours or days increases after consumption, the pollen concentration value decreases. As a result, some pollen can be excreted up to one month after ingestion as pollen tends to get caught in the intestinal luminal folds.

Sobolik (1988b) analyzed human paleofeces from Baker Cave, Texas, and provided evidence that high pollen concentration values (e.g., more than 100,000 pollen grains/gram) indicate intentionally eaten (economic) pollen types that were ingested recently. Lesser concentrations of economic pollen suggest they were ingested days before the sample was deposited. Most paleofeces also contain a variety of unintentionally ingested background or contamination pollen. Therefore, the lower the overall concentration of pollen, the harder it is to recognize which types were intentionally ingested.

Other areas of more recent research include analyzing phytoliths from paleofeces to help determine dietary items that may be missed with macro and pollen analyses (Danielson 1993; Meade 1994), assessing prehistoric nutrition and health through analyses of paleofecal contents (Sobolik 1988a, 1990; Cummings 1989), and ascertaining meals and cuisine through cluster analysis (Sutton 1993; Sutton and Reinhard 1995). The newest paleofecal research has focused on identification of sex of depositor through hormonal studies (Sobolik et al. 1996) and DNA content (Sutton et al. 1996). This research will be highlighted in later sections of the book, but it revolves around an important issue in paleonutrition research: the search for the diet and nutrition of individuals and small groups within a larger population.

Direct and Indirect Data

Paleonutrition data are derived from many divergent sources, including skeletal materials, the study of plant and animal remains, paleobiochemistry, and others. Such data can be characterized as either direct or indirect (following Sutton 1994). Direct data are those where no inference is necessary; the remains are directly linked to human paleonutrition (such as constituents in paleofeces or nutritional pathologies in bone). On the other hand, indirect data require an inference to link them to human paleonutrition; for example, a deer bone from a site infers consumption of deer, but does not directly demonstrate it. Some archaeologists view indirect data as the technology (e.g., grinding stones) used in food processing, a category subsumed under the definition outlined here.

Indirect data constitute the vast majority of paleonutritional data from archaeological sites. Most researchers pursue single lines of investigation, relating the results of their particular research to the paleonutrition of a particular population. For example, those working on paleofeces (e.g., coprolites) detail diet but only rarely integrate those findings with the skeletal evidence of health and nutrition of the same population, partly since such complementary data sets are rare (but see Cummings 1989; Ericson et al. 1989; Sobolik 1994a). Nevertheless, to move toward a full understanding of the paleonutrition of a population, multiple data sets are necessary—and the greater the number of complementary data sets, the better.

Current studies related to paleonutrition are overwhelmingly concerned with diet and how diet affects health. To understand how diet and health are related, however, it is necessary to understand the entire subsistence system. Subsistence is "the procurement [strategies, tactics, and technology] of those materials that are necessary for the physiological well-being of a community," whereas diet is "what is eaten" and nutrition is "a measure of the ability of the diet to maintain the body in its physical and social environment" (Dennell 1979:122). Health is a reflection of nutrition and other stress experiences. These components are intertwined and an understanding of all of the components is necessary for an understanding of the whole individual (also see Greene and Johnston 1980; Sept 1992).

Direct and indirect data relating to prehistoric diet, nutrition, and health are present in the archaeological record in three basic forms: macroremains, microremains, and chemical remains. Macroremains are those that are large enough to be distinguished with the naked eye or with relatively little magnification. The majority of faunal and botanical remains, such as seeds, bones, and preserved impressions, fall into this category. Most of these remains are collected from screens (or sieves) in the field or through some specialized laboratory processing such as flotation (also usually with screens) (see chap. 4).

Microremains, such as pollen and phytoliths, are those that must be identified with the use of specialized microscopy equipment and/or techniques. These include light microscopy (simple and compound, reflected, polarized, confocal scanning, interference, and Fourier transform infrared methods), electron microscopy (transmission electron, scanning electron [SEM; see Parkes 1986, Meeks 1988, and Olsen 1988 for discussions of SEM uses in archaeology], and emission microscopy), X-rays, and acoustic microscopy (refer to Rochow and Tucker [1994] for detailed descriptions of each type). Light and electron techniques are the most widely utilized for archaeological applications.

Chemical remains are those substances that are not identifiable by visual means, and so must be identified through chemical analyses. Such remains fall into two basic categories: visible but unidentified organic residues and nonvisible chemical constituents. The first category of remains has received considerable attention from the physical sciences, and the identification of materials through gas chromatography (GC), mass spectrometry (MS), gas chromatography/mass spectrometry (GC/MS), optical emission spectroscopy, and/or infrared spectroscopy is becoming increasingly sophisticated (see Parkes 1986:197–199; Pollard and Heron 1996:20–74; Young and Pollard 1997). The second category includes stable isotope analysis, trace element analysis, immunochemistry, ancient DNA (aDNA) analysis, soil chemistry, hair composition analysis, and amino acid analysis. This latter category consists of data that preclude "the need for individuals to be pathological before dietary assumptions can be made, and they can make use of fragmentary, nondiagnostic materials" (White 1999:xii).

Future Areas of Research

The future areas of paleonutritional research will revolve around interdisciplinary analyses in which a variety of archaeological assemblages are used to assess not only the paleonutrition of a population, but also the paleonutrition of small groups and subgroups within the larger population context. This type of analysis is important because the diet, health, and nutrition of small groups within a larger population are diverse in modern cultural groups, indicating that such must have been the case in the past. To ascertain small-group paleonutrition, analysts will need to tease out information on these groups from the archaeological record. New technological advances will aid in this endeavor, such as DNA and hormonal studies, but the main pursuit will rest with the researcher and the types of questions and avenues of research that he or she seeks.

Summary

The study of paleonutrition is becoming more complex and information is continually being generated by both new data and the reanalysis of old data. As the details of the information increase and the level of analysis becomes more sophisticated, we will be able to expand upon our under-standing of past diet and behavior. Moreover, the future holds the prom-ise that additional paleonutritional data will generate new ideas, theories, and insights that would have been fanciful only a few years ago.

This volume provides detailed discussions of various aspects of paleo-nutrition and showcases specific analyses of paleonutrition among eth-nographic and prehistoric groups in various parts of North America and Africa. These case studies include analyses of Great Basin subsistence models based on single-leaf pinyon (*Pinus monophylla*), east African highland foraging techniques and the importance of honey, children's health in the American Southwest as a possible consequence of agri-culture, dietary stress among prehistoric populations in northern Sudan, and cuisine in the northern Coachella Valley of California as evidenced in paleofeces.

CHAPTER 2

The Paleonutrition Data Base
Direct Data

IN THIS CHAPTER, we discuss the kinds of data that relate directly to human paleonutrition, or those data that do not require an inference to be linked to human diet and health (see Sutton 1994). Direct data are relatively uncommon components of archaeological sites and are currently limited to two basic categories: (1) the study of human remains, including the analysis of pathology and chemistry, and (2) the study of human paleofeces.

Human Remains

Human remains consist of the bones, soft tissue, hair, and/or chemical products of humans and may contain direct evidence of paleonutrition. Most human remains studied by anthropologists consist of skeletal materials and a great deal of effort has been invested in studying bones, including cremations. Unfortunately, the skeleton is probably the least sensitive indicator of nutritional status, particularly for adults (e.g., Allen 1984). Fragmentary human remains, especially those commingled with other materials, from a site pose additional challenges, and an analytical approach similar to that of faunal remains could be productive (Outram et al. 2005).

The majority of work on human remains has been focused on paleopathology where evidence of specific diseases, trauma (including injuries related to warfare), deformation, and nutrition may be identified. Paleopathology employs a variety of data sets, primarily the analysis of bone and soft tissues, but may include other inferential data. Recent reviews of this field were provided by Bush and Zvelebil (1991), Ortner (1991), Roberts (1991), Boyd (1996), Larsen (1997, 2000, 2002), Aufderheide and Rodríguez-Martín (1998), Lovell (2000), Walker (2001), Roberts and Manchester (2007), and Waldron (2007). Several interesting case studies drawing on diverse lines of biological data were presented by Wright and White (1996) and Larsen (1994, 1998).

Disease is the most significant factor in human morbidity and mortality. The detection and identification of diseases in individuals and of disease patterns in populations are primary goals in paleopathological analyses. Juveniles are more heavily impacted by disease than adults and an understanding of juvenile morbidity and mortality can serve as an indicator for the health of the population as a whole (see Martin et al. 1991:125).

Skeletal Analysis

In life, the human skeleton will "respond to a broad range of stimuli, ranging from environmental and hereditary stresses to mechanical usage" (Stout 1989:41), and will preserve a unique record of past metabolic events. Morphological features on bone may contain a patterned record of five basic phenomena: "general growth; mechanical usage during growth and adult life; nutrition; genetics; and general health and acquired disease" (Frost 1985:222). Some of the inferences that can be gained from the analysis of skeletal remains include living conditions, cultural interactions, population movements, and changes in nutrition and health over time (see Huss-Ashmore et al. 1982; Larsen 1987, 1997, 2000, 2002; Ribot and Roberts 1996; Mays 1998; Goodman and Martin 2002). Examples of changes over time may include shifts in economic bases, such as from general hunting and gathering to specialized hunting and gathering (Lambert 1993) or from hunting and gathering to agriculture (Cohen and Armelagos 1984).

The general techniques utilized in the analysis of individual skeletons include metric measurements to determine gross morphology (such as stature and sex), methods to measure bone development, and methods to determine and describe pathology (such as disease, trauma, deformation, and nutritional stress). The skeletons of subadults (adolescents, children, and infants) are morphologically different than those of adults and present their own analytical challenges (Scheuer and Black 2004; Baker et al. 2005).

At the population level, demographic data, including stature, sex, age at death, and cause of death, can provide information regarding behavior in life, general health and diet, and a variety of other issues. Wood et al. (1992) cautioned, however, that these issues are complex and the translation of

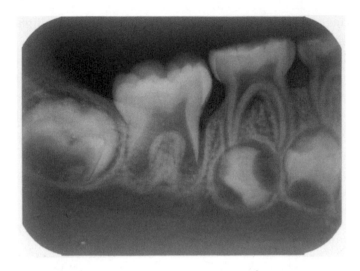

FIGURE 2.1. Radiograph of partially erupted and unerupted teeth (tooth buds) of an infant from an archaeological site in southern California (photo of an X-ray provided by the office of Dr. Jerry Woolf at Woolf Dental in Bakersfield, California).

skeletal data directly to conclusions on ancient demography and health is not straightforward, creating an "osteological paradox" in which these problematic issues could result in flawed conclusions. Recent work in bioarchaeology, both in methods and in analysis, provides optimism that these problems can be resolved (Wright and Yoder 2003; also see Larsen 2006).

A variety of specialized techniques are available to study and evaluate the skeleton, including radiography, magnetic resonance imaging (MRI), computerized axial tomography (CAT) scans, positron emission tomography (PET) scans, photon absorbiometry, gravimetric techniques, thin sections (dry and stained), microradiographed thin sections, macromeasurements, and micromeasurements. Each of these techniques was discussed in some detail by Martin et al. (1985:236–253; also see Frisancho 1990; Buikstra and Ubelaker 1994:165; Chege et al. 1996; Lynnerup et al. 1997). Probably the most useful technique in skeletal analysis is radiography. Radiographs can show features not visible to the naked eye, such as some healed traumas, bone density (e.g., osteopenia or osteoporosis), unerupted teeth (fig. 2.1), and many other aspects of the skeleton.

Since there is no danger of overexposure to the bone, multiple radiographs may be taken.

Skeletal analysis is not without limitations. Many results that indicate stress do not specify what kind of stress. Also, the older an individual was at death, the more difficult it is to determine age at death, so the ages of older individuals tend to be underestimated (see Aykroyd et al. 1999; Schmitt 2004; Baker and Pearson 2006). Thus, population profiles can be skewed, with cohorts spanning longer and longer age ranges as one moves up the scale. It is also possible that differences in preservation and/or disposal techniques could create sampling bias.

Cremations

In addition to inhumation (burial) in which significant portions of the skeleton can be recovered and analyzed, cremation is another common method of disposal of the dead. While selected skeletal remains can (and often do) survive the cremation process, this type of treatment presents a set of problems and opportunities quite different from those of inhumations. On the negative side, the bone is usually highly fragmented and often badly calcined and distorted, making it difficult to obtain complete metric and nonmetric data or even to identify specific elements. In addition, cremation practices often included procedures, such as the stirring of a fire, that cause further fragmentation and scattering of the bone. On the positive side, burned or calcined bone resists weathering better than unburned bone and so may preserve longer. Also, some artifacts, such as basketry, might be charred and fairly well preserved in cremation features. Lastly, the usual presence of large quantities of charcoal in cremations makes radiocarbon dating of such features easier, without having to conduct destructive analyses on the human remains themselves.

A number of studies have dealt specifically with cremations, although few have been conducted on remains from North American sites. Only within the last few decades have anthropologists anywhere considered cremated human remains to be of sufficient scientific value to merit their collection and evaluation (e.g., Gejvall 1970; Mays 1998; McKinley 2000). Many of these analyses, as well as discussions related to the study of cremated bone, have taken place in Europe (Wells 1960; Brothwell 1981) but several important contributions have been made by American scholars (Merbs 1967).

Histological Analyses of Bone

Bone histology (see Martin et al. 1985; Martin 1991) emphasizes histo-morphology, the microscopic analysis of bone structure, to deduce a variety of conditions, including "skeletal growth, pathology, maintenance, and repair" (Martin 1991:55) and diagenesis (Bell et al. 1991). The goals of histological analyses are to examine bone remodeling in populations and to relate those patterns to age (e.g., Macho et al. 2005; Pfeiffer et al. 2006), sex, stature, pathological conditions, and cultural affiliation so that differential health statuses can be addressed (Martin 1991:55). Histological analysis of bone should include "measure of *bone quantity* (cortical thickness, cortical area, and rate of remodeling) and *bone quality* (quantification of the size, distribution, and level of mineralization of discrete units of bone)" (Martin 1991:55, italics in original).

Another histological approach is the study of the skeletal intermediary organization (IO) of bone between the level of the cell (osteon) and the organ (the bone structure) (Stout 1989:41). The basic functions of the IO are "growth, modeling (changes in geometry of bones), remodeling [e.g., pathology], repair, and homeostasis" (Stout 1989:41), and an understanding of the IO may permit the inference of a variety of factors, including disease, nutrition, and mechanical usage (Frost 1985:211; also see Marchi et al. 2006). It may also be possible to use bone histology to identify the species of origin of bone (Davenport and Ruddell 1995; Martiniaková et al. 2006) and to even identify disease (e.g., von Hunnius et al. 2005).

Skeletal Pathologies

Most pathologies in skeletal remains are the result of congenital malformation, disease, trauma, deformation, and/or nutritional deficiencies. The most common skeletal pathology is related to degenerative disease, with trauma ranking second (White and Folkens 2005:312). Congenital malformations, trauma, and deformations typically do not relate to diet or nutrition and so are not considered further herein (but see Wells 1964:37–44; Turkel 1989; Brothwell 1999; Roberts and Manchester 2007). The other two categories of pathology, disease and nutritional deficiency, are discussed below. An excellent and comprehensive review of human skeletal pathology was presented by Roberts and Manchester (2007; also see

Steinbock 1976; Ortner and Putschar 1981; Goodman et al. 1984; Işcan and Kennedy 1989; Buikstra and Ubelaker 1994:107–158; Ortner 1994; Larsen 1997; Aufderheide and Rodríguez-Martín 1998; White 2000; White and Folkens 2005). Dental pathology is discussed separately below.

Disease Pathologies.   Most diseases are not long-lived enough to result in the formation of distinct lesions on the skeleton, although such evidence is sometimes recovered and recorded (e.g., Williams 1985; Hershkovitz et al. 1998; Roberts and Manchester 2007). Some chronic conditions will result in the formation of periosteal reactions, or lesions on the surface of the bone, but such lesions are usually nonspecific (Rothschild and Rothschild 1997) and poorly understood (Miller et al. 1996; Lewis 2004). Periostitis can thus provide an indicator of general infection (see Martin et al. 1991:125–146). A few diseases will produce diagnostic bone lesions (table 2.1) and so can be identified in individuals and populations. A potential and relatively new approach to the identification of disease in bone is the possibility of detecting specific pathogen proteins using enzyme-linked immunosorbent assay (ELISA; Smith and Wilson 1990), other immunological methods (Tuross 1991), and ancient DNA (aDNA; Likovsky et al. 2006). Discussions of diseases represented in the skeleton were provided by Steinbock (1976), Morse (1978), Ortner and Putschar (1981), Brothwell (1981:127–151), Kelley (1989), Larsen (1997:64–108), Aufderheide and Rodríguez-Martín (1998), and Roberts and Manchester (2007).

Perhaps the most common affliction reflected in the skeleton is bone loss (deossification), either osteopenia or the more severe osteoporosis. Bone loss can be caused by a number of disorders, including dietary factors (Huss-Ashmore at al. 1982:423–432). Osteoporosis affects both men and women, but affects women earlier in life. This will result in a variety of problems, with fractures being the most common, particularly rib fractures (e.g., Brickley 2005). Bone density may also reflect stress in juveniles (see McEwan et al. 2005).

Bone density can be measured using a variety of techniques, the best being dual-energy X-ray absorptiometry (Arabi et al. 2007:1060), but digital photodensitometry (Symmons 2004), metacarpal radiogrammetry (Ives and Brickley 2005), and quantitative computerized tomography (Gonzalez-Reimers et al. 2007) are also used. It is important to point out,

TABLE 2.1. Selected Diseases and Corresponding Skeletal Pathologies[a]

Disease	General Cause	Skeletal Pathology
Acute osteomyelitis	Infection	Lesions in the interior, then exterior, distal ends of long bones, sometimes in other sites
Chronic osteomyelitis	Infection	Capsulated abscesses
Chronic osteomyelitis (arthritis)	Infection	Fusion of joints
Trephonemal disease: venereal syphilis	Infection	Severe infection, osseous lesions, often in cranium
Trephonemal disease: endemic syphilis (bejel)	Infection	Moderate infection, osseous lesions, rarely in cranium
Trephonemal disease: yaws	Infection	Slight infection, osseous lesions, primarily in tibia
Tuberculosis	Infection	Lesions in vertebral column, pelvis, joints, and fingers (skeletal involvement rare)
Leprosy	Infection	Lesions and/or osteoporosis in extremities and face
Smallpox	Viral infection	Destruction of metaphyseal bone in arms, particularly in elbow; no involvement in adults
Anemias	Various causes	Porotic hyperostosis, cribra orbitalia
Dietary osteopenia: scurvy	Vitamin C deficiency	Ossification of healed hematomas, diaphysis fractures
Endocrine osteopenia	Hormone deficiencies	Osteoporosis
Stress osteopenia: atrophy	Lack of mechanical stress	Location-specific osteoporosis
Rickets	Vitamin D deficiency in subadults	Nonmineralization of osteoid, light and brittle bones, deformities
Osteomalacia	Vitamin D deficiency in adults	Deformities of weight-bearing bones; skull rarely involved
Arthritis	Age, mechanical stress, injury, infection	Osteoporosis, bone and connective tissue destruction, bone-on-bone wear, cysts
Tumors	Various	Bony lesions and cysts

[a] Compiled from Steinbock (1976) and Ortner and Putschar (1981).

FIGURE 2.2. Bone lipping (osteophytic growth) on the vertebrae of a modern adult discovered in southern California (photo provided by Jill K. Gardner).

however, that diagenesis of archaeological specimens must be considered in any interpretation (Berna et al. 2004).

Arthritis, or the inflammation of the joints, is another condition associated with aging and to some degree body mass (Weiss 2006). However, arthritis is also associated with workload and mobility and can be employed in studies dealing with these issues (e.g., Hemphill 1999; also see Baker and Pearson 2006; Lieverse et al. 2006). Osteoarthritis is the destruction of the cartilage in a joint and the formation of adjacent bone. The visible pathology is often manifested as polished bone surfaces (eburnation, from direct bone-on-bone wear), the formation of bone along the edges of the joint (lipping; fig. 2.2), and/or bone spurs (exostosis) in and around the joint. This disorder is commonly visible in vertebrae. Spondylolysis (degeneration of the articular surface of the vertebrae) may also be identified in skeletal populations (e.g., Gunness-Hay 1981; Merbs 2002).

Skeletal evidence of the four major treponemal diseases (venereal syphilis, endemic syphilis [bejel], yaws, and pinta) is widespread but it is very difficult to distinguish among the four (see Rothschild and Rothschild 1996, 1997; Roberts and Manchester 2007), although histological identification may be possible (e.g., von Hunnius et al. 2005).

Other diseases may also manifest themselves in the skeleton. Tuber-culosis has now been identified in the skeletal remains of individuals around the world based on evidence in bone (e.g., Fink 1985; Micozzi and Kelley 1985; Sumner 1985; Arriaza et al. 1995; Conlogue 2002; Mays and Taylor 2002; Matos and Santos 2005) and using molecular analy-ses (e.g., Faerman et al. 1997; Mays and Taylor 2003; Zink et al. 2004). Skeletal evidence of leprosy has been noted from burials in England (Manchester 1981), Scotland (Taylor et al. 2000), the Czech Republic (Likovsky et al. 2006), and India (Robbins et al. 2009). Manchester (1991) discussed the evidence for the interaction of these two diseases. An osteo-sarcoma (cancerous tumor of the bone) was identified from an individual in Germany (Alt et al. 2002).

Nutritional Deficiency Pathologies.   Nutritional stress on an individ-ual may also be expressed in bone (see Larsen 1997:29–56; Hoppa and FitzGerald 1999; dentition is discussed separately below). Protein-energy deficiencies will manifest themselves in general ways (and so be difficult to diagnose), while some vitamin-related deficiencies may be more specific. Martin et al. (1985:230) argued that skeletal indicators of prehistoric diet should be analyzed at the population level, concentrating on "juvenile and premature osteoporosis, differential remodeling rates of cortical and trabecular bone, growth arresting (Harris lines) of the long bones, and iron deficiency anemia" and further noted that, in general, "the skeletal response to nutritional stress is an increase in resorption and a decrease in formation resulting in a net loss of bone" (Martin et al. 1985:234). Another indicator of developmental stress is fluctuating asymmetry (e.g., DeLeon 2006).

Bone microstructure can provide a partial record of past nutritional events (see Martin 1981; Martin et al. 1985:230–236) as the body responds to nutrient deficiencies by borrowing materials from bone that, in turn, will recycle reserves at the cost of lowered resistance (Martin et al. 1985:234). Thus, nutritional stress can be related to premature bone loss (see Martin and Armelagos 1986). However, bone preservation must be assessed before conclusions based on microstructure can be made (Mar-tin et al. 1985:236).

Vitamin-related nutritional deficiencies (see Huss-Ashmore et al. 1982; Stuart-Macadam 1989; Brickley et al. 2005, 2006) may also be reflected in the skeleton, generally resulting in osteopenia. For example, scurvy (vitamin C deficiency) results in bone thinning and pathological fractures and lesions in fast-growing portions of bones, is most notable in children, and has been identified in infant skeletons (Brickley and Ives 2005). A deficiency in vitamin D prevents the proper mineralization of bone proteins and the resulting condition—called rickets in subadults and osteomalicia in adults—causes bent and distorted bones, often the limbs. Both rickets (Ortner and Mays 1998; Mays et al. 2005; Roberts and Manchester 2007) and osteomalicia (Brickley et al. 2005, 2006) have been identified in skeletal populations. Rickets is often seen among agricultural groups dependent on grain crops due to a lack of calcium absorption caused by the grain chemistry (e.g., Ivanhoe 1985). Stuart-Macadam (1989) provided a discussion of both scurvy and rickets and outlined the archaeological evidence for each.

Porotic Hyperostosis and Cribra Orbitalia.   The best-studied manifestation of nutritional deficiency is porotic hyperostosis. Porotic hyperostosis is the skeletal manifestation of any anemia, including both nutritional and hereditary (e.g., sickle cell) anemia (see discussions in Martin et al. 1985:265–269; Stuart-Macadam 1985, 1988, 1989:212–219, 1992a,b; Ascenzi et al. 1991; Martin et al. 1991:149–162; Larsen 1997:30–40; Facchini et al. 2004; Roberts and Manchester 2007:225–232). Anemia can be defined as the "subnormal number of red blood cells per cubic millimeter . . . subnormal amount of hemoglobin in 100 ml. of blood, or subnormal volume of packed red blood cells per 100 ml. of blood" (Kent 1992:2). The condition of anemia will stimulate the production of red blood cells (RBCs), resulting in an expansion of marrow and a thinning of the outer layer of the bone and exposing the trabecular (spongy) interior. These lesions may be visible in a variety of locations where thin bone is present, including bones of the orbit (cribra orbitalia) and cranium (fig. 2.3).

The etiology of porotic hyperostosis and cribra orbitalia is a synergistic reaction revolving around dietary insufficiency and malnutrition. Diets dependent on corn agriculture are deficient in a number of essential amino acids, as well as iron. With the increased dependence on corn agriculture, as in the American Southwest, iron-deficiency anemia can develop in individuals who rely too heavily on corn and so are not getting a diverse enough nutrient intake. With fluctuating climatic conditions and environmental changes, such as periods of drought, a heavy reliance

FIGURE 2.3. Porotic hyperostosis lesions on the skull of an individual (photo courtesy of Clark Spencer Larsen).

on corn as a dietary staple can result in an increase in iron-deficiency anemia.

Other causative agents in this synergistic cycle include the prevalence of disease and parasites. Disease tends to be spread in larger, more sedentary populations with poor sanitation. Disease also tends to increase in populations that are malnourished, in essence proliferating anemia in individuals who are already malnourished. In addition, it has been observed (Reinhard 1985) that prehistoric populations in the American Southwest were infested with a number of potentially debilitating parasites. Parasite infestation robs the body of much-needed nutrients and may block the absorption of iron, again participating in the proliferation of iron-deficiency anemia. A similar case has been made for the prehistoric Northwest Coast (Bathurst 2005).

Severe porotic hyperostosis tends to be found more frequently in infants and children because their bones are thinner and not fully mineralized, whereas adult bone is more resistant. In addition, by six months of age, children have depleted the accumulated iron stores obtained from their mother *in utero* and are trying to triple their blood supply (hematopoietic activity); therefore, they need more iron (El-Najjar et al. 1976). The increased need for iron confounded by malnutrition and the lack of iron in their diet produces severe iron-deficiency anemia. If a child with porotic hyperostosis survives into adulthood, the lesions and pitting can remain with that individual for a long time, eventually becoming healed and remodeled and less evident on the bone (El-Najjar et al. 1976).

Anemia can occur at any time in life and can affect bone. Production of RBCs occurs throughout life, but the distribution of RBC-producing tissue differs between adults and children. Among adults, RBC production is limited to "red" bone marrow that may be found in a number of the flat and irregular bones, such as the vertebrae, sternum, innominate (especially the ilium), and cranial vault bones. It is among the latter that adult-onset anemia is best known.

The two most frequently acquired anemias are iron deficiency and anemia of chronic disease (Kent 1992:2). It is commonly assumed that iron-deficiency anemia in prehistoric populations was generally the result of dietary deficiencies (Kent 1992:3), often due to a dependency on maize (also see Von Endt and Ortner 1982). Stuart-Macadam (1998) noted that the condition postdates the adoption of agriculture and that the pattern of females being more susceptible to the condition is fairly recent. In addition, there is now reason to believe that diet may not be the major factor affecting anemias but that some chronic disease (or the absence of defense against such disease) is a prominent factor in the presence of porotic hyperostosis (El-Najjar et al. 1975, 1976; Lallo et al. 1977; Mensforth et al. 1978; Kent 1992:13; Stuart-Macadam 1992a, 1992b:155–156; Reinhard 1992a:251–252; Wadsworth 1992; Schultz et al. 2001; but see Garn 1992:34, 53; Holland and O'Brien 1997). In sum, current research suggests that porotic hyperostosis cannot be explained by dietary factors alone.

Harris Lines.   During times of nutritional stress, normal bone growth may be interrupted, resulting in the formation of lines (or bands) of alternatively thinner and denser bone mineralization in the growth areas of the bone (fig. 2.4). These lines are usually deposited transverse to the length of the bone, and are generally referred to as "Harris lines" (Larsen 1997:40–43), probably the second most commonly studied nutritional deficiency. Harris lines may be visible either by radiograph or in cross

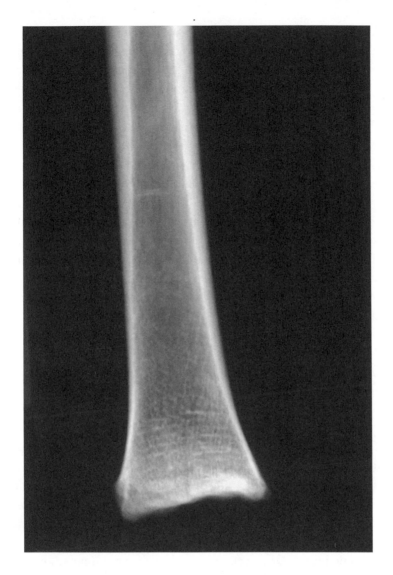

FIGURE 2.4. Harris lines on the tibia of a juvenile (photo of an X-ray provided by Dr. Oscar W. Rico at Kern Radiology in Bakersfield, California).

section. They form only during bone growth, when the individual is relatively young, and so reflect the nutritional stresses of childhood. Due to
bone remodeling during the adult years, evidence of Harris lines fades
with age and, since most studies of Harris lines have been conducted on
adults, the results may not reflect the nutritional status of the individuals
in adolescence (Vyhnanek and Stoukal 1991). Thus, it is important that
all segments of a population be studied (Martin et al. 1985:258–259).

Harris lines appear most frequently in long bones, and the tibia (particularly the distal tibia), femur, and radius are the best bones for study
(Martin et al. 1985:259). The location of the lines relative to the epiphyseal ends may be used to estimate the age at which the individual was
stressed, although this is a difficult process (Martin et al. 1985:261–263)
due to problems in accurately dating the events relative to the age of the
individual. Mays (1995) studied skeletons from a Medieval site in England and concluded that Harris lines and other stress indicators were best
utilized in the study of juveniles.

Harris-line data can also be used to study the nutritional status of
populations through time. In a study of 102 individuals from diverse time
periods in California, McHenry (1968) argued that Harris lines decreased
through time, suggesting a general improvement in health and nutrition.

Dentition

Dental health and condition can be correlated with diet and stress within
populations (see Goodman et al. 1984; Cruwys and Foley 1986; Goodman
1988, 1991; Lukacs 1989; Kelley and Larsen 1991; Martin et al. 1991:164–206;
Hillson 1979, 1996; Larsen 1997:43–56; Langsjoen 1998). Like bone, teeth
record a partial history of nutritional stress and morbidity during their
growth period (prenatal to eighteen years). As enamel is not resorbed, the
record is permanent and so the "biological adequacy of childhood diets
[by age and sex] can thus be inferred from the dentition of adults" (Rose
et al. 1985:282).

Whether due to dietary factors (such as the consumption of refined
sugars) or poor maintenance, poor oral hygiene may result in gum disease, caries, abscesses, tooth loss, and general infection (spread through
the bloodstream). Dental problems can alter the normal diet and lead to
nutritional problems that might appear unrelated to dental pathology. As

a result, "population morbidity and mortality levels are directly affected to some degree by the prevalence of dental health, which is in turn influenced both directly and indirectly by dietary factors" (Powell 1985:308).

Developmental Defects of Enamel (DDE).   Developmental abnormalities in tooth enamel include hypocalcifications and hypoplasias (Federation Dentaire Internationale 1982; Rose et al. 1985; Duray 1990; Goodman and Rose 1990, 1991; Skinner and Goodman 1992). Both kinds of DDE form only during tooth development and enamel growth in young individuals.

Hypocalcifications are discolored patches in the enamel and can form during mild disruptions of the mineralization process. The relationship of hypocalcification to diet is unclear. A hypoplasia is any deficiency in the amount or thickness of the enamel (Goodman and Rose 1990:64) and can result in linear creases, pitting, and even the absence of enamel observed on the exterior of the tooth. Hypoplasia can result from several conditions, primarily localized trauma, heredity, or systemic metabolic disruption during the growth of a tooth (Goodman and Armelagos 1985:479). An episode of trauma would be localized, affecting only a few teeth, while hereditary hypoplasia would affect all teeth. A hypoplasia caused by metabolic disruption should show up as a simultaneous event in many teeth, relative to the development of the teeth. Enamel is not subject to remodeling and so the record of these stresses is preserved (Goodman and Armelagos 1988; Goodman and Rose 1990:59), including in deciduous teeth (Blakely and Armelagos 1985).

Metabolic stress of just a few days may cause short-term disruption of enamel growth, which may result in slight alteration of the matrix of the enamel. These episodes may be visible in thin section as small, linear bands of discolored enamel, commonly called Wilson bands. As normal tooth growth sequence is well understood, the location of Wilson bands in the enamel matrix can be used to deduce the age of the individual at the time of the metabolic disruption. A recent study of contact period materials from Florida (Simpson 2001:175, also see Simpson 1999) found a number of defects in enamel microstructure, suggesting that severe dehydration due to weaning diarrhea was a serious health problem in early mission times.

If metabolic stress lasts from weeks to months, the enamel will stop developing, resulting in thinning of the enamel. These episodes may

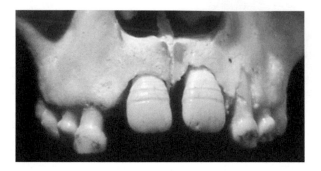

FIGURE 2.5. Linear enamel hypoplasia on the teeth of a juvenile (photo courtesy of Clark Spencer Larsen).

be visible on the surface of the tooth and are commonly called linear enamel hypoplasia (LEH). Once the stress is removed, the enamel will continue its normal growth, leaving the region of thin enamel on the tooth (fig. 2.5). Estimating the age of the individual at the time of the stress is difficult (Goodman and Song 1999).

While general associations are known between LEH and a variety of clinical conditions, diseases, and malnutrition (see Rose et al. 1985:284–285), there is not a "clear and consistent relationship between dietary deficiency and the formation of enamel defects" (Goodman 1994:171; also see Neiburger 1990). Some studies have found a relationship between diet and LEH (e.g., Hutchinson and Larsen 1995:95; Mays 1995; Lukacs and Walimbe 1998; Lukacs et al. 2001), but others have not (e.g., McHenry and Schulz 1976). One must always exercise caution in the diagnosis of these conditions, however, since enamel defects may be produced by chemical and/or developmental abnormalities, rather than by nutritional stress (see Dahlberg 1991; Duray 1996:276), and different teeth have different susceptibilities to growth disruption (Goodman and Armelagos 1985:491), making interpretations difficult. LEHs might also be produced as the result of other stressors, such as diseases, warfare, population pressures, and the like as a result of contact with Europeans (Wright 1990; Hutchinson and Larsen 2001). LEH may also be used to measure developmental stress on some domestic animals (e.g., pigs [Dobney and Ervynck 2000]), providing information on resources employed in raising them or on hunted animals with implications on subsistence (e.g., Niven et al. 2004).

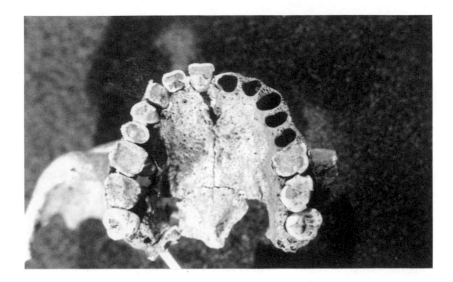

FIGURE 2.6. Tooth wear on the maxilla of a young adult from an archaeological site in southern California (photo provided by Jill K. Gardner).

Dental Pathologies.   Dental pathologies can take several forms, most notably tooth wear (some of which is not pathological), caries (cavities), and periodontal disease (see Powell 1985; Hillson 1986, 1996; Lukacs 1989; Buikstra and Ubelaker 1994:47–68; Langsjoen 1998). Dental pathologies may reflect a variety of circumstances, including general health, some aspects of diet, techniques of food preparation, use of teeth as tools and for decoration, and even geochemistry (e.g., fluoride in groundwater [Hildebolt et al. 1988; Yoshimura et al. 2006]).

Wear of the enamel crown occurs throughout life through a combination of erosion (chemical dissolution), attrition (tooth-on-tooth contact), and abrasion (tooth-to-foreign-substance contact) (Williams and Woodhead 1986). Some degree of tooth wear is normal, even beneficial, and is not pathological, while excessive wear can cause considerable problems (fig. 2.6). The amount and type of abrasion depend on occlusion (e.g., Begg 1954), the types of food consumed (e.g., those species containing a significant number of phytoliths may cause excessive wear [Puech and Leek 1986; Reinhard and Danielson 2005; but see Sanson et al. 2007]), the technology involved in food preparation (e.g., presence of grit from the use of stone milling tools; but see Wolfe and Sutton 2006), and the other uses to which teeth are subjected.

Attrition and abrasion may be distinguished by wear patterns observed microscopically (Powell 1985:308; Cross et al. 1986; Harmon and Rose 1988; Lukacs and Pastor 1988; Teaford 1991; Larsen 1997; Teaford et al. 2001) and can be employed to determine broad dietary patterns in humans (Walker 1978; A. Walker 1981; Newesely 1993; Lubell et al. 1994). Skinner (1996, 1997) identified differences in dental wear between Neanderthal and Upper Paleolithic infants, indicating that Upper Paleolithic infants received supplemental foods earlier than their Neanderthal counterparts, and suggested that this dietary difference may have influenced a population increase in the Upper Paleolithic. Dental microwear can also be employed to determine the general diet of ancient livestock (Mainland 1998).

Another mechanism creating tooth wear is their use as tools, such as grasping cordage, chewing hides, or holding pipe stems (Molnar 1971, 1972; Schulz 1977; Larsen 1985; Sutton 1988a; Kennedy 1989:table 1; Milner and Larsen 1991). In addition, teeth may have been purposefully modified (engraved and/or colored) for cosmetic reasons or removed (technically a trauma) for various purposes (see Merbs 1989:172).

The degree of tooth wear has been utilized as a method of determining the age of an individual at death (e.g., Oliveira et al. 2006). Age is only one of the variables in tooth wear, however, and while it is fair to suggest that a significantly worn tooth belongs to an adult, the aging of skeletons based solely on general tooth wear is not advisable. On the other hand, a recent study of crown height on molars on a skeletal population of nineteenth-century Dutch of known age at death (Mays 2002) revealed a linear relationship between crown wear and age at death, suggesting that molar wear might be a good indicator of age within a homogeneous population. Nevertheless, it currently seems imprudent to rely solely on dental wear as indicators of age at death.

The presence of plaque, calculus, and caries (see Hillson 1986:283–303) on the teeth may also give clues to diet. Plaque, a combination of bacteria and proteins from the saliva, forms on the surface of teeth. The bacteria consume sugars and other materials present in the mouth as food is consumed by the person and acid is produced as a waste product. If sufficient acid is produced, the pH of the plaque is lowered to the point that the enamel of the tooth begins to decalcify, producing a caries. If the pH level remains high enough, the plaque will not impact the enamel but will instead mineralize to form calculus, a layer of calcified minerals and organic materials (Jin and Yip 2002:426) next to the tooth, with a layer of plaque on top of the calculus. This calculus can actually serve to protect the tooth, lowering the frequency of caries. If at some point the pH of the plaque is lowered enough, however, the calculus may become decalcified, allowing plaque to penetrate the enamel and cause caries.

Only relatively simple sugars can be processed by oral bacteria. As food enters the mouth, saliva begins the digestion process by rapidly breaking down sugars and converting simple carbohydrates into sugars. These sugars provide the nutrition needed by the oral bacteria, and so diets high in sugars and simple carbohydrates encourage the growth of oral bacteria and the formation of plaque. Other foods, such as complex carbohydrates, protein, and/or fat, are not converted to sugars in the mouth, are not available as nutrition to oral bacteria, and are much less conducive to plaque formation (see Powell 1985:313–314, 316; Meiklejohn et al. 1988).

Left unchecked, caries can evolve into abscesses, resulting in tooth loss, bone loss, general infection, and even death. Many caries and abscesses are easily visible in ancient dentition (although not always measured consistently; see Hillson 2001), and evidence of bone resorption may be present. The link between caries and diet is clear but there are a number of other factors to consider, such as enamel disruptions that may increase the susceptibility to caries (Duray 1990). Other factors, including food texture, chemical composition, and frequency of consumption, also influence rates of caries (Powell 1985:320).

Another dental pathology that can be detected in ancient teeth is periodontal disease (e.g., Delgado-Darias et al. 2006), a bacterial infection of the tissues surrounding a tooth. Untreated infections can result in the erosion of gum tissue, abscess, tooth loss, and bone resorption. In most instances, periodontal disease is linked to poor oral hygiene, although it is possible to have a genetic predisposition to the disease.

Interestingly, the plaque and calculus preserved on ancient dentition are not commonly studied, perhaps partly due to the difficulty in directly linking them to dietary intake (e.g., Lieverse 1999; Delgado-Darias et al. 2006:664). Nevertheless, plaque and calculus can contain important nutritional data, as particles—such as food, pollen, phytoliths, starch grains, grit, and tephra—can become incorporated into them. These materials can then be recovered and analyzed, and preliminary studies (e.g., Dobney and Brothwell 1986; Magennis and Cummings 1986; Fox et al. 1996; Brothwell and Brothwell 1998; Reinhard et al. 2001; Yohe and Cummings 2001) suggest that the approach holds considerable promise in paleonutrition studies. Some work has also been done on the chemistry of calculus (Capasso et al. 1995) in an attempt to develop a data base for paleonutrition studies.

Dentition may be used as a partial measure of the subsistence economy and pathology related to nutritional stress. For example, changes in tooth wear and pathology could be used to infer shifts in diet among hunter-gatherers (e.g., Walker and Erlandson 1986; also see Walker 1978), to infer the transition from hunting and gathering to agriculture (e.g., Turner 1979; Larsen 1983; Smith 1984; Schmucker 1985; Schneider 1986; Larsen et al. 1991; Lillie 1996; Lukacs 1996; Lillie and Richards 2000; Eshed et al. 2005; but see Tayles et al. 2000), to delineate differences in the diet of agriculturalists due to relative status (Whittington 1999; also see Storey 1992, 1999; Valentin et al. 2006), or to infer seasonality of hunting prey species (Rivals and Deniaux 2005).

Soft Tissue Analysis

Soft tissue comprises most of the human body, including all of the organs, muscles, and hair. The majority of human pathology and disease is manifested only in soft tissues (see Martin et al. 1985), since with many diseases the host dies before the bone can be impacted by a pathogen. As a result, the identification of disease from skeletal remains is limited (at least with current methods, but see Smith and Wilson [1990] and Tuross [1991]). Thus, the recovery and analysis of preserved human soft tissue is a relatively rare opportunity that can provide a great deal of information currently unavailable from the analysis of skeletal remains alone.

Except under unusual circumstances, most soft tissues are subject to rapid decomposition and are not commonly recovered from the archaeological record, although it is now apparent that hair is quite resilient and can preserve in recognizable form in open sites for long periods of time (e.g., Bonnichsen 1996; Bonnichsen et al. 2001). The majority of preserved human soft tissues is found in mummified remains. These include artificially mummified bodies found in places such as Peru, Chile (e.g.,

Arriaza 1995), and Egypt (see Yohe and Gardner 2004) or the naturally mummified bodies found in hot deserts (Peru, North America, northern Africa, and China), in cold deserts (e.g., the Arctic and Asian steppes), in waterlogged contexts (e.g., the "bog" bodies of northern Europe and the materials from the Windover site in Florida), or in other unusual conditions, such as "catacomb mummies" (Aufderheide and Aufderheide 1991). A general review of preserved human bodies was provided by Aufderheide (2003; also see Brothwell 1987).

Methods employed to examine preserved human soft tissue remains (see Aufderheide 2003) include endoscopic examination (Tapp et al. 1984; Schäfer et al. 1995), radiography (e.g., Sutton 1980; Notman 1995), xeroradiography (selenium impregnated radiographs), MRI (Wallgren et al. 1986), PET and CAT scans (Sutton 1980:1230–1307; Vahey and Brown 1984; Notman 1986; Pahl 1986; Lewin 1991; Wisseman 1994), and various combinations of the above (Notman and Lupton 1995; Notman 1998). One of the more interesting aspects of determining soft tissue characteristics is when none is recovered on a skeleton and a reconstruction of the soft tissue is undertaken based on the skeletal data. For example, the face of the Kennewick Man was approximated through the use of well-established techniques for facial reconstruction (Chatters 2001).

Soft Tissue Paleopathology

Researchers have examined many thousands of mummies for soft tissue pathologies, and numerous studies have dealt with the various cases of pathology that have been observed (see Cockburn 1971:52; Whitehouse 1980; Cockburn et al. 1998; Aufderheide 2003). For example, Wells (1964:67–70) briefly noted the discovery of arteriosclerosis in mummies from Egypt and Peru, suggesting a variety of ailments including heart disease, stroke, and lung diseases, while the discovery of perforated eardrums in an Egyptian mummy led Lynn and Benitez (1974) to suggest the incidence of defective hearing.

Zimmerman et al. (1981) conducted a medical examination of an Aleutian mummy, concluding that the person suffered from pulmonary and ear infections, atherosclerosis, pediculosis, degenerative joint disease, and anthracosis (a common affliction due to the use of indoor fires). Rothhammer et al. (1985) performed autopsies on twenty-two Chilean mummies, nine of which showed clinical manifestations of Chagas' disease, a parasitic infection, transmitted by insect bites, that can affect the heart and intestines and can be fatal. These findings suggested that the parasite became a serious problem after ca. 500 B.C., when human populations became sedentary in that location. Aufderheide et al. (2004) discovered that Chagas' disease was present in Peru as early as 9,000 B.P. Blackman et al. (1991) detected a variety of renal problems in an Andean mummy.

Several additional examples of soft tissue analysis of paleopathologies are illustrative. Bourke (1986) undertook a number of medical examinations on Lindow Man, including radiography, MRI, xeroradiography (also see Connolly 1986), and CAT scans (also see Reznek at al. 1986), and discovered a number of pathologies. Later, Brothwell et al. (1990) took radiographs and CAT scans on the Huldremose Woman bog body (found in Denmark) to locate the intestinal tract for sampling purposes. Finally, Ammitzbøll et al. (1991) conducted detailed X-ray analyses of eight mummies discovered at Qilakitsoq, Greenland, and identified a variety of pathologies and disease. Radiographic, CAT, and MRI scans, coupled with SEM observations, were conducted on 8,000-year-old preserved human brain matter from the Windover site in Florida (Hauswirth et al. 1991, 1994).

Also of interest is the rare discovery and analysis of tumors (Gerszten and Allison 1991) and cancers (Pahl and Undeutsch 1991; Tenney 1991) in soft tissues. In addition, pathogens have been discovered in mummified soft tissue remains (see Lewin 1991) using microscopy. Some pathogens also have been identified in bone (see Smith and Wilson 1990; Tuross 1991), as have some ancient enzymes (Etspüler et al. 1996). Further, studies of zoonoses—disease organisms that can move back and forth between humans and other animals—have provided important discoveries (e.g., Bell et al. 1988). Examples of such diseases are rabies and tuberculosis. Brothwell (1991) provided a discussion of zoonoses and their relevance to paleopathology.

Analyses of some inorganic materials can be conducted on soft tissues, including stable isotopes and trace elements. In addition, renal and bladder stone diseases are implied by the presence of stones (Steinbock 1985; also see Blackman et al. 1991). The two conditions appear to be related, at least in part, to diet; thus, the presence of such stones in burial populations could be a source of paleopathological and dietary information. Other soft tissue calcifications, such as pleural plaques, leiomyomas of the uterus, and lymph nodules, may also assist in determining disease and other anomalies in prehistoric populations (Baud and Kramar 1991).

Analysis of Hair.   Hair (which includes fingernails and toenails) contains a diachronic record of the metabolism of an individual that is stored in the internal (endogenous) portion of the hair during its growth phase. In contrast, the exterior (exogenous) component consists of materials that accumulated, at some point in time, on the surface of the hair (see Hopps 1974; Sandford 1984:58; Sandford and Kissling 1993). An analysis of the exogenous component of hair can reveal details regarding external environmental conditions, while the endogenous component can provide data on a number of issues, including diet, pollution, and toxicology (e.g., Benfer et al. 1978). Sandford (1984:97–268) suggested that calcium, magnesium, iron, zinc, copper, and manganese are the six primary elements to study in hair.

Hair may be preserved in a variety of circumstances, such as that attached to mummies or other skeletal remains, loose materials found in soils, and that attached to (or as part of) artifacts. The first two circumstances are of special interest, as the hair can be associated with specific individuals, and associations between analytical results and the age, sex, and/or pathologies of the individual can be made.

Sandford (1984) conducted a study of hair from 168 individuals from two Sudanese Medieval Christian period cemeteries, one from the early Christian period (A.D. 550 to 750) and one from the late Christian period (A.D. 750 to 1450). She determined that there had been little change in the diet between the two periods (see Case Study 4 in chap. 6). In addition, iron deficiency was identified as the likely cause of lesions in the orbits (cribra orbitalia; see above) in the population (Sandford et al. 1983). In another study, Bresciani et al. (1991:164) employed X-ray fluorescence to determine the quantities of trace elements in the hair from the mummies discovered at Qilakitsoq, Greenland, showing the general increase in heavy metal pollutants over the last five hundred years. Hair has also been used to identify other compounds, including drugs; for example, Balabanova et al. (1995) identified cocaine and nicotine in the hair of a Peruvian mummy. Isotopic analysis of hair from Nubian mummies (Schwarcz and White 2004) revealed a pattern in the use of stored foods.

It is also possible to recover hair from general archaeological site deposits. Hair has been recovered from soils at a number of sites (e.g., Grupe and Dörner 1989; Bonnichsen 1996) and can be utilized to generate information regarding diet and nutrition of the population of a site. Hair can also be radiocarbon dated and the hair follicles analyzed for aDNA to reveal the genetic imprint of the inhabitants (e.g., Bonnichsen et al. 2001). More recently, carbon and nitrogen isotope analysis of hair can help reveal details about past diet (Knudson et al. 2007).

Ectoparasites.   Ectoparasites (e.g., lice) found on preserved human remains (or in preserved clothing) may be useful in the inference of general health conditions. Gill and Owsley (1985) conducted an analysis of head lice found on a historic adult male mummy from Wyoming and discovered an extensive infestation. They suggested that the level of infestation was the result of a decrease in normal grooming activities, perhaps as a consequence of social stress related to Euroamerican expansion (e.g., starvation, warfare). Mummy II/7 from Qilakitsoq, Greenland (Bresciani et al. 1991:162), was heavily infested with head lice, suggesting "an extremely low hygienic standard, and perhaps, to some extent also, low resistance to the attack of lice." Lice were also discovered in the feces of the individual, indicating the probable consumption of lice, as has been observed ethnographically (Bresciani et al. 1991:162; also see Sutton 1988b, 1995). Lice-infested mummies also are known from other areas of the world (e.g., Fry 1976; Cockburn and Cockburn 1980).

Human ectoparasites also may be vectors of disease. Fleas were the prime transmitters of bubonic plague in Europe during the Middle Ages and continue in this role (see Buckland and Sadler 1989). Along with lice, mites, midges, mosquitoes, and other disease vectors, fleas also carry typhus, malaria, and other maladies. In addition, some people have allergies to particular insect bites and a number of people die each year from bee stings. A discussion of ectoparasites and humans was presented by Busvine (1976).

Analysis of Ancient DNA

The application of techniques to recover, isolate, amplify, and identify ancient DNA (aDNA) holds the potential to revolutionize archaeology (e.g., Pääbo 1985a,b, 1990, 1993; Thuesen and Engberg 1990; Brown and Brown 1992; Persson 1992; Richards et al. 1993; Tuross 1993; Hagelberg 1994a; Herrmann and Hummel 1994; Thuesen 1995; O'Rourke et al. 1996, 2000; Mays 1998:197–206; Renfrew 1998; Pääbo et al. 2004; Mulligan 2006). Today, DNA testing/typing is used in a variety of forensic applications, such as the identification of war casualties (Holland et al. 1993), including those from the American Civil War (Fisher et al. 1993).

As DNA is originally present in virtually all organic materials, including bone (Hagelberg et al. 1989; Persson 1992; Hagelberg 1994b; Hummel and Herrmann 1994; MacHugh et al. 2000), its recovery in ancient specimens could be used to address many research questions. These include the identification of pathogens in human remains (Salo et al. 1995a; Baron et al. 1996; Taylor et al. 1996, 2000, 2001; Braun et al. 1998; Faerman et al. 1998; Dixon and Roberts 2001; Sallares and Gomzi 2001; Mays and Taylor 2002; Spigelman et al. 2002; Soren 2003; Aufderheide et al. 2004; Bathurst and Barta 2004; Likovsky et al. 2006), population migrations (Pääbo et al. 1988; Torroni et al. 1992; Stone and Stoneking 1993, 1996; Kaestle 1995; Kolman et al. 1995; Fox 1996; Kaestle and Smith 2001), ethnicity and lineage (Nielsen et al. 1994; Torroni et al. 1994; Salo et al. 1995b; Parr et al. 1996; Richards et al. 1996; Vargas-Sanders et al. 1996; Dudar et al. 2003), the sex of human remains (Hummel and Herrmann 1994; Thuesen et al. 1995; Lassen et al. 1996; Sutton et al. 1996; Colson et al. 1997; Brown 1998, 2001; Götherström et al. 1998; Matheson and Loy 2001; Mays and Faerman 2001), the identification of species of food remains (Loy 1991, 1996; Hillman et al. 1993; Hardy et al. 1997; Butler and Bowers 1998; Barnes et al. 2000; Burger et al. 2002; Newman et al. 2002), the identification of species processed on stone tools (Kimura et al. 2001; Shanks et al. 2001, 2005), and the identification and tracking of domesticates (Brown et al. 1993; Goloubinoff et al. 1993; Rollo et al. 1994; Loreille et al. 1997; Schlumbaum and Jacomet 1998; Bar-Gal et al. 2002). The latter three uses of DNA are particularly appropriate when dealing with issues of paleonutrition. A consideration of the protocols in using skeletal materials in aDNA analysis was presented by DeGusta and White (1996).

The two major problems in aDNA analysis are preservation and contamination (see Kolman and Tuross 2000; Mulligan 2006). While it is clear that some aDNA survives over time, even over millions of years (e.g., DeSalle et al. 1992), it is not clear in what form such molecules survive, if they might have been altered, and whether they can be correctly identified (Eglinton and Logan 1991; Hedges and Sykes 1992; Richards et al. 1995; Rogan and Salvo 1995; Handt et al. 1996; Chalfoun and Tuross 1999; Poinar and Stankiewicz 1999; Rollo et al. 2002; Yang and Watt 2005; Gilbert et al. 2006). Even if well preserved, aDNA samples can be easily contaminated by a variety of organisms, especially bacteria and fungi, before the sample is recovered; after recovery, contamination by the researcher is possible (Richards et al. 1993:19–20).

Paleodemography

Paleodemography is the study of ancient populations—their size, birth rate, life span, population structure, growth, morbidity, and mortality (all by sex and age). Diet and nutrition are fundamentally linked to these demographic components. Most paleodemographic studies are based on the analysis of archaeological skeletal populations, which, in turn, are subject to a number of assumptions and limitations (as detailed by Buikstra and Mielke 1985:362–367; also see Boddington 1987; Corruccini et al. 1989; Holland 1989; Konigsberg et al. 1989; Jackes 1992; Roth 1992; Verano and Ubelaker 1992; Wood et al. 1992; Meindl and Russell 1998; Milner et al. 2000; Wright and Yoder 2003; Bello et al. 2005). These include an assumption of the uniformity of biological processes, an incomplete understanding of small-group population dynamics, archaeological sampling biases, and accuracy of sex and age-at-death estimates. Another critical concern in paleodemography is that many of the models employed were developed by demographers on the basis of analogies from modern data that may translate to ancient populations.

Several measures of nutritional deficiencies in human populations can be utilized in studies of paleodemography, including studies of long-bone growth curves and of adult stature (see Huss-Ashmore et al. 1982:410–414; also see Danforth 1999). Such studies can be used to show general trends of nutrient availability at the population level, or by age, sex, and/or gender. Skeletal remains can be used to determine sex and age at time of death (see chap. 4), data critical to demographic analysis (see Guy et al. 1997; Aykroyd et al. 1999; Wright and Yoder 2003:47–49).

Human Paleofeces

Preserved human fecal materials, collectively known as paleofeces (fig. 2.7), are a source of significant information regarding the ingredients of prehistoric diet, including condiments (e.g., Trigg et al. 1994; Sutton and Reinhard 1995), possible nutrition (Cummings 1994), health (Reinhard and Bryant 1992), behavior (see Reinhard and Bryant 1992:270–273), pharmacology (e.g., Hillman 1986:103; Reinhard et al. 1991; Sobolik and Gerick 1992; Trigg et al. 1994; but see Dean 1993; Reinhard 1993), and processing technology (Callen 1967b; Robins et al. 1986; Rylander 1994). Most researchers credit Eric Callen (see Callen and Cameron 1960; Bryant and Dean 2006) for the initiation of serious paleofecal studies. Recent reviews of paleofecal studies are available in Fry (1985), Hillman (1986), Sobolik (1990), Reinhard and Bryant (1992), Holden (1994), and Bryant and Dean (2006).

Paleofeces provide direct evidence of substances consumed, although cess (see below) may be mixed with other materials. Materials can enter the digestive system and end up in feces in a number of ways. The most

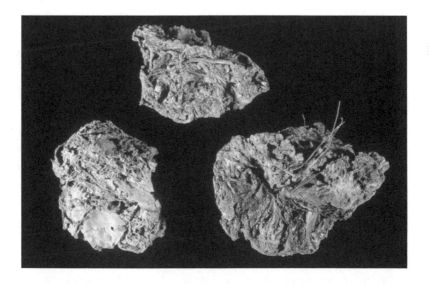

FIGURE 2.7. Coprolites (one of the three types of paleofecal material) from Hinds Cave, Texas (photo provided by Kristin D. Sobolik).

common and obvious method is by intentional ingestion, as food, medicine, part of religious activities, or even for entertainment purposes (such as swallowing goldfish as part of a fraternity initiation). Accidental ingestion can also occur, for example, if an unseen item is attached to material that was intentionally consumed, if something is unknowingly eaten by mistake, or even if the mouth is left open too long (e.g., swallowing a winged insect). Paleofeces may also contain parasites and/or postmortem intrusive materials (discussed below).

Human paleofeces are the end result of the digestive process and may be classified into six primary components (Fry 1985:128):

1. Food residues and undigested dietary components
2. Intestinal and digestive secretions not destroyed or reabsorbed
3. Substances excreted into the digestive tract, primarily phosphates, calcium, salts, iron, and other metals
4. Bacteria and their metabolic products
5. Cellular elements, which in pathological cases may include blood, pus, mucus, serum, and parasites and their ova
6. Enteroliths, gallstones, and pancreatic calculi

Bacteria comprise some 25 percent to 50 percent of a paleofecal specimen (Fry 1985:128) while the ratios of the various dietary components will vary with the specific diet. Both color and odor of specimens will also vary; a diet high in meat will be darker in color and highly aromatic while a diet high in vegetal matter will be lighter in color and less aromatic (Fry 1985:128–129).

Archaeologists or paleoecologists studying human paleofeces make a number of assumptions, often with great merit, regarding the nature and origin of the specimens. For both intestinal and disassociated specimens it is assumed that (1) the materials present in a specimen were intentionally ingested by the person from which the sample came, (2) such materials can be readily identified, and (3) the identified materials represent at least part of the subsistence aspect of diet. Substances ingested for ceremonial and/or medicinal purposes (Hillman 1986:103; Shafer et al. 1989; Reinhard et al. 1991; Sobolik and Gerick 1992; Trigg et al. 1994) are more difficult to identify and interpret. For disassociated specimens, it is further assumed that (4) constituents present in a specimen represent the materials consumed within the twenty-four-hour period preceding its deposition (e.g., Fry 1985:128), although this may not be the case (e.g., Sobolik 1988a:207; Jones 1986a), and are likely a combination of several meals (e.g., Watson 1974:240), and (5) each specimen represents a unique elimination event and is not mixed or combined with other such events. Despite these assumptions, however, specimens possibly representing separate events are sometimes grouped together for analysis, a practice that should be avoided as it could result in the mixing of specimens from different events or individuals.

Other factors are of note in paleofecal analysis (see Sobolik 1988b:114). As only the undigested part of the diet is visually identifiable, a visual analysis results in only a partial catalog of the original dietary constituents. With the use of protein residue (e.g., Newman et al. 1993) and aDNA (e.g., Sutton et al. 1996; Poinar et al. 2001) analytical techniques, a more complete inventory of constituents is possible. Further, taphonomic problems (e.g., digestion, processing, preservation) associated with paleofeces are not well understood, although there has been some work accomplished in that area (e.g., Calder 1977; Jones 1986a; Rylander 1994; Butler and Schroeder 1998). Finally, in spite of a listing of constituents in a paleofecal sample and some understanding of the nutritional content of foods, the ability of the body to break down and absorb such nutrients is not fully understood (see papers in Taylor and Jenkins 1986:232–258).

Of some nutritional interest is the "second harvest," the practice of picking out undigested seeds from dry feces and reprocessing and (re)consuming them. This practice was reported by Aschmann (1959:77) among Native Americans in the Central Desert of Baja California. This practice would seem to be a rather desperate measure and is probably indicative of considerable resource stress.

Paleofeces take one of (at least) three basic forms (Greig 1984:49; Holden 1994:65–66): (1) gut contents, the intestinal contents of preserved human bodies; (2) coprolites, fecal material excreted by a live individual; and (3) cess, disaggregated fecal material recovered from locations such as cesspits and privies. A fourth category, perhaps best considered a subcategory of gut contents since it may be associated with a specific individual, might include the materials recovered from soil samples taken from the stomach/intestinal area of bodies from burials. Unfortunately, both human bodies and human fecal materials are very fragile and are rarely recovered archaeologically.

Gut Contents

Gut contents are the materials recovered from the intestinal tract, including the stomach, of a preserved (e.g., mummified) human body. These materials are generally preserved due to desiccation, freezing, or waterlogging (e.g., in peat). Unlike coprolites or cess, information from the analysis of the gut contents of preserved individuals can be coupled with knowledge of the sex, age, and general health of the individuals, allowing correlation of these factors with diet (see Reinhard and Bryant 1995; Reinhard 1998a). In addition, the general order of constituents ingested can be determined by their location in the intestinal tract; in some cases, the "last meal" can be deduced, as in the case of Lindow Man (Hillman 1986; Holden 1986; West 1986). Brothwell et al. (1990) proposed a protocol for sampling preserved gut contents with minimal damage to the body (also see the methods used by Holden [1986] in sampling the gut contents of Lindow Man).

Studies on preserved gut contents have been conducted in Peru (for a summary see Holden 1994:66), Chile (Holden 1991), Africa (Smith and Jones 1910b; Cummings 1989), North America (Zimmerman 1980, 1998; Gill and Owsley 1985; Bresciani et al. 1991), and Europe (Hillman 1986; Holden 1986; Jones 1986b). There has also been some effort to recover "stomach" contents from primary inhumations by taking soil samples from the area of the abdomen (e.g., Williams 1985; Shafer et al. 1989; Reinhard et al. 1992; Berg 2002). The success of these efforts depends on a number of conditions, including bioturbation, preservation, sampling procedure, processing methods, and analysis. Using electron spin resonance (ESR) spectroscopy, Robins et al. (1986) were able to conclude that some of the gut contents of Lindow Man were cooked, some of which was baked bread.

Coprolites

Coprolites are the distinct, formed, and preserved fecal materials excreted by a live individual. The word *coprolite* was originally meant to refer to the fossilized feces of ancient animals (Fry 1985:127) and the term is still often used to refer to the preserved feces of any animal. For our purposes, the term refers only to human coprolites.

Coprolites generally preserve through desiccation or freezing, but sometimes charred specimens are discovered (Hillman 1989:228; Hillman et al. 1989:164–166). As coprolites are disassociated from a particular person, they contain much less information on sex, age, health, and other meals than is available from the gut contents of specific individuals. Being excreted from a live person, coprolites cannot be the "last meal" of a person; such a meal would still be in the gut of the deceased.

The discovery of coprolites is complicated by at least two factors. First, coprolites are difficult to recognize in a general site matrix. Coprolite specimens may have decomposed too much, they may be of a color similar to that of the surrounding soil, or they may just be undetected. In addition, other materials can sometimes be misidentified as coprolites (e.g., Sutton et al. 2006). Second, ethnographic data (e.g., Lee 1984:31–32) suggest that most latrine areas are located away from living areas (where most excavations are conducted), making their discovery even more difficult.

Coprolites may be discovered singly or in concentrations that probably represent latrines. While the human population responsible for a latrine coprolite deposit generally is assumed to be homogeneous, this may not be the case. If a particular segment of the population (e.g., based on age, sex, or status) used a specific latrine, the sample would not be demographically homogeneous and interpretations based on that assumption would be incorrect. Latrine use over time may be an additional concern. Since these factors cannot currently be controlled, however, most researchers tend to assume sample homogeneity.

Cess

Cess is an accumulation of disaggregated fecal material, often mixed with other debris, recovered from locations such as cesspits and privies, and can be in varying states of decomposition (Greig 1984:49). Cess deposits form when numerous excretory events occur at the same location, such as in a privy, or where such materials are transported to a central location, such as a cesspit or other sewage facility. Being a mixture of numerous feces events, cess cannot be used to reconstruct individual diet, and since it often is mixed with other debris, including undigested and/or discarded food remains, it is considered an indirect source of dietary data. In some cases, animal waste has been discarded into a cesspit (Pike 1975:347; Wilson 1979), mixing with human waste and making dietary reconstructions particularly problematic.

Cess deposits can be identified by the regular patterning of botanical and other remains in a confined area (Knörzer 1984:331); in many circumstances, the preservation of organics can be very good (e.g., McCobb et al. 2001). In addition to the remains of dietary items, the eggs of parasites can be recovered from cess deposits (Taylor 1955; Pike and Biddle 1966; Pike 1967, 1968, 1975; Greig 1983:194), providing data regarding the general health of the population.

A number of interesting studies have been conducted with cess deposits. Dennell (1970) identified seeds from sewer deposits, Greig (1981) recovered a wide variety of faunal and botanical remains in a barrel latrine, and Knights et al. (1983) discovered that a defensive ditch at a Roman fort in Scotland also served as a cesspit and were able to identify some foodstuffs. Knörzer (1984) reported the analysis of materials from fifteen cesspits from three different temporal periods, in which the composition of the diet, the first appearance of cultivated plants, changes in cultivated plants, the importation of fruit, and the history of the immigration of weeds were documented. Working with cesspit materials from different time periods in Amsterdam, Paap (1984) documented some dietary variation with regard to social differences.

A Note on Animal Dung

With the exception of most rodent material, animal dung recovered at an archaeological site would most likely be present only if the animals were in close association with humans. This close association could mean that some of the animals, such as dogs, were eating human food and/or waste; thus, an elucidation of the diet of those animals could be useful in understanding human diet. Other animals, such as domesticated herbivores, would have a different diet, but one that would still be informative about human activities and resource procurement and allocation (e.g., Robinson and Rasmussen 1989; Panagiotakopulu 1999; Hunt et al. 2001). Further, an examination of animal dung and site soil samples may reveal the presence of fecal spherulites, microscopic crystalline structures produced in the guts of some animals. The presence of spherulites can be used to infer the presence of ruminant herbivores and even the conditions of their pastures (Canti 1997, 1998, 1999).

Analysis of Paleofeces

Prior to about 1960, the materials within paleofecal samples were extracted either by cutting open the dry samples and identifying the visible contents or by grinding the samples through screens. Both of these procedures result in considerable damage to the constituents within the specimen and a resultant loss of data. Rehydration of the specimens also results in damage to the contents, particularly botanical and parasitological, as they would swell too rapidly and disintegrate.

Callen and Cameron (1960) developed a method of rehydrating paleofecal specimens by refining similar techniques developed by Benninghoff (1947) for rehydrating herbarium specimens and by van Cleave and Ross (1947) for rehydrating zoological specimens. The method involves rehydrating the paleofecal sample in a mild solution (e.g., 0.5 percent) of trisodium phosphate. This technique permits the botanical specimens within the fecal matrix to gently rehydrate with little damage and allows the matrix to deflocculate and be easily screened. This method, still used today, revolutionized the science of paleofecal analysis. Jouy-Avantin et al. (2003) developed a standardized method for the description of coprolite specimens.

Holden (1994:69–70) proposed three primary categories of food tissues (macroremains) that could be visually identified in paleofeces. The first category is tissues that generally survive in recognizable form, such as bone, chitin, hair, some types of shell, feathers, large tendons, and cartilage. The second category is that of tissues that may or may not survive the digestion process, depending on specific conditions; this category includes some plant parts, such as unmilled maize kernels. The third category is tissues that do not survive except under unusual circumstances, such as those that pass through the gastrointestinal system at high speed.

Several data sets can be used to determine seasonality of consumption and thus site occupation, particularly pollen (Reinhard and Bryant 1992:251–252; Gremillion and Sobolik 1996). Seasonality estimates based on paleofeces are problematic, however, since many resources

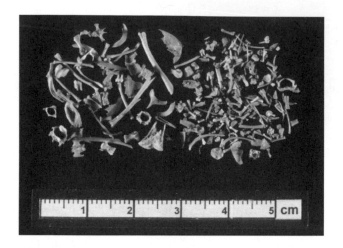

FIGURE 2.8. "Hard-tissue" faunal remains recovered from a coprolite in Hinds Cave, Texas (photo provided by Kristin D. Sobolik).

are storable and can be consumed at any time. As with many aspects of any analysis, the more concordant the data, the greater the strength of the interpretation.

Macrofaunal Remains in Paleofeces

A variety of "hard tissue" faunal remains may be present in paleofeces, including bone (fig. 2.8), feathers, hair, eggshell fragments, marine and freshwater shell fragments, insect exoskeletons, egg/pupal casings, and/or fish or reptile scales. These remains are typically identified using visual techniques; however, some "soft tissue" remains also may be present, such as muscle fibers and chemicals. The identification of these remains is becoming easier and will increasingly contribute to the data sets.

The bones of most large animals are too large to have been consumed whole, so they are most often eaten in some processed form. On the other hand, the bones of many small animals, including birds, bats, rodents, and reptiles (Sobolik 1993), can be consumed whole. One would expect, then, that the identification of faunal remains in paleofeces would be skewed toward smaller animals. Even if consumed, bone (especially fish bone) can be significantly degraded by the digestive process and may not

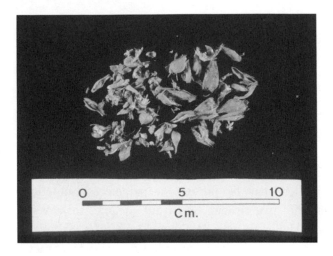

FIGURE 2.9. Botanical remains (onion fibers) recovered from a coprolite in Hinds Cave, Texas (photo provided by Kristin D. Sobolik).

pass through in a recognizable form (Jones 1986a; Butler and Schroeder 1998). This can obviously impede the identification of animals that are consumed by people, although the discovery of bones impacted by the digestive process may facilitate the identification of latrine areas.

Macrobotanical Remains in Paleofeces

Many intact and visually identifiable macrobotanical remains may be present in paleofeces (fig. 2.9), either as undigested materials (e.g., unmilled maize kernels) or indigestible remains (e.g., fruit pits). Other macrobotanical remains that are not so easily identified may also be present and analyzed using specialized techniques (see Butler 1988; Prior 1988; Smith 1988; Neumann et al. 1989; Sobolik 1992; Hillman et al. 1993; van de Guchte and Edging 1994; Pearsall 2000:170–188). Botanical remains are discussed further in chapter 3.

Some macrobotanical remains may contain evidence of processing techniques. For example, using scanning electron microscopy, Rylander (1994) identified traces of grinding on maize endocarps in coprolites from several sites in the American Southwest, suggesting that a variety of preparation techniques were used (also see Sutton and Reinhard 1995).

Rylander (1994) further suggested that variable preparation techniques could affect the nutrition available from a particular meal.

Microbotanical Remains in Paleofeces

Microbotanical remains recovered from paleofeces consist of two primary constituents: pollen and phytoliths. Both of these are discussed in more detail in chapter 3.

Pollen.   Pollen may be present in paleofeces, sometimes in very large quantities (see reviews by Bryant 1974b,c, 1975; Wilke 1978:70; Bryant and Holloway 1983; Williams-Dean 1986; Sobolik 1988a; and Reinhard et al. 1991). Pollen recovered from paleofeces may be used to determine plants consumed, employed in seasonality determinations, and used to supplement other botanical data. For example, Scaife (1986) identified cereal pollen in the gut of Lindow Man, complementing the macrobotanical evidence of grain consumption.

Phytoliths.   Phytoliths may also be found in paleofeces. While not actually organic in nature, phytoliths can be used to identify some of the plant species consumed (cf. Bryant and Williams-Dean 1975; Rovner 1983; Fox et al. 1996; Scaife 1986:134; Piperno 1988, 1991, 2006a; Reinhard and Bryant 1992:252–253; Piperno et al. 2000; Tyree 2000).

Other Microbotanical Remains.   The study of fungi (mycology) in paleofeces can sometimes provide useful data. Fungi often preserve well and "provide insights into the preservation conditions of coprolites" (Reinhard and Bryant 1992:250). The recovery of certain taxa in human paleofeces may provide indirect evidence of the consumption of species that those fungi inhabit (e.g., lagomorphs, rodents, and maize; see Reinhard and Bryant 1992:251). Scaife (1986:133) reported the recovery of fungal spores in the gut of Lindow Man.

Several attempts have also been made to identify bacteria and viruses from paleofeces. Although early efforts proved negative (Sneath 1962; Tubbs and Berger 1967), Fry (1976:24) identified cocci bacteria from several specimens, Colvin (in Stiger 1977:45) succeeded in culturing some cyst-forming anaerobic types from several specimens, and Williams-Dean

(1978:224–225) discovered an unidentified virus in a specimen from Hinds Cave, Texas, dating between 2,300 and 3,700 years ago. This avenue of research remains to be explored fully.

Endoparasites and Ectoparasites in Paleofeces

Endoparasites, primarily helminths (round, flat, thorny-headed worms), may be present in many human populations. Evidence of such infestations is present in paleofeces in the form of eggs, ova, and even adult parasites (e.g., Samuels 1965). Such parasites live inside the host and disrupt the absorption of nutrients, weakening the individual and leading to a variety of health problems. Evidence of parasitic infection may be found in all forms of paleofeces, including mummy gut contents (Zimmerman 1980:123, 1998:149–150; Gill and Owsley 1985; Jones 1986b), coprolites (Reinhard et al. 1987; Reinhard 1988, 1992b; Faulkner 1991;), and cess (Pike and Biddle 1966; Pike 1967, 1968, 1975; Reinhard et al. 1987:635). Reviews of endoparasites in paleofecal remains (archaeoparasitology) are available in Fry (1985:138–141), Horne (1985), and Reinhard (1992b, 1998b).

Early parasitological analyses of paleofeces were primarily from the Great Basin in Utah. These studies include works by Fry and Moore (1969), Fry (1970a, 1976), Hall (1972), and Reinhard et al. (1985). Other parasitological analyses were conducted by Hall (1977) on paleofecal material from Oregon, by Patrucco et al. (1983) on samples from Peru, by Fount (1981) on pre-Columbian mummies representing diverse populations, by Williams (1985) on soil around the pelvic area of a burial in the Plains, and by Bathurst (2005) on coastal shell middens.

The analysis of endoparasites in paleofeces can be used to infer a variety of behaviors (Reinhard 1992b), including (1) the health of the individual and/or the general health conditions under which the individual lived, (2) population movements (also see Kliks 1990) and trade, and (3) changing nutritional and social conditions associated with the transition from hunting and gathering to agriculture (e.g., Faulkner 1991). For example, the presence of hookworms suggests both a health danger and unsanitary conditions (see Reinhard and Bryant 1992:254). Even in the absence of the actual remains of a parasite itself, other conditions might imply their presence. For instance, Dunn and Watkins (1970:177)

reported Charcot-Leyden crystals from a Lovelock Cave, Nevada, coprolite, suggesting an infection by diarrhea-causing endoparasites.

As mentioned in chapter 1, differences have been noted between the
prevalence of parasitic disease in hunter-gatherers and agriculturalists
(Hall 1972). A number of debilitating and possibly life-threatening parasites have been identified from agriculturally based paleofeces from the
southwestern United States (whipworms, giant intestinal roundworms,
threadworms, beef tapeworms, dwarf tapeworms, and pinworms),
whereas only the pinworn (*Enterobius vermicularis*) has been identified
from hunter-gatherer paleofeces (e.g., Fry 1970a,b; Reinhard et al. 1985).

Agriculturalists and hunter-gatherers have very different subsistence
bases and lifeways that seem to influence the types of diseases found
in each group and the types of parasites that infect them. Studies suggest that increased sedentism (Nelson 1967), increased population size,
poor sanitation practices (Walker 1985), and close proximity to crops and
domesticated animals (Dunn 1968; Fenner 1970) may all result in an
increased parasitic load in prehistoric populations.

In addition to indications of the health of the host, the presence of
certain parasites in human feces provides indirect evidence of people eating animals that those parasites inhabit (called false parasitism [Reinhard
1992b:234]). For example, fish tapeworm eggs recovered from coprolites
in Peru suggested the consumption of raw fish, some eggs in Egyptian
specimens were derived from the consumption of beef and pork, and
the presence of other parasite species in Great Basin specimens suggested the consumption of insects and/or rodents (Reinhard and Bryant
1992:253). Other examples of false parasitism were provided by Reinhard
(1992b:236–237).

Ectoparasites (e.g., lice, roundworms, fleas) might also sometimes
be found in paleofeces and can be used to infer general health conditions and the types of species afflicting people at a point in space and
time. For example, Kenward and Carrott (2001) reported the presence of
the human whipworm (*Trichuris trichiura*) in paleofecal material from
an archaeological site in London that dated to the sixteenth and sev-
enteenth centuries. Whipworm, a type of round worm that infects the
large intestine, causes trichuriasis, which is a parasitic disease common
in countries with warm, humid climates. It primarily affects children,
who may become infected if they consume soil contaminated with eggs

of the whipworm. In some cases, it can result in bloody diarrhea and iron-deficiency anemia.

Analytical Approaches to Paleofecal Studies

Chemical Studies

The study of paleofecal chemistry is a growing subfield of analysis. In addition to visible remains, paleofeces can be expected to contain three main categories of organic compounds (Wales and Evans 1988:406):

1. Nitrogenous substances, mainly proteins and their constituent amino acids
2. Lipids that can be divided into three groups: (a) simple lipids, such as fats, oils, and waxes; (b) complex lipids, including phospholipids and glycolipids; and (c) derived lipids, including cholesterol, steroids, and vitamins
3. Carbohydrates, such as sugars, starch, and cellulose

Paleofeces are also likely to contain a range of minerals. Each of these categories, among others, has been investigated and is considered in chapter 3. A problem common to most of these avenues of inquiry is an incomplete understanding of the chemical impact the digestive process may have on the compounds (e.g., Wales and Evans 1988:407–409; Wales et al. 1991:340), although bile acids are known to survive and have been identified (Eneroth et al. 1966a,b; Kukis et al. 1978).

Wakefield and Dellinger (1936) conducted analyses of the percentages of nitrogen, calcium, magnesium, sodium, potassium, and phosphorus from paleofecal samples derived from a mummy in the southeastern United States; Zimmerman (1980:130) identified ammonia and phosphates in the feces of an Aleutian mummy; and Fry (1976:22–24, tables 16–18) analyzed twenty-seven paleofecal specimens from Hogup Cave, Utah, for basic chemistry (nitrogen, sodium, calcium, and potassium). None of these studies reported unusual results, although Fry (1976:22–23) reported a high percentage of sodium, likely the result of high concentrations in drinking water and salt-tolerant plants that were eaten.

Using protein residue analysis, Newman et al. (1993) were able to identify the presence of proteins in several coprolite samples. It is thought that these proteins originated in consumed foods and survived the digestive process. If verified, this technique could be used to address that portion of the diet that is "invisible" in traditional paleofecal studies. More work is needed on this aspect of analysis. (See chapter 3, under "Immunochemistry," for more information on protein residue analysis.)

The presence of numerous assemblages of apparently butchered human bone in the American Southwest is suggestive of cannibalism (e.g., White 1992; Turner and Turner 1999; Hurlbut 2000; Lambert et al. 2000; Novak and Kollmann 2000; Kuckleman et al. 2002; but see Reinhard 2006), although there is always the question of whether the materials represented ritual or other activities. Using materials from a small Puebloan (Anasazi) site in southwestern Colorado, Marlar et al. (2000) made the connection between butchered human remains, the presence of human proteins on cutting tools, human myoglobin in ceramic cooking vessels, and human myoglobin within a coprolite—all from the same context—to demonstrate the actual consumption of human flesh by other humans.

The hormonal content of paleofecal samples can now be measured using gas chromatography and radioimmunoassay (Sobolik et al. 1996). So far, this method has been used only to determine the sex of the depositor by measuring the levels of testosterone and estradiol. Although both of these steroids degrade through time, it appears that their ratios can still be used to determine sex. In the future, such work may also be utilized to study endocrine function and hormone metabolism. This method can also be employed as a cross-check to aDNA analyses for sex determination (see "Integrated Analyses" below); once the sex is determined, analyses of the sample constituents can help detect differences in diet between the sexes. It is possible that hormone levels could be used to discriminate between pre- and postpubescent females, but no such studies have been conducted.

Experiments in the recovery and identification of human aDNA in paleofeces have been undertaken (Sutton et al. 1996), initially merely to determine the sex of the depositor. More recently, analysis of three coprolites from Hinds Cave, Texas (Poinar et al. 2001), resulted in the identification of four animal and eight plant species, plus haplotype identification of the depositors. Clearly, this approach can be very productive.

Lipids (steroids/cholesterols) have been identified in modern human fecal samples in a number of studies (Eneroth et al. 1964, 1966a,b;

Miettinen et al. 1965; Martin et al. 1973) and have also been found in paleofecal materials. Wales et al. (1991:340) warned, however, that due to the digestive process, the identified lipids may not have anything to do with the food consumed. Lin et al. (1978) identified steroids in several coprolites from Lovelock Cave, Nevada, and lipid analysis has been used to identify cess in archaeological soils (Knights et al. 1983; Evershed and Bethell 1996).

Using visible infrared spectrometer and gas chromatography methods, Wales et al. (1991) identified beeswax in several coprolite samples from an Epipaleolithic site in Syria. Wales et al. (1991) argued that since waxes pass through the digestive process chemically intact (while lipids are altered), waxes may be useful in identifying their sources (such as plant taxa) in a fecal specimen.

Analyses of the odors detected from both modern and ancient rehydrated fecal specimens have identified some of the substances consumed (Moore et al. 1984, 1985). This technique utilizes both gas chromatography and gas chromatography/mass spectrometry analyses and has discovered compounds characteristic of licorice and apple in modern fecal specimens of individuals who had eaten those foods (Moore et al. 1985). A variety of other components have been identified in ancient specimens (Moore et al. 1984; also see Trigg et al. 1994:213–214, appendix 11.1).

Medical Analyses

In theory, fecal material should contain "signatures" of some health conditions. Relatively few medical studies on paleofeces have been conducted, however, although it seems that this aspect of paleofecal research has considerable potential.

Dunn and Watkins (1970) conducted a series of medical analyses on 168 coprolites from Lovelock Cave, Nevada (also see Heizer and Napton 1969; Napton 1970:240–241). These tests included bacteriological studies, the discovery of Charcot-Leyden crystals, and the identification of parasites (mites [also see Radovsky 1970], rhabditoid nematodes, and some unidentified worm eggs). Fry (1976:24) reported the results of medical tests of five specimens from Danger Cave, Utah. These tests included lipid-class gas chromatography (which indicated no significant differences between ancient and modern specimens), guaiac test for blood (all negative), the Sudan HCAA (heat and acetic acid) test for hydrolyzed fat (positive in three samples), and Gram-stain examination for bacteria (all negative for rods but all positive for cocci). Williams-Dean (1978: 77–78, 223) conducted a number of unsuccessful tests to identify blood in several paleofecal specimens from Hinds Cave, Texas. Finally, in an attempt to identify potential diarrhea-toxin-producing taxa, Williams-Dean (1978:96–97, 216–222) pinpointed the remains of two types of algae in specimens from Hinds Cave, Texas. While neither was a diarrhea-causing taxon, the same types were identified in nearby water sources, suggesting the use of those water sources in antiquity.

Integrated Analyses

The analysis of paleofeces is rapidly evolving away from a simple list of constituents found in a sample. The integration of new analytical approaches is beginning to produce a much more detailed picture of diet and health. Standard midden-derived subsistence data (e.g., faunal and botanical remains) can be combined with materials recovered from paleofeces as visible constituents (e.g., Sutton 1993), protein residues (Newman et al. 1993), aDNA (Sutton et al. 1996; Poinar et al. 2001), and hormones (Sobolik et al. 1996; Rhode 2003). In these ways, a great deal of information can be generated, including the sex of the depositor and the identification of materials not visually detectable.

Once these data have been obtained, statistical analysis of constituents can generate information on meals and cuisine, and that information can then be used to address questions of diet, health, and status (Sutton and Reinhard 1995; Sutton 1998). This wealth of data has only just been tapped.

Summary

Direct data present the most conclusive evidence in the paleonutritional data base for determining diet and health among prehistoric populations. Such data are those archaeological and biological materials that are clearly related to human paleodiet and nutrition. Direct paleonutritional data come in two forms: human remains (including bones, soft tissue, hair, and chemical components) and human paleofeces. By analyzing these direct data, aspects of paleonutrition can provide information regarding diet, nutritional stress, health, disease, and a variety of other paleopathologies. In turn, this information can elucidate issues of human morbidity, mortality, disease patterns and causes, and changes in subsistence regimes, among others.

These issues are ultimately relevant to the modern world. If we can determine how past peoples managed resource shortages, disease progression, and other dietary challenges, we may be able to employ the techniques archaeological cultures used to help people today. For example, among specific modern North American native groups (such as the Pima of Arizona), the prevalence of non-insulin-dependent diabetes mellitus (NIDDM) has been the subject of what has been termed the "thrifty" genotype (Wendorf and Goldfine 1991). This genotype, believed to have originated among North American Paleoindians who practiced a lifestyle of hunting and gathering, "allowed a selective advantage during the periods of fasting that occurred between big game kills" (Wendorf and Goldfine 1991:161). This advantage was then compromised when people adopted a more sedentary lifestyle and food resources became more constant. In other words, this genotype "has a selective advantage in a food-scarce environment [but] can contribute to NIDDM in a food-abundant environment" (Wendorf and Goldfine 1991:164; also see Lieberman 2003).

The promise of such research is clear and vital. As the example above demonstrates, the archaeology of nutrition around the world often presents a perspective on studies of diet and health today that is different and essential. This example also shows the exciting research potential for DNA analyses in archaeology as our techniques continue to improve. Working together, archaeologists and modern medical professionals can provide links between prehistoric health responses and medical mysteries of modern-day populations.

CHAPTER 3

The Paleonutrition Data Base
Indirect Data

INDIRECT DATA ARE THOSE that cannot be directly and unequivocally attributed to human consumption and so can only be used to infer aspects of human paleonutrition. Such data form the majority of information considered by archaeologists (see Sutton 1994). Categories of indirect data include visible faunal and botanical remains, most chemical remains, technological remains, and evidence regarding the use of landscapes. Unlike the direct data sets discussed in chapter 2, indirect data can only be used to infer human consumption and/or use of foods and other materials. It also is important to remember that, at least in most circumstances, the ecofactual remains recovered from a site do not represent the entire range of materials used by prehistoric peoples. This is due to processing in prehistory, preservation in the archaeological record, and the recovery techniques employed by archaeologists (see the discussion of taphonomy in chap. 4).

Faunal Remains

Faunal remains are the remains of animals in archaeological sites—*all* animals, not just the large ones (and including humans; see White 1992). Recent reviews of faunal studies are available in Klein and Cruz-Uribe (1984), Parmalee (1985), Davis (1987), Crabtree (1990), Brewer (1992), Lyman (1994a, 2008), Reitz and Wing (1999), O'Connor (2000), and Redding (2002). Faunal remains include a variety of materials, primarily bone, but also shell, soft tissues, blood, proteins, chitin, and even impressions in a matrix. Zooarchaeologists, those who study faunal remains, tend to focus on bone and shell and often do not look for or recover other materials, except in unusual circumstances. After recovery (the recovery of faunal remains is discussed in detail in chap. 4), materials must be properly classified and interpreted (for more complete discussions of this aspect of faunal studies, see Lyman 1982, 1987a,b, 1994b; Parmalee 1985; Brewer 1992; Reitz and Wing 1999).

The principal goals in the analysis of faunal remains as related to paleonutrition are (1) the reconstruction of human subsistence, including behavior and technology associated with subsistence and other aspects of culture, and (2) the reconstruction of paleoecology and biogeography. In addition, information regarding the use of animals for other than strictly subsistence purposes (e.g., entertainment, ritual, pets) also is important. Some of the questions an archaeologist may ask about faunal remains include:

> Which taxa [species] were regularly eaten, which were rarely eaten, and which were never eaten [and why]? Which taxa contributed most to the diet? When were particular taxa hunted? How much food did different taxa provide? Were particular age groups or one sex of a taxon preferred over others? Did age, sex, or individual selection vary intertaxonomically? Where were food animals hunted and how were they hunted [or otherwise obtained]? [Lyman 1982:335].

Archaeologists also need to understand a number of issues regarding the use of animals as food, including (1) the dynamics of divisions of labor, both gender and age related, involved in the procurement of food animals, (2) understanding the combinations of foods that were preferred to allow a reconstruction of cuisine, and (3) whether there was some sort of differential access to certain foods based on age and/or gender. Further, it should be kept in mind that animals were used for purposes other than as food, such as for raw materials (e.g., dung, hides, and fibers), as pets, as labor (transport and traction), and in ceremonies.

Virtually every part of an animal is potentially usable, although not all human groups use all parts. The general categories include hide, hair, meat, blood, marrow, sinew, bone, and viscera (see Lyman 1987a:table 5.1). Faunal remains may take a variety of forms, such as endoskeletons (bone), exoskeletons (e.g., shell, insect parts), soft tissue (e.g., mummified or otherwise preserved remains), and residual chemicals (e.g., proteins). Any or all of these materials may be encountered in an archaeological site; however, bone and shell are the most commonly recovered faunal remains.

Faunal materials enter an archaeological deposit through a number of mechanisms, with human activity being only one. Many animals (e.g., rodents, badgers) live their entire lives in sites, die there, and become incorporated into the site deposit. When the site is excavated, their bones are collected by archaeologists, along with the bones of animals used for food by the human inhabitants of the site. In some cases, the natural and cultural remains may be the same species of animal. Of the cultural remains, not all are the result of dietary activities. Various animal products (or the live animals themselves) were used for nonfood purposes and so enter the record along with the dietary remains.

Vertebrates

Vertebrates (phylum Chordata) are animals with backbones (vertebral columns and spinal cords). In most inland sites, most faunal remains are vertebrates. Terrestrial (land-dwelling) vertebrates share a common general skeleton and many of the bones (elements) have the same names. The most common elements will share a basic shape; that is, a humerus (upper arm or foreleg) looks similar from species to species.

The primary categories of vertebrates are fish, amphibians, reptiles, birds, and mammals. Fish are aquatic animals with gills and fins. Bony fishes possess full skeletons of bone, whereas cartilaginous fishes (e.g., sharks, rays, and skates) have a skeletal system of cartilage that is often reinforced by calcium in heavy load areas (e.g., vertebrae, jaws). Many of these reinforced elements will preserve in the archaeological record, such as vertebrae, jaws, otoliths, and scales. Each of these elements can be informative regarding species, size, season of capture, and even water temperature (see Casteel 1972, 1976:38–71; Wheeler and Jones 1989:145–146, 158; Colley 1990:214; Higham and Horn 2000).

Amphibians (e.g., frogs, toads, and salamanders) and reptiles (e.g., crocodiles, turtles, tortoises, lizards, and snakes) are ectothermic animals that lay eggs. Many amphibian and reptile skeletal elements are the same as in mammals. However, turtles and tortoises have bony shells that, if fragmented, may appear to be large mammal cranial parts. A discussion of amphibian and reptile remains from archaeological sites was presented by Olsen (1968; also see Sobolik and Steele 1996).

Birds are feathered, winged animals, although some are flightless. In general, bird bones tend to be rather thin relative to mammal bones and thickness of long bones is a key to the initial identification as bird. While birds share some skeletal elements in common with mammals, many elements are unique. A general treatment of bird remains in archaeology

TABLE 3.1. Mammalian Orders

Order	General Description	Comments
Flying		
Chiroptera	Bats	—
Marine		
Cetacea	Whales, dolphins, porpoises	Fishlike, fins and tails, no hair or external ears
Pinnipedia	Walruses, sea lions, seals	Standard-looking limbs, hair, and external ears
Terrestrial		
Marsupialia	Kangaroos, opossums	Pouched
Insectivora	Shrews, moles	—
Edentata	Sloths, anteaters, armadillos	—
Lagomorpha	Pikas, rabbits, hares	—
Rodentia	Chipmunks, marmots, squirrels, prairie dogs, mice, rats, beavers, voles, porcupines	—
Carnivora	Dogs, coyotes, wolves, foxes, bears, raccoons, weasels, skunks, lions, lynx, bobcats	—
Proboscidea	Mammoths, mastodons, elephants	—
Sirenia	Manatees	—
Perissodactyla	Horses, burros, hippos	Odd-toed, hoofed
Artiodactyla	Pigs, camels, elk, deer, moose, caribou, pronghorn, cows, bison, goats, sheep	Even-toed, hoofed

was presented by Serjeantson (2009), and several keys to the identification of some of the more common North American (Olsen 1979; Gilbert et al. 1981) and British (Cohen and Serjeantson 1986) species are available. Fragments of bird eggshells may also be present in a faunal collection.

Mammals are endothermic, (usually) hairy animals who bear live young and whose mothers produce milk to feed their young. Mammals are divided into three major types—flying, marine, and terrestrial (table 3.1)—and share a generally similar limb structure, with common elements. Many mammals were used for food and other purposes in antiquity; among terrestrial mammals, artiodactyls, lagomorphs, and rodents were the most widely used and are common constituents in site assemblages in many parts of the world.

Invertebrates

Invertebrates (animals without backbones) vastly outnumber vertebrates in sheer number of species and individuals, but are relatively uncommon in inland archaeological collections. Archaeologists typically recognize the remains of mollusks in sites and these remains are usually collected, although other invertebrate remains (e.g., insects) usually are either not recognized or ignored. Mollusks (phylum Mollusca, commonly called shellfish) are animals with soft bodies, often within shells, and include clams, oysters, snails, slugs, squids, and octopi. Waselkov (1987) provided a discussion of the study of shellfish in archaeological contexts (also see Meighan 1970; Bailey 1975), and Evans (1972) discussed land snails in archaeological contexts.

Archaeologists rarely deal with the insect remains from a site, usually considering them to be intrusive. However, virtually all peoples have eaten and/or used insects in some way and their remains are sometimes present in sites. Even if insect remains are recovered, several problems exist in their analysis, including taxon identification (there are few comparative collections) and quantification (primarily since they tend to be highly fragmented). Reviews of insect remains in archaeological contexts were presented by Elias (1994) and Sutton (1995).

The remains of other invertebrates, including crabs (Losey et al. 2004), lobsters, shrimp (marine and freshwater), spiders, scorpions, and worms also may be found in archaeological sites. These animals must be fully considered in any faunal analysis.

Botanical Remains

The remains of plants (from logs to pollen) found in archaeological sites are called botanical remains, although the terms *plant, floral, archaeobotanical,* and *paleobotanical* are sometimes used. The term *phytoarchaeology* (Brooks and Johannes 1990) refers to a broader realm that looks at the relationship between vegetation and archaeology and includes the study of ethnobotanical materials, contemporary plant distributions, and remote sensing to discover traces of the past from the distribution of plant communities. Plants include trees, shrubs, herbs, ferns, mosses, liverworts, and lichens, among others. The most obvious use of plants by humans is as food, but there are many other uses, such as shelter, bedding, textiles, cordage, firewood, medicine, and ceremonies. Nonartifactual botanical remains are classified as ecofacts, although many tools were manufactured from plant materials, in which case the remains are artifacts. Recent summaries of botanical remains in archaeology have been presented by Smith (1985), Miksicek (1987), Hastorf and Popper (1988), Hillman et al. (1993), Fritz (1994), Bryant and Dering (1995), Gremillion (1997), Hastorf (1999), Pearsall (2000), and Miller (2002).

In many cases, the plant remains from sites (at least those excavated prior to the development of more sophisticated techniques) were incidentally recovered using methods designed to find artifacts, such as while screening (the recovery of botanical remains is discussed in detail in chap. 4). Until recently, the collection and analysis of samples designed specifically for the recovery of botanical remains were relatively uncommon. An exception to this is flotation samples taken from features or other contexts. Even in those circumstances, however, only large floating remains were collected (the material that did not float, called the "heavy fraction," was often discarded). As the discipline has become more sophisticated, the existence and value of microremains are becoming more apparent to researchers.

Macrobotanical Remains

Macrobotanical remains are defined as those that are visible to the naked eye, such as seeds, charcoal, and fibers, but may also include roots and tubers (see Hillman 1989:215; Hather 1994). Such remains are usually recovered from archaeological sites only if they have been carbonized to some degree or preserved in dry or waterlogged contexts. In open sites, uncharred botanical remains are likely to be recent in origin. In circumstances of unusual preservation, a much greater diversity of remains may be recovered. In addition to the use of traditional visual comparative methods, identification of botanical remains may take several specialized avenues (see Hillman et al. 1993; Pearsall 2000:170–188), including thin-section microscopy (both optical and electron [e.g., Neumann et al.

1989; Tomczýnska 1989]), electrophoresis, isotopic analysis, morphometric analysis by computer (Mangafa and Kotsakis 1996), and by various chemical means (e.g., Ugent 1994; Fankhauser 1994).

Seeds

Most of the seeds from prehistoric sites will have been charred (otherwise, they would not have been recognized and recovered) and will be brittle and black in color. Some fresh seeds also are black, however, so the texture of the seed must be carefully examined to determine if it is charred. Seeds come in varying sizes, from very tiny to the size of maize cobs. Some of the most economically important seeds in antiquity are quite small (e.g., tobacco) and are unlikely to be recovered in normal field screening.

Caution must be exercised in the interpretation of seed remains (see Minnis 1981; Miller and Smart 1984; Pearsall 2000:240–242). Charred seeds are typically viewed as cultural in origin (Minnis 1981:147; Miksicek 1987:234–235), often associated with dietary activities; however, they may enter, or be moved around in, site soil by a variety of means, including by rodents and ants (e.g., Gasser and Adams 1981; Lawlor 1992, 1995).

Seeds, even of known economic plants, also may be incorporated into a site as the result of the use of a plant itself, rather than the seed, for nondietary purposes such as construction material or fuel (Minnis 1981; Miller and Smart 1984). For example, if the superstructure of a house was constructed of plant materials that contained seeds (e.g., juniper) and the house burned, charred seeds could enter the record in large numbers. Clearly, such seeds would not be of dietary significance. Such an issue might be resolved if the context of the seeds was considered (e.g., Pearsall 1988) and if additional botanical analyses were conducted on the remains of the structure, perhaps linking the seeds and charcoal as the same species. Such a technique could be applied to hearths as well, attempting to tie in seeds with firewood. Thus, while charcoal generally is not considered a dietary constituent, its identification and interpretation could be helpful in determining if certain other materials actually were dietary remains (also see Smart and Hoffman 1988; Wright 2003).

Another example is the presence of wild seeds in animal dung used as fuel. Such seeds could be charred in the fire and, if recovered in an excavation or hearth sample, might be wrongly interpreted as representing species used by humans as food (Hastorf and Wright 1998). It is imperative, therefore, that investigators consider predepositional, depositional, and postdepositional processes related to plant usage before assigning meaning to macroarchaeobotanical assemblages.

Charcoal

Charcoal is the burned, carbonized remains of plants, usually the woody parts (burned seeds usually are considered separately). Charcoal can enter a site in a variety of ways, from campfires (ancient and modern) to natural fires. Context is important in making this distinction (see Smart and Hoffman 1988).

Archaeologists tend to assume that most of the charcoal in a site is anthropogenic. One relative measure of activity from layer to layer is the quantity of charcoal in the midden. Some archaeologists do not save charcoal from screens, however, so this information must be obtained from soil samples. Quantification of charcoal (by volume and weight) from archaeological contexts is important, as it can aid in the interpretation of carbonized materials as they relate to the intensity of use, disposal, and cultural significance of a site.

It is possible to identify some wood represented by charcoal to the genus and perhaps even to the species level (see Thompson 1994; Pearsall 2000; but see Wright 2003). Identified plant species can be used to reconstruct the general environment, thus providing information regarding subsistence potential. In addition, the identification of the taxon of charcoal from a hearth feature can demonstrate which plants were being used for firewood, charcoal from a burned structure can indicate what was being used for the construction of houses, and so forth.

Microbotanical Remains

Microbotanical remains are those plant materials that are visible only with the aid of magnification, primarily pollen and phytoliths (see chap. 2). Some studies have been conducted on the identification of plant tissue remains based on micromorphology (Briuer 1976; Körber-Grohne and Piening 1980; Körber-Grohne 1981; Tomlinson 1985; Hillman 1989:215;

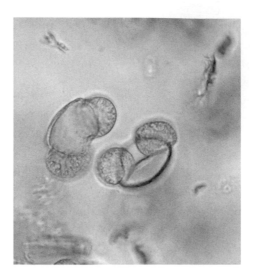

FIGURE 3.1. Photo of a pollen grain from pinyon (*Pinus edulis*) (photo courtesy of PaleoResearch Laboratory, Golden, Colorado).

Neumann et al. 1989; Hather 1991, 1993, 1994; Sobolik 1992; Ancibor and de Micou 1995), and this is a promising avenue of research. Preserved plant cuticles, the outer protective layer of many leaves, can provide additional information about plants (see Palmer 1976). In addition, starch grain analysis can be used to identify various root crops (see Loy 1991, 1994; Barton et al. 1998; Piperno and Holst 1998; Haslam 2004; Horrocks 2005; Piperno 2006b) and the relationship between tool type and function (Perry 2004).

Pollen

Pollen (fig. 3.1) is, in effect, the sperm cells of plants, and palynology is the study of pollen (see Bryant and Holloway 1983; Dimbleby 1985; Holloway and Bryant 1986; Moore et al. 1991; Fægri et al. 2000; Pearsall 2000:249–353). The spores of nonpolleniferous plants and fungi are sometimes considered with pollen. Pollen is ubiquitous in the environment, being distributed by a variety of mechanisms. Most pollen is airborne dispersed and settles onto all exposed surfaces in a "pollen rain." Pollen usually preserves quite well (but see Bryant and Holloway 1983:195–198;

Pearsall 2000:348–349) and is commonly incorporated into soils, including midden soils, thus forming a record of past vegetation. Much pollen is identifiable to genus and so can be used to delineate at least some of the species of plants in an area and/or those utilized by past peoples.

The analysis of pollen can be used to address a variety of research issues, including reconstruction of past natural environments, detection of anthropogenic and/or managed landscapes (Maguire 1983; Flenley 1994; Haberle 1994; Kelso 1994), presence of domesticates (Maloney 1994), and dietary studies. In the reconstruction of past diets, pollen data may constitute either indirect or direct evidence. Indirect pollen data can be used as a supplement to other botanical data to infer ecological conditions at a site and to delineate potential resources within the site region. Pollen data also can be used in the identification of room use (Hill and Hevly 1968), the contents of vessels (Jones 1993), and materials processed on tools, such as pollen recovered from a metate. Pollen may also be identified directly as a dietary constituent in human paleofeces (Bryant 1975; Wilke 1978:70; see chap. 2). The same basic principles also apply to phytoliths (cf. Rovner 1983; Piperno 1988, 1991, 2006a; Pearsall 1994; see below).

Pollen analysis should be approached with caution, however. Pollen records are easy to contaminate (e.g., through sampling or bioturbation) and pollen can travel great distances, potentially skewing the record for a given area. For example, the pollen record of a lakebed will contain pollen from the entire watershed of the lake, not just the immediate area.

Pollen may also be present on the surface of some artifacts and may be evidence of the processing of particular plants. For instance, maize pollen may be present in large quantities on milling implements used to grind maize. The detection of such pollen would indicate the species of plants processed and the function of the tool. Similar studies are possible on such artifacts as bedrock mortars, basketry, and ceramics (see Bryant and Holloway 1983:214–216). However, it seems clear that additional research on pollen deposition and taphonomy will be needed to make behavioral inferences from pollen data (Geib and Smith 2008).

Phytoliths

Phytoliths (see Rovner 1983; Piperno 1988, 2006a; various papers in Rapp and Mulholland 1992; Piperno and Pearsall 1993; discussions in

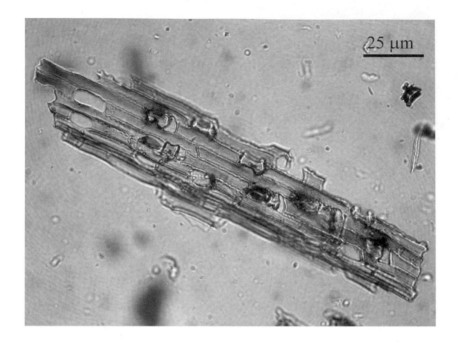

FIGURE 3.2. Epidermal sheet element from green needlegrass (*Stipa viridula*) with long-cell and short-cell phytoliths *in situ* (photo courtesy of PaleoResearch Laboratory, Golden, Colorado).

Pearsall 1994, 2000:355–496) are the microscopic silica bodies that form within individual plant cells (fig. 3.2). They develop when the minerals in groundwater accumulate within cells (the same residue seen as water spots on glasses caused by hard water) where they may form floating bodies within the cell or "shells" in the shape of the cell. When the plant dies, the biological tissues decompose in the soil, leaving the phytoliths intact, which then enter the soil in large numbers. In addition to soils, phytoliths may also come to reside on tools, teeth, containers, and other archaeological materials. Being inorganic, phytoliths usually preserve well, and in cases of poor organic preservation, they may constitute the sole botanical record (e.g., Powers 1988). Like pollen, phytoliths are commonly incorporated into soils, including midden soils. Unlike pollen, phytoliths are generally not transported far and so form a local record of past vegetation.

Phytoliths are usually identified using a general morphological typology, although recent efforts in computer-assisted morphometrics (Ball et al. 1996) are improving identification. Archaeologists are just beginning to learn how to properly recover, process, and identify these remains, but considerable work is still required to make the method more reliable (see Tsartsidou et al. 2007).

As with pollen, phytoliths can be used to address a variety of research topics, including reconstruction of past natural environments (Rovner 1983:242–247; Piperno 1988:200–217, 2006a:165–186; Fredlund 1993), detection of anthropogenic landscapes (Piperno 1988:189–192, 208–220), documentation of the presence of domesticates (Rovner 1983:249–253; Piperno 1988:169–184, 2006a:45–79; Fujiwara 1993; Rosen 1993; Umlauf 1993; Pearsall 1994; Pearsall et al. 2003; Harvey and Fuller 2005; Trombold and Israde-Alcantara 2005; Mbida et al. 2006), and dietary studies (Piperno 1988:197, 2006a:163–164; Pearsall 1993). Phytolith data can supplement other botanical data to imply past ecological conditions at a site (Lewis 1981; Rovner 1983:247–249; Piperno 1988:184–195; Dinan and Rowlett 1993) and to delineate potential resources within an area (Piperno 1988:195–197). Phytoliths recovered from tool surfaces can help identify tool function and plants processed (Rovner 1983:254–256; Piperno 1988:198, 2006a:163–164; Ryan 1995; Kealhofer et al. 1999), specimens found in vessels can help identify vessel use (Jones 1993) or content (Tyree 2000; Thompson 2006), and those found in association with features can help identify the species of stored plants. Phytoliths may cause distinctive wear on teeth, allowing inferences regarding diet (Rovner 1983:253), and they may also be discovered within dental calculus, indicating the consumption of those species (Rovner 1983:253; Ryan 1995). Phytoliths recovered from human paleofeces may be used to identify plants that were consumed, either as food or for other reasons (see chap. 2).

Although they are not phytoliths, calcite crystals can also sometimes form within plant tissues and may have some utility in the identification of plant species. For example, Freitas and Martins (2000) identified calcite crystals from storage facilities in Brazil and identified maize and cassava.

Biomolecular Archaeology

Chemical methods are increasingly important in the analysis of archaeological materials (Barraco 1980; Hedges and Sykes 1992; Loy 1993; Sandford 1993b; Lambert 1997; also see various articles in *World Archaeology*

25[1] 1993). The methods used to characterize and study organic remains is herein called biomolecular archaeology (following Barraco 1980) to distinguish them from the analyses of inorganic materials. This is clearly a multidisciplinary field that includes chemists, biologists, geneticists, physicians, geologists, biological anthropologists, and archaeologists. The techniques of biomolecular archaeology are applicable to a variety of research questions, such as human evolution; the paleobiology, paleogeography, and paleodemography of humans; human diet, food webs, and subsistence systems; artifact use studies; site formation processes; and environmental reconstruction (Thomas 1993:2–3). Of particular interest herein are those techniques that can be used to identify specific ancient foods, general dietary patterns, domesticates, diseases, general health patterns, and aspects of technology related to subsistence.

Analyses of Organic Residues

Organic residues are amorphous materials lacking clearly identifiable morphological features that would distinguish them as bone, wood, seeds, or other biologic materials (Heron and Evershed 1993:249; Pearsall 2000:178–183). Such residues may be visible on the surface of an artifact or absorbed into the matrix of the artifact, especially ceramics (Heron et al. 1991a; Heron and Evershed 1993:250; Evershed and Tuross 1996; Evershed et al. 2000; Craig et al. 2005) and milling stones (Jones 1989). Organic residues may represent materials processed (such as foods) or manufactured (such as mastics and textiles) (e.g., Jones 1993; Sobolik 1996; Hardy and Garufi 1998).

In addition to macroscopic and microscopic methods used to identify pollen, phytoliths, and/or tissues, organic residues may be analyzed with a variety of chemical techniques, including elemental analysis, stable isotope analysis, infrared spectroscopy, nuclear magnetic resonance spectroscopy, thin-layer chromatography, high-performance liquid chromatography (HPLC), gas chromatography (GC), gas chromatography/mass spectrometry (GC/MS), laser microprobe mass analysis (LAMMA), and pyrolysis. Reviews of these various techniques are available in Shearer (1988), Jones (1989), Biers and McGovern (1990), Evershed et al. (1990, 1992), Heron et al. (1991b), Heron and Evershed (1993), Fankhauser (1994), Ugent (1994), and Pollard and Heron (1996).

The usual approach in the identification of ancient organic materials is to characterize their chemistry and to compare those biomarkers to modern known species (see Heron and Evershed 1993:267–270). Much research in this area has focused on the use of lipids as biomarkers (Evershed 1993). This research has succeeded in identifying plants and animals (Evershed 1993; Fankhauser 1994; O'Donoghue et al. 1996; Dudd et al. 1999), food residues in vessels (Needham and Evans 1987; Marchbanks 1989; Charters et al. 1997), food residues (stains) on teeth (Oxenham et al. 2002), crop species in the Pacific (Hill and Evans 1988, 1989), and the importation of Dead Sea asphalt for use in embalming Egyptian mummies (Nissenbaum 1992). Identification of some plant species may also be possible with chromatography and spectrophotometry (Ugent 1994; Malainey et al. 1999a,b).

These analytical techniques are also utilized to identify drugs—ingested throughout prehistory for numerous purposes—in ancient tissues. The identification of such substances aids in our understanding of ethnopharmacology, religion, forensics, trade, and perhaps even recreation. For example, psychotropic drugs have been discovered in pre-Columbian New World mummies (Balabanova et al. 1995) and European bog bodies, perhaps used for ritual purposes (see discussion in Hillman 1986:103). In a controversial finding, Balabanova et al. (1992) identified the drugs cocaine and nicotine in ancient Egyptian mummies. Since these compounds are supposedly New World in origin, their presence in Old World mummies cannot be explained at this time, but may involve problems in sampling, contamination, and/or laboratory procedures.

Blood and Lipids

The presence of preserved blood on artifacts and/or other archaeological materials can be detected using visual and/or specific chemical methods. Less specific chemical methods to detect general proteins other than blood protein (e.g., hemoglobin) are also used by archaeologists and are discussed below. If preservation is good enough, individual blood cells can be observed microscopically from mummified human tissues (Zimmerman 1973), on artifacts (Loy 1983, 1991; Newman and Julig 1989; Newman et al. 1996; Loy and Dixon 1998; Shanks et al. 2001), and on raw lithic material (e.g., Hortolà 2002). In some cases, identification of the origin of the blood is possible, even to species. Such residues can some-times even be radiocarbon dated (D. Nelson et al. 1986).

A number of chemical methods are also available to detect blood residues (described by Loy and Dixon 1998). Several general tests are available to screen for hemoglobin, including guaiac paper tests to detect blood in feces (Fry 1976:24; Williams-Dean 1978:77–78, 223) and/or soils (e.g., Moffat 1988) and the Ames Hemastix test. A dot-blot test can also be employed to detect mammalian blood. Studies by Manning (1994), however, have cast doubt on the accuracy of the Hemastix and dot-blot tests for blood residues. If blood is identified, the species of origin can be determined using several methods, including isoelectric focusing (Oshima et al. 1982), hemoglobin crystallization (Loy and Wood 1989; Loy and Dixon 1998:28–30; but see Smith and Wilson 1992; Remington 1994), and aDNA characterization.

The ELISA (enzyme-linked immunosorbent assay) technique is also useful in the identification of blood. Smith and Wilson (1990) success-fully used ELISA to detect and identify hemoglobin in human bone tissue. Tuross (1991) was able to extract and identify serum-derived and bone-cell-produced proteins from human bone, and Tuross and Dillehay (1995) identified the species of origin of blood residues. Cattaneo et al. (1994) identified the blood protein albumin in 4,000-year-old human bone. But, as noted by Smith and Wilson (1990; also see Brandt et al. 2002), the degradation of blood proteins over time is a limiting factor in interpreting ELISA results. On the other hand, proteins may be quite resilient, as when Cattaneo et al. (1995) reported the recovery of albumin from ancient human bone that had been cremated.

The study of blood-cell antigen groupings is useful in studying pop-ulation genetics and population movements (see Henry 1980; Aufder-heide 1989). Most such studies have been conducted on soft tissues and a number of analytical problems are known, including poor preservation and misidentification of remains. Albumin appears to be the most use-ful blood protein for genetic investigation (Smith et al. 1995:68). Several studies have identified blood groups in mummies, such as those from the Arctic (Zimmerman 1980:130, 1998:149), from Egypt (Flaherty and Haigh 1986), and from Lindow Man (Connolly et al. 1986:74).

All human tissues possess a human leukocyte antigen (HLA) system, which is important in modern medicine to match transplant donors and recipients. The tissue types of family members tend to be similar and, in an attempt to determine relatedness between individuals, Ammitzbøll et al. (1991:89–94) analyzed the tissue types of eight mummies from Qilakitsoq, Greenland, suggesting that many of the individuals were related.

Lipids include a wide variety of compounds, although most archaeological studies have concentrated on fatty acids, such as steroids and cholesterols (e.g., Evershed 1993:75–76; Fankhauser 1994:228). Evershed (1993:93; also see Gülaçar et al. 1990) reviewed the general "properties, origins, means of detection, characterization, modes of preservation and decay, and application to archaeological investigation" of lipids. The recovery and analysis of lipids from human tissues could reveal a variety of information, such as general organic preservation and hormone levels (see Sobolik et al. 1996).

Lipids have been discovered in the tissues of bog bodies (Connolly et al. 1986:73; Evershed 1990, 1991; Evershed and Connolly 1994) and mummies (Gülaçar et al. 1990). The usefulness of lipids is not limited to human tissues. Lipids may also be used to identify the origin of samples, such as fecal materials (Bethell et al. 1993) and plant remains (McLaren et al. 1991; O'Donoghue et al. 1996).

Proteins

Very small quantities of proteins can be preserved in the archaeological record, and these proteins can be recovered and identified, sometimes to the genus level (for recent reviews of this work see Child and Pollard 1995; Bernard et al. 2007). Ancient preserved proteins can be present on stone tools, in human tissues, in human paleofeces, and in soils. A number of techniques, generally referred to as immunochemistry, can be used (see Cattaneo et al. 1993:table 2), but crossover immunoelectrophoresis (CIEP) is probably the most common. These techniques, often erroneously confused with blood residue analysis (see above), identify proteins not just from blood, but from the tissues of any living thing—animals, plants (but see Leach 1998), and even pathogens (Tuross 1991; Child and Pollard 1992).

Some researchers are skeptical about the applicability of immunochemical methods (e.g., Cattaneo et al. 1993; Downs and Lowenstein 1995; Eisele et al. 1995; Fiedel 1996, 1997; Brandt et al. 2002) while others are much more optimistic (e.g., Hyland et al. 1990; Newman 1990; Yohe et al. 1991; Kooyman et al. 1992; Newman et al. 1993, 1997, 1998; Tuross 1993; Shanks et al. 1999; Reuther et al. 2006). It is possible that aDNA analysis may be employed to determine the species represented in a sample (Loy 1993:52–56, 1996; Newman et al. 1998, 2002; Burger et al. 2002) and may be used to supplement or even replace immunochemical techniques.

Immunochemistry faces a number of technical problems and limitations. An understanding of whether proteins can actually preserve on archaeological materials is a major issue. While there is no question that proteins are initially present on, for example, an artifact used to butcher a deer, proteins are degraded by exposure to ultraviolet radiation (Tuross et al. 1996), and it is not clear how long they can preserve in recognizable form; however, preservation for at least hundreds of years has been documented (e.g., Newman et al. 1998). Another problem is that we can currently only test for several dozen species, meaning many species identifications will be missed. As more antisera are developed, however, this situation will improve.

Recent work has indicated that the standard methods employed for the recovery and storage of samples for immunochemical testing are destructive to the proteins (Cummings et al. 1996). Typically, proteins have been removed from specimens using ammonium hydroxide, which breaks the bonds of the proteins from the matrix and places them into solution; however, if left too long in solution, the bonds will break down too much, degrading the protein to the point where it cannot be recognized. In addition, the solution is commonly stored in glass vials but the proteins in solution will bond with the silica in the glass and further decrease the effectiveness of the test. The problem can easily be solved by placing the ammonium hydroxide in plastic vials and freezing the vials immediately after the proteins have been removed from the specimens. As pointed out by Marlar et al. (1995), some standardization of laboratory procedures is needed to make the results comparable.

The most significant problem in immunochemistry seems to be with the interpretation of results. The testing provides either negative or positive results. If the results are negative, it may mean that (1) proteins were never present in the sample, (2) proteins were present but did not survive in detectable form, or (3) proteins were present but the correct species was not tested for. It is currently not possible to distinguish between these three alternatives.

It is therefore necessary to deal only with positive results. If the result is positive, several interpretations are possible. First, the identified protein was in the sample as a result of cultural activity, such as yucca proteins being present on a grinding stone because yucca was processed on that tool in antiquity. Second, it is possible that the identified protein was in the sample as a result of contamination and is not related to cultural activity. For example, if a mouse urinated on a grinding stone, one might get a positive reaction to mouse but that would not mean that mice were ground up on the stone. This possible error can be minimized by processing soil samples collected from the vicinity of the artifact to test for contaminants. Proteins might also be present on artifacts from handling, so great care must be taken during excavation and analysis. Third, it is possible that the protein identified in the sample was either misidentified or that a false positive was obtained. Some species will cross-react with others and this possibility must be considered. These problems remain unresolved and great caution must be exercised in the interpretation of immunochemical results.

Immunochemistry can have important analytical implications. It is now possible to identify proteins on specific tools, thus aiding in the functional interpretation of those tools. For example, milling stones (metates) usually are regarded as seed-processing tools; however, Yohe et al. (1991) identified various animal proteins on such tools, indicating that particular animals were processed on the milling equipment. Not only did this provide evidence of resource use and associated technology, it also shed light on the processing of the bones from those animals, whose visibility in the conventional faunal record was much reduced (also see Sobolik 1993). In addition, it may be possible to identify pathogens in preserved human tissues, aiding in the understanding of past human diseases (also see Buikstra and Williams 1991).

Another important application of the technique is to expand our knowledge of the breadth of resources identified at a particular site (or region), resources that may not be present in the traditional (macro) dietary record. The following example illustrates the value of the technique. The macrofaunal analysis of the materials from a 3,400-year-old site (CA-SBR-6580) in southern California resulted in the identification of only turtle (*Clemmys marmorata*) and "large mammal" (Sutton et al. 1993). In the immunological analysis of both flaked and ground stone artifacts from the site, however, pronghorn (*Antilocapra americana*), deer (*Odocoileus* sp.), waterfowl, fish, rodents (rat), lagomorphs, and either porcupine or squirrel were identified, indicating the use of a variety of animals (Newman 1993). Nevertheless, the lack of visible faunal remains from similarly aged sites in the region has led researchers to suggest a reliance (specialization) on plant resources (cf. Moratto 1984:153). In light of these new data, the identification of a wider range of utilized animal resources suggests that the subsistence adaptation of the prehistoric people in this region should be reevaluated. More recently, Kooyman et al. (2001) used protein analysis to identify horse (*Equus* sp.) from a Clovis-age site in Alberta.

Inorganic Remains

The analyses of inorganic (elements, minerals, and some compounds such as water and carbon dioxide) remains typically include techniques to chemically characterize (or source) materials such as glass and metal (e.g., Henderson 2000). While such analyses can provide important information on various aspects of human behavior (e.g., trade and manufacturing processes), other types of inorganic materials related to diet and nutrition are contained within the foods people consume. These inorganic remains become incorporated into the tissues of the body and a number of these materials can be detected and measured. It should be noted, though, that the study of these elements cannot be used to directly "reconstruct" ancient diet, since they may have environmental origins. Rather, they can be used to deduce the general profiles of the different foods consumed in life. The major tissue utilized in these analyses is bone (e.g., Lambert et al. 1989, 1991; Lambert and Grupe 1993). These studies are conducted much less frequently than more traditional approaches, such as faunal or botanical analyses, and so are considered here in some detail.

Stable Isotope Analysis

Many elements exist in a number of isotope states; that is, in the number of neutrons in their nucleus. Depending on conditions, isotopes are either stable or unstable (radioactive). Stable isotopes do not change over time, making them ideal for measurement, while radioactive isotopes do change over time (but this is the basis of radiometric dating). Stable isotopes tend to be absorbed into tissues differentially, due to their unique molecular weights. Different types of plants tend to take up different isotopes, and animals that eat plants will absorb those isotopes in the same ratios as the plants. In theory, humans who eat animals will reflect the basic isotopic ratios of those animals. Finally, the stable isotopes within a tissue sample can be measured, plotted, and used to deduce the diet of the animal (including humans) from which the sample was taken. Conversely, isotopic ratios can originate in a number of ways unrelated to diet (see Hayes 1982), such as in the biological processes of the consumer, which can distort the analytical results (Schoeller 1999; Hedges 2003).

Of the stable isotopes, ten are of biological interest, with carbon, nitrogen, and oxygen generally being employed to infer aspects of paleonutrition (e.g., DeNiro and Epstein 1978, 1981; Sullivan and Krueger 1981; Schoeninger and DeNiro 1984; Turnlund and Johnson 1984; Parkes 1986; DeNiro 1987; Aufderheide et al. 1988a; Keegan 1989; Price 1989b; Schoeninger 1989; Tieszen and Boutton 1989; Gearing 1991; Pollard et al. 1991; Schwarcz 1991; Schwarcz and Schoeninger 1991; Katzenberg 1992; Schoeninger and Moore 1992; Ambrose 1993; Goldberg 1993; Pate 1994, 1997; Tieszen 1994; Katzenberg and Harrison 1997; Larsen 1997:271–290; Mays 1998:182–190, 2000; Ambrose and Krigbaum 2003; also see Goldberg 1993:table 3 for a list of other studies). Isotopes of carbon, nitrogen, and strontium appear to be the most useful in paleonutrition studies, although sulfur (e.g., Krouse and Herbert 1988; Craig et al. 2006; Privat et al. 2007), hydrogen (Schwarcz 1991), and calcium (Clementz et al. 2003) have the potential to provide clues related to past diet.

Isotopes are initially taken up by plants (see Tieszen 1991) and are concentrated in their tissues depending on the metabolic pathway used (see below). In general, isotopic values will increase (about 3 to 5 percent with $\delta^{15}N$; Bocherens and Drucker 2003) by trophic level. Thus, plants will have an isotopic signature, herbivores an enriched signature, and carnivores a further enriched signature (e.g., Minagawa and Wada 1984), although this enrichment may also be influenced by taxon within a trophic level (Sponheimer et al. 2003; Codron et al. 2005). Thus, all animal tissues contain an isotopic signature that reflects, at least in part, the

TABLE 3.2. Some Isotopic Values for δ¹³C and δ¹⁵N[a]

Material	General δ¹³C Value	General δ¹⁵N Value
Carbonate standard	o	N/A
Normal atmosphere	−7	—
Amazon rainforest atmosphere (at ground level)	−15.5	—
C₃ plants (e.g., beans, squash, manioc, trees, shrubs, cool-season grasses)	−27	+3
C₄ plants (e.g., amaranth, maize, warm-season grasses)	−12.5	+3
CAM[b] plants (e.g., cacti, agave)	−10 to −22	—
Browsing herbivores	−21	+5.3
Mixed feeding herbivores	−12	—
Grazing herbivores	−7	—

[a] Liberally adapted from van der Merwe (1982:table 1), Schoeninger and Moore (1992:fig. 1), and Hard et al. (1996:264–265).
[b] CAM = crassulacean acid metabolism.

food consumed. By measuring the isotopes in tissues, usually either bone collagen or apatite, a number of attributes of the diet may be deduced, although the preservation (see DeNiro 1985), transport, and retention of isotopes from food to tissues is not fully understood (e.g., Lee-Thorp and van der Merwe 1987; Schoeninger 1989:40–48; Ambrose 1993; Ambrose and Norr 1993). Further, DeNiro et al. (1985) demonstrated that extreme heating will alter the ratios and suggested that anomalous readings not be utilized in dietary reconstructions.

The systematics of carbon isotopes in the food chain are the best known (O'Leary 1981; Krueger and Sullivan 1984). Plants incorporate carbon into their tissues in one of three known pathways, each of which results in a distinct ratio of stable carbon isotopes (¹³C/¹²C, with ¹⁴C being unstable). The three pathways are (1) the Calvin (or "C₃") pathway where the three-carbon acid, ribulose bisphosphate, is the marker; (2) the Hatch-Slack (or "C₄") pathway in which the four-carbon acid, phosphoenolpyruvate (PEP), is the marker; and (3) the pathway characterized by crassulacean acid metabolism (CAM), via either the C₃ or C₄ path (see table 3.2). Experiments by Ambrose and Norr (1993) suggested that the C₄ contribution to the diet may be consistently and substantially underestimated (also see Schwarcz 2000). It was further argued by Heaton (1999) that $\delta^{13}C$ values on C_3 could vary enough to cause difficulties in interpreting small changes in archaeological samples. In addition, it was suggested by van Klinken et al. (2000) that marine foods played a lesser role in prehistoric diets in Europe, making the interpretation of carbon and nitrogen ratios from European samples more difficult.

Work by Fogel and Tuross (2003) indicated that the $\delta^{13}C$ values in the amino acids of samples could be used to differentiate the carbon signals derived from plants and animals. Thus, the total carbon intake relative to the total protein intake can be measured and the degree of omnivory could be calculated.

Nitrogen isotopes derive mostly from protein in the diet (Schoeller 1999; also see Ezzo 1993:14), and the ratios of $^{15}N/^{14}N$ can be used to deduce breastfeeding (Katzenberg et al. 1996), trophic level (Hedges and Reynard 2007), and the relative contribution of plant and animal proteins in the diet. Nitrogen ratios in bone may also be useful in deducing past climates (Heaton et al. 1986; but see Ambrose and DeNiro 1987).

Nitrogen values in tissues are measured in reference to the international standard of atmospheric nitrogen (ambient inhalable reservoir, AIR). Values of about +4 indicate that the protein was derived primarily from plants, whereas values in the +11 to +12 range suggest primarily animal sources. Values between these two poles indicate mixed protein sources. Thus, the use of a ratio of carbon and nitrogen values permits the modeling of the relative contributions of plant, terrestrial animal, and marine animal foods in human diets, although there is some evidence to suggest that the roles of terrestrial and marine resources may be reversed in some cases (deFrance et al. 1996).

Analyses of oxygen isotopes are useful in environmental reconstruction (e.g., Ayliffe and Chivas 1990; Bryant et al. 1994; Stephan 2000), to source fish (Dufour et al. 2007), and as indicators of seasonality of shellfish (e.g., Kennett and Voorhies 1996; Andrus and Crowe 2000); oxygen-isotope analyses have also been found suitable in detecting breastfeeding and weaning (e.g., Wright and Schwarcz 1998, 1999). Isotopic analysis can also be used to identify plant materials unidentifiable by more traditional means (DeNiro and Hastorf 1985).

Various assumptions are made in isotope analysis (and in trace element analysis; see below), including (1) that the isotopic composition of possible foods is known and does not vary, (2) that isotopic levels in human tissues reflect those in the diet, (3) that levels are distributed predictably across the diet, (4) that storage and preparation do not alter the levels, (5) that diagenesis does not alter the levels, (6) that isotopic levels can be accurately measured, and (7) that sampling is not an issue (Sullivan and Krueger 1981; Krueger and Sullivan 1984; Kyle 1986; B. Nelson et al. 1986; Buikstra et al. 1989:155–156; Grupe et al. 1989; Schoeninger et al. 1989; Schwarcz 1991; Schwarcz and Schoeninger 1991; Ambrose and Norr 1992; Hard et al. 1996:265–266; also see Parkington 1987; Armelagos 1994; Armelagos et al. 1989; Sillen 1989; Bocherens 2000; Grupe et al. 2000; Hedges and van Klinken 2000; Lee-Thorp 2000; Pfeiffer and Varney 2000; Schoeninger et al. 2003a,b). The broader the diet, the more difficult it is to interpret the measurements, and much work is still needed to gain an understanding of their anthropological meaning (Sillen et al. 1989), particularly in poorly understood ecosystems (e.g., Lam 1994). Further, Ambrose (1991) argued that nitrogen isotopic values will be higher in hot, arid environments than in cool, wet ones, suggesting that an understanding of the environment is necessary to properly evaluate results. Experimental results reported by Ambrose (2000), however, suggested that this model was not correct.

Isotope data have been plotted in a number of ways (fig. 3.3), including pointlike distributions to illustrate overall similarity in diet, a linear distribution to plot the relative contributions of two foods, or a diffuse plotting, such as the three-component isotopic diet model proposed by Bumsted (1985:542–547; also see Morton et al. 1991).

The majority of stable isotope work has been conducted on bone, usually collagen, as bone is the most common archaeologically available tissue, although other materials (such as seeds) can be used. Krueger and Sullivan (1984; also see Lee-Thorp et al. 1989) suggested that the differences in isotopic ratios between collagen and apatite could be useful indicators of paleodiet. While the preservation of collagen is not well understood (e.g., Collins et al. 1995; Semal and Orban 1995), it may preserve better than apatite (Ambrose 1987; Grupe et al. 1989), as it appears to be less susceptible to contamination (van Klinken 1999); thus, it may produce numbers more representative of diet (Tieszen and Fagre 1993a; but see Lee-Thorp et al. 1994). A problem in using bone is that it reflects only an average of the concentrations of the various elements over a

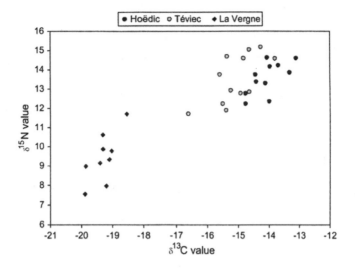

FIGURE 3.3. Plot of isotope data from human bone recovered from three archaeological sites in France. The higher nitrogen and lower carbon signatures from Hoëdic and Téviec indicate a greater reliance on marine resources (adapted from Schulting et al. [2008]; reproduced by permission).

ten- to thirty-year period (the bone replacement rate; see Hard et al. 1996:264). However, the use of tooth enamel, which does not remodel, for isotopic studies can be fruitful (e.g., Balasse 2002; Al-Shorman 2004; Clayton et al. 2006; L. Wright 2005; Tafuri et al. 2006).

The carbonate fraction of bone apatite seems to be more susceptible to diagenesis and thus may produce less reliable numbers (Schoeninger and DeNiro 1982; Lee-Thorp and van der Merwe 1991; Wright and Schwarcz 1996; Koch et al. 1997; Garvie-Lok et al. 2004), although not all researchers agree on that point (Krueger 1991). One method to test the integrity of bone collagen was developed by Parsche and Nerlich (1997). Tykot et al. (1996) noted that in order to obtain an understanding of all but the most simple food webs, isotope analysis should include measurements from bone collagen, bone apatite, and tooth enamel (also see Wiedemann et al. 1999; Lee-Thorp and Sponheimer 2003), coupled with baseline measurements from the plant and animal resources of that area (e.g., Schoeninger 1995).

Nielsen-Marsh and Hedges (2000a) suggested that bone diagenesis was site dependent, with site hydrology having a strong influence and bone porosity being the most important factor in bone preservation. In a further study, Nielsen-Marsh and Hedges (2000b) concluded that only histologically well-preserved bone would return reliable dietary data, but Koch et al. (2001) suggested that weathering did not alter the isotopic ratios in bone collagen. Ambrose (1990) proposed a protocol for the sample collection, processing, analysis, and reporting of isotopic data. Some work has been done on isotopic analysis of food residues (e.g., Morton and Schwarcz 2004; but see Hart et al. 2007) and this may be a promising avenue of research. More recently, isotopic analysis has been conducted on fossilized hominid bone (Drucker and Bocherens 2004; Lee-Thorp and Sponheimer 2006), suggesting that isotopic signature can preserve for a considerable time.

Few baseline data are available on isotopic values (but see DeNiro and Schoeninger 1983). Balasse et al. (1999) fed cattle specific diets and found that dietary changes could be detected using isotopic analysis (also see Balasse et al. 2001). Hare et al. (1991) conducted a controlled feeding experiment to determine isotopic concentrations in modern animal bone as a comparative base, and Richards et al. (2003a) determined that sulfur isotopic signatures in horses varied depending on the amount of protein in their diet. A similar experiment using pigs (Howland et al. 2003) showed the relationship between foods consumed and isotopes, cholesterol, and amino acids in the pig bone. Tieszen and Chapman (1995) plotted the isotopic signatures for many of the major resources in the Atamaca Desert in northern Chile for use as baseline data for prehistoric studies. O'Connell and Hedges (1999) compared hair and bone to collagen and keratin from the same individuals and found that the values varied greatly between the two sample types. Dufour et al. (1999) tested the isotopic concentrations of the same species of fish from lakes in a number of European locations and found that values varied, suggesting that no single baseline data set could be used to evaluate archaeological samples.

Witt and Ayliffe (2001) characterized the isotopic values in the diets of red kangaroos, compared those values to the isotopic values in the bone collagen, and determined that only adults reflected the diet accurately. Nursing infant kangaroos, they found, exhibited skewed isotopic ratios, seemingly due to metabolic pathway differences in the production of mother's milk, a situation that may also relate to humans. An isotopic study by O'Connell et al. (2001) on modern human tissues (hair and bone collagen) showed different isotopic values between the two sample types in the same individual, suggesting that consistency in isotopic signatures between sample types cannot be assumed. Further work on these problems is necessary to resolve these issues.

Isotopic analysis has also been used to ascertain the ratios of terrestrial to marine foods in the diet (Tauber 1981; Schoeninger and DeNiro 1984; Price et al. 1985; Sealy 1986; Walker and DeNiro 1986; DeNiro 1987, 1988; Hayden et al. 1987; Keegan and DeNiro 1988; Sealy and van der Merwe 1988; Parkington 1991; Goldberg 1993; van der Merwe et al. 1993; Bourque and Krueger 1994; Gilbert et al. 1994; Lubell et al. 1994; Tieszen et al. 1995a; McGovern-Wilson and Quinn 1996; Mays 1997; Richards and Hedges 1999; Coltrain et al. 2004; Eriksson 2004; Newsome et al. 2004; Prowse et al. 2004; Yoneda et al. 2004; Corr et al. 2005; Müldner and Richards 2005; Jay and Richards 2006; Keenleyside et al. 2006; Richards et al. 2006; Valentin et al. 2006; Bocherens et al. 2007; but see Harritt and Radosevich 1992; Day 1996; Katzenberg and Weber 1999; Richards et al. 2003b; Schulting et al. 2008), the ratios of plant to animal resources consumed (Bumsted 1981, 1985; Bocherens et al. 1991, 1999; Harrison and Katzenberg 2003; Richards et al. 2003c; White et al. 2004a; Lillie and Jacobs 2006), the types of animals that were eaten (van der Merwe et al. 2000), whether animals that were consumed were raised locally or imported (Klippel 2001; also see Barrett et al. 2008), whether animals were foddered (Noe-Nygaard et al. 2005; Pechenkina et al. 2005; Makarewicz and Tuross 2006), the role of dairy resources (Mulville and Outram 2005; Bocherens et al. 2006), the taxonomic identification of faunal remains (Balasse and Ambrose 2005), and for determining the general categories of foods eaten (van der Merwe 1982; Hastorf and DeNiro 1985; Ambrose and DeNiro 1986; Antoine et al. 1988; Chisholm 1989; Lee-Thorp et al. 1994; White and Schwarcz 1994; Tieszen et al. 1995b; White 1995; Iacumin et al. 1998; Richards et al. 2000; van der Merwe et al. 2003; Yesner et al. 2003; Thompson et al. 2005; Bösl et al. 2006).

Other isotopic studies have tackled larger issues such as group mobility (Sealy and van der Merwe 1985, 1986; Balasse et al. 2002; Bentley et al. 2004; Haverkort et al. 2008), general residence location (Hoogewerff et al. 2001; Burton et al. 2003; White et al. 2004b; Knudson et al. 2005), migration and mobility (White et al. 2000; Dupras and Schwarcz 2001; Schweissing and Grupe 2003; Ubelaker and Owsley 2003; Hodell et al.

2004; L. Wright 2005; Tafuri et al. 2006; Prowse et al. 2007), social and economic status (e.g., Schurr 1992; Reed 1994; Ubelaker et al. 1995; Richards et al. 1998; Schutkowski et al. 1999; Cox et al. 2001; Ambrose et al. 2003; Polet and Katzenberg 2003; Tomczak 2003; Le Huray and Schutkowski 2005; Dürrwächter et al. 2006; Honch et al. 2006), population variation (Katzenberg 1993), diets based on age (e.g., breastfeeding and weaning: Katzenberg et al. 1993; Schurr 1997, 1998; Herring et al. 1998; Wright and Schwarcz 1998, 1999; Richards et al. 2006; Bourbou and Richards 2006; Turner et al. 2006), the transition to agriculture (Papathanasiou 2003; Hu et al. 2006), intensification among hunter-gatherers (Bartelink 2006), the use of fertilizer on ancient fields (Commisso and Nelson 2007), crop management (Bogaard et al. 2007), and crop yields (Araus et al. 2001).

As noted above, isotopic data may be employed to deduce social structure. For example, using isotopic data on human bone from two separate Mesolithic cemeteries in coastal Brittany, Schulting and Richards (2001) detected differences in the consumption of marine foods between the two populations. Even more interesting, they concluded that young women had consumed fewer marine foods and suggested that these women had come to the coast later in life, possibly reflecting an exogamous, patrilocal marriage pattern. Another possible explanation may be differential access to certain foods based on sex or status.

In addition, isotopic data can be used in the reconstruction of paleoenvironment (van der Merwe 1989; Schoeninger et al. 2000; Schoeninger et al. 2003a) and the paleoecology of animals (Jahren et al. 1998; Bocherens et al. 1999; Sponheimer and Lee-Thorp 1999). Such studies have included the diet of domestic dogs (Cannon et al. 1999; White et al. 2001a) and camelids (Finucane et al. 2006), wild deer that feed on crops (Emery et al. 2000; White et al. 2001a), and even where crops were grown (Benson et al. 2003). Katzenberg et al. (2000; also see Schwarcz and White 2004) employed a combination of bone chemistry (isotopic and trace element) data, hair analysis, and experimental data on food known to have been consumed to reconstruct the diet of a large sample of skeletons from a historic cemetery in Canada. This study also provided comparative baseline data useful for studies of paleodiet.

One of the major research directions using isotopic data has been to understand the role of maize (a C_4 plant) in the diet (e.g., Vogel and van der Merwe 1977; van der Merwe and Vogel 1978; Burleigh and Brothwell

1978; van der Merwe et al. 1981; Boutton et al. 1984; Buikstra et al. 1988; Katzenberg 1988; White 1988; Ericson et al. 1989; White and Schwarcz 1989; Burger and van der Merwe 1990; Buikstra and Milner 1991; Boutton et al. 1991; Schurr and Redmond 1991; Blake et al. 1992; Larsen et al. 1992; Katzenberg et al. 1993; Lee-Thorp et al. 1993; Tieszen and Fagre 1993b; Chisholm and Matson 1994; Katzenberg et al. 1995; Little and Schoeninger 1995; Norr 1995; Ubelaker et al. 1995; Hard et al. 1996; Tykot et al. 1996; Larsen et al. 2001; Webb et al. 2004). Similar efforts have been made in the analysis of trace elements (see Aufderheide et al. 1988b; Armelagos et al. 1989; Aufderheide 1989; Buikstra et al. 1989; Price 1989a), and isotopic data have been combined with other data sets, such as trace elements (Spielmann et al. 1990; Katzenberg et al. 2000), paleofecal materials (Matson and Chisholm 1991), faunal remains (van der Merwe et al. 2000), and archaeobotanical specimens (Tuross et al. 1994; Hard et al. 1996), in order to broaden the perspective.

Evershed et al. (1995) reported the recovery of lipids (steroids and cholesterols) from samples of archaeological bone and suggested that measurements of ^{13}C isotopes from the lipids could be used in conjunction with ^{13}C measurements from collagen in isotopic analysis. Additional studies in the analysis of cholesterol from bone (e.g., Scott et al. 1999) have suggested that it may retain a more reliable isotopic signature than collagen and may better represent past diet. Finally, isotopic analysis can be used to source wood (Reynolds et al. 2005), to source irrigation water (Williams et al. 2005), and to trace the origin of some traded materials, such as shell (Vanhaeren et al. 2004), glass (Henderson et al. 2005), and textiles (Benson et al. 2006).

Trace Element Analysis

Trace elements are those that occur in minute amounts and may be present in the body by being ingested with food or from environmental exposure. A number of elements may have potential in the study of paleodiet, but it may be that only barium and strontium can be utilized (Ezzo 1994a,b). General reviews of trace element analyses were provided by Klepinger (1984), Buikstra et al. (1989), Sandford (1992), Ezzo (1994a), Sandford and Katzenberg (1995), Larsen (1997), Mays (1998:190–196), and Sandford and Weaver (2000). In general, there is considerable concern that trace elements may not be very useful (or may be misleading) in the reconstruction of paleodiet due to biogenic changes in concentrations having little to do with diet and in diagenesis of archaeological materials. Nevertheless, efforts to refine the technique continue.

To be useful in studies of paleonutrition, a trace element must follow the basic principles of the strontium model (Comar et al. 1957; Toots and Voorheis 1965), and Ezzo (1994a, 1994b:610) suggested that a trace element must meet at least six criteria. The trace element must (1) be measurable, (2) correlate to dietary intake, (3) concentrate in bone, as bone is the most common archaeological material, and (4) not be an essential nutrient so as to have an independent concentration, but should (5) imitate the movement and activity of an essential nutrient and (6) be stable. Some controlled experiments have been conducted to determine trace element concentrations in animal bone (Lambert and Weydert-Homeyer 1993a,b), although there has been relatively little work accomplished to ascertain baseline data in human bone (Hancock et al. 1989, 1993).

Some trace elements are essential for metabolic processes, and serious health problems may occur if they are lacking. Others are toxic at even very low levels. Several trace elements are absorbed into the body but serve no metabolic function. For example, calcium (Ca) is absorbed into the body and incorporated into bone. If present in food, however, the body will absorb some strontium (Sr) and/or barium (Ba) and incorporate them into bone in place of some of the Ca and the ratios of Sr and Ba to Ca will diminish by trophic level. Thus, many have argued that the levels of Ca and the ratios of Sr/Ca and Ba/Ca can be used to determine dietary constituents (e.g., Blakely 1989; Sillen 1992; Sillen et al. 1995), including marine resources (Burton and Price 1990, 1991). It is also important to realize that the Sr/Ca and Ba/Ca ratios are affected by a number of other factors, including diets high in calcium and differences in culinary practices (Burton and Wright 1995). In addition, Burton et al. (1999:609) argued that Ba/Ca and Sr/Ca ratios vary too much in natural plant assemblages to be used in a "quantitative assessment of plant/meat ratios" (also see Burton and Price 1999, 2000).

The majority of work on trace element analysis has been performed on soft tissues, although most of the archaeological work has been conducted on bone (see Gilbert 1985:347–352; Aufderheide 1989:237–253), primarily collagen. On the other hand, Coyston et al. (1999:222) suggested that "bone apatite, which is the mineral phase of bone, may provide a more reasonable estimate of the composition of the whole diet," and Grupe (1988) argued that compact bone was the best type to sample. Hair and nails are probably more sensitive materials since they reflect very short-term exposures. Tooth enamel develops during childhood and contains a record of trace elements and so reflects childhood diet. As it does not remodel during adulthood, tooth enamel is the material of choice for trace element analysis and dietary reconstruction (e.g., Ericson 1993; Rink and Schwarcz 1995; Richards et al. 2002).

Strontium (see Sealy et al. 1991; Sillen and LeGeros 1991), barium, zinc, and lead are the primary trace elements examined in bone (Aufderheide 1989; Burton 1996). Strontium apparently does not fractionate by trophic level and can be very useful in the identification of residence location, particularly of children (as the strontium signature of childhood is "locked" in the tooth enamel throughout life). However, Ambrose (1987) suggested that strontium may be more susceptible to diagenesis than generally thought, although Aufderheide and Allison (1995a; also see Sillen and Sealy 1995) argued that bone contaminated to the point of altering Sr/Ca ratios can be detected and eliminated from a sample. More recent work (Hoppe et al. 2003) has not been as optimistic with bone but has suggested that enamel may be the best material to use in strontium analysis. While other elements may be useful (e.g., Lambert et al. 1979, 1984; Farnum et al. 1995), Ezzo (1994a,b) argued that only strontium and barium are productive since the levels of other elements are determined by cellular function, rather than just diet.

Anthropological interest in trace elements centers on issues of diet, health, and behavioral correlates (Aufderheide 1989:240–241). Trace element concentrations in human tissues and bone may be employed to investigate a variety of ecological, dietary, and social questions. The relative contribution of plant and animal foods (trophic levels) in the diet can be estimated (Sillen and Kavanagh 1982; Gilbert 1985:346–347, table 11.1; Ericson 1989; Spielmann et al. 1990; Baraybar and de la Rua 1997; Little and Little 1997), although some plants may provide a disproportionate amount of calcium, skewing estimates of plant/meat ratios (see Burton 1996).

Trace element data have been used to infer similarity of diet by sex (Lambert et al. 1979:121, 127; Cook and Hunt 1998), social status (e.g., Schoeninger 1979; Aufderheide 1989:246; Vuorinen et al. 1990; Cook and Hunt 1998; Schutkowski et al. 1999), the contributions of marine resources (Sealy and Sillen 1988; Francalacci 1989; Burton and Price 1990, 1991; Aufderheide and Allison 1995b; Baraybar 1999), migration and mobility (Katzenberg and Krouse 1989; Price et al. 1994a,b, 2000; Grupe 1995; Sealy et al. 1995; Ezzo et al. 1997), identification of group affinity (e.g., Verano and DeNiro 1993; Safont et al. 1998), residence patterns (Ericson 1985; Aufderheide et al. 1995; Baraybar 1999), whether a woman might have been pregnant or lactating (Blakely 1989), weaning patterns (Sillen and Smith 1984), and perhaps seasonality (Herrmann 1993). Trace element analysis has also been employed to deduce dietary deficiencies since levels of various elements that are too high or too low may have serious health consequences (Aufderheide 1989:table 1).

In addition, some aspects of pollution can be measured through trace element analysis (e.g., Bresciani et al. 1991:164–167). For example, Pyatt et al. (2000) measured copper and lead concentrations in various samples from the area of a copper mine used during Nabatean, Roman, and Byzantine times in southern Jordan and discovered that heavy metals not only polluted the area during those times, but continue to do so today. High concentrations of some trace elements, such as lead, can be used as a measure of industrial activity (e.g., Ericson et al. 1979, 1991), ethnicity (e.g., Carlson 1996), status differences (Aufderheide et al. 1981, 1985, 1988b; Corruccini et al. 1987), and even behavior related to toxicity (Kowal et al. 1991; Farrer 1993; Beattie 1995; Keenleyside et al. 1996).

A number of methods may be employed to measure elements (see Gilbert 1985:351–352; Aufderheide 1989:241–243, table 2). The most sensitive methods are electroanalysis, mass spectrometry, and neutron activation analysis (NAA). Spectrographic (emission, absorption, plasma), atomic absorption, and various X-ray methods are also common analytical methods (e.g., Lambert et al. 1979; Bethell and Smith 1989; Winter and Marlow 1991; Pollard and Heron 1996). A new method to analyze elements is inductively coupled plasma mass spectrometry (ICP-MS).

Problems abound in using trace elements in dietary analyses (see Kyle 1986; Runia 1987; Hancock et al. 1989; Sillen et al. 1989; Schwarcz and Schoeninger 1991; Ezzo 1994a; Klepinger 1994; Katzenberg and Sandford 1995; Sandford and Katzenberg 1995). The primary problems are (1) whether element concentration is dependent on diet or whether biogenesis has altered the concentration, (2) sampling procedures, and

(3) whether the measured concentrations have been altered by diagenesis (e.g., Ambrose 1987; Pate and Hutton 1988; Grupe and Piepenbrink 1989; Tuross et al. 1989; Lambert et al. 1990; Schwarcz and Schoeninger 1991:287; Ezzo 1992; Radosevich 1993; Sandford 1993a; Farnum et al. 1995), although it appears that it may be possible to mitigate the diagenesis problem (Price et al. 1992; Edward and Benfer 1993). The impact of cremation on trace element concentrations in bone is also an issue (Grupe and Hummel 1991). Other issues include incomplete data on trace element contents for certain resources, the usually large variety of foods consumed, the shifting percentages of consumed resources, the consumption of some resources high in trace elements (e.g., nuts and berries) overwhelming the signature of other resources, and the usually small archaeological sample size.

Using ICP-MS, Cordell et al. (2001) measured soil chemistry in three sample cornfields in New Mexico, grew corn on those fields, and were able to match the corn chemistry to the fields, developing a method to trace the geographic location where corn was grown. Ultimately, they hope to trace archaeological materials found in the Chaco Canyon area to their sources to test the hypothesis that some of the corn had been traded in from other regions.

Soil Chemistry Analysis

People and animals alter site soils, resulting in anomalous concentrations of some chemicals, including calcium, magnesium, nitrogen, phosphates, and potassium, and they can alter soil pH (Cook and Heizer 1962, 1965; Eidt 1973). On a large scale, soil chemistry, particularly phosphate concentrations, can be used to locate sites (see Woods 1977; Weymouth and Woods 1984; Parkes 1986:232–236; Bethell and Máté 1989).

Within a site, soil chemistry can be used to detect a variety of structures, with phosphate levels being a primary tool to define midden concentrations, to locate various activity areas (e.g., Chaya 1996; Schlezinger and Howes 2000), to identify latrine areas (e.g., an increase in nitrogen), and even to detect plowed soils or agricultural fields (Leonardi et al. 1999).

Morgan et al. (1984) conducted analyses on soils from an Arctic site and identified "fats" derived from seals, the predominant taxa in the faunal assemblage (also see Nolin et al. 1994). Davies and Pollard (1988) tested the soils around a human burial and detected higher-than-background levels of organics, including lipids, suggesting that soil analysis may be useful in detecting burials where bone does not preserve. Research conducted by Bethell (1991; also see Bethell and Smith 1989) on the concentrations of elements in soils showed that this could also be an effective method to detect "shadow burials" (no bones, just a stain that in proper context can be identified as a burial). Evershed and Tuross (1996) identified proteins and amino acids in some soils, associated with ceramic vessels.

Other Data Sources

The technology of food production, procurement, processing, transport, storage, and consumption can yield a great deal of information regarding paleonutrition. For example, artifact assemblages are often used in support of certain interpretations regarding hunting, plant processing, or other subsistence practices. If the function of certain tools is simply assumed, however, their evidentiary power to deduce dietary patterns may be compromised. In addition, the function of features, such as those used for storage, can provide considerable insight into diet. Some information may also be gleaned from written and/or oral accounts of disease (e.g., Andersen 1991; Chase 1991; Kelley 1991) and depictions of disease and/or pathologies in art (e.g., Dequeker 1991; Filer 1995:29–39), such as imprint paintings of hands that seem to be missing fingers (Wells 1964:32–35, figs. 4, 14).

Certain landscape modifications, such as irrigation features, cleared fields, and/or deforested areas, might be used to infer some aspects of an economic and/or settlement system. In addition to physical features in the landscape, conventional ecofactual data (e.g., faunal and botanical remains) could contribute information to landscape studies. Using archaeobotanical analyses, carbon-isotope studies on cattle bones, and shifting settlement patterns, Reddy (1991) postulated an increasing emphasis on pastoralism and adoption of drought-resistant summer crops in the late Harappan of India and Pakistan.

Among hunter-gatherers, burning was a common technique to modify and manage landscapes, for both ritual and subsistence purposes (see Lewis 1982). As such, the detection of landscape burning could imply the presence, absence, and availability of certain resources, as well as which resources were emphasized. Westbroek et al. (1993) suggested that burning by hunter-gatherers over the last million years was the impetus for large-scale climatic change.

Summary

As discussed in this chapter, indirect data in paleonutrition studies include faunal and botanical remains, biomolecular materials, inorganic remains, technology related to food acquisition and processing, and landscape modifications. While such data are more open to interpretation than direct data are, they nonetheless provide critical information regarding human nutrition during prehistory. Ideally, direct and indirect data should be used in tandem, leading to a more comprehensive understanding of paleonutrition.

For example, a recent study combining paleofecal, aDNA, immunological protein residue, radiocarbon, obsidian hydration, geoarchaeological, artifactual, botanical, and faunal analyses provided data on some of the earliest evidence of human occupation in the Far West (Jenkins 2007). At Paisley Caves in south-central Oregon, the recovery of human coprolites prompted this multidisciplinary study to verify the identification, context, and age of the coprolites. Along with the other data from the site, the study indicated that initial occupation of the site took place by at least 12,000 years ago.

The Jenkins study is ongoing, and subsequent analyses at Paisley Caves have the potential to contribute information regarding nutrition in far western North America during Paleoindian times. The point here is that if archaeologists plan for such multidisciplinary studies, the data base related to paleonutrition (as well as other aspects of human behavior) will be greatly enhanced. Only then will we be able to have a more detailed understanding of diet and nutrition among prehistoric populations.

CHAPTER 4

Issues in the Recovery of Paleonutritional Data

THERE ARE A VARIETY of methods used to recover archaeological materials important for paleonutritional analyses. These methods are dependent on the type of site that is being excavated, the types of matrix and strata from which the remains are recovered, and the kinds of research questions being asked. The most important step in the recovery of such materials is that the paleonutritionist be involved from the very beginning. The paleonutritionist should be a part of the research design and should help plan where excavations will take place and how excavations should proceed in order to assist in the recovery of the various materials that are necessary for paleonutritional assessments. During actual excavations, the paleonutritionist should be present to collect at least some of the samples and to observe depositional conditions and recovery. In this way, the paleonutritionist will be able to assess taphonomic factors and conditions as well as modify the basic plan of recovery if needed.

The least innovative, but productive, way to recover biological materials is to have a technician collect random, unspecified samples from the field and send them in a bag to the paleonutritionist, along with a map of the field grid indicating where each sample was collected. The problem with this method is that the paleonutritionist has no indication of potential taphonomic factors, the kinds of cultural or environmental conditions that may have influenced deposition and preservation, whether samples were collected from unambiguous cultural features/horizons/ zones, whether the "best" samples were collected, or how the samples fit in with the entire site. If the paleonutritionist conducting the analyses had never been to the site during excavation and/or had not been a part of the excavation design and sample recovery, the analysis of the samples may become nothing more than technical identification with little or no interpretation. If paleonutritionists wish to contribute to the understanding of prehistory and the importance of biological material in the reconstruction of past lifeways, they should be involved in the actual recovery process at all stages. The major issues facing the paleonutritionist in the interpretation of materials collected from an archaeological site are a clear understanding of taphonomy, the identification of cultural versus noncultural materials, and a recognition of how recovery methods may have influenced what materials were recovered from a site.

Taphonomy

Taphonomy is the study of site formation processes as they affect the preservation, inclusion, and distribution of biological components from archaeological sites. Efremov (1940), a paleontologist, defined the term *taphonomy* (*taphos* [tomb] and *logos* [law]) as the study of the transition of animal remains from the biosphere to the lithosphere. Because the term was defined by a paleontologist, most taphonomic studies have focused on the recovery and analysis of bone remains, although the taphonomy of plant (and other) remains is just as important for archaeological inter-pretations. Since its inception, the definition of taphonomy has been altered to fit the needs of both paleontology and archaeology. Today, the study of taphonomy has evolved to include the postfossilization period (Lyman 1994a), and the scope of taphonomy now encompasses the his-tory of biological remains, including their collection and curation (see Sobolik 2003).

Because of the broad array of biological, environmental, and human agents affecting the preservation, inclusion, and distribution of biological remains in archaeological sites, taphonomy should be the first concern of all archaeologists and paleonutritionists before they even begin to recover these remains. Before walking onto a site, before screening for bones, before floating for seeds and charcoal, the archaeologist should be thinking about all the agents that could be responsible for the assemblage and that may have affected the archaeological site overall. In this chapter, we discuss why it is important for the paleonutritionist (and archaeologist) to be aware of taphonomic processes at every step of an investigation, particularly what types of taphonomic factors could be influencing their assemblages and how they might account for these factors in the overall analysis and interpretation. As Bunn (1991:438) observed, "Taphonomic studies of mod-ern analogs have shown the complexity of the processes that affect bones; but rather than despair, we should recognize that the processes likely to have operated at a particular archaeological site, and the likely range of variability in the patterned effects of those processes, are specifiable."

Some of the ways that archaeologists and paleonutritionists can help determine the taphonomic processes of a site or assemblage are with the aid of experimental archaeology and ethnoarchaeology. Experimental archaeology and ethnoarchaeology provide avenues for testing hypotheses about site formation processes and artifact assemblage preservation, movement, and origin.

In experimental archaeology, researchers can conduct staged experiments, as well as observe modern natural factors, to determine various environmental and cultural elements affecting their site and/or assemblages. With experimental archaeology, we can stage or observe phenomena that relate to what we see in the archaeological record. In this way, it is possible to formulate ideas about how archaeological sites actually become formed and what types of impacts various factors have on the formation process. For example, in a study of bone movement by wood rats, Hoffman and Hays (1987) introduced bone from six different animal taxa into an active wood rat den and recorded how the rats influenced the culturally controlled assemblage. Bocek (1986) observed modern rodent ecology to determine the potential effects of rodents on archaeological sites. For this study, the experiment was not controlled, but rather the observations of those effects were the basis for the analysis and interpretations (Bocek 1986).

Another way in which archaeologists and paleonutritionists measure the taphonomy of sites or assemblages is through the use of ethnoarchaeology. Ethnoarchaeology is the study of living human communities by archaeologists for the purpose of answering archaeologically derived questions. Data from these studies are particularly useful to taphonomists because such studies are, in essence, living demonstrations of the cultural processes involved in site formation. For example, in a study of modern Aché hunter-gatherer camps, Jones (1993) indicated that short-term camps have a pattern that is distinct from long-term camps in that the former have a fire-focused assemblage pattern in which debris is in primary context. We can then infer that short-term camps of prehistoric people with a similar cultural pattern may contain artifacts in primary context, whereas long-term camps may exhibit more assemblages in secondary context (see below).

There are limits to the use of ethnoarchaeological data since modern societies have different behaviors and customs that can create artifact and site patterns that are different from those of past societies. In addition, prehistoric (and modern) human behaviors vary through time and across space, so comparing the assemblage patterns of contemporary hunter-gatherers in Africa to Paleoindians in North America may be problematic. What ethnoarchaeological studies do offer is an arena for observing cause-and-effect relationships between humans and their environment that cannot be obtained through other means. For the rest of this section, we discuss the different components of archaeological sites that can affect the taphonomy of biological assemblages used in paleonutritional assessments.

Of primary importance to an archaeologist is the determination of whether an archaeological assemblage is actually cultural, whether it was deposited and/or modified by humans. There are a variety of ways in which biological remains can become deposited in archaeological sites that have nothing to do with humans. For the analysis and interpretation of human behavior, it is important to ascertain which part of the site and which assemblages are due to human behavior and which are not. After determining which assemblages are cultural, the researcher can then assess whether that cultural material is in primary or secondary context; that is, whether this cultural material is in the context in which prehistoric humans placed it (primary) or has been moved or modified by other processes such as fluvial action, dogs, tree throws, or modern vandals (secondary). If it is determined that the assemblage is in secondary context, then it is necessary to determine whether analysis of that assemblage will be useful to the overall research agenda and/or questions.

Preservation

Preservation of materials in archaeological contexts is the intersection of recognition and recovery, both of which are dependent on the research design, field methods, training, laboratory analyses, and skill. Organic materials in a site degrade, often to the point that the field archaeologist is unable to visually recognize them. Thus, in the eyes of the archaeologist, such materials did not preserve. It may also be that the methods used in the excavation of a site preclude the recovery of some items; for example, the size of the screen mesh used will greatly influence the recovery of animal bone and small artifacts (Thomas 1969; Gobalet 1989; Shaffer 1992; Shaffer and Sanchez 1994; Nagaoka 2005). As we learn more and refine our methods, such as using finer screens and chemical analyses, we may discover that many more data are "preserved" in a site than we thought.

Nevertheless, organic materials do degrade due to a variety of factors, including biological, environmental, and cultural issues. In this section, we address some of these factors, although this discussion is not intended to be exhaustive. It is up to each archaeologist and paleonutritionist to analyze and experiment with the types of preservational factors that may have influenced or may continue to be influencing the site. Each site is different and was formed under unique conditions that affect the ease by which data from the site can be recovered.

Biological Preservation Factors

There are a great number of biological factors that influence the preservation potential of biological remains from archaeological sites. The most important biological factor is the presence of saprophytic organisms. Saprophytic organisms are plants and animals that live on dead matter and obtain all their nutrients for growth (nitrogen compounds, potassium, phosphates, oxidation of carbohydrates) by breaking down organic matter. Saprophytic organisms can include larger scavengers and rodents, but the term refers mainly to small organisms such as earthworms, insects, fungi, bacteria, and microbes. These organisms consume organic materials, including biological materials from archaeological sites. The environments in which these organisms flourish greatly influence whether biological assemblages will be preserved (see below).

Other important factors that determine whether biological remains preserve include their robusticity, durability, and/or density. The more durable a bone or plant part is, the longer it will survive decay by saprophytic organisms and chemical decomposition. Carbonization (burning) of plants makes them more resistant to destruction since the carbonization process converts the chemical constituents of wood and plants to elemental carbon, a durable substance that offers no nutrients for saprophytic organisms. Therefore, in many regions of the world in which archaeological plant remains are usually degraded, charred plant remains may survive in recognizable form and be recovered.

Burned animal bone, representing various stages from slightly singed to calcined, will also preserve better than unburned bone under certain conditions. Burning removes protein and alters the calcium content of bone. Calcined bone is pure white, friable, and porous, whereas bone that is not quite calcined (gray to white in color) is quite durable. Calcined or almost calcined bone preserves well in areas with acidic soils where unburned bone is degraded through chemical action (see "Environmental Preservation Factors" below).

Plant remains that are more frequently preserved and recovered by paleonutritionists are those that contain elements having a structural or protective role for the plant and are therefore more durable. Such elements include cellulose (to a lesser degree), sporopollenin (the main component of pollen), silica (the main component of phytoliths), lignin, cutin, and suberin, all of which may be found in pits, seeds, rinds, spines, woody components, resin, pollen, and phytoliths. Plant parts that do not contain these durable elements tend not to preserve as well in archaeological sites and their potential absence should be taken into consideration.

Bone, horn, antlers, teeth, hooves, hide, and shell are the most frequently observed animal remains from archaeological sites. These materials are more resistant to decay because they are made of robust structural elements such as keratin and collagen (horn and hooves), phosphatics (bone, antlers, teeth), and chitin (insect and crustacean exoskeletons) or are calcareous (shell) (table 4.1). A shell midden site may contain many thousands of durable and well-preserved oyster shells, or a Puebloan site in the American Southwest may contain large numbers of carbonized corn cobs. It should be noted, however, that the quantity of these well-preserved remains does not demonstrate that prehistoric peoples were eating nothing but oysters or corn at such sites. Preservation affects biological remains differentially; some remains will be well preserved and others will be far less preserved, so keep in mind that field methods and basic recognition of remains are always factors in preservation.

Although bone is the most frequently observed animal remain from archaeological sites, some bone is more resistant to decay and destruction than others. Various bone elements, as well as bone elements from different species, have different structural densities. Larger animals tend to have bone with greater density than medium and small animals, so their

TABLE 4.1. Chemical Foundation and Decay Resistance of Animal Remains[a]

Remains	Chemical Foundation	Decay Resistance
Bone	Phosphatic	High
Antler	Phosphatic	High
Ivory	Phosphatic	High
Teeth	Phosphatic	High
Horn	Keratin and collagen (protein)	Low
Hoof	Keratin and collagen (protein)	Low
Hair	Keratin and collagen (protein)	Low
Hide	Keratin and collagen (protein)	Low
Leather	Keratin and collagen (protein)	Low
Turtle shell	Keratin and collagen (protein)	High
Arthropod exoskeleton	Chitin (protein)	High
Mollusk shell	Calcareous	Medium/high
Bird eggshell	Calcareous	Low/medium

[a] Compiled from Carbone and Keel (1985:table 1.1, 9).

remains tend to be preferentially recovered from archaeological sites. Some exceptions include beaver, whose dense bone has a greater durability than most carnivores and other medium-sized mammals. Mammal bone also tends to be denser than fish and bird bone and thus is more frequently recovered. Denser elements include the mandible, femur, humerus, tibia, calcaneus, and astragalus. These bones will also be recovered with greater frequency than less dense elements (Lyman 1994a). In addition, adult bones tend to preserve better than those of infants (Guy et al. 1997), making paleodemographic reconstructions more difficult.

Another important and often underrated influence on the taphonomy of biological assemblages, particularly bone, is dogs. Dogs have been associated with humans for at least ten thousand years and their remains are found in numerous archaeological sites around the world. Unfortunately, ethnoarchaeological studies have demonstrated that dogs can be very destructive to modern bone assemblages. In her study of domestic dogs in a modern Aka hunter-gatherer camp in central Africa, Hudson (1993) observed that dogs consumed between 74 percent and 97 percent of the bone elements brought into camp. Due to their bone density, skull elements, limb shafts, and the bones of larger animals survive canine assaults best.

Environmental Preservation Factors

The environment in which plant or animal remains are deposited greatly influences their decomposition and whether they will be preserved in recognizable form for a month, a year, ten years, a thousand years, or longer. Because saprophytic organisms are the main cause of biological material destruction, preservation depends mainly on what types of depositional environments are conducive to or inhibiting to these organisms. Carbone and Keel (1985) listed four environmental factors that influence preservation of biological assemblages: soil acidity, aeration, relative humidity, and temperature. In addition, other geological conditions may also be important for biological preservation.

Saprophytic organisms are intolerant of highly acidic soils and live almost exclusively in alkaline soils. Therefore, acidic soils tend to preserve biological materials (organic components) because these materials are not consumed by microorganisms, whereas alkaline soils tend to have poor preservation of biological materials. This can be seen in the potential for pollen preservation in the Southwest. Because soils in the southwestern United States are highly alkaline, preservation of organic materials in open areas tends to be poor. Pollen has a strong outer covering (called exine) made of sporopollenin, one of the strongest natural substances known. However, alkaline soils are conducive to fungi and bacteria that eat pollen, with the result that those species whose pollen contains more sporopollenin in its exine will tend to preserve better.

While alkaline soils usually contain more saprophytic organisms that consume organic assemblages (plant remains and organic components of bone), the chemistry of such soils fosters the preservation of bone and shell (mineral components) better than that of acidic soils. Bone is made up of minerals (hydroxyapatite, calcium carbonate, and trace elements) and organics (collagen, bone protein, fats, and lipids) in an approximately 2:1 ratio. The organic components of bone will tend to be eaten by saprophytes in alkaline soils, leaving mineral bone components intact. Therefore, the structural components of bone are preserved and can be recovered in alkaline conditions. Bone does not survive well in acidic conditions because acids dissolve the structural bases of minerals, leaving only organic traces of bone in the soil. Calcareous shell and antlers are preserved under the same conditions as bone.

For example, soils in Maine tend to be acidic, which limits the preservation potential of bone. Bone preservation in interior sites is mostly limited to specimens that are calcined or almost calcined (see above). Although only small pieces of calcined bone are preserved in interior sites with acidic soils, bone (mainly uncalcined) is prevalent from archaeological shell midden sites along the coastal regions of Maine. Bone preserves in these sites because weathering and degradation of the calcareous shell matrix produces an alkaline environment conducive to preservation of the mineral components of bone. Therefore, the level of preservation at archaeological sites in Maine depends upon their location and soil alkalinity. Although alkaline soils (such as in a shell midden) preserve bones better, they will continue to undergo decay, degradation, and alteration through time.

Soil pH is not the only factor that influences preservation of biological assemblages. For example, while the soil acidity in Maine tends to preclude bone preservation, these acidic soils should preserve other organics, such as botanical remains, as the acidity inhibits saprophytic organisms that eat organics. This is not the case, however, because the seasonal freezing/thawing cycle mechanically degrades chemical composition and the moisture-rich soil tends to be conducive to saprophytic organisms. In many such cases, however, preservation of organics can be obtained when they have been carbonized or burned.

One example is the preservation of carbonized botanical remains discovered in a fire hearth in an archaeological site in an interior region of Maine, revealing the earliest evidence of squash agriculture in the region (e.g., Peterson and Asch Sidell 1996). Another example comes from the southwestern United States. As previously discussed, alkaline soils in the American Southwest are not conducive to pollen preservation, although this region is famous for the preservation of other biological remains due primarily to high temperatures, extreme aridity, and relative lack of humidity. Saprophytic organisms do not thrive in hot, dry conditions and therefore biological preservation in these areas tends to be excellent. Preservation of organics in open areas of this region, on the other hand, is not as good as in enclosed areas (e.g., caves, rockshelters, pueblos) because of the increased exposure to weathering (wind, erosion, rain). Bone preserves better in this alkaline environment than other biological assemblages, although preservation of all organics in this region is excellent.

In addition to hot temperatures, cold temperatures also limit the amount of decay of biological remains because saprophytic organisms cannot thrive in extreme temperature environments. Biological assemblages in the Arctic can be as well preserved as in hot, arid regions; however, most archaeological sites in the Arctic are surface sites with little or no subsurface deposits. Because of this constant exposure to weathering, some biological remains will become degraded and will not preserve well over time. For example, large animal bone remains are ubiquitous at these northern sites, whereas botanical remains are less likely to be recovered (recovery is also due to cultural impacts; see "Cultural Preservation Factors" below).

Aeration can also affect the preservation of biological materials. Saprophytic organisms cannot live without oxygen, so anaerobic (lacking oxygen) environments are more conducive to preservation. Such environments include peat bogs, which are famous for the preservation of bog bodies and other biological materials (e.g., Stead et al. 1986; Brothwell 1987), and waterlogged sites, which have been known to contain preserved wooden stakes representing the remains of prehistoric weirs for trapping fish (e.g., Ames 1994).

Anaerobic conditions may also exist under deep layers of clay or silt deposits, providing a good environment for preservation of biological materials. One reason carbonized botanical remains were preserved from the Little Ossipee North Site in Maine (e.g., Sobolik and Will 2000) is that soon after humans made and used fire hearths at the site, there was a flooding event of the Saco and Little Ossipee Rivers that capped the site with clay and silt deposits, preserving botanical remains in a relatively anaerobic environment. The depth of deposit of biological materials is an important component of preservation in such environmental conditions; the deeper the material is buried and the more anaerobic the environment is, the better the preservation potential.

For instance, a few years ago, a llama farm in Maine donated a llama skeleton to the zooarchaeology collection at the University of Maine on one condition: The skeleton was to be dug up and collected by the university. The llama had been buried for three years in what the owners termed a "shallow" grave. One weekend, one of us (KDS) took a group of graduate students to the farm to dig up the llama under the assumption that a llama buried for three years in a shallow grave in the wet soils of

Maine would be nothing but bones. The llama turned out to be deeply buried (1.5 to 2 meters) and was in pristine condition with little decomposition of fur or muscle. The depth of burial produced a relatively anaerobic environment that inhibited saprophytic activity and thus inhibited decay and decomposition. The owners were informed that the research team would be back in ten years.

Anything that disturbs an anaerobic environment, however, can introduce sources of oxygen and change the environment from one of good preservation to one in which saprophytic organisms can thrive and cause decomposition. After the head portion of the llama was exposed, for example, oxygen was introduced, aerating the soil around the llama. Because of this disturbance, the head portion of the llama will probably decompose more rapidly than the undisturbed hind portion that maintained its relatively anaerobic burial conditions. Nonhuman disturbance factors will also affect preservation by introducing aerated matrix regions into relatively anaerobic environments, such as rodents or other animals that dig deep burrows or pits, worms and insects that dig into the ground, plant roots that burrow into the ground, and tree throws that expose previously undisturbed environments to the aerobic environment.

In addition to introducing aerated soil into anaerobic environments, tree throws are also problematic because they mix up and disturb the cultural and noncultural components of a site (fig. 4.1). After the tree decays, there may be little evidence to indicate that a major disturbance took place in this area of the site. Not only do tree throws move cultural and noncultural materials around in a site, they can also introduce objects from younger deposits into older areas of the site, making it difficult to obtain meaningful radiocarbon dates or biological (and other cultural) materials in appropriate cultural zones. Rodents and other burrowing animals also move cultural material around, mix younger deposits with older deposits, aerate anaerobic environments, and introduce noncultural materials into cultural zones.

Cultural Preservation Factors

Humans also affect the preservation potential of biological materials. Before biological remains are deposited, humans can affect their robusticity and structure, either decreasing or increasing their potential for

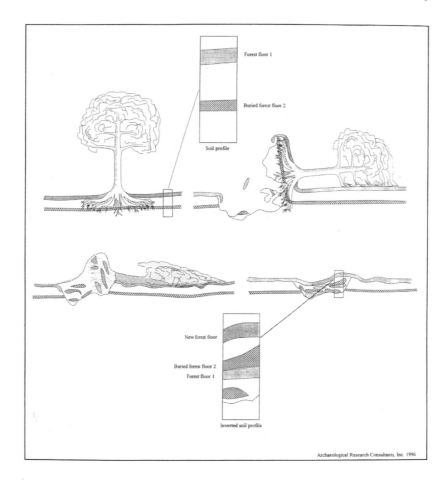

Forest floor 1

Buried forest floor 2

Soil profile

New forest floor

Buried forest floor 2
Forest floor 1

Inverted soil profile

Archaeological Research Consultants, Inc. 1996

FIGURE 4.1. Graphic showing how a tree throw can invert soil profiles and transport older materials upward in the soil column (from Will et al. [1996], courtesy of James Clark; reproduced by permission).

preservation. Humans burn plants and bones, either intentionally or unintentionally, increasing the probability that such remains will be preserved (see "Biological Preservation Factors" above). In addition, humans break apart, macerate, pound, chop, and boil biological materials before deposition, which decreases their chance of preservation. For example, humans break bone to gain access to marrow, sometimes pounding the bone into little pieces and boiling it in water to obtain the fat content.

Humans also dig pits for various purposes, causing exposure of under-lying archaeobiological assemblages to a more aerobic environment, potentially reducing their preservation (see "Environmental Preservation Factors" above). This type of cultural transformation is seen more fre-quently in larger, multicomponent, and/or stratified sites (where human activity was more extensive and diverse and thus can affect culturally older deposits) than in small, single-component sites (where the evi-dence of human activity tends to be more centralized).

Ultimately, the main factor that affects whether biological materials will become deposited in archaeological sites is whether humans used that material or even brought it to a site. The types of materials (includ-ing materials other than biological remains) humans use and bring back to a site indicate what type of site it is, such as a base camp, hunting camp, or butchering site. Archaeological bone is mainly the result of meat- and tool-gathering behaviors of humans. Gathering meat involves disarticulation and skinning of scavenged or hunted prey and defleshing of bone. In the case of a large animal, much of this activity may take place outside the base camp; therefore, not all bone from an animal will be brought back to the base camp and become deposited in the archaeo-logical record (the "schlepp effect" [Daly 1969:149]).

Another example of cultural preservation is the processing of agave plants by prehistoric and historic peoples of the southern plains and southwestern deserts of North America. Agave is a desert succulent that has long, flat, sharp leaves aboveground and a nutritious, compact "heart" belowground. The nutritional value of the "heart" peaks just before the plant is ready to send up its reproductive stalk, so it is at this time that humans would dig up the plant. First, the sharp leaves would be cut from the rest of the plant and then the "heart" would be dug up. The "heart" would then be roasted in earthen ovens for at least forty-eight hours to make it edible. People would eat parts of the agave "heart" at the earthen oven site and then take the rest back to camp to share and eat there. Numerous chewed pieces of agave, called quids, have been found in base-camp sites. From this example, we can see that remains of agave will be found at procurement sites (leaves), at earthen oven sites (remains of agave in the ovens as well as surrounding the site), and at base camps (quids). In addition, people used agave leaves for items such as basketry, sandals, paintbrushes, twining, and clothing, so the fibrous remains of agave would probably be found in any site at which agave was used.

Cultural versus Noncultural Assemblages

Some of the many factors that can affect the preservation potential of biological materials were discussed above. When biological remains are recovered, they need to be assessed as to whether they are cultural or noncultural in origin. A cultural context is defined as a setting that has been physically altered or added to as a result of human activity. Evidence of this activity may include features (e.g., postholes, hearths, buildings), portions of stratigraphic layers (middens, living surfaces), and/or artifact concentrations. Noncultural archaeological contexts are those for which human activity is not indicated. Most sites have within them both cultural and noncultural contexts; that is, sites are commonly formed by a combination of cultural and noncultural processes. Therefore, the archaeologist needs to determine which portions of a site are cultural and which are not. The paleonutritionist can contribute greatly to this determination by analyzing which biological assemblages are cultural and which are not.

Most taphonomic studies addressing the issues involving cultural and noncultural material have focused on accumulation and modification of faunal remains. These studies have indicated that there are a large number of factors, such as carnivores, rodents, owls, and raptors, that influence bone assemblages deposited at archaeological sites. All of these animals accumulate bone and may deposit bone not used by humans into archaeological sites. This noncultural bone is usually distinguishable from cultural, human-deposited bone.

Carnivore influence on a bone assemblage can be recognized by the surface attributes of individual bone specimens. When chewing or gnawing, animals leave characteristic marks on bone. Microscopic examination of bone can reveal incisions, scratches, gouges, punctures, and pitting. Some of these marks are exclusively of human origin, while others are clearly of noncultural origin. Punched holes, striations, scoop marks, and crunching/splintering are examples of tooth marks left on bone by animals. For example, canids will create shallow grooves or channels transverse to the longitudinal axis on long bones because the long and thin shape of these bones prevents bone from being gnawed in other directions. Punched holes, or tooth perforation marks, occur where hard bone is thin or soft, such as at the blade of the scapula or the ilium. These marks may appear as small hollows if the tooth did not fully pierce the bone surface. Striations occur on bone surfaces where carnassial teeth have scraped the surface in an attempt to reach the marrow cavity. Tooth scratches tend to follow the surface of the bone, deeper on convex surfaces and shallower on concave surfaces.

In contrast, cut marks of human origin tend to be uniform in depth. Where the epiphysis has been removed, scratches that are parallel or diagonal to the longitudinal axis of the bone may be present on the diaphysis. Compact bone may also be gnawed away to gain access to spongy bone, leaving overlapping striae and a scooped-out appearance on bone surfaces. Finally, marrow is reached by larger animals by crunching through bone, causing longitudinal splintering. Smaller canids will remove epiphyses to weaken bone structure prior to crunching through the diaphysis.

Humans mark bone while butchering, skinning, and preparing food. Cuts are purposely placed for a desired result. Skinning an animal can leave cut marks on the underside of the mandible and cut marks that encircle the distal ends of limb bones. Since cultural marks are created on bone in butchering, cut marks cluster around articular surfaces or in areas of major muscle attachment. Marks will differ between species due to variances in joint strength. Bone struck with stone tools will leave crescent-shaped notches at the point of impact and bones broken during butchering by "grooving and snapping" have heavy incisions along the broken edges. Differences between the shapes of cut marks from tools and those from carnivore tooth damage are also readily identifiable. Tool marks are characterized by fine striations within the furrow made by cutting action. These striations are thought to be created by irregularities on the working edge of the tool. Tooth marks lack striations but exhibit ridges perpendicular to the direction of the mark, caused by uneven force applied by the animal to the bone. These are often called "chatter marks."

Another way that archaeologists and paleonutritionists distinguish cultural from noncultural bone is the presence of small animals, particularly rodents, in the assemblage. Small animals excavated from sites are often considered noncultural or contaminants by some researchers;

however, to disregard them as possible human food refuse may underestimate the importance of small animals to the dietary inventory of prehistoric peoples. A wide variety of small animals have been recovered from paleofeces, indicating that they were eaten by prehistoric people; thus, their bone remains in archaeological sites may be due to cultural factors (Sobolik 1993). For instance, numerous paleofeces from archaeological sites in southwest Texas contain bone remains from small animals; 333 paleofeces have been analyzed for their macrocontents, 245 (74 percent) of which contained small bone remains and 123 (33 percent) specifically contained rodent remains (Sobolik 1988a).

Other ways to determine cultural versus noncultural bone are through analyses of potential taphonomic agents in a particular region. Research on taphonomic factors that may have influenced site depositional processes and biological assemblage preservation and incorporation must be regional, site specific, and fairly inclusive, because different factors are at work in different areas and time periods. It is not as useful to focus on one aspect of taphonomy at a site and ignore other possible influences. For example, one of us (KDS) conducted a taphonomic study of the faunal remains from a prehistoric hunter-gatherer base camp in Big Bend National Park, Texas. The factors that influenced faunal deposition at the site were rodent burrowing and carnivore scat deposition. Other potential taphonomic factors that were not as important were fluvial deposition and/or modification and raptor pellet deposition.

Because of the wide variety of taphonomic factors that may have influenced the biological assemblages in an archaeological site and the importance of understanding taphonomic history, many paleonutritionists may become fixated on data collecting at the quantitative level without looking at the big picture. Before examining 5,000 bone fragments for the presence of cut, tooth, or gnaw marks, it is necessary to assess whether such analysis is necessary for the overall research goals. As an example, Shipman (1986) examined more than 2,500 bones under a scanning electron microscope looking for human and nonhuman marks. She observed numerous instances in which human cut marks were made over scavenger tooth marks, allowing her to conclude that early humans (hominids) were actually scavengers rather than hunters; they obtained meat by scavenging portions after other carnivores had made the kill. Shipman's painstaking analysis was for a purpose—it contributed to the big picture. Although not all of our analyses may have such grandiose or far-reaching implications as Shipman's, we need to be constantly thinking of how our data fit into the big picture and what research goals we may help answer.

Context

Ultimately, the question of whether a biological assemblage is cultural or noncultural is one of context. Interpretation of context occurs at all stages of research, from excavation to analysis. During excavation, the presence of artifacts (such as stone tools or ceramics) in direct archaeological association with biological materials provides evidence that they may have a cultural origin.

Disturbances to context should be evaluated critically. Potential disturbances are numerous and can include tree throws and carnivore or other animal modification as evidenced by the presence of scat, burrows, and gnaw marks on bone. Rodent burrows are commonly identified intrusions into archaeological contexts and are often easy to recognize during excavation. Rodents are notorious for introducing noncultural bone into archaeological sites, as well as moving cultural material out of their primary contexts. The actions of these agents can displace, introduce, or remove artifacts or ecofacts from their original point of deposition. As previously discussed, humans, both prehistorically and in modern times, disturb archaeological contexts and move cultural materials from a primary to a secondary context.

Biological materials can be disturbed and moved into or out of a site by numerous agents of accumulation, such as water and wind. For example, these materials can be removed from their primary context in an archaeological site and redeposited in a secondary context by fluvial processes. Typical fluvial contexts are channels, floodplains, lake margins, point bars, and coastal settings. Because water can move artifacts out of their primary context, many times archaeological sites have been "discovered" when, in fact, they are nothing more than artifacts in secondary context. Will and Clark (1996) conducted an experimental archaeology study in which it was documented that artifacts can be moved great distances along lakeshores due to wave action and ice movement. This study helped to explain why numerous sites were recorded during the initial survey along a large impounded lake, but, upon excavation, some of these sites consisted merely of surface lithic debris. Although the experiment was conducted on lithic artifacts, the same could hold true for biological materials as well.

Fluvial action can move cultural remains out of a site as well as deposit noncultural materials into a site. Fluvial effects on bone have been extensively studied, whereas such effects on botanical materials are not as well known. Surface abrasion and rounding of bone surfaces are attributes of bones that have been transported by water. Orientation may also be a sign that bone specimens have been moved by fluvial processes—heavier ends of elongate elements point upstream. Elements with low density, low weight, and a high surface-area-to-volume ratio, such as innominates and scapulae, are more likely to be transported long distances. Shape will also influence transportability—long, flat bones are more likely to be transported than round ones.

In a classic study on the effects of fluvial action on bone, Voorhies (1969) experimented with bones from medium-sized animals to determine their transportability in flowing water. Faunal elements were divided into groups, placed in a flume, subjected to flowing water, and their movements charted. Group I elements included ribs, vertebrae, sacrum, and sternum. These elements were immediately moved by slow-moving currents. Group II was composed of the femur, tibia, humerus, metapodia, pelvis, and radius, which were gradually carried away in a moderate current. A few elements, including the scapula, ulna, and phalanges, were between Groups I and II. The skull and mandible belonged to Group III and were only moved by strong currents, while the mandibular ramus was intermediate to Groups II and III. Thus, Voorhies (1969) demonstrated that an assemblage composed of elements representing all of the groups was probably not affected by fluvial action. However, if an assemblage consists only of elements from one group, fluvial action should be considered as contributing to the taphonomy of the assemblage.

Discussion

Determining the taphonomy of biological materials recovered from an archaeological site is the first and most important step an archaeobiologist takes in the analysis and interpretation of such remains. It is critical to determine how the botanical or faunal remains became deposited in a site and all the potential factors influencing that deposition. The archaeologist must ask whether the biological remains from a particular site are cultural or merely represent deposition through noncultural agents. If remains are determined to be noncultural, they may be useful in analyses of paleoenvironment but they are not useful for direct analyses of human activity. Even if biological materials are considered to be deposited as a direct result of cultural activity, they may be out of primary context due to postdepositional factors, such as vandalism, animal burrowing, and human digging. Depending on research goals, biological materials out of primary context may not be useful for analysis and interpretation, even if they are considered cultural; the time, money, and effort spent on their analysis may be too great for many research projects.

In all stages of an archaeological project, decisions need to be made regarding the effectiveness and potential of each step. It is up to the archaeologist to determine which sites are to be tested or analyzed further and which will yield the most information during the typically short field season. After the archaeologist has made these decisions and the site has been excavated, it is up to the paleonutritionist (who, it is hoped, has been involved during all phases of excavation) to determine which materials from a site are worth the expenditure of diminishing supplies of time and money. In other words, the paleonutritionist must determine which materials will help answer research goals, which will assist in interpretations of past human lifeways, and which are cultural and in good context. Understanding taphonomy will help to answer these questions. Paleonutritional analyses and interpretation cannot profitably proceed without this understanding.

Archaeological Recovery Methods

Materials related to paleonutrition can be recovered in the same fashion as other archaeological remains; during normal excavation and screening, such remains can be removed from the matrix or picked up in the screen. The majority of archaeological sites are excavated using dry and/or wet field screening. The use of 1/4-inch mesh screen to process site soils is commonplace but is a rather crude method for the recovery of biological data (and even for some artifacts). Because these materials may be too small to be observed with the naked eye during excavation or to be caught in traditional screens, most biological materials are recovered during fine-screening and flotation (usually in the laboratory). Biological materials that are collected during normal excavation procedures should be bagged separately from those recovered during fine-screening and flotation.

Numerous studies have demonstrated that the use of fine screens (1/8-inch or 1/16-inch screens) and flotation devices is essential for an adequate recovery of paleonutritional materials. Studies on the efficiency of various screen sizes have shown that the loss of data increases in percentage as the type of animal (or element) gets smaller and as the screen size gets larger (Thomas 1969; Gobalet 1989; Shaffer 1992; Shaffer and Sanchez 1994; Nagaoka 2005). In fact, some species may be missed entirely (table 4.2).

The importance of flotation techniques in the recovery of botanical remains has also been realized through a number of research projects; the study by Struever (1968) is usually cited as the first thorough discussion. Flotation uses water to separate lighter (less dense) material, usually organics, from heavier (more dense) material, usually inorganic matrix but also including some bone. Although flotation was used sporadically prior to the 1960s, the development of the "new archaeology" (Binford 1962, 1968), with its emphasis on the recovery and interpretation of ecological and environmental remains from archaeological sites, led to the acceptance of flotation as an important tool for botanical data recovery.

If entire taxa are not recovered due to the use of large-mesh screens, a miscalculation of the relative importance of particular species can easily result in the development of a spurious subsistence model (e.g., Gordon 1993). As the analytical aspects of dietary models become more sophisticated, it is astonishing to see the continued (and customary) use of 1/4-inch screen in the field in many parts of the world (and even no screening in some places!), including some regions of North America.

Fine-screening is a simple technique in which a known quantity of matrix is passed through a fine-mesh screen (usually 1/8- or 1/16-inch mesh). This can be done by using a separate fine screen by itself or placing the screen within or underneath the framework of an existing coarse screen (usually 1/2- or 1/4-inch mesh), thereby screening the same matrix with coarse and fine screen. This type of screening method is easiest when dealing with dry matrix. When fine-screening wet matrix such as

TABLE 4.2. Comparison of Results from Screen Size and Faunal Recovery Rate Studies

Study and Taxon	Size of Live Animal	Bone Recovery Percentages		
		1/4-inch screen	1/8-inch screen	1/16-inch screen
Shaffer and Sanchez (1994:tables 1 and 2)				
Least shrew (*Cryptotis parva*)	4–7 g	3%[a]	3%[a]	—
Deer mouse (*Peromyscus* sp.)	18–35 g	3%[a]	29%[a]	—
Ground squirrel (*Spermophilus* sp.)	140–252 g	18%[a]	53%[a]	—
Cottontail rabbit (*Sylvilagus* sp.)	600–1,200 g	47%[a]	68%[a]	—
Fox (*Vulpes* sp.)	4,500–6,700 g	76%[a]	91%[a]	—
Thomas (1969:393, table 1[b])				
Mouse-sized mammals	<100 g	16%	81%	100%
Squirrel-sized mammals	100–700 g	40%	82%	100%
Rabbit-sized mammals	700–5,000 g	53%	97%	100%
Coyote-sized mammals	5,000–25,000 g	98%	100%	100%
Deer-sized mammals	>25,000 g	99%	100%	100%
Kobori (1979)				
Unspecified mammals	—	8.3%[c]	51.3%[c]	—
Gobalet (1989:table 2)				
Tule perch (*Hysterocarpus traskii*)	<16 cm TL[d]	6%[e]	—	94%[e]
Sacramento perch (*Archoplites interruptus*)	60 cm TL[d]	4%[e]	—	96%[e]

[a] Percentage of element category (e.g., skull, femur, carpal) represented.
[b] Calculated from the materials from all levels at Smoky Creek Cave, Nevada.
[c] Percentage of total bone recovered from combined excavation units 2 and 5.
[d] TL = total length.
[e] Percentage of total number of elements recovered.

clay or mud, it is easier to water-screen the samples so that the matrix can be easily broken apart, water-cleaned, and identified. In clay or muddy soils, biological remains may turn the same color as the matrix, making identification difficult.

The advantage of fine-screening and water-screening is the increased recovery of smaller remains. The main disadvantage of these types of screening techniques is that fragile biological remains, such as seeds, charcoal, and small bone, are easily broken down due to the mechanical nature of screening and the impact of high-pressure water on the sample. Because of this disadvantage, flotation is usually the method of choice by paleonutritionists to recover fragile botanical remains. There are a wide variety of flotation methods, with each analyst tending to prefer a specific technique. A review of the types of flotation methods employed by various projects around the world was presented by Pearsall (1988). Some of these techniques are reviewed here. Whatever method is used, it remains important to properly analyze the results (e.g., P. Wright 2005).

Flotation Techniques

The initial flotation method employed by Struever (1968) was called the "immersive method" or the "apple method" and was useful in areas where there was running water in which to float the samples. For this method, one would use washtubs with screens welded in the bottoms and partly immerse the tub in the water source (e.g., creek, river, pond, lake). The archaeological soil is then added to the tub and all floating material is skimmed off with cheesecloth. For this method, it is possible to use multiple people and tubs to keep the process going, resulting in the ability to float great volumes of material rapidly. The heavy fraction (the material that sinks to the bottom of the tub) is then dumped in a bucket of zinc chloride (1.9 specific gravity) and separated further (some material that originally sinks will float in zinc chloride). The disadvantages of this method are that you have to strain the zinc chloride in cheesecloth after each use to prevent contamination, the process makes bones and calcium carbonates foam due to the hydrochloric acid in the zinc chloride preparation, it is costly, and it irritates skin and eyes.

Helbaek (1969) developed a similar technique to float samples in areas in which water is scarce. In this method, soil is dumped into a bucket full of water, the soil is stirred, and the top portion of the water is poured onto a fine-mesh screen to collect the light fraction. The heavy fraction at the bottom of the bucket is either discarded (not the preferred option) or dried for later examination. The process is repeated with new water for each sample. In addition to this process, Helbaek used carbon tetrachloride rather than water because it has a higher specific gravity (1.8), which increases organic material recovery. Carbon tetrachloride is costly, however, and we now know that it is carcinogenic.

FIGURE 4.2. Example of a SMAP flotation system used at the NAN Ranch Ruin, New Mexico, under the direction of Harry J. Shafer (photo provided by Kristin D. Sobolik).

A frequently used flotation method in archaeology today is the oil drum method. This technique is also called the "SMAP" (Shell Mound Archaeological Project) flotation method and was first used by Watson (1976). It involves pumping water from a nearby source into the bottom of a 55-gallon drum that has a screen-bottomed bucket inset at the top. Archaeological soil is dumped into the screen-bottomed bucket; the light fraction floats and the heavy fraction is caught at the bottom of the bucket. The light fraction is skimmed off the surface with a coffee strainer and dumped onto newspaper to dry and then be sorted. This technique can process a great deal of soil even when water is limited because water in the 55-gallon drum can be reused from sample to sample.

A similar technique was used at the NAN Ranch, a Mimbres puebloan site in southwest New Mexico (Sobolik et al. 1997). A 55-gallon drum was filled with water from a hose (fig. 4.2). The drum had a large hole in the bottom that was closed with a screw-top. This hole was used to drain water and the heavy fraction once it had been utilized a number of times. Water entered the drum through a hose attached to a ring aeration system, creating a frothing, moving system that churned the soil and induced organics to float to the top. Soil was dumped into the drum; the light fraction floated to the surface with the aid of the aeration system, where it ascended a slanted spout, attached to the top edge of the drum, into cheesecloth on a catchment area. The light fraction in the cheesecloth was then hung to dry on a clothesline before being sorted and analyzed. The heavy fraction sank to the bottom of the drum, where it was periodically drained through the large hole in the bottom.

A potential problem with this technique and other mechanical techniques is that numerous samples are often floated using the same water, possibly introducing contamination from sample to sample. Unless you have access to large amounts of water and time, it is not feasible to empty the drum after every sample. If the water is reused, each sample can be "run" or floated for longer periods of time in an attempt to eliminate light-fraction contamination.

Recovery of Fine-Screen/Flotation Specimens

The easiest method for recovery of biological remains from archaeological sites combines fine-screening and flotation in one simple step. This method is time efficient, does not create the potential for contamination, can be accomplished by one person, uses small amounts of water, does not use potentially dangerous chemicals, and is sensitive to individual soil sample types. Referred to here as the "combination method," it originates from the first basic manual flotation techniques generated before archaeologists and paleonutritionists started using more "scientific" techniques. The technique does not have the limitations of the more sophisticated methods and retains all of the positive characteristics. For more detailed descriptions of this technique and its modifications, see Pearsall (2000:35–50).

The combination method involves a basic plastic or metal bucket in which the bottom has been removed and a fine screen (1/8-inch or 1/16-inch mesh) attached in its place. The bucket is set into a tub or directly into a sink (if flotation is being conducted in the laboratory) or outside in an area that can become very wet without damaging the site (if flotation is being conducted in the field). The bucket is placed in the tub with approximately five inches remaining at the top above the tub. A hose or a faucet runs water into the bucket and then into the tub. A known quantity of soil is added slowly into the bucket. The light fraction will float to the surface where it is collected with a fishnet and dumped onto a labeled, paper-lined tray for drying. The light fraction is collected continuously until organics stop floating to the surface. Flotation is assisted manually as the operator churns the soil with his/her hand to induce organics to float to the surface and soil to pass through the screen at the bottom. This step allows each individual sample to be floated for a greater or lesser period of time and to be manually assisted to some degree.

After all of the light fraction has been collected, the bucket is removed from the tub and the material caught in the bottom screen portion is placed on a separate labeled tray for drying. This sample is called the heavy (and fine-screened) fraction. The bucket and tub are then rinsed clean and new water is added to the system for the next sample, thus eliminating potential contamination from sample to sample. This system can be operated by one person and can be run continuously, allowing numerous samples to be processed in a short period of time.

Recovery of Pollen and Phytolith Samples

As noted in chapters 2 and 3, pollen and/or phytolith samples should be taken throughout the site for analysis of human dietary patterns, as well as from areas surrounding the site for possible paleoenvironmental analysis (table 4.3). Pollen and/or phytolith sample collection from archaeological sites involves the retrieval of matrix samples from a column in exposed stratigraphic profiles. Because the focus of sample collection in archaeological sites is to understand human activity, samples should be chosen from areas of the site that have good cultural context. In most cases, individual samples should not be randomly collected throughout the site; a column sampling technique from a fully excavated stratigraphic profile should be used so that potential changes through time can be delineated. In many cases, good cultural context is not known until after excavation; therefore, pollen column samples should be taken from a variety of areas throughout the site.

TABLE 4.3. Basic Flotation/Fine-Screening Sampling Procedures

---

Flotation and Fine-Screen Sampling

1. Randomly select 1- by 1-m pits for sample collection. As excavation area grows, randomly add pits from which to sample.
2. Select one quad of the pit for sample collection, such as the SW quad. Systematically collect a 2-liter sample from each level of that quad using a bucket with the 2-liter volume clearly delineated (or with whatever volume you want to use delineated).
3. Collect samples from any archaeological feature encountered, such as hearths, pits, caches, floors, and other anomalies, carefully recording sample volume. Samples should only include feature matrix, not surrounding matrix.
4. Collect samples from noncultural deposits for a comparison with cultural deposits and as a standard, carefully recording sample volume.
5. Provide each sample with a separate, unique field sack or lot number.

Pollen and Phytolith Sampling

1. Select an exposed profile of material in good cultural context from a pit that has been entirely excavated.
2. Establish how many samples you are going to collect from the profile in column fashion. You can collect one or two samples from each cultural zone, from each stratigraphic level, or every 5 to 10 cm along the column. Label bags according to the location of each potential sample and provide a separate field sack or log number for each.
3. Prepare for sample collection, making sure all of your materials are handy as collection needs to take place quickly and efficiently to avoid environmental pollen and phytolith contamination. Materials include a trowel, spoon or other small collecting device, water, towel, and labeled plastic bags.
4. Start taking approximately 100- to 200-ml samples from the bottom of the column working to the top. The trowel and spoon should be cleaned before each sample collection with clean water and dried with a clean towel. Each sample should be taken after the profile area has been scraped clear with a trowel. The samples are taken with a spoon and placed into a clean, labeled bag. The trowel and spoon are rewashed for the next sample collection.
5. Back at the laboratory, the sample can be split for pollen and/or phytolith processing.

Pollen and phytolith samples are taken after excavation has been completed in an area and a stratigraphic profile has been exposed (Dimbleby 1985; Piperno 1988; Horrocks 2005). In most cases, pollen and/or phytolith samples should be taken in a contiguous fashion so that the samples are close together and will represent a range of pollen deposited from that time period that will overlap with the range observed from samples taken below and above the strata (assuming the strata are not mixed). Therefore, samples are usually taken 5 to 10 centimeters apart. Sometimes, however, samples can be taken strictly following the natural stratigraphy, particularly if the natural strata occur in levels less than 10 centimeters.

Because pollen and phytoliths are ubiquitous in the natural environment, contamination is an important issue. During sample collection, all recovery equipment must be cleaned and wiped to avoid modern pollen and phytolith contamination from the air as well as contamination from one sample to the next. All supplies needed for sample collection should be on site and plastic bags should be prelabeled (each with its own field sack or lot number). Supplies needed include a trowel, spoon, water, cloth or towel, and prelabeled plastic bags. Sample collection should proceed from the bottom of the column up to avoid contamination from upper deposits. The trowel should be washed and dried and then used to scrape the profile clean. At each designated sample collection spot, a newly washed and dried spoon (or other useful collection device) is used to retrieve approximately 100 to 200 milliliters of newly exposed matrix that is immediately placed into the appropriately labeled bag. The profile of the next sample collection spot is then cleared with a newly cleaned and dried trowel and a newly washed and dried spoon is again used to collect the next sample. Because of the destructive process sampling has on the profile, it is recommended that such sampling take place after excavation and profile mapping have been completed.

In addition to samples derived from stratigraphic profiles, pollen and/or phytolith specimens can also be collected individually from archaeological features, such as pits, caches, hearths, burials, and floors, to ascertain potential human activity from these areas. To better understand whether pollen and/or phytoliths from an archaeological site are related to human activity or basic environmental conditions, samples should also be taken away from the site so that an understanding of environmental conditions in relation to human-modified conditions can be achieved. Such samples usually include collecting modern matrix from the surface to compare with archaeological samples. For this, a number of 100- to 200-milliliter matrix samples should be collected, or the "pinch" method can be used in which a number of "pinches" of matrix are collected from around the site and combined for a single modern pollen sample. Another collection method involves taking pollen samples from a natural profile away from the archaeological site to use as a time/depth comparison to samples within the site. To do this effectively, however, both sample areas need to have good chronological control, usually through radiocarbon dating.

Recovery of Paleofecal Remains

As noted in chapter 2, paleofeces are desiccated human feces that can be preserved in arid or frozen conditions and contain the food remains of what past peoples consumed. Paleofeces tend to be recovered in desert regions of the world (including the frozen Arctic desert), as well as in caves and rock shelters with constant temperature and minimal contact with water and wind. During normal excavation procedures, paleofeces (generally in the form of coprolites) are difficult to recognize if the excavator does not know what to look for (see fig. 2.7). Many paleofecal specimens may have been thrown out in the backdirt piles if excavators thought they were clumps of dirt. Coprolites have been recovered singly from midden deposits or in large quantities from room blocks, surfaces, or areas of a site that were used as latrines. In a latrine situation, coprolites may be distinguishable as separate entities or they may be found as a large horizon.

Excavation of these unique specimens should focus on the recovery of individual samples, which should be placed in separately labeled bags. Each sample represents short-duration food intake by a single individual, so recovery of individual samples is preferred to the excavation of large clumps of latrine areas, which represent the dietary intake of a number of individuals. Due to new analytical methods, it is now possible to recover DNA and hormones from paleofeces (Sobolik et al. 1996; Sutton et al. 1996), providing a wonderful data base by which to answer research questions. To conduct analysis of human DNA from paleofeces, the samples must not be touched (contaminated) by humans. Therefore, paleofeces should be collected using sterile, latex gloves, and each sample should be placed in a separate, clean bag to avoid contamination. The samples should not be handled, breathed on, or removed from the bag until they are analyzed in the laboratory. The identification of paleofeces was discussed in detail in Fry (1985).

Recovery of Human Skeletal Remains

Human skeletal remains are usually encountered as burials or partial burials in many areas of excavation, in the midden, under house floors, and in pits scattered throughout the site. Human bone can also be encountered randomly, in situations that do not resemble a burial pattern. Recovery of human skeletal remains should proceed with the utmost care and caution in order to retrieve as much information, material, and remains as possible. Burials should be treated as a separate "feature" or entity of the excavation, and all materials and remains associated with a particular burial should be labeled, boxed, and curated separately. Burials should be recorded and mapped *in situ*, and each bone or portion of the burial should be removed carefully, usually using small brushes, picks, and forceps. Care should be taken that the bones receive as little trauma as possible during excavation and removal, not only out of respect for the deceased, but also because researchers need to analyze the surface structure of the bone for possible health and nutritional indicators. Bones should be wrapped in some type of cushioning material and should be placed only in boxes containing other bones from that particular burial. Burial matrix should not be coarse-screened; all matrix from a burial should be collected for fine-screen/flotation and pollen and/or phytolith analyses.

Excavation and Sampling

Even using the quick, easy, and efficient flotation and fine-screening method described above, fine-screening and flotation are still time consuming and costly, so it is not usually feasible to collect all or even a large quantity of the matrix from an archaeological site through such a system. Therefore, a sampling strategy needs to be employed to determine which biological samples will be collected for fine-screening and flotation and the locations from which they will be taken. As discussed previously, the answers to these questions rely heavily on site taphonomy and the research design.

To understand issues of paleonutrition, human diet, and subsistence, collected samples should be clearly associated with cultural areas of the site, again realizing that it is not likely that all portions of a particular site were deposited and/or modified by humans. If one of the research goals is paleoenvironmental reconstruction, it is best to collect samples in areas that are not considered cultural and/or modified by humans; therefore, sample collection should take place away from the archaeological site so that the information obtained is focused primarily on environment and not on human selection. If the research interest is in human impacts on paleoenvironment (and vice versa), then samples should be collected in both cultural and noncultural contexts.

Most archaeologists and paleonutritionists are interested in some aspect of human use of plants and animals. For that research goal, biological samples should be collected in areas of the site that are considered cultural zones, horizons, and levels. In some cases, cultural affiliation can be determined on the basis of artifacts and biological samples; therefore, such samples should be taken from a variety of areas of the site. Since cultural affiliation can be difficult to determine, it is best to collect as many samples as possible. In addition, biological samples can help to ascertain whether different areas of a site are cultural or noncultural, whether rodents were ubiquitous in an area, and/or whether deposition represents carnivore habitation or alluvial deposition rather than human occupation. The basic procedures for sample collection presented here should be modified to fit the needs of each researcher and the vagaries of each site.

In most archaeological sites, biological samples should be collected from sequential excavation levels so that a progression of samples is obtained from an area. Samples do not have to be collected from every level of every excavation unit, but once an excavation unit is chosen for fine-screen/flotation sample collection, samples should be retrieved from every level of that unit. The archaeologist can determine what excavation levels are ascribed to the same cultural zones depending on stratigraphy, dating, and midden formation. Nevertheless, it is still necessary to collect biological samples from every level to help in cultural-zone determination and to be able to develop a progression of plant and animal use through time, assuming that the deposits represent cultural zones in chronological order.

Fine-screen/flotation samples can be collected from every level by using one of the quadrants from a 1- by 1-meter square designated for collection of samples. One quadrant from each level can be chosen from which to collect all samples, but any quadrant is sufficient as long as collection procedures are consistent. The sample recovered from each level should have the same volume so that concentration comparisons can be made. A 2-liter sample is usually of sufficient volume to obtain a representative sample from each level, but the volume collected can be increased if necessary. It is important, however, to always record the volume collected, with each level bagged and recorded separately. Each bag is then taken to the in-field flotation center or back to the laboratory for flotation and fine-screening.

In addition to sample collection in each level of specified units at a site, biological samples should also be taken from any feature or specific cultural context that is encountered, such as hearths, floors, caches, pits, and any anomalies. The materials from such features should be collected separately from the unit in which level samples are collected. Most, if not all, of a small feature should be collected for flotation and the sample volume should be carefully recorded.

The most important part of collecting samples from features is to include only matrix from the feature itself; matrix from surrounding deposits should not be included in the sample. Therefore, excavation and sample collection surrounding and including features should proceed using natural rather than arbitrary stratigraphy. If excavations are being conducted using arbitrary levels, excavation procedure should change to natural levels when features or other natural stratigraphy are encountered, particularly if biological samples are to be taken in that area.

Archaeological Laboratory Methods

Paleonutritional analyses involve a significant amount of technical expertise that is learned through training, experience, and many hours of analysis. Because analyses are time consuming and involve a great deal of experience, many paleonutritionists are specialists or experts in a particular area or on particular botanical or faunal taxa, such as plants, pollen, mammals, fish, gastropods, or specific domesticates. Technical expertise is the backbone of paleonutritional analysis, and technical identification and analysis can be the most time consuming and often most tedious step. Without that expertise, however, it would not be possible to answer a broad range of questions about the biological materials, including botanical and faunal remains, of a particular archaeological site or region. The most rewarding aspect of paleonutrition is not when a certain plant or animal bone has been identified (although such small victories are exciting), but when the identification of an entire biological assemblage leads to new discoveries, answers previously unanswered questions, or indicates that a modification of a hypothesis is necessary.

A critical component of biological analyses is the use or generation of an extensive reference collection of modern plants and/or animal bones to use for comparative purposes. Paleonutritionists should be familiar with the plants and animals in an area in which archaeological samples are collected and should have an extensive reference collection from that area before proper identification and analysis can take place. One of the reasons paleonutritionists should be involved in the overall project and be present during excavations is that they can collect modern reference samples from the surrounding area.

For paleoethnobotanists, collecting reference specimens involves the retrieval of a wide variety of complete plants from different seasons so that the life cycle of the plant is represented in the sample. Complete plants can be collected in a plant press and dried for preservation. Other reference samples should include pieces of wood, nuts, seeds, berries, roots, and phytoliths from all parts of each plant. Pollen reference samples are also collected from individual plant flowers during the appropriate season. The processing of modern plants needs to be undertaken to remove pollen and phytoliths for reference samples. The most important part of collecting modern species to use as comparative reference samples is that the modern species need to be definitively identified or they are useless and potentially problematic.

For zooarchaeologists, reference-sample collecting involves defleshing animals to recover all the bones. Animals can be obtained, usually with an appropriate permit, via the collection of roadkills or through taxidermy businesses. A number of animals are on the endangered species list, however, and cannot be legally collected, whereas others (e.g., carnivores) may carry diseases such as rabies and should be avoided. A list of these endangered species, as well as collection permits, can usually be obtained through the U.S. Fish and Wildlife Service or the state's wildlife office or other similar state agency. Reference collections can also be obtained through the use of existing laboratory comparative material.

The most important aid to technical identification of biological remains is comparative reference collections. In addition, a number of identification guides or atlases are available to further aid in identifications, but these can and should be used in conjunction with, never in place of, a comparative reference collection (see below for examples of reference guides). Analysts should know where various collections are housed and be able and willing to use them if necessary.

Laboratory Analysis of Botanical Remains

Botanical remains recovered during coarse screening should be sorted into similar categories or groups from which identification can proceed. All of the material, however, should continue to be labeled and associated with the particular field sack or lot number assigned to the botanical remains from that excavation provenience and level in the field. Samples should not be washed or modified through brushing or removing adhering matrix unless required for identification.

The most tedious and time-consuming aspect of botanical analysis is the sorting of flotation samples. Depending on the volume of material, samples can be split into different sizes by screening them through nested geological sieves (2-millimeter size and less), which can make it easier to sort. Samples should be sorted using a magnifying lens or microscope (10X, 20X), with all botanical remains sorted into recognizable entities such as seeds, charcoal, sticks, fiber, wood, leaves, and miscellaneous unidentified items. Care should be taken to make sure that all sorted and identified items are correctly bagged and labeled.

After the remains have been sorted, they can be identified to particular taxon and element using comparative collections, with the aid of identification guides. Some useful identification guides for botanical remains include Martin and Barkley (1961), Appleyard and Wildman (1970), Western (1970), Leney and Casteel (1975), Gunn et al. (1976), Montgomery (1977), Dimbleby (1978), Core et al. (1979), and Catling and Grayson (1982). The samples can then be quantified to aid in analysis and interpretation. Different paleoethnobotanical recording techniques and a fairly extensive list of references on the identification of domesticates can be found in Pearsall (1988).

Quantification

The quantification of plant remains is a significant problem in the identification of archaeobotanical materials. The main reason for this is that
many researchers use different quantification methods, and few comparative papers have been published on the different procedures for quantifying archaeologically derived botanical remains and assessing their
strengths and weaknesses (for exceptions, see Hastorf and Popper 1988).

The presence/absence (or ubiquity) method incorporates the frequency with which each taxon occurs within a group of samples. Either
a taxon is present in a sample or it is absent. No matter what other kinds
of quantification methods are employed during analysis, every study uses
presence/absence. Since it is a nearly universally used technique, this
type of quantification allows for easy comparison between different samples. As a technique, the presence/absence method reduces the effects of
differential preservation and sampling, although the number of samples
and groupings within a sample will affect results; the more groups that are
recognized in a sample, the more important a common botanical constituent will seem and the less important an infrequent botanical constituent
will seem. This is also the case as the sample number is increased.

In the percentage-weight method, all of the botanical constituents in
a sample, including both flotation and coarse-screened samples, are separated and weighed. The weights are compared directly or are reflected as
a percentage weight of the total. As the weight technique is a frequently
utilized method for quantification, analyses conducted with this method
are easier to compare with other studies. The major drawback of this
method is that it underestimates the lighter contents, such as fiber, and
overestimates the heavier contents, such as charcoal.

Another frequently used quantification technique is the percentage-
count method, in which the botanical remains of a specific taxon are
counted and compared to the total botanical count. This method tends
to overestimate botanical remains that are easily broken or contain more
fragments to begin with, such as fiber particles and charcoal. This technique is useful, however, in that it provides a quantification method that
is not time consuming, is relatively easy to accomplish, and is additive
in that analyses can be added to each other without having to change

numbers (similar to the NISP quantification method for faunal remains; see below).

In the percentage-volume method, all materials from the sample are separated and placed into similar containers. The number of containers each constituent fills is then compared to the total. This technique is fairly sufficient in estimating the amount of each item in a sample, although it is very cumbersome and imprecise. Thus, this method uses more "guestimation" than other quantification methods. It is also not widely used in archaeology, making comparisons difficult.

For the percentage-subjective method, all of the botanical constituents in a sample are aligned in their proper order, from most frequent to least frequent, and are then placed into preset percentage groups. These percentage groups provide a range of error, without any bias being introduced. Each constituent is placed into these different percentage groups when the sample is being sorted and separated. This technique is the least time consuming and most cost efficient and does not provide the drawbacks of the other quantification techniques. The percentage-subjective method does not overestimate larger items or items that are broken into numerous pieces. The problems with this technique are threefold: (1) quantities are presented as a range so data cannot be easily manipulated statistically, (2) it is not cumulative so more samples cannot be added to the total analysis, and (3) it is not widely used, making comparisons between different studies difficult.

Pollen Analysis

Pollen analyses from archaeological sites and other environmental conditions can offer a diversity of information on prehistoric populations and subsistence practices that cannot be determined through the sole analysis of other biological remains. Pollen is prevalent in the environment, has a sturdy structure, and can be recovered from many sample types. A number of research avenues can be pursued with pollen, including paleoenvironmental reconstruction, archaeological dating techniques, and paleodiet.

Pollen is a sturdy structure due to its exine (outer layer), which is composed partly of sporopollenin, a strong, resistant substance. The inner layer of pollen (intine) consists of cellulose, which is easily degraded after a short length of time, such as in archaeological deposits. When the cellulose layer of the intine is degraded, only the outer layer containing sporopollenin remains. However, this layer is often sufficient for identification because the exine contains distinct sculpturing patterns and aperture shapes, allowing for pollen identification to be made, to the species level in some instances.

Pollen types are divided into insect-pollinated plants (zoophilous) and wind-pollinated plants (anemophilous). Insect-pollinated plants produce few pollen grains and are usually insect specific to ensure a high rate of pollination. Such plants generally produce fewer than 10,000 pollen grains per anther (Fægri et al. 2000). These pollen types are rarely observed in the pollen record due to their decreased occurrence in nature and method of pollination. Wind-pollinated plants, on the other hand, produce large amounts of pollen to ensure pollination and are frequently found in the pollen record. An example of the enormous quantity of pollen that is produced by some plants was provided in the study conducted by Mack and Bryant (1974), who found pine pollen percentages over 50 percent in modern deposits where the nearest pine tree was more than 100 miles away. Fægri et al. (2000) stated that an average pine can produce approximately 350 million pollen grains per tree.

It is important to recognize the difference between pollination types in archaeological samples, because a high frequency of wind-pollinated pollen types most likely indicates natural environmental pollen rain rather than human activity. High frequencies of insect-pollinated pollen types, however, may indicate human use and modification of that particular plant. Understanding the context of samples is imperative to understanding potential human depositional patterns.

There are a variety of ways to process pollen samples, although the basic procedure involves removing organics, silicates, and carbonates. A basic procedure by which to extract pollen from soils is provided in table 4.4. Pollen extraction should be done by trained technicians who realize the potential problems and dangers with each step and take appropriate precautions to avoid damage to the sample or injury to the analyst.

As with any other identification, pollen identification must proceed using a modern comparative collection from representative pollen types in the region from which the samples originated. Like the study of faunal remains, learning to identify pollen is time consuming and takes practice

TABLE 4.4. Standard Pollen Extraction Procedure[a,b]

Step I: Removal of Large Organic or Mineral Particles

1. Remove 30 to 50 ml of soil from the sample collected. If samples come from heavily weathered areas or alluvial sediment, use 100 ml of soil.
2. Screen samples through a 1-mm mesh screen into a beaker. Discard material caught in screen.
3. Add 1 to 2 *Lycopodium* spp. spore tablets, carefully recording number of spores per tablet.

Step II: Removal of Carbonates

4. Add concentrated HCl (38%) to remove carbonates and dissolve calcium bonding in spore tablets. Stir and allow reaction to take place. If reaction causes foam, use fine spray of ethanol to disperse.
5. Pour off and discard liquid fraction. Add 1,000 ml of distilled water to sediment in beaker and stir. Let solution settle for 2 hours. Repeat this step 2 more times. Place remaining sample in 50-ml centrifuge tubes.
6. Centrifuge the residue at 2,000 rpm for 15 seconds. Discard liquid fraction.

Step III: Removal of Silicates

7. Transfer remaining sediment into plastic beakers and add small amounts of 70% HF[c] acid until matrix sample is covered. Stir occasionally and sit overnight.
8. Add distilled water to beaker and stir. Let solution settle for 2 hours. Pour off and discard liquid fraction in fume hood sink. Repeat this step at least 2 more times. Place remaining sample in 50-ml centrifuge tubes.

Step IV: Removal of Organics

9. Rinse residue in glacial acetic acid to remove water. Centrifuge and decant.
10. Prepare acetolysis mixture: 9 parts acetic anhydride, 1 part sulfuric acid.
11. Add acetolysis mixture to samples, stir thoroughly, and place in a boiling water bath for 5 minutes. Do not mix water from water bath with acetolysis mixture! Remove, centrifuge, and decant. Repeat.
12. Wash sample in distilled water. Centrifuge and decant. Repeat.

Step V: Slide Preparation

13. Place remaining residue in a small vial with glycerin for curation. Label.
14. Take a small portion of glycerin-mixed residue and place on a microscope slide. Place coverslip over sample and secure with nail polish or other sealant. Identify and count pollen.

[a] Table taken from Sobolik (2003).
[b] Pollen extraction techniques involve the use of toxic chemicals. Extraction should never be attempted without a fully functioning fume hood and protective coat, gloves, and goggles. Processing should be done by a trained technician.
[c] Use of HF must be restricted to a fume hood. HF fumes are very harmful and can cause permanent damage to lungs and nose if inhaled. Contact with HF can be fatal so always wear plastic coat, plastic gloves, and plastic face mask.

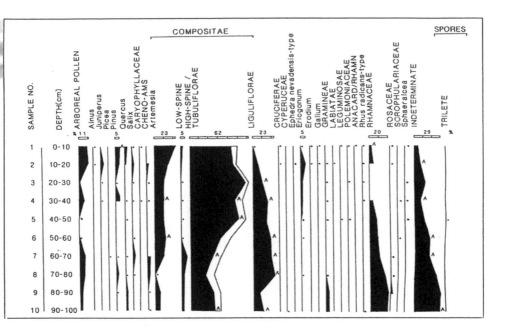

FIGURE 4.3. Pollen diagram from the Guapiabit site in southern California (from Cummings [1996:fig. 1]; reproduced by permission).

and experience. After analysis, pollen data can be illustrated in a variety of ways, but most data are presented as a pollen diagram (fig. 4.3). Most diagrams present data in stratigraphic and chronological order, with the bottom of the diagram representing the deepest (and hopefully oldest) deposits and the top representing the youngest, and in many cases the modern, deposits. Pollen taxa are listed along the top border with their observed percentages from each sample provided in black. Because this sample represents a stratigraphic profile or column, the data are presented as a change through time; therefore, the pollen percentages are filled in black from one sample (or pollen zone) to another.

A second example (fig. 4.4) illustrates pollen identified from individual paleofecal samples, rather than from a continuous pollen and stratigraphic profile. This type of presentation can also be used for individual pollen samples, such as surface samples or samples from archaeological features, rather than pollen stratigraphic column samples. In this diagram, the individual samples and associated radiocarbon dates are presented

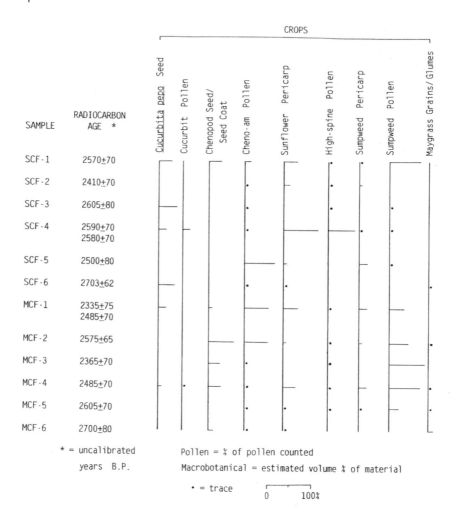

FIGURE 4.4. Pollen diagram from Mammoth Cave paleofeces (modified from Gremillion and Sobolik [1996]; reproduced by permission).

on the left axis. Pollen taxa are presented across the top and their percentages as observed in each sample are illustrated. In this particular case, crop pollen is designated separately from wild plant pollen (which is not shown here), and pollen concentration values are indicated by the relative lengths of the horizontal lines.

Pollen concentration values are determined through the analysis of the number of prehistoric pollens versus the *Lycopodium* sp. tracer spores added to each sample before processing (e.g., Sobolik 1988a). Concentration of pollen in the sample is determined through a simple formula in which the amount of spore grains added is multiplied by the amount of prehistoric grains counted in the sample. This number is divided by the number of spore grains counted multiplied by the amount of sediment processed. Concentration values are important for pollen analysis in that they help determine the amount of prehistoric pollen present in a sample and can help assess depositional rates (for soil samples) and possible pollen ingestion (for paleofecal samples).

Phytolith Analysis

As with pollen, different plants produce diverse, and often unique, morphological phytolith types. Unlike pollen, it has been observed that different parts of the plant produce morphologically different phytolith types, making the use of comparative collections from all plant parts essential. However, in some areas in which pollen analysis is not distinctive (such as with grasses), phytolith analyses can produce excellent results. Phytoliths can also be preserved in environmental conditions in which pollen is degraded or absent, and they can be used in conjunction with pollen analyses for a more complete paleoenvironmental and archaeological picture. For extensive information on identification and interpretation of phytoliths see Piperno (1988, 2006a), Rapp and Mulholland (1992), and Piperno and Pearsall (1993).

There are a variety of ways in which phytolith analysts process samples. As Pearsall (1988) noted, side-by-side tests need to be conducted on the various processing techniques to determine what works best under which conditions. All basic phytolith processing, however, involves floating phytoliths from matrix using heavy density separation. Steps surrounding heavy density separation vary from analyst to analyst. The basic procedure used by Piperno (1988) is outlined in table 4.5.

Laboratory Analysis of Faunal Remains

Most faunal remains are recovered from archaeological sites through coarse screening, but also from columns and other samples. Faunal remains should be analyzed in the same basic fashion as botanical materials. These remains

TABLE 4.5. Phytolith Extraction Procedure[a,b]

Step I: Separation of Phytoliths and Removal of Clay

1. Defloculate soil samples with 5% solution of Calgon or sodium bicarbonate.
2. Screen with 53-μm mesh screen. Keep the sample caught in the screen.
3. Place remaining sample (which passed through the screen) in large beakers and add water to 3/4 full. Stir vigorously. Let solution settle for 1 hour. Pour off and discard liquid fraction. Repeat at least 5 times.
4. Place remaining sample in 100-ml beakers and add water. Stir, let settle for 3 minutes, and pour off supernatant liquid into a 1,000-ml beaker (this separates fine and coarse silt fractions). Repeat, allow to settle for 2 minutes, and pour off supernatant liquid into the same 1,000-ml beaker. Repeat at least 5 times.

Step II: Removal of Carbonates

5. Place 1–1.5 g of each silt sample and the screened sand sample (3 samples total) in test tubes; rinse with distilled water.
6. Add HCl (10%) to remove carbonates, centrifuge at 500 rpm for 3 minutes, and pour off liquid fraction. Repeat until no reaction is observed. Rinse with distilled water.

Step III: Removal of Organics

7. Add hydrogen peroxide (3%) or concentrated nitric acid to remaining sample. Place in boiling water bath until reaction stops. Repeat.
8. Conduct heavy density separation with zinc bromide, specific gravity 2.3. Mix 10 ml of heavy density solution to samples and centrifuge at 1,000 rpm for 5 minutes. Remove liquid (containing phytoliths) to a second centrifuge tube. Remix initial sample and repeat centrifugation. Remove liquid to second centrifuge tube. Repeat if necessary.
9. Add distilled water to liquid portion in 2.5:1 ratio. Centrifuge at 2,500 rpm for 10 minutes, decant, and discard liquid. Repeat twice.
10. Wash in acetone.

Step IV: Slide Preparation

11. Place remaining residue in a small vial with Permount for curation. Label.
12. Take a small portion of Permount-mixed residue and place on a microscope slide. Place coverslip over sample and secure with nail polish or other sealant. Identify and count phytoliths.

---

[a] Compiled from Piperno (1988).
[b] Phytolith extraction techniques involve the use of toxic chemicals. Extraction should never be attempted without a fully functioning fume hood and protective coat, gloves, and goggles. Processing should be done by a trained technician.

should not be washed unless they have matrix adhering to them that hinders identification (clean bones are almost always easier to identify than dirty ones). When bones can be easily identified, washing, brushing, or other modifications should be avoided because this may cause bone to break or crumble and may add marks on the bone that can obscure prehistoric modifications (such as cut marks and gnaw marks). In fact, Sutton (1994) recommended that most artifacts, including archaeobiological remains, should never be washed because it may damage or destroy important evidence such as organic and protein residues. In addition, our increasing awareness of nonvisual remains associated with archaeological samples, such as aDNA, makes it clear that the less we handle and modify any archaeological materials, the better.

Sorting fine-screen samples for smaller faunal remains can be quite time consuming. If there is a great deal of matrix associated with the fine-screen sample (which has been recovered with flotation samples and essentially water-screened), then the sample may be passed through nested geological sieves to separate the sample into size groupings for ease in sorting and identification. The samples recovered from fine screens are smaller and thus may be harder to identify. A good comparative collection of all sizes of animal species is particularly important for this stage of analysis, including smaller fish, rodents, shrews, bats, reptiles, amphibians, and small birds. The species diversity recovered from a site usually increases dramatically once fine-screening has been completed and the samples are analyzed (Reitz and Wing 1999). After the remains have been sorted, they can be identified to taxon and element using comparative samples. In some instances, identification guides can be a useful adjunct for identification. Some useful faunal identification guides include Olsen (1968), Casteel (1976), Gilbert et al. (1981), McGinnis (1984), Cannon (1987), Gilbert (1990), Sobolik and Steele (1996), and Claassen (1998).

Quantification

Quantification in zooarchaeological studies has been conducted with more precision and frequency than in paleoethnobotanical studies, and papers on the subject are more prevalent (Krantz 1968; Bökönyi 1969; Casteel 1976; Lyman 1979; Gilbert and Singer 1982). The most frequently used techniques are presence/absence (ubiquity), number of identified specimens (NISP), and minimum number of individuals (MNI). Other quantification techniques that have been used include minimum number of elements (MNE), meat weight, and various taxonomic diversity and richness indices (Reitz and Wing 1999). Some of these techniques are discussed below (for more detailed discussions, see Grayson 1984; Klein and Cruz-Uribe 1984; O'Connor 2000).

The presence/absence (or ubiquity) method is inherent in all faunal analyses and allows different samples to be easily comparable. The use of this method reduces the possibility of errors in interpretation due to differential preservation of the sample as well as by increasing the number of sample divisions. As the sample is increasingly divided into smaller groups or the sample size is increased, constituents that occur more frequently will seem to be more important, whereas constituents that are less frequent will occur in fewer samples and will be considered of minimum importance. Presence/absence information has proven useful for zoogeography and paleoenvironmental reconstruction as well as dietary purposes.

The use of NISP is also common in faunal analyses and involves a raw count of the bones from each taxon. NISP numbers can be obtained from different analytical units, from a single excavation level to the entire site. One drawback to NISP is that it tends to overestimate the frequency of taxa in an assemblage. NISP can increase with bone breakage (either by prehistoric activity or due to postdepositional factors), thus inflating the number of animals thought to be represented at a site. In addition, some animals contain more elements than others, such as turtles and alligators (teeth), and their NISPs will therefore be higher. Such inflation of NISP could lead to an overestimation of the contribution of particular taxa to the human diet.

Another frequently used quantification technique is MNI, which is a measurement of the minimum number of animals that are present in a sample by calculating the most abundant element of each taxon identified. MNI may also be calculated according to number of different sides (left or right) of the most abundant element, matching elements, sex, and age. This type of quantification reduces the possibility of overestimating the number of individuals when it is assumed that each element or fragment represents a different animal. The MNI quantification method is not biased toward animals with more bony parts (e.g., crocodiles, turtles, and armadillos), animal bones that are more fragmented (e.g., due to bone marrow processing), or animals that were brought to a site in fragmentary form (e.g., hindquarters or ribs) (Klein and Cruz-Uribe 1984).

Several problems can arise from the use of MNI. One is that different aggregation techniques will produce different MNI counts (Grayson 1984). As the faunal sample is divided into smaller aggregates (e.g., analytical units, such as a level in an excavation unit), the MNI for each taxon increases because the most abundant element of each taxon could be different for each aggregate. Another problem with the MNI method is that animals that occur in low numbers will tend to be overestimated, whereas more commonly represented animals will be underestimated. For example, when one bird bone is observed, the MNI for birds is 1. If ten different rabbit bone elements are observed, the MNI for rabbits could also be 1, even though there is a high probability that the rabbit bones are from more than one animal.

In addition, different investigators will determine the MNI differently. Some will calculate the most abundant element, whereas others will distinguish left from right elements, and will even try to match different elements according to size, age, and sex of the animals. At Baker Cave, for example, MNI was determined using the most abundant element of each taxon, as well as left/right sides and age determination (Sobolik 1991). Some of these issues can be mitigated by the use of statistical methods (Orchard 2005).

Simple quantification figures on bone do not necessarily reflect economic importance. For example, if a particular faunal collection contains the remains (MNI) of ten small mammals and one large mammal used as food, which animal was more important to the diet in prehistory? A simple numeric calculation would show a 10:1 ratio in favor of small mammals. However, if the small mammals weighed one pound each (a total of ten pounds) and the large mammal weighed one hundred pounds, the ratio would be 10:1 in favor of the large mammal. Clearly, such calculations can be important to interpretation.

There have been studies conducted for mammals (e.g., White 1953; Stewart and Stahl 1977; Lyman 1979; Stahl 1982) and fish (e.g., Casteel 1974) to calculate the live weight, available meat (food utility index [see Metcalfe and Jones 1988], the live weight minus bone and hide), and

TABLE 4.6. Estimated Edible Meat for Selected Species

Common Name	Scientific Name	Total Edible (g)	Reference
Canada goose	*Branta canadensis*	2,089	White 1953
Mallard duck	*Anas platyrhynchos*	653	White 1953
California quail	*Callipepla californicus*	130	White 1953
Siberian husky (dog)	*Canis familiaris*	10,432	White 1953
		17,000	Stewart and Stahl 1977
California sea lion	*Zalophus californianus*	130,550	White 1953
Ringed seal	*Phoca hispida*	64,774	White 1953
		27,760	Stewart and Stahl 1977
Elephant seal	*Mirounga angustirostris*	1,305,500	White 1953
Walrus (male)	*Odobenus rosmarus*	522,200	White 1953
Prairie dog	*Cynomys* spp.	560	White 1953
Ground squirrel	*Spermophilus* spp.	373	White 1953
Eastern grey squirrel	*Sciurus carolinensis*	440	White 1953
		162	Stewart and Stahl 1977
American beaver	*Castor canadensis*	13,335	White 1953
		6,134	Stewart and Stahl 1977
Pack rat	*Neotoma* spp.	261	White 1953
Jackrabbit	*Lepus* spp.	1,120	White 1953
Cottontail rabbit	*Sylvilagus audubonii*	653	White 1953
Mule deer	*Odocoileus hemionus*	37,300	White 1953
Pronghorn antelope	*Antilocapra americana*	20,515	White 1953
Bison (male)	*Bison bison*	335,700	White 1953
Bison (female)		147,200	
Armadillo	*Dasypus novemcinctus*	2,798	White 1953

usable meat (what people might actually eat) for a number of species. While these measures are approximate and not widely used in analysis, they do provide some general idea about animal size and meat contributions (see table 4.6). It should be remembered, however, that recovery techniques (especially the use of 1/4-inch screens) are biased toward large animals and that body weight calculations may serve to increase the bias.

A variety of other data from zooarchaeological remains can be obtained to add further detail to understanding prey populations, the human impact on these populations, and human adaptations. These include age profiles, mortality profiles, sex differences, and the like (see

Reitz and Wing 1999:171–238). For example, the sex and age profiles in domesticated populations should be quite different than in wild populations. In domesticated populations, only a few males are needed to breed with the females and many of the young males would be killed for their meat and hides. The females would not be killed but retained for breeding and milking purposes. Thus, the age and sex profiles in the skeletal materials from a site should show many young males, a few old males, a few young females, and many old females.

Laboratory Analysis of Paleofeces

Prior to analysis, paleofecal specimens must be dissected and the constituents identified. Great care must be exercised in this process to avoid ruining the data. As most specimens are dehydrated, they must be rehydrated. Rehydration in trisodium phosphate solution (0.5 percent) for at least forty-eight hours is the typical method used, as dry-screening and water-screening tend to damage fragile components, reducing the ability to identify them. Observations of the color, odor, and surface film of paleofecal rehydration liquid should be made. If possible, one-half of each paleofecal sample should be conserved for future analyses and, it is to be hoped, better techniques.

The rehydrated samples should then be screened with 850- and 250-micrometer (0.03- and 0.01-inch) mesh screens to retain macrobotanical and macrofaunal materials. The materials caught in the mesh screens should be placed on drying paper and allowed to dry before analysis. The dried macroremains should be sorted and analyzed under a microscope, usually at 10X or 20X magnification. The debris that passes through the micrometer mesh screens should be caught in a beaker and allowed to settle for at least three hours. The liquid should then be siphoned off, leaving the heavy sedimentation that may contain pollen, phytoliths, and endoparasites. Processing for pollen and phytoliths from paleofeces should continue using normal processing procedures (see tables 4.4 and 4.5).

Processing for endoparasites involves concentrating the heavy sedimentation material with the use of a centrifuge and placing it into vials in a solution of acetic formalin alcohol (AFA), which prevents fungal and bacterial growth. The material should be allowed to settle via gravity. Once settled, the upper portion should be siphoned with a pipette

and microscope slides made with this upper portion and glycerol. Microscope slides should be scanned at 400X on a stereoscopic microscope for
possible endoparasitic remains.

Quantification

Quantification and analysis of paleofecal constituents continue to be an
issue (see discussions in Fry 1985:142–143; Bryant 1994:155) for a variety of
reasons. First, the visible constituents represent only a portion of the diet,
those materials that, for whatever reason, survived digestion. An emerging solution to this problem lies in the chemical identification of constituents, allowing for a more complete inventory of materials consumed.

The second issue is the need to measure the quantities of the materials identified in the specimen. Such approaches include a general estimate of abundance per specimen and then overall percentage (Yarnell
1969:45), an actual count of macrofossils per specimen (Jones 1988:23),
and quantification by weight (Napton 1969).

The final issue is translating quantities of identified constituents into
quantities of food originally consumed. This continues to be difficult, as
the process of the reduction of mass of consumed foods in the digestive
process is unknown, likely resulting in some constituents being overrep-
resented and others being underrepresented. There have been attempts,
however, to correct the ratio of quantities of fecal constituents to quantity
of food consumed by applying a conversion factor (Fry 1985:142; Holden
1990; also see Holden 1994:73–74). Still, most researchers generally disregard these problems and focus on the constituents present in a paleofecal
specimen, where they are usually listed and discussed as to their importance (relative abundance is assumed to represent relative importance)
in the diet.

There have been some recent efforts to statistically analyze the patterns of resource combination and utilization (e.g., intra-specimen variation; Sutton 1993, 1998; Sutton and Reinhard 1995) in order to determine
patterns of food preferences and combinations (cuisine). This work is
ultimately based on old-style quantification, however, and suffers from
the same basic limitations. Most paleofecal analysts tend to quantify
macroremains with the same methods used by paleoethnobotanists in
their quantification of botanical remains.

Laboratory Analysis of Human Remains

Most archaeological human remains consist of bones, although pre-served tissues (such as flesh, hair, and/or chemicals) may also be recovered. Human remains comprise an important source of information regarding a wide variety of anthropological questions, including diet and nutrition, health, social status, cultural practices, and paleodemography. The study of human remains is also important from the standpoint of forensics (Dailey 1983; Cox and Mays 2000).

Recovered human remains are frequently from the intentional disposal of the dead, either as inhumations or cremations. Many materials are recovered from a variety of other contexts, however, such as the "Iceman" discovered in 1991 in the Alps of central Europe who died *in situ* and was not intentionally buried (e.g., Sjøvold 1992).

Inhumations are bodies that are buried or entombed unburned. A primary inhumation is a burial located in the place in which it was originally interred. A secondary inhumation is a burial that has been interred long enough for the soft tissues to decompose, after which the bones are disinterred and reburied in another location, perhaps in a container such as a ceramic vessel or in an ossuary. The catacombs in Paris and Rome, where the bones of hundreds of thousands of individuals are interred, are examples of ossuaries. In these facilities, the bones of specific individuals tend to become mixed with those of other individuals, reducing the interpretive value of the remains for anthropological study. In spite of these problems, considerable information regarding past populations can be gained by the study of ossuary remains (Ubelaker 1974).

Cremations are bodies that have been intentionally burned. The efficiency of such burning is variable and there may be significant quantities of bone that survive. Like inhumations, a cremation may be primary (buried in the pit in which it was burned) or secondary (interred away from the cremation pit, as in western societies). The bones (or bone fragments) that survive the process of cremation can often be productively analyzed (see chap. 2).

Individuals may be interred (either as inhumations or cremations) singly (isolated interments) or in groups (multiple interments). Cemeteries usually consist of a number of individual and/or multiple interments within a specific area. Over time, interments may infringe upon one another, creating confusion regarding which remains and offerings belong to which body and at which time.

Identification and Analysis

The data points used in the identification and classification of human remains are fairly extensive (see Buikstra and Ubelaker 1994:177–182; White and Folkens 2005:67–74) and generally follow those used in the analysis of faunal remains. Basic skeletal data include the identification of the element, the side of the body, which end of the bone (proximal or distal), the degree of epiphyseal fusion in long bones, the condition of any articular surfaces, metric data, nonmetric data (such as modifications and pathologies), and the minimum number of individuals in the collection (number of identified specimens [NISP] is not typically employed in reference to human remains). Extensive discussions and descriptions of human bone and their identification can be found in Bass (1987), White (2000), and White and Folkens (2005).

The skull consists of thirteen major and sixteen minor bones. The skull minus the mandible comprises the cranium, and the skull minus the facial bones comprises the calvarium. Skull bones are relatively thin, often curved, and possess a number of distinctive characteristics, such as sutures, sinuses, foramina, passages, and dentition. Humans normally possess thirty-two teeth: twelve molars, eight premolars, four canines, and eight incisors. Infants are generally born with unerupted teeth that erupt within the first few years. These teeth are deciduous ("baby teeth") and are lost as the permanent teeth replace them. The general timing and sequence of tooth eruption is well known and can serve as an important method to determine age. Deciduous teeth can be easily distinguished from permanent teeth, since they are smaller, often lack roots, and have thinner enamel (see Bass 1987:263; White and Folkens 2005:136). As each person loses a set of deciduous teeth during life, the presence of such teeth at a site is not necessarily indicative of a burial. Patterns of tooth wear can be informative as to the diet, health, and age of a population (see below).

In an adult, the postcranial skeleton consists of 177 bones. Twenty-seven of these are single bones, such as the vertebral column and the sternum. The remaining 150 are paired left and right bones. In humans (after Bass 1987:7), the long (limb) bones are tubular in cross section and are relatively long (greater than 20 centimeters). Short bones are small (less than 10 centimeters) tubular bones and include the clavicles and the bones of the hands and feet. Flat bones include the pelvis, scapulae, ribs, and sternum. Irregular bones include the vertebrae, carpals, tarsals, and patellae.

Analytical Approaches

Metric Analysis.   Many measurements can be made on the skeleton and some of these measurements can be combined to produce indices that serve to describe the bones. Absolute measurements are useful for some purposes, such as the determination of stature, while various indices are used for other purposes. The basic measurements include the maximum length of the bone, the diameter of the midpoint of tubular bone, and the maximum width of the ends of the bones (for detailed discussions, see Brothwell 1981; Bass 1987; Buikstra and Ubelaker 1994; White 2000; White and Folkens 2005).

Nonmetric Analysis.   Nonmetric variations are those that cannot be discovered by simple measurement. These include variations in the number of teeth, crowding or impaction of teeth, variation in the shape of the bones, variation in the number and placement of various foramina, degree of ossification, variation in the interior structure of the bone, presence or absence of some features, and many other traits. Many nonmetric traits may be related to environmental influences or to circumstances relating to the life of the specific individual, such as joint wear in people who walked a great deal and changes in the leg bones of someone who sat cross-legged for long periods.

Estimations of Age, Sex, Stature, and Race.   There are various ways to estimate age in an individual at death (see Buikstra and Ubelaker 1994:21–38; Hoppa and Vaupel 2002; White and Folkens 2005:363–385). These methods include changes in the pubic symphysis (Suchey and Brooks 1986a,b), the metamorphosis of the auricular surface of the ilium (Lovejoy et al. 1985a,b; but see Storey 2006), basiocciput osteometrics (Tocheri and Molto 2002), sternal rib-end morphology (e.g., Yoder et al. 2001), and epiphyseal closure (the fusing of the ends on the shaft of a long bone). Unfused epiphyses indicate an infant or early juvenile, while fully fused bones are likely those of adults. Closure of cranial sutures, both endocranial and ectocranial, is also indicative of age (see Meindl and Lovejoy 1985; White and Folkens 2005:369–372), although suture closure and obliteration schedules seem to vary considerably with race and sex (Rogers 1984). Recent research has indicated, however, that these methods may not be suitable for all populations (Schmitt 2004). Bone histology is also a useful technique for age determination (see Stout 1992; Ericksen 1997; Macho et al. 2005).

Dental attributes may also be useful to determine age at death. The analysis of dental eruption is also employed as both the sequence and timing of tooth eruption and replacement are reasonably well known and can help (coupled with other indicators) to estimate age of juveniles and subadults (see Smith and Avishai 2005). General tooth wear is also an indicator of age (e.g., Brothwell 1981:71–72; Walker et al. 1991; Miles 2000; Oliveira et al. 2006), but diet is also a major factor. Tooth microstructure (FitzGerald and Rose 2000) and the dimensions of the pulp chamber within teeth (e.g., Luna 2006) may also be used to estimate skeletal age.

The methods generally employed to estimate skeletal age may be biased, reflecting the age structure of the reference sample (Bocquet-Appel and Masset 1982), one of the paradoxes noted by Wood et al. (1992). Recent work on a new technique called transition analysis (e.g., Boldsen et al. 2002), however, holds promise for being more objective and accurate by attempting to resolve some of the problems associated with estimating adult age.

The determination of the sex of an individual is also of great analytical importance. In humans, sexual dimorphism in the skeleton is not great and so is not a clear indicator of sex, although, in general, the skeletal elements of females tend to be smaller and less robust than those of males and analysis of large skeletal series can provide good probabilities for general analyses.

The sex of adults can be determined by several basic techniques, including the size of the "passage" through the complete pelvis, width of the sciatic notch, measurement of the subpubic angle, visual characteristics of the os pubis (e.g., Phenice 1969), and discriminant analysis of the femur and humerus (Dittrick and Suchey 1986). Other bones useful in

sexing a skeleton are femoral neck diameter (e.g., Stojanowski and Seidemann 1999) and hand and foot bones (e.g., Wilbur 1998). In addition,
new statistical techniques have been developed for dealing with sexing
of fragmentary skeletal material (Kjellström 2004).

The sex of prepubescent individuals is much more difficult to determine, although aDNA analysis can now be employed for that purpose
(Hummel and Herrmann 1994; Faerman et al. 1995, 1998; Stone et al.
1996; Colson et al. 1997; Cunha et al. 2000; Stone 2000; Matheson and
Loy 2001; Mays and Faerman 2001; Smith and Avishai 2005). For more
detail on sexing techniques, refer to the discussions in Bass (1987:200–206),
Buikstra and Ubelaker (1994:16–21), and White and Folkens (2005:385–398).

Stature (height) is estimated by the measurements of bones applied
to a formula (e.g., that of Trotter 1970; also see Raxter et al. 2006). Unfortunately, populations vary widely and there is no single, valid measure.
Stature tables for American whites (male and female), American blacks
(male and female), and Mesoamericans (male and female) were provided by Bass (1987:22–29).

Based on current knowledge, race can only be estimated from the
skull and dentition (Bass 1987:83). The skulls of Caucasoids, Negroids,
and Mongoloids (including American Indians) exhibit a number of distinguishable characteristics (see Bass 1987:83–92). One of the indicators
of Mongoloids is the presence of shovel-shaped incisors, a depression
present in the lingual aspect of the maxillary incisors.

Pathologies.   Pathologies in skeletal remains are the result of congenital
malformation, disease, trauma, deformation, and/or nutritional deficiencies,
with the two most common forms being those related to degenerative
disease and trauma (White and Folkens 2005:312). Discussions of disease
and nutritional pathologies were presented in chapter 2.

Postmortem Alterations.   Bone is modified during life in various ways,
through genetic control, pathologies, and stress (e.g., robust muscle
attachments in an individual who was used to heavy work); however,
postmortem modifications also occur. Many of these modifications will
occur as natural processes, such as decomposition of the tissues, soil
conditions, roots, and animal gnawing. Cultural postmortem modifications also may occur and manifest themselves on the skeleton. Examples

include cremation and breakage patterns and/or tool marks that might indicate cannibalism (see White 2000:477–489).

Other Analyses.   A variety of other techniques are employed in the analysis of human remains. These include radiography, microscopy, bone chemistry, and DNA analysis. Each of these approaches was discussed in detail in chapter 2.

Summary

Excavation and recovery of biological samples and pollen and/or phytolith samples from archaeological sites for paleonutritional assessments can follow a basic procedure from site to site. Modifications to this procedure may be made depending on site type, environmental conditions, time and money constraints, and research design. It is always best, however, to collect more samples than needed for analysis for a particular project. Excavation is destructive and there are no second chances. Fifty years from now, other researchers may need particular samples to help answer a research question, or an additional sample may be needed from a particular area of an excavated site in the event that samples were not collected from that area and such samples are needed to complete the analysis. Having matrix samples sitting on a shelf for possible future analysis is preferable to having samples lost in the backdirt pile.

No matter what types of paleonutritional analyses are conducted at a site, the most important aspect of interpretation is integration between the various assemblages and analyses conducted (Sobolik 1994a; Reitz et al. 1996). A more complete picture of prehistoric lifeways and paleoenvironmental changes can be revealed through the integration of biological analyses. Integration between different assemblages can be difficult given the diverse ways in which biologists identify, analyze, and interpret various archaeological remains. In many of the case studies presented in this book (see chap. 6), the researchers have attempted to integrate diverse biological analyses, despite the fact that the basic techniques (such as quantification) were not uniform across disciplines or even between analysts. Paleonutritional reconstructions can rarely be effective, encompassing, and broad based without integration.

Integrative paleonutritional research does not always mean that a number of separate analyses should be combined into some conclusion. Integration can and should involve research on modern species ecology, as well as ethnographic and/or ethnohistoric information where feasible. Ultimately, integration must take place at the site or regional level as the paleonutritionist works with the archaeologist (although they may be the same person) to synthesize all of the information obtained from a site excavation into a cohesive final statement.

CHAPTER 5

Interpretation and Integration

MANY OF THE ARCHAEOLOGICAL data currently available on past human behavior are related to food acquisition and consumption. These data include ecofacts (e.g., seeds, bones), artifacts (e.g., procurement and processing tools), architectural remains (e.g., storage features), and settlement patterns (e.g., the distribution of food procurement sites across the landscape). As such, diet is one of the more obvious aspects of human behavior observable in the archaeological record and thus lends itself more readily than others to investigation. The interpretation and integration of dietary data vary in complexity from lists of resources to models of behavior, with the latter ultimately being more informative about questions related to paleonutrition.

A number of approaches have been undertaken in attempts to correlate human behavior with diet, nutrition, and/or subsistence within particular populations. These include ecological perspectives, gender studies, ethnicity, sociopolitical organization, resource intensification, and biological reconstructions. In this chapter we describe these different approaches and provide specific examples of some of these studies. This discussion is not intended to constitute an all-inclusive list of such approaches; rather, it provides a sampling of the possibilities that exist for examining issues of diet and nutrition among prehistoric populations.

Ecological Perspectives

Ecology is the study of the interaction of an organism with its environment. Human ecology is the study of the interaction of humans with their environment. Cultural ecology, a subdiscipline of human ecology, is the study of the interaction of culture on human adaptations (see Sutton and Anderson 2010). Given that many of the data available in the archaeological record are dietary, a number of theoretical approaches based on ecology are used to interpret the past. Among these approaches are evolutionary ecology and evolutionary archaeology, both of which apply biological selection theory to the study of archaeological data.

Within archaeology, however, there has been considerable debate about how closely the strict biological model of selection can be applied to the study of past cultures (e.g., Spencer 1997; Boone and Smith 1998; Lyman and O'Brien 1998; Neff 2000; Flannery 2002). Culture is a powerful force in adaptation, and any evolutionary explanation must include the role of culture, such as behavior, decision-making, and sociopolitical factors. Mechanisms of change include invention, diffusion, social and political upheavals, and migrations and diasporas.

Evolutionary Ecology

Evolutionary ecology begins with the supposition that societies function like organisms and that varying cultural practices, including diet, are traits upon which selection acts (see Smith and Winterhalder 1992; Winterhalder and Smith 1992). Cumulative selection pressures then act on societies and complexes, depending on the outcome of their choice of practices (e.g., Richerson and Boyd 1992).

The approach used most often in evolutionary ecology is optimization, primarily through the application of some model of optimal diet (e.g., Maynard Smith 1978; Stephens and Krebs 1986). Such models are used to explain some aspects of behavior related to the utilization of resources (Jochim 1983:157) and are generally derived from optimal foraging theory, which emphasizes net efficiency (a least-cost hypothesis) and minimization of risk as its guiding principles. Optimization models were originally developed by economists, borrowed by biologists to predict the behavior of animals in relation to their diet and feeding strategies, and then applied to humans by anthropologists (see Winterhalder 1981; Smith 1983).

Most optimization studies have been conducted on hunter-gatherer groups rather than agriculturalists, apparently because hunter-gatherers are supposed to behave like other animals, foraging for their food and wandering about the landscape (Ingold 1987:11). Conversely, agriculturalists are food-producing landholders who are viewed as somehow set apart from nature, making the application of optimization models less attractive (but see Gregg 1988).

All optimization models have four basic components (Gardner 1992:18). Each requires (1) an actor (e.g., people) to choose among the different alternatives, (2) a currency (e.g., calories or protein) by which the payoff on the decisions can be measured, (3) a variety of available resources from which to choose, and (4) a set of constraints, factors that limit the alternatives and payoffs. The primary optimization models used are (1) diet breadth (e.g., Simms 1984, 1985), (2) patch choice (e.g., Smith 1983), (3) central place foraging (e.g., Bettinger 1991), (4) linear programming (e.g., Gardner 1992), and (5) focal-diffuse (e.g., Cleland 1976).

Optimization models contain two inherent problems: The environmental conditions and constraints of the study are rarely understood, and the models really only test biological responses, not cultural behavior. This situation is constantly improving as more detailed data become available and are incorporated into new studies. For example, the productivity of different species of pinyon can vary significantly and it is important to use the correct species to model diet in the past (see Case Study 1 in chap. 6).

It must be remembered that simple optimization models adopted directly from biology cannot account for the diversity of cultural behaviors and factors influencing economic decision-making processes (see Jochim 1998:23–26). On the other hand, such models are not designed to investigate cultural factors; in reality, they are designed to account for the biological aspect of behavior so that the cultural side can be isolated and investigated by other means.

Even with these limitations, optimization models can be very useful and are often employed as at least a "first pass" by archaeologists reconstructing past societies (Winterhalder and Smith 1981). It is necessary to work through the various issues, identify and deal with problems, and refine the models and data accordingly. The goal is to learn about the past, and optimization models are tools to accomplish this. Within evolutionary theory, optimization models appear to be the best, if not the only, current way to explore the interaction between people and their environment (e.g., O'Connell 1995; Broughton and O'Connell 1999).

An important product of the use of optimization models by archaeologists is the unification of research efforts working with botanical and zoological remains. The use of a model that can be applied to both data sets means that both plants and animals can be considered in the same study, providing a much greater depth of understanding of paleonutrition (e.g., Gardner 1992:12).

Evolutionary Archaeology

Another ecological approach is evolutionary archaeology. This method adopts a strict perspective of Darwinian evolution (Maschner 1996; O'Brien 1996; O'Brien and Lyman 2000; Leonard 2001) to explain culture change as the result of direct selective processes on the variation among artifact types and frequencies, resulting in the change of those types and frequencies over time.

In this approach, archaeological traits are treated as if they were biological traits, with selection acting (positively or negatively) on artifacts, systems, and behaviors. Selective pressures on these traits will then translate to selective pressure on cultures as a whole. While evolutionary ecology and evolutionary archaeology share a basic approach, evolutionary archaeology tends to be more focused on material culture rather than diet. With this in mind, a considerable amount of material culture is devoted to fulfilling nutritional needs, so evolutionary archaeology can be very important in studies of paleonutrition.

To illustrate the application of evolutionary archaeology to a prehistoric population, in a study of agricultural engineering and technology in the American Southwest, Maxwell (1995) examined the nature and distribution of fields that were covered in gravel. It was determined that the gravel had been intentionally placed on the fields as a mulch of some sort. Gravel can store excess heat and slow the evaporation of water. Maxwell (1995:122) concluded that the rock mulch could "offer an advantage in crop production to farmers living in regions with periods of low or variable rainfall and low temperatures." The region in which the rock-mulched fields were discovered was an area of both low precipitation and low temperature. As a result, it was determined that the use of rock mulch was an adaptive trait that enabled the farmers to be more successful.

In their evolutionary perspective on prehistoric hunting in California, Hildebrandt and McGuire (2002:231) observed that increased population densities during the middle and late Holocene may account for the "imbalances between human populations and the availability of highly ranked food resources." As a result of these imbalances, according to optimal foraging theory, foraging efficiency should decline while reliance on smaller prey should increase. In contrast, Hildebrandt and McGuire (2002:231) argued that large-game procurement throughout California was actually increasing during the middle and late Holocene.

On that assumption, Hildebrandt and McGuire (2002:231–232) posed the question "why, when there is a consensus that human populations were increasing and subsistence activities intensifying, would there be a corresponding *increase* in the taking of higher-ranked, large-animal taxa, at the expense of lower-ranked small animals?" They suggested that it may have to do with conferring fitness on males in that it would increase mating opportunities, provide favored treatment for their offspring, and facilitate communication with allies and adversaries (Hildebrandt and McGuire 2002:232). In other words, it was linked to sexual selection and prestige (also see Bettinger 1991:200–201), or what Hildebrandt and McGuire (2002:235) referred to as "show-off hunting" (also see Broughton and Bayham 2003; Hildebrandt and McGuire 2003).

Gender Studies

Meyers (2003:190) defined gender as "the social construction or cultural interpretation of sexual difference, especially as it results in assigning individuals, artifacts, spaces, and bodies to categories." In the anthropological sense, gender is defined differently than sex. Sex is an individual's chromosomal makeup; that is, a female has two X chromosomes and a male has an X and a Y chromosome, with a few exceptions based on genetic anomalies. Gender refers to a social category of behavior in which an individual's role and/or status are typically defined as either "male" or "female" regardless of their chromosomal makeup; as such, gender is typically a function of socialization and can be self-assigned. Gender roles other than male or female, such as homosexuals or transvestites, exist in many societies and are often considered normal; in fact, in some cultures, they are thought to be imbued with special insight. Gender concepts change through time within a culture, and some cultures assign greater significance to gender differences than do others. The gender of an individual can be recognized by others within a given society through appearance (e.g., clothing, hairstyles, adornment), activities ("male" and "female" work), and/or styles of social interaction (see Case Study 2 in chap. 6).

Archaeologists attempt to identify genders in past cultures, to determine their importance within a particular group, and to interpret the meaning of gender within the worldview of that group. To study gender in past cultures, archaeologists can employ evidence from various sources, including ethnographic analogy, historical documents, dietary data, skeletal and mortuary data, and representational art (Costin 1996:116–117, 2002). During the last few decades, there has been much archaeological interest in gender, more specifically the theoretical perspective of gender in both prehistoric and historical contexts (e.g., Conkey and Spector 1984; Ehrenberg 1989; Gero and Conkey 1991; Wylie 1992; Little 1994; Wall 1994; Wright 1996; Conkey and Gero 1997; Nelson 1997; Grauer and Stuart-Macadam 1998; Hill 1998; Price 1999; Dowson 2000; Schmidt and Voss 2000; Claassen 2002). In archaeological contexts, for example, some artifacts are typically assigned to gender-specific tasks. For example, milling stones (e.g., manos and metates) are usually regarded as "female" tools, while projectile points are considered "male" tools. Of course, it is not that simple, as many gender-ascribed tools were used throughout prehistory for multiple purposes by both males and females.

Although most dietary data cannot currently be linked with specific individuals, it is now possible to identify, using aDNA (Sutton et al. 1996) and hormonal evidence (Sobolik et al. 1996), whether a paleofecal specimen was from a male or a female. Once the sex of an individual has been determined, the specifics of the diet can then be detailed, thus elucidating differences between male and female diets and cuisine. Such information has the potential to inform archaeologists about differential access to various foods, medicines, and other consumables, indicating power and prestige relationships between the sexes. As such, gendered archaeology enlightens us about the past lives of men as well as women. As Meyers (2003:185) pointed out, "Because people have rarely lived gender-segregated lives, learning about one gender provides information about the other."

In a study conducted by White et al. (2001b), stable carbon isotope and nitrogen isotope data for bone collagen and apatite on Maya skeletons in Belize were employed to interpret social complexity and food systems. Spanning the time between the Preclassic and Postclassic periods, several shifts in the consumption of C_4 foods (tropical grasses, particularly maize) demonstrated differential access between males and females, in that males consumed more meat and C_4 foods than females did (White et al. 2001b:371). High status was also indicated by the consumption of large quantities of C$_4$ foods among some individuals.

In his discussion of the role of insects in the human diet of hunter-gatherer groups around the world, Sutton (1990:195) noted a pattern of differential access to protein sources in some contemporary societies, such as the Yanomamo of northwestern Brazil and the Tukanoan of the northwest Amazon. In these societies, males obtained most of their protein from vertebrates while females consumed a much larger proportion of insects. Observing the same pattern in modern-day chimpanzees, Sutton (1990) suggested that this pattern may have its roots in antiquity, perhaps as early as the Plio-Pleistocene. At that time, hominid females may have focused on insects for protein in response to male-dominated use of vertebrates. Because of their abundance and easy availability, a reliance on insects by some females "may have resulted in a greater success of those individuals and their offspring, and such differential success may (in part) have led to the development of the genus *Homo*" (Sutton 1990:195). Testing this idea archaeologically could take two forms: (1) trace element or stable isotope analysis of human bones to detect the consumption of insects and (2) the recovery of fossilized insect parts and/or the tools used to process insects (Sutton 1990:203).

Ethnicity

Ethnicity is a difficult concept to define. Bloch-Smith (2003:402–403) defined it in terms of ethnic groups, or "a group of people larger than a clan or lineage claiming common ancestry" related by descent and kinship. Ethnicity can be conveyed by way of various characteristics, including language, ritual behavior, physical features, material culture, and dietary choices (Finkelstein 1996:203). Nevertheless, it is difficult to delineate ethnic boundaries, even among modern societies, because there is "no simple one-to-one relationship between ethnic units and cultural similarities and differences" (Barth 1969:13–14; also see Finkelstein 1996:203). This is an even more formidable task when dealing with past cultures, as only selected cultural materials will preserve and/or be discovered in the archaeological record.

From an archaeological perspective, it may be possible to detect ethnicity through analyses of what foods people consumed and how the foods were consumed (see Case Study 5 in chap. 6). As Finkelstein (1996:206) noted, "Culinary practices often rival ideology and religion in terms of cultural conservatism, and food is one of the primary symbols manipulated by people seeking to maintain their cultural identity and group solidarity." Many factors can influence dietary patterns within a particular ethnic group, including acculturation, culture contact, and the availability of resources.

Ethnicity is often determined based on trait lists that are thought to be ethnically distinct markers. But such trait lists rely on "fragments from the cultural whole . . . on the basis of an evolving routinization of ethnographic genres" (Hannerz 1992:21). The definition and determination of ethnicity are also problematic in that it is difficult to determine whether ethnicity is ascribed from within the group itself or by outside groups. As such, it has been argued either that ethnic groups are a myth or that they are artificial constructs (e.g. Miller 2004:56).

In an attempt to identify the Israelites who opposed the Philistines from the twelfth through the early tenth centuries B.C., Bloch-Smith (2003:415–416) observed that there were four distinguishing traits of Israelites: circumcision, maintaining a short beard, abstaining from eating pork, and military inferiority. The taboo on pork has typically been considered a way of differentiating archaeologically between Israelites and Philistines through analyses of pig bones. However, in a study of pig bones from Israel, Syria, Iraq, eastern Anatolia, and Egypt, Hesse and Wapnish (1997) concluded that interpretations of the absence of pig remains as an ethnic marker for the Israelites must be tempered by sociocultural, economic, and temporal factors. In other words, "It is not sufficient to show that a people did not consume pork, but one must also demonstrate how this abstinence was integrated into the social life of their community" (Gandulla 2000:657).

In his study of subsistence practices at five French colonial sites in North America, Becker (2004) observed that the types of food people eat can be determined both by cultural practices and by the environment in which a particular ethnic group lives. For example, cultural (or ethnic) identity can be inferred though selective consumption—that is, consuming certain foods to the near exclusion of others. Selective consumption can also provide information regarding social distance between people. As a result of his analysis of variation in the subsistence patterns of the groups at these five sites, Becker (2004) argued that it was possible to view the different ways in which cultural identities were expressed at each site.

In an analysis of the faunal remains from prehistoric Iroquoian and Algonquian sites along the St. Lawrence estuary between about 500 and 1,000 years ago, St. Pierre (2006) argued that these two populations developed different patterns of resource exploitation within the same environment. The faunal remains from Iroquoian sites contained a much larger proportion of sea mammal bones, whereas those from Algonquian sites consisted primarily of land mammals. There were also differences in the proportions of harbor seals and harp seals between the two groups, with Algonquians primarily hunting the former and Iroquoians the latter (St. Pierre 2006:4). In addition to issues regarding ethnicity, these patterns offered clues regarding the negotiation of borders and resource exploitation between these two populations (St. Pierre 2006:5).

Scott (2001) documented what she believed to be ethnic differences in food consumption among French, Anglo-American, and African American groups between 1820 and 1890 at Nina Plantation, a sugar and cotton plantation in central Louisiana. She also compared the differences in diet among the plantation inhabitants during the pre-Emancipation and post-Emancipation years. While the differences were not always distinct, Scott (2001:671) argued that her evidence demonstrated "the relations of power that existed on the plantation as well as the ways in which ethnicity and economic class affected diet."

Sociopolitical Organization

Social organization refers to the ways in which individuals and social units interact to form a society (see Case Studies 2 and 3 in chap. 6). It includes, but is not limited to, such social institutions as marriage, kinship, family, social stratification, settlement, and subsistence practices. Political organization is the myriad of ways that people have devised to maintain order internally and externally and includes warfare, trade, and culture contact, to name a few. Because they are intimately tied to each other, these two terms are often combined and called sociopolitical organization. Many of these facets of sociopolitical organization are closely tied to diet and nutrition, such as social stratification (e.g., differential

access to preferred food resources), settlement (e.g., farming versus foraging food resources), warfare (e.g., external conflict over food resources),
and trade (e.g., exchange of local for nonlocal food resources).

For example, differential access to important resources, such as water,
food, weapons, and information, can reveal a great deal about diet and
nutrition. Archaeologically, this can be observed in faunal assemblages
and human skeletal remains in terms of who is consuming what, which
ultimately may tell us why those differences existed. This difference in
access frequently results in social, economic, and/or political inequali-
ties within a specific group or between adjacent and/or related groups.
The degree of stratification and inequality in a society is one aspect of its
sociopolitical organization and complexity.

In a study that examined the faunal assemblage from the site of Colha
in northern Belize, Shaw (1999:83) argued that the Preclassic period
Maya (250 B.C. to A.D. 250) engaged in "considerable experimentation
and variation in the strategies used to acquire meat for food." The strategies that focused on meat procurement and resource control provided
support for the large populations of the late Classic period, which ultimately resulted in the development of social and economic inequality.
This shift in faunal procurement strategies suggests that the inhabitants had the ability, "through social and economic means, to remove
[themselves] from the relative subsistence autonomy of earlier periods
and move to a strategy of indirect procurement through trade or tribute"
(Shaw 1999:97).

While noting that postcontact pressures have disturbed the distributions of plant and animal resources in the Great Basin, Fowler (1986:64)
attempted to delineate the role of plants and animals in the diets of ethnographic groups in this region, including how certain species were
manipulated and the role different species played in the worldview of
the cultures that resided there. She observed that the acorn did not play
as significant a role in the Great Basin as it did in California; rather,
pine nuts were of greater importance. Fowler (1986:93–95) observed that
while the subsistence regime of most Great Basin groups was related to
resources that could be hunted and gathered, most groups manipulated
the environment in a number of ways, including burning to increase
yields, broadcast sowing of seeds, pruning, watering, and some irrigation of the natural vegetation. These practices indicate a significant and

detailed knowledge of the environment, a critical component of socio-political organization.

Resource Intensification

The concept of resource (or subsistence) intensification is typically defined as having two related components: "an increase in productivity per areal unit of land" along with "an associated decrease in productive efficiency" (Broughton 1999:5). It was first applied to historical agricultural groups as a means of explaining human population growth (Boserup 1965). Since that time, the application of resource intensification models has become relatively common in explaining the subsistence economics of prehistoric hunter-gatherer groups (e.g., Bartelink 2006; Broughton 1994, 1999; Raab 1996; Wohlgemuth 1996; see Case Study 5 in chap. 6). According to Raab (1996:66), resource intensification models predict two related trends: "the addition of increasingly 'marginal' food species to the diet . . . and increasing investments in the technologies required to exploit the new food items in a cost-effective way." Such models are typically associated with population-resource imbalances and higher levels of sedentism during the late Holocene (Bartelink 2006:4; also see Broughton and O'Connell 1999).

Broughton's (1999) study of resource intensification employed prey body size as a measure of prey profitability in his analysis of the Emeryville Shellmound along San Francisco Bay, where he observed that sturgeon, which was the largest fish from the site, declined in relative abundance through time. This decline was also apparent among various large mammal species, including deer and elk, during the approximately 600-year occupation span of Emeryville. Then, beginning about 2,000 years ago, this trend was reversed, with deer dramatically increasing in abundance until about 700 years ago. This reversal was thought to be due to "an increasing use of distant less-depleted deer patches in the hinterlands of the region and was supported by a variety of faunal data" (Broughton 1999:viii).

In another example, mollusks from the Quoygrew site in Orkney, Scotland, led Milner et al. (2007:1461) to suggest a trend toward the intensification of marine resources at the end of the first millennium A.D. The stratified midden of the site, which dated from approximately the tenth to the thirteenth centuries, contained predominantly limpets, thought to have been used to bait fish. These limpets demonstrated a reduction in size through time. To test whether this reduction in size was related to intensification in exploitation, Milner et al. (2007) conducted an analysis of limpet shoreline location. They also used age data to demonstrate a lowering of average age, which suggested intensification in gathering during the eleventh and twelfth centuries at the site (Milner et al. 2007:1461).

Biological Reconstructions

Biological archaeologists can examine the question of diet in human populations through studies of human remains, such as skeletal data, paleofecal studies, and isotope analyses (see Case Studies 3 and 4 in chap. 6). Teeth and bones can provide valuable data for interpreting the lifeways of past cultures, although "many American archaeologists have not appreciated the full potential of osteological research as a source of information on biocultural behavior and human adaptation" (Owsley et al. 1989:122; also see Larsen 1997). Such information can then be used to develop biological reconstructions, which include analyses of age, sex, stature, pathological conditions, and paleodemography within a specific population or between two or more populations.

For example, using stable carbon and nitrogen isotopic analysis on skeletal specimens from the Stillwater Marsh, Schoeninger (1995:102) noted that some individuals consumed a large amount of C_4 foods, despite the fact that none of the identified plants were C_4. While this suggests that nonlocal C_4 foods were exploited, "two of the faunal samples [hare and duck] have $\delta^{13}C$ values indicating that up to 70 percent of their diet was a C_4 plant (or plants) or a CAM plant with a C_4 signature." The study also revealed that, based on isotope analysis, there was no obvious patterning within the group under analysis in terms of age at death or sex (Schoeninger 1995:102). The conclusion of the study was that prehistoric peoples of the Carson Desert ate a variety of foods, with distinctly different diets at various times throughout the occupation of the region (Schoeninger 1995:105).

Based on the skeletal remains from two archaeological sites located on the island of northern Ambergris Cay, Belize (San Juan and Chac

Balam), Glassman and Garber (1999:123) observed that, despite a small sample size, a pattern seemed to emerge demonstrating that the stature of individuals assigned to the elite members of the population averaged 167.1 centimeters compared to an average of 162.0 centimeters for individuals assigned to the middle and low status groups. This suggested to Glassman and Garber (1999:123) that, in some highly stratified societies, individuals in higher social positions had better diets and were thus healthier than individuals of lower social standing. Other morphological indicators of nutritional stress among the Ambergris populations included Harris lines, dental enamel hypoplasias, and porotic hyperostosis (Glassman and Garber 1999:126).

The results of an isotopic analysis of burials from the Mesolithic sites of Téviec and Hoëdic in Brittany, France, demonstrated the significant use of marine resources by the inhabitants of these two sites (Schulting and Richards 2001). On the other hand, there were unexpected differences between the two sites, as the people of Hoëdic received up to 80 percent of their protein from the sea, whereas the people of Téviec made relatively equal use of marine and terrestrial proteins. Further, at both sites, women (especially young women) consumed fewer marine resources, suggesting an exogamous, patrilocal marriage pattern (Schulting and Richards 2001).

Summary

As the above examples demonstrate, there are a number of theoretical approaches that can be used to extract data from the archaeological record in order to provide information on past human behavior related to diet and nutrition. With the exception of biological reconstructions, which can provide direct evidence of diet, most of these approaches are indirect indicators of diet, such as inferences regarding differential access based on gender, ethnicity, and/or status. In tandem with a variety of archaeological data, however, such studies offer valuable insights into the dietary and nutritional patterns of past populations.

Future Directions

As the examples in this book have illustrated, we currently have a great deal of data about past diet and nutrition and have begun to integrate these data toward an understanding of human behavior. The gaps in our knowledge remain considerable, however, and basic baseline data on diet and nutrition are still needed for many groups worldwide. Some researchers have a tendency to discontinue seeking baseline data when they begin to see a pattern of redundancy, believing that there is nothing left to learn about a particular group. We would argue, however, that even redundant data are important and should continue to be sought. Understanding stability is as important as understanding variation or change in the environments and/or behaviors of human groups. We learn something in either case.

Information about paleonutrition exists in a number of data sets, including faunal, botanical, and bioarchaeological, but we rarely recover complete data sets for any particular group in an archaeological context. In other words, we may know something about the faunal utilization of Group A, the plant usage of Group B, and the aDNA of Group C, but we do not often have the luxury of controlling all three of these sets of data within one group. There is a considerable need to generate complementary data sets for each group under study so that comparisons can be made and concordant data for hypothesis testing can be generated.

Paleonutrition studies continue to become greater in scope and sophistication. There is an increasing trend to combine botanical and faunal data from archaeological excavations to gain a more complete picture of the resources that were used by a group. Analytical technology—such as gas chromatography/mass spectrometry—is now commonly utilized to generate new data sets, often in combination with traditional faunal and botanical studies. The application of aDNA data to problems in paleonutrition studies—such as population movements—is very exciting and promises to move us into realms of knowledge only imagined a few decades ago.

Our understanding of paleonutrition must be expanded beyond behaviors related to obtaining food to include a series of other behaviors related to the consequences of diet. For example, environmental conditions will influence choices made by a group about the types and quantities of foods that can be obtained, which in turn will influence certain behaviors within a group (e.g., within the theory of evolutionary archaeology, which animals get hunted using which tactics and with what technology). Surpluses or shortages of resources could influence sociopolitical organizational responses (e.g., who has what power), which can influence the equality of subgroups (e.g., different genders) within a group.

Ultimately, studies that combine and integrate suites of data sets—including faunal and botanical, isotopic, aDNA, pathology, technology, settlement patterns, ecology, sex and gender, and socioeconomic—will provide a much richer understanding of the past than we currently have. Studies of paleonutrition can lead the way.

CHAPTER 6

Case Studies

THIS CHAPTER PRESENTS five case studies on paleonutrition and related issues. Three of these case studies come from North America, including the Great Basin, the American Southwest, and the northern Coachella Valley of California. Two come from Africa, one from east Africa and one from northern Sudan. The topics of these case studies cover a wide range of research, including some of the personal research of the authors. One of the studies, of contemporary east African foragers, illustrates the applicability of the study of contemporary groups to the study of prehistoric populations.

Case Study 1, "*Pinus monophylla* and Great Basin Subsistence Models," is a reanalysis of previous data on pinyon, with a different interpretation on the value of pinyon to prehistoric peoples in the Great Basin. Case Study 2, "East African Highland Foragers," demonstrates the importance of the combination of hunting and honey collecting among east African highland groups, primarily the Okiek. In Case Study 3, "Children's Health in the Prehistoric Southwest," a slightly different approach is taken. In this study, the authors first synthesize the previous research on the topic of children's health in the Southwest and then provide an analysis of the data that is first seen in this volume. Case Study 4, "Complementary Paleonutritional Data Sets: An Example from Medieval Christian Nubia," highlights dietary stress during the Medieval Christian period (ca. A.D. 550 to 1450) in northern Sudan (once known as Upper Nubia), as evidenced in mummies recovered during archaeological excavations. The final case study, No. 5, "An Evolving Understanding of Paleodiet in the Northern Coachella Valley, California," is a comparison of models related to diet among the prehistoric and ethnographic Cahuilla in the Coachella Valley of California, and how paleodiet and other factors may have contributed to settlement shifts.

It is hoped that these case studies will stimulate future such analyses among archaeologists (and related professionals) and aspiring students in the field. Such studies could also lead to additional reanalyses of previous research, possibly leading to new interpretations of old ideas based on more recent information. The future of paleonutritional research is an open door inviting all interested scholars to enter.

Case Study 1: *Pinus monophylla* and Great Basin Subsistence Models

In formulating models of human adaptation, it is important that the environmental parameters be understood and that accurate information be employed. This case study illustrates the use of information regarding the behavior of one species of pinyon to model the behavior of another. This study led to a miscalculation of the availability and productivity of the species in question and an underestimation of the value of pinyon in Great Basin subsistence systems (see Sutton 1984).

In a landmark study, David H. Thomas (1971, 1973) formulated a model (called Basin I) of prehistoric central Great Basin subsistence and settlement patterns based on ethnographic data gathered by Julian Steward (e.g., 1937, 1938) and others. Thomas concluded that from about 5,500 B.P. to the time of historic contact, the archaeological record of the Reese River Valley in central Nevada reflected the same basic land-use system that characterized the ethnographic period. To create Basin I, Thomas modeled the availability and productivity of the suite of resources utilized by the ethnographic Western Shoshone. The exploitation of single-leaf pinyon (*Pinus monophylla*) was an integral part of that adaptation, and the ethnographic pattern of its use was a key element in the archaeological predictions derived from the model. Similar models, also employing pinyon, have been used in other subsistence studies in the Great Basin (e.g., Bettinger 1975; Thomas 1983) and, at least partly as a result of these models, pinyon has gained the reputation of having been an erratic and unpredictable aboriginal food source.

To understand how pinyon was used by the prehistoric inhabitants of the Great Basin, it was necessary to understand the behavior of pinyon. The species of pinyon that grows in the central Great

Basin is *P. monophylla*. At the time of the Reese River Valley study, however, specific data on *P. monophylla* were lacking. As a proxy, Thomas used ecological data from the Colorado pinyon (*P. edulis*) for his simulation of pine nut harvests over a 200-year period. Based on Little (1938), Thomas (1973:160) "assumed that the behavior of *Pinus monophylla* [was] comparable to that of *P. edulis*." Using the behavioral data from *P. edulis*, Thomas modeled cone crop frequency and yield, seed (food) yield, and harvest estimates on pinyon. The model was then run through a computer to produce a reconstruction of the environment to be compared to the archaeological record. Based on the expectations produced by the model and on the archaeological data obtained from the study area, Thomas concluded that the cultural adaptation recorded in ethnographic times was substantially the same for the last 5,500 years.

Unfortunately, the assumption that the behavior of *P. edulis* was basically the same as that of *P. monophylla* was in error, as shown by data compiled on *P. monophylla* after Thomas had completed his study. The use of *P. edulis* as a proxy resulted in a considerable underestimation of the productivity of *P. monophylla* and a misunderstanding of the use of this resource by Great Basin peoples. The points of error are discussed below (also see table 6.1).

Habitat and Description

The range of *P. monophylla* (fig. 6.1) is confined primarily to the central and southwestern Great Basin, including western Utah; northeastern, central, and southern Nevada; the eastern slopes of the Sierra Nevada; and interior southern California (Sargent 1922; Mirov 1967). The species is adapted to semi-arid desert mountains ranging in elevation from about 1,500 to 2,300 meters (Britton 1908; Mirov 1967). The range of *P. edulis* (fig. 6.1) is confined to Colorado, eastern Utah, Arizona, New Mexico, and parts of Texas and Wyoming (Sargent 1922; Mirov 1967). *P. edulis* is adapted to the drier mountain ranges at elevations from about 1,800 to 2,400 meters (Britton 1908). Generally speaking, *P. monophylla* trees are bigger and have larger cones than *P. edulis*, and the two species have a

TABLE 6.1. Comparative Data on *Pinus monophylla* and *Pinus edulis*

	P. monophylla	P. edulis
Tree height	6 to 15 meters[a]	3 to 12 meters[a,b]
Cones mature in	Late August[c]	September[a,c]
Cones fall in	September to October[c]	September[c]
Average cone length	4.0 to 6.5 centimeters[a]	2.0 to 5.0 centimeters[d]
Crop frequency	1 to 2 years (avg., 1.5 years)[a]	2 to 5 years (avg., 3.5 years)[d]
Unshelled seeds per bushel of cones	1.7 to 4.7 pounds (avg., 3.2 pounds)[a]	3.3 pounds[a]
Average shelled seed length	1.5 centimeters[b]	1.2 centimeters[b]
Number of unshelled seeds per pound	1,100[a]	1,900[a]
Percentage of seed weight taken up by the shell	30[a]	42[a]
Edible seeds per pound of unshelled seeds	0.70 pound	0.58 pound
Average edible seed yield per year (edible seeds divided by crop frequency)	0.47 pound	0.16 pound
Calories per pound[e]	2,250	3,190
Bottom Line: Average calories available (yield times calories) per year	1,057	510

[a] Schopmeyer (1974).
[b] Britton (1908).
[c] Ligon (1978).
[d] Little (1941).
[e] Farris (1982:table 2).

differential geographic distribution. It is also important to note that the cones of both species mature in their third growing season (Ligon 1978).

Species Behavior

Cone Crop Frequency

Citing the work of Little (1941), Thomas (1971) estimated that a *P. edulis* tree will produce cones (cone crop frequency) at two to five years. These

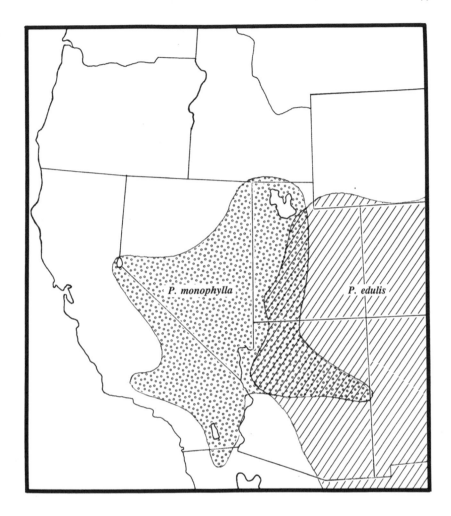

FIGURE 6.1. Distribution of *Pinus monophylla* and *Pinus edulis* in the Great Basin (from Sutton 1984:241; reproduced by permission).

data have been replicated more recently (Schopmeyer 1974) and a cone crop frequency of two to five years for *P. edulis* appears to be confirmed. The cone crop frequency for *P. monophylla* was extrapolated by Thomas (1971) using the *P. edulis* data, as there were no independent data available for *P. monophylla* at that time. Specific data on the cone crop frequency of *P. monophylla* are now available (Schopmeyer 1974) and show that the cone crop frequency of *P. monophylla* is one to two years, a substantial difference from *P. edulis*.

Other quantitative data on *P. monophylla* cone crops seem to indicate frequent cone crop production. Forcella (1978) examined a small sample of trees in eight *P. monophylla* stands (five trees per stand) in southern Idaho and northern Nevada and estimated cone production over a ten-year period. He concluded that "the overall cone crops in pinyon communities are highly irregular" (Forcella 1978:171), but added that seed crops measured in his study exceeded the overall ten-year sample average in two or three years, with such crops followed by average yields in about half of the study plots. Poor crop yields (below the ten-year average) were also recorded. Forcella (1978) suggested that variation in cone crop size might serve as a defense against the pinyon cone moth (*Eucosma bobana*) by not allowing the moths to concentrate in particular stands over successive years. The life cycle of the pinyon jay (*Gymnorhinus cyanocephalus*), which subsists primarily on pinyon nuts (Lanner 1981), suggests that the crops of *P. monophylla* must occur often and be at least somewhat consistent.

It is clear that pinyon cone crops do fail, but such failures are probably confined to specific stands (cf. Lanner 1983). Unfortunately, there is no clear definition of what a "stand" is or how large "stands" are. Crop failures of radical proportions do occur but may be quite limited in geographical extent. Widespread crop failures might be quite rare, and none were reported by Forcella (1978). While the above data are not conclusive, they do support the suggestion that cone crop frequencies of *P. monophylla* are higher than those of *P. edulis*.

Cone Crop Predictability

It takes three seasons for a pinyon cone to mature. During the second growing season, more than a full year prior to their maturity, small cones often are plainly visible on the tree. They are virtually right next to the near-mature cones of the current crop and should have been easily observable during pinyon harvests (cf. Wheat 1967:116; Sutton 1984:fig. 2). There should, therefore, have been little problem in estimating the crop for the next year, making the crop of the following year highly predictable. Monitoring of the cones throughout the year would add to the reliability of the predictions.

Seed Yield

Based on sample plots throughout the range of pinyon, the pounds of seeds per bushel of cones has been estimated for the two species (Schopmeyer 1974:622–623). The data indicate that the seed yield (pounds per bushel) in *P. monophylla* is sometimes larger but perhaps more erratic than that of *P. edulis*.

The seeds of *Pinus monophylla* are substantially larger than those of *Pinus edulis*. According to an analysis of yield data (Schopmeyer 1974:622–623), *P. monophylla* averages 1,100 unshelled seeds per pound of seeds while *P. edulis* averages 1,900 seeds per pound. In addition, the shells of *P. edulis* comprise an average of 42 percent of the seed weight whereas the shells of *P. monophylla* average 30 percent of the total weight (Lanner 1981). As a result, *P. monophylla* produces about 12 percent more edible material per pound of seeds than *P. edulis*, a substantial difference.

A nutritional analysis of several species of pine, including *P. monophylla* and *P. edulis*, was reported by Farris (1982). Several major differences exist between *P. monophylla* and *P. edulis*, including a higher fat and protein content in the latter and a higher carbohydrate content in the former. The seeds of *P. edulis* have a higher caloric value and would seem to have more of several important minerals (Farris 1982). On the other hand, *P. monophylla* contains larger proportions of twelve of twenty-two amino acids (see Madsen 1986:table 2).

Good Years and Bad Years

The model proposed by Thomas predicted that Great Basin peoples could expect a "good" crop of pine nuts every 7.7 years with an "acceptable" (good or fair) crop every 5.4 years (Thomas 1971:26). Crop failure (undefined by Thomas) could, by implication, be expected in most years. The criteria of "good" and "fair" used by Thomas (1971, 1972) were based on mid-1940s Forest Service estimates of seed yield (on *P. edulis*) from a field station near Tucson, Arizona. These data were originally intended to measure harvests in modern economic terms, not in aboriginal economic terms, and are somewhat confusing. A "good" harvest to the Forest Service in Arizona was 100,000 pounds of seeds per township (4.34

pounds per acre), the equivalent of 30,000 pounds (1.3 pounds per acre) for Great Basin pinyon densities (after Thomas 1971:30). A "fair" seed crop would have been 50,000 pounds for Arizona, or 15,000 pounds (0.65 pound per acre) for the Basin. Pinyon crop failure for the Basin would apparently be less than 0.65 pound of seeds per acre.

Based on the data provided by Thomas (1971:30) for aboriginal population density and pinyon needs (21 persons per township [36 square miles] requiring a total of 6,300 pounds of seeds [0.27 pound per acre] per year), there could be a serious failure based on the Forest Service standard, although there would be ample pinyon seeds still available to support the aboriginal population. While there were certainly local cone crop failures and "bad" years, it is difficult to see how P. monophylla could have been an unreliable food source. The use of modern standards to predict prehistoric conditions of pinyon appears to have been a serious flaw.

Discussion

The behaviors of P. edulis and P. monophylla are quite different. Thus, the predictions of central Great Basin pinyon crops made by Thomas based on the behavior of P. edulis were incorrect, and it seems that P. monophylla would have been at least twice as productive in average available calories as P. edulis (see table 6.1). The use of modern standards to define crop failures in aboriginal times compounds the issue. One could argue that the conclusions reached by Thomas were based on incorrect data, and the conclusions based on those data are probably not valid. To construct and use models, one must begin with accurate data. If not, the results of the models will be unsatisfactory and could distort our understanding of the societies involved.

In the Great Basin, the conclusions of the Basin I study are widely held as "gospel" and much of the interpretation of the prehistory of the region is based on the premise that there was some sort of cultural continuity in the central Great Basin for the past 5,500 years. This has had a profound effect on a number of issues, most notably linguistic prehistory. The model of an expansion of Numic groups across the Great Basin beginning about 1,000 years ago (see Madsen and Rhode 1994) has been countered by an alternative model suggesting that Numic groups originated in the central Great Basin (Aikens and Witherspoon 1986). This latter model was based, in a large degree, on the premise of a cultural continuity in the central Great Basin.

The new pinyon data would, no doubt, greatly alter the original conclusions of the Thomas (1971) study and call into question all of the work that used those conclusions as their baseline premise. Having a good understanding of pinyon biology could have a profound impact on interpretations of Great Basin prehistory.

Case Study 2: East African Highland Foragers

The foragers turned pastoralists of the east African highlands subsisted mainly on hunted foods supplemented by honey, a small amount of gathered plants, and some traded domesticated foods (Cronk 2004). Wild game has always been considered extremely important to diet and nutrition by these peoples, whereas the importance of honey has been considered mainly symbolic or religious in nature (Blackburn 1971, 1982a,b). Honey consists primarily of carbohydrates, one of three sources of caloric energy (the other two being protein and fat). The ubiquitous combination of hunting and beekeeping in the eastern African highlands most likely has served the purpose of providing alternative energy sources with ingestion of carbohydrate-rich honey. As such, honey is an essential dietary item providing a unique source of caloric energy. Combining honey and hunting in this region is therefore nutritionally adaptive.

Recent attention has focused on the nutritional adequacy of diets, whether relating to modern cultural groups (Farris 1982; Kuhnlein et al. 1982; Ramos-Elorduy de Conconi et al. 1984), prehistoric populations (Dennell 1979; Ezzo 1994c; Sobolik 1994b), or processes of hominid evolution (Bumsted 1985; Sealy and van der Merwe 1985). Protein is an integral component of proper nutrition and, as noted above, one of three sources of caloric energy. Speth (1989, 1990) and Speth and Spielmann (1983) observed that there seems to be an upper limit in the amount of caloric energy that can be acquired through protein sources without the consequences of deleterious health effects. This maximum limit has been defined as approximately 50 percent (or 300 grams) of total ingested calories obtained from protein. Therefore, other sources of caloric energy are important in maintaining a nutritional balance and avoiding the ill effects of a high-protein diet.

Human Energy Requirements

Energy is the essential outcome of the body's use of dietary constituents. Energy requirements for human growth are obtained through the ingestion of protein, fat, and carbohydrates. One gram of fat provides 9 kilocalories of energy, whereas 1 gram of carbohydrates or 1 gram of protein provides 4 kilocalories of energy. Although fat is the most concentrated source of energy (Shahied 1977), carbohydrates are actually the least expensive source of energy (Sherman 1941; Roehrig 1984; Guthrie 1986). This assessment is based on the thermic effect (or specific dynamic action) of foods. The thermic effect of carbohydrates is only 6 percent (Speth and Spielmann 1983), indicating that for every 100 grams of carbohydrates ingested 6 grams are used to drive metabolism. This is in contrast to a 6 percent to 14 percent thermic effect for fat and 30 percent thermic effect for protein (Speth and Spielmann 1983). Protein, therefore, is the least efficient energy source while carbohydrates are the most efficient.

Humans can convert glycerol fats and amino acids to glucose, relieving the body of its need for carbohydrates, although the best source of energy and glucose is through carbohydrate ingestion (Committee on Dietary Allowances 1980). Carbohydrates are found mainly in plant food sources, and an intake of at least 100 grams of carbohydrates a day is recommended, primarily to prevent an increased ingestion of protein as an energy source (Guthrie 1986). The lack of carbohydrates in the diet leads to breakdown of tissue protein, ketosis, dehydration, and loss of cations (Committee on Dietary Allowances 1980).

Recent nutritional studies have indicated that in optimal conditions, 15 percent of caloric intake should be derived from protein, 30 percent to 35 percent from fat, and 45 percent to 55 percent from carbohydrates (Lloyd et al. 1978; Cahill 1986; Guthrie 1986; Poduch et al. 1988). Caloric intake percentages vary among societies. For example, it has been estimated that modern Americans acquire 43 percent to 58 percent of their energy from carbohydrates, 12 percent from protein, and 30 percent to 45 percent from fat (Guthrie 1986). Hunter-gatherer groups, however, tend to consume larger amounts of protein. The !Kung San of Botswana receive 16 percent of their calories from protein (Lee 1979), and the northern Ache of Paraguay derive 39 percent of their calories from protein (Hill 1988). The highest percentage of protein consumption occurs in arctic and subarctic regions, however, with a range between 15 percent and 45 percent (Sinclair 1953; Draper 1977, 1980; Schaefer 1977). Researchers analyzing prehistoric hunter-gatherer diets have estimated that early humans received between 25 percent and 34 percent of their caloric intake from protein, 45 percent to 60 percent from carbohydrates, and only between 15 percent and 21 percent from fat (Robson and Wadsworth 1977; Eaton and Konner 1985).

Dietary protein can originate from either plants or animals; however, protein derived from animals is most useful for human dietary requirements because of the diversity and variety of amino acids in animals, whereas plant protein may be deficient in one or more essential amino acids (Hegsted 1978; Guthrie 1986). The highest percentage of protein in the diet of modern human populations has been calculated to be less than 50 percent of total caloric intake. This intake level seems to be a crucial cutoff point in the amount of protein that humans can ingest without deleterious effects. Protein consumption above 50 percent of total calories may surpass the level at which the liver can perform amino acid metabolism, as well as the amount of urea the body can synthesize and excrete (Noli and Avery 1988; Speth 1990). Some deleterious effects of increased protein consumption include dehydration, electrolytic imbalance, calcium loss, elevated levels of blood ammonia, and hypertrophy of the liver and kidneys (Miller and Mitchell 1982; Cahill 1986; McArdle et al. 1986; also see Speth 1990).

Speth (1989) argued that meat (and meat protein) from larger game sources was probably not an important aspect of early hominid dietary practices; dietary energy was probably achieved through the ingestion of plant foods and smaller insects and animals. Larger African ungulates are particularly lean and devoid of fat, with average fat levels reaching 4 percent during optimal times (Speth and Spielmann 1983; Speth 1987) and decreasing to 1 percent to 2 percent during lean times (Speth 1987). Due to the inefficiency of protein as an energy source, as well as the deleterious effects resulting from high protein intakes, Speth (1989) argued that lean African ungulates were probably not sought as a preferable food source, particularly during times of resource stress. Vegetable foods, many of which are rich sources of fat and carbohydrates, would probably have been their primary foraging targets.

In another study, Speth and Spielmann (1983) hypothesized that, again due to the inefficiency of protein and the detrimental effects of high protein consumption, hunter-gatherers may have been forced to decrease their emphasis on hunting larger ungulates during times of stress. During lean times, "protein is simply an expensive source of calories" (Hegsted 1978:64). Larger ungulates would also be nutritionally stressed and their fat content would decrease, resulting in a larger portion of animals containing pure protein rather that a mixture of protein and fat. Speth and Spielmann (1983) discussed other possible strategies for capturing alternative energy sources during times of stress, such as the selective procurement of animals with high fat content, building up a reserve of body fat during optimal times, applying labor-intensive techniques of bone grease acquisition, and foraging for and/or storing carbohydrate-rich plant foods.

The Nutritional Value of Honey

Honey has been and continues to be an important food source for various prehistoric and historical cultural groups throughout the world (Fraser 1951; Cipriani 1966; Turnbull 1966; Pager 1973) and was used for thousands of years before the introduction of cane or beet sugar (Crane 1975). Today, honey is a key commercial trade product, as honey is a staple resource on its own and not necessarily as an ingredient in other foods (Perlman 1974; Crane 1975, 1980). In 1973 alone, the United States produced 107,985 tons of honey, exporting 7,985 tons and importing 4,854 tons (Crane 1975).

The sweet composition of honey depends on two main factors: the composition of different plant nectars, which vary in types and concentrations of sugars, and external factors such as weather, climatic conditions, and beekeeper practices (Crane 1975). There are a variety of vitamins

TABLE 6.2. Nutrients in Honey in Relation to Human Requirements[a]

Nutrient	Average Amount (100 g of honey)	U.S. Recommended Daily Intake
Energy	304 kcal	2,800 kcal
Vitamins		
B$_1$ (thiamine)	0.004 to 0.006 mg	5,000 mg
Riboflavin	0.02 to 0.06 mg	1.5 mg
Nicotinic acid	0.11 to 0.36 mg	20 mg
B$_6$ (pyridoxine)	0.008 to 0.32 mg	2.0 mg
Pantothenic acid	0.02 to 0.11 mg	10 mg
C (ascorbic acid)	2.2 to 2.4 mg	60 mg
Minerals		
Calcium	0.004 to 0.05 g	1.0 g
Chlorine	0.002 to 0.02 g	—
Copper	0.01 to 0.1 mg	2.0 mg
Iron	0.1 to 3.4 mg	18 mg
Magnesium	0.7 to 13 mg	400 mg
Manganese	0.02 to 10 mg	—
Phosphorus	0.002 to 0.06 g	1.0 g
Potassium	0.01 to 0.47 g	—
Sodium	0.006 to 0.04 g	—
Zinc	0.2 to 0.5 g	15 g

[a] Taken from Crane (1975).

and minerals found in honey (table 6.2), although carbohydrates (sugars) contribute the largest amount of nutrients (Perlman 1974; Crane 1975, 1980). The average carbohydrate content of honey in the United States is 78.10 percent, while the average found in African honey is 76.18 percent (table 6.3). The energy value of honey is 304 kilocalories per 100 grams (table 6.3), or 1,380 kilocalories per pound (Watt and Merrill 1963). Acids, minerals (ash), protein and amino acids, trace elements, and enzymes are also present in honey, but only in minor amounts (Anderson and Perold 1964; Crane 1975). Most carbohydrates that are found in honey are monosaccharides, predominantly the sugars laevulose and dextrose, which make up 85 percent to 95 percent of honey carbohydrates (Crane 1975). Disaccharides are also present in honey, but are very rare (White and Hoban 1959; White et al. 1962).

TABLE 6.3. Average Percentage Carbohydrate Composition of Honey from the United States and Africa[a]

Country	General Carbohydrate	Specific Carbohydrates				
		Dextrose	Laevulose	Sucrose	Maltose	Dextrin
Angola	78.62	33.9	36.4	0.86	6.48	0.98
Mozambique	77.57	32.0	36.2	1.10	6.51	1.76
Portuguese Guinea	77.72	31.2	38.3	1.06	6.36	0.80
Sao Tome and Principe	73.57	31.0	34.8	0.61	5.97	1.19
South Africa	73.44	31.5	35.5	0.54	5.40	0.50
United States	78.10	31.3	38.2	1.30	7.30	—

[a] Taken from Crane (1975), Anderson and Perold (1964), and White et al. (1962).

The Lifestyle of East African Highland Foragers

Forager/pastoralists of the east African highlands include as many as three dozen diverse groups located throughout the forests of Kenya and Tanzania (Blackburn 1974). Although these groups were once commonly referred to as "Dorobo," it is now widely understood that this is a derogatory term without validity as a tribal designation. The groups are more properly referred to by their individual names, such as the Mukogodo just north of Mount Kenya and the Okiek of the Mau Escarpment and some other areas (fig. 6.2). These groups share similar technologies, social structures, belief systems, and subsistence strategies (Blackburn 1974). Many of them have recently made the transition from a mobile hunting and gathering way of life to one primarily of pastoralism (Huntingford 1953; van Zwanenberg 1976; Blackburn 1982a,b; Cronk 1989a,b,c, 2004). For the Mukogodo, this transition began immediately after the turn of the twentieth century, with the most significant change occurring between 1925 and 1936 (Cronk 1989b, 2004).

The most valuable data available on the diets of these groups while they were still hunter-gatherers have come from studies of the Okiek of northern Tanzania and southern Kenya. Due to overall similarities of the subsistence economies of these groups, however, the same insights into the dietary role of honey likely apply to the non-Okiek beekeeping groups as well. The combination of hunting and beekeeping is widespread in the forager subsistence of this region. Hunting provides most of

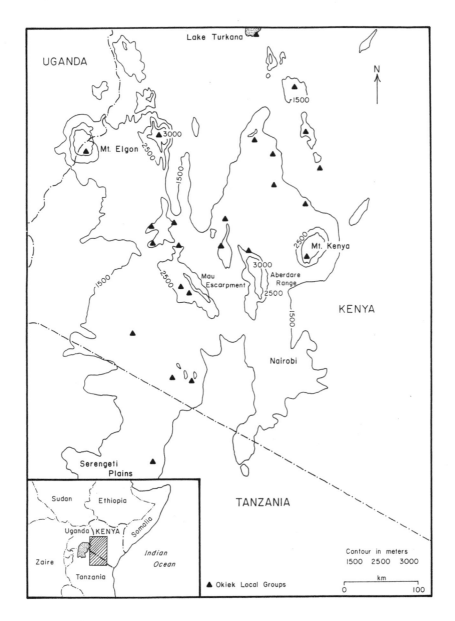

FIGURE 6.2. Location of the various Okiek groups in east Africa (redrawn from Blackburn [1982b:fig. 13.1]; reproduced by permission).

the dietary energy required by the population, although beekeeping and honey consumption play an essential role in both forager subsistence and symbolism (Blackburn 1971; Cronk 1989a). Moreover, although hunting provides the most calories, foragers spend a great deal of their foraging time in the acquisition of honey and the upkeep of beehives (Blackburn 1971, 1982a,b). Before the shift to pastoralism, the main source of food came from hunting and trapping, collecting honey, and gathering wild plant foods. Blackburn (1971) indicated that the Okiek estimated that 70 percent of their diet came from meat, 15 percent from honey, 14 percent from domestic foods acquired from other tribes, and less than 1 percent from wild vegetables or fruits.

Blackburn (1982a:13) observed that "honey-gathering is the most important activity of the Okiek," mainly because of its symbolic significance. Honey is considered sacred, and a variety of taboos and rituals are associated with gathering and consuming honey (Huntingford 1953, 1955; Blackburn 1971). The symbolic nature of honey is also indicated by the amount of time and energy spent in collecting and storing honey (Blackburn 1971, 1982a,b).

Honey is obtained from both natural and man-made hives (Cronk 1989a), although the majority of Okiek honey comes from the latter (Huntingford 1955). Man-made hives are constructed after a tree has been cut down and a section taken from the tree and hollowed out (Huntingford 1955; Blackburn 1982a). The hollowed section is sealed with wooden boards at two ends, and a small notch is made at one end to allow entrance for bees, as well as for prying it open to get at the honey (Cronk 1989a). The hive is placed in the branches or crotch of a tree, avoiding trees with low branches so that the honey badger cannot get the honey (Huntingford 1955; Blackburn 1982a). The honey is collected using smoking sticks to calm the bees. Men do not wear protective clothing and bee stings are common but rarely serious (Blackburn 1982a; Cronk 1989a).

Honey is eaten by the gatherer's family, used in trading partnerships, made into a fermented drink, or stored for later use (Huntingford 1953; Blackburn 1982a,b; Cronk 1989a). The Mukogodo store honey by leaving it to harden in sealed containers. Traditionally, containers of honey were placed in caves whose locations were kept hidden from other members of the tribe (Cronk 1989a). Honey may have been kept in the cave for a couple of years before it was used. The ability to store honey probably increased the importance of honey to the diet (Cronk 1989a).

Since their recent subsistence change to pastoralism, people in the east African highlands rarely hunt, and the importance of wild plant and animal foods has been replaced by traded cultivated crops and livestock. Among the Okiek, the percentage of the diet from meat has decreased to approximately 30 percent, honey has decreased to 10 percent of the diet, and the largest percentage (60 percent) consists of posho (cooked maize meal) and milk (R. Blackburn, personal communication 1990). Blackburn (1971) also estimated that as much as 75 percent of the diet may include garden crops. Similar protein contributions to total caloric energy have also been observed for other pastoralists in the area. Masai pastoralists have a protein intake of 30 percent to 35 percent of calories (Ho et al. 1971; Taylor and Ho 1971), and Turkana pastoralists average between 21 percent and 30 percent protein intake of calories (Galvin 1985).

Honey is still an important dietary item, however, although its significance has decreased in recent times. Okiek informants stated that they prefer honey over meat and posho (R. Blackburn, personal communication 1990), and when honey and meat are brought home from a foraging expedition, honey is the favored commodity (Blackburn 1971). Blackburn (personal communication 1990) estimated that an adult male consumes 400 pounds of honey per year (table 6.4), although he had earlier placed the average at 300 pounds of honey per year (Blackburn 1971). Blackburn's Okiek informants also stated that males eat as much as 4 pounds of honey per week to 2 pounds per day if it is available. Blackburn (1971) also noted that during hunting/foraging expeditions, men may eat as much as 3 pounds of honey per day, although this large amount of honey consumption is confined to actual expedition days.

An estimation of the caloric contribution of honey to Okiek diet during the traditional foraging time period is indicated in table 6.4. This table illustrates that Okiek males ingest, on average, between 787 and 4,347 kilocalories per day of honey, a range of 28 percent to 155 percent of their daily caloric requirements. Higher estimates most likely indicate consumption during honey expeditions rather than average daily intake. Assuming that the average Okiek male requires 2,800 kilocalories per day, an assumption that may be incorrect due to cultural, environmental, and physical differences among populations (Stini 1975; Srinivasan 1981;

TABLE 6.4. Estimated Male Okiek Honey Ingestion[a]

Honey Ingestion[b]	kcal/day (avg.)	Percentage of Required 2,800 kcal/day
Pastoral Society (10% of diet)		
400 lb/year	1,518	54
300 lb/year	1,134	41
4 lb/week	787	28
3 lb/day (if available)	4,140	148
2 lb/day (if available)	2,760	99
Traditional Society (15% of diet)		
420 lb/year	1,587	57
315 lb/year	1,191	43
4.2 lb/week	828	30
3.15 lb/day (if available)	4,347	155
2.1 lb/day (if available)	2,898	104

[a] From Blackburn (1971; personal communication 1990).
[b] Honey provides 1,380 kcal/lb.

Seckler 1982; Messer 1986), a large portion of Okiek caloric requirements is met by the ingestion of honey. In fact, the average amount of honey (and therefore carbohydrates) ingested by Okiek males approximates the amount of carbohydrates that nutritional sources suggest normal diets should contain—between 45 percent and 55 percent (Cahill 1986; Guthrie 1986; Poduch et al. 1988).

One of the significant points in this discussion of honey ingestion is the reliance on data from Okiek males. Data on honey consumption are limited mainly to male informants (R. Blackburn, personal communication 1990), and males usually consume the most honey, particularly during the honey-gathering season (Blackburn 1971). During honey season, men travel into the forest to collect honey. During these expeditions, a large part of the honey collected may be consumed by males, and portions that are brought home are "retained by the owner for his children, for selling or trading and for making wine" (Blackburn 1971:78). One-third of the honey that is brought back is usually given to children, and "the wife takes little or none for herself" (Blackburn 1971:80). The amount of honey that females consume is unknown; therefore, the importance of carbohydrate ingestion in relation to protein for the entire population cannot be calculated or even assumed.

Discussion

Honey is an extremely important dietary resource for east African highland foragers, particularly males. During traditional foraging periods, if honey is not available, most of the human caloric energy requirement would be met through the ingestion of protein. Admittedly, fat would also contribute to the total caloric energy requirement through ingestion of fatty animal meat; however, this contribution would be minor in comparison to that of protein. Most caloric energy of modern-day pastoralists is provided by agricultural or garden crops, consisting mainly of carbohydrates. Honey has always been important in the traditional forager diet of this region of Africa, because it is an extremely substantial source of carbohydrates, an energy food source that can complement the energy provided by protein.

Honey collecting and hunting are recurrent themes observed throughout foraging societies in east Africa (Blackburn 1971; Cronk 1989a). This combination is probably essential due to the extensive amount of protein provided by a hunting subsistence pattern. If the contribution of protein to the total caloric energy requirement exceeds approximately 50 percent, then the population will probably experience a variety of deleterious health effects (Speth and Spielmann 1983; Speth 1989, 1990). In this part of the world, honey has always provided an easy and important energy alternative. More than 75 percent of the content of honey consists of carbohydrates, an excellent and efficient source of energy, and honey is a highly ranked resource for this reason. The combination of honey collecting and hunting, particularly in east Africa, is a nutritionally efficient strategy.

Case Study 3: Children's Health in the Prehistoric Southwest

Children's health in the prehistoric American Southwest has been the subject of a number of studies, particularly given the relative abundance of well-preserved human skeletal remains excavated from the region. Most researchers, however, have addressed the question of children's health from a very local, site-specific perspective rather than from a broader, southwestern perspective. For this case study, we synthesize data from previously analyzed human skeletal remains in different cultural contexts (Anasazi, Mogollon, Hohokam, Sinagua, Mimbres, and Salado), site sizes (small and large), and time periods (A.D. 1 to the protohistoric period) in order to address the issue of children's health from a broader perspective (Sobolik 2002). This synthesis reviews and discusses the main health indicators that are observable on human skeletal material and attempts to ascertain any patterns of children's health through time and across cultural boundaries in the prehistoric Southwest.

Southwestern archaeologists have long speculated on the human biological consequences of the adoption of corn agriculture. There is strong evidence that the climate in the Southwest was almost always marginal for subsistence reliance on corn agriculture (Ford 1968; Rose et al. 1981; Wetterstrom 1986). Human diet and health eventually suffered as a result of such reliance, with conditions progressing from bad to worse as the agricultural subsistence base increased in importance through time, inducing "endemic nutritional inadequacy" (Palkovich 1984a:436) for populations in the Southwest. Stodder (1990) also indicated that health problems increased through time and at larger sites as populations became more sedentary, reliance on corn agriculture became more pervasive, and the rate of infectious disease transfer increased. Population aggregation and the subsequent increase in site size associated with increased reliance on corn agriculture have also been cited by Walker (1985) as probable causes for increased health problems such as anemia.

Therefore, many researchers believe that the health of prehistoric Southwest populations deteriorated through time as people became more sedentary, aggregated in larger sites, and became more reliant on corn agriculture. The health of children in such a setting is viewed as potentially disastrous as infant mortality rates increased. Differences in health status within Southwest populations through time, from small and large sites and from different cultural affiliations, are analyzed in this case study in order to discern the effects of these differences on children's health.

Methods

To obtain information on children's health throughout the Southwest, the literature on analyzed human skeletal remains was reviewed. In particular, reports of subadult burials, stature estimates, and pathologies relating to health were examined. This review did not include studies where relevant information was not listed, such as number of subadult burials and pathological analyses. We realize that although we present a large number of analyzed assemblages, we do not have the entire published scope of human skeletal analyses from the Southwest. Most likely, a number of analyses reside in contract archaeology reports as well as in other published literature of which we are unaware. It is hoped that the analyses we did review are representative of the studies that have actually been conducted.

In total, 9,703 human remains from the Southwest were reported from various sites (table 6.5). Individuals were categorized by the site from which they were excavated, the site size as recorded by the analyst, cultural affiliation, and time period. Anasazi human remains were the most frequently recovered and reported, and an analysis of differences in children's health due to site size and time periods was conducted with this large sample using chi-square analysis. Due to small sample sizes for Mogollon, Hohokam, Sinagua, Mimbres, and Salado burials, analyses of significant differences in site size and time periods cannot be accomplished with these samples at this time.

Health Indicators

There are a variety of indicators directly related to the health of an individual that can be obtained from a human skeletal sample. To specifically analyze children's health, it should be noted that health patterns revealed on adult skeletons are, in many cases, the result of that individual's health as a child. Therefore, studies of children's health involve an analysis of all the individuals in the population and of the population's health in general. Health indicators used in this study are childhood mortality rates, adult stature, evidence of anemia through porotic hyperostosis and cribra orbitalia, growth-arrest indicators through linear enamel hypoplasias and Harris lines, and evidence of infection (periostitis).

TABLE 6.5. Human Skeletal Information from Selected Southwestern Sites

Site	Site Size[a]	Cultural Affiliation	Time Period	Number of Individuals[b]	Reference
Black Mesa	Small	Anasazi	BM II (200 B.C.–A.D. 200)	7	Martin et al. 1985, 1991
Puerco Valley	Small	Anasazi	BM III (A.D. 750–850)	17	Wade 1970
Mesa Verde region	Small	Anasazi	BM III–early PII (A.D. 600–975)	168	Stodder 1984
Yellowjacket sites	Small	Anasazi	BM III–P III	52	Swedlund 1969
Puerco Valley	Small	Anasazi	P I–early P II (A.D. 850–1000)	19	Wade 1970
Black Mesa	Small	Anasazi	A.D. 800–1050	49	Martin et al. 1985, 1991
Glen Canyon sites	Small	Anasazi	P II (A.D. 1000–1150)	40	Ryan 1977
Mancos Canyon sites	Small	Anasazi	P II–P III (A.D. 900–1275)	53	Robinson 1976
Mesa Verde region	Small	Anasazi	Late P II–late P III (A.D. 975–1300)	276	Stodder 1984
Puerco Valley	Small	Anasazi	Late P II–early P III (A.D. 1000–1150)	96	Wade 1970
Black Mesa	Small	Anasazi	A.D. 1050–1150	111	Martin et al. 1985, 1991
Chaco Canyon (Bc59)	Small	Anasazi	P II–P III (A.D. 900–1156)	32	El-Najjar et al. 1976
Chaco Canyon (Bc51, 53, 59, Kin Neole)[c]	Small	Anasazi	A.D. 1050–1130	218	Palkovich 1982
Sundown	Small	Anasazi	A.D. 1100–1200	26	Merbs and Vestergaard 1985
Glen Canyon sites	Small	Anasazi	P III (A.D. 1150–1250)	35	Ryan 1977
Carter Ranch Pueblo	Small	Anasazi	P III (A.D. 1100–1225)	34	Danforth et al. 1994
Puerco Valley	Small	Anasazi	P III (A.D. 1150–1250)	39	Wade 1970
Mesa Verde	Small	Anasazi	A.D. 750–1300	179	Miles 1966
Chaco Canyon[c]	Small	Anasazi	Wide age range	135	Akins 1986
TOTAL Anasazi small-site individuals				1,586	

Canyon de Chelly	Large	Anasazi	BM II–BM III (A.D. 400–700)	136	El-Najjar et al. 1976
Mesa Verde	Large	Anasazi	BM III–P III (A.D. 450–1350)	202	Bennett 1975
Navajo Reservoir	Large	Anasazi	P I–P II (A.D. 700–1100)	92	El-Najjar et al. 1976
Canyon de Chelly	Large	Anasazi	P I–P III (A.D. 700–1300)	78	El-Najjar et al. 1976
Pueblo Bonito	Large	Anasazi	A.D. 1020–1120	112	Akins 1986; Palkovich 1982, 1984b
Mesa Verde, Site 34	Large	Anasazi	P III (A.D. 1250–1300)	27	Reed 1965
Cochiti sites	Large	Anasazi	ca. A.D. 1225–1550+	174	Heglar 1974
Inscription House	Large	Anasazi	P III (A.D. 1250–1300)	24	El-Najjar et al. 1976
Glen Canyon sites	Large	Anasazi	Late P III (A.D. 1250–1300)	103[d,e]	Ryan 1977
Zuni Pueblo de los Muertos	Large	Anasazi	A.D. 1280–1320	26	Wheeler 1985
Gran Quivira	Large	Anasazi	P IV–PV (A.D. 1315–1673)	361	El-Najjar et al. 1976; Reed 1981
Arroyo Hondo Pueblo	Large	Anasazi	A.D. 1300–1425	120	Palkovich 1980
Tijeras Pueblo	Large	Anasazi	A.D. 1300–1425	64	Ferguson 1980
Kechipawan site	Large	Anasazi	A.D. 1300–1600	54	Lahr and Bowman 1992
Paa-ko	Large	Anasazi	A.D. 1300–1600s	57	Ferguson 1980
San Antonio	Large	Anasazi	A.D. 1300–1600s	28	Ferguson 1980
Old Walpi	Large	Anasazi	After A.D. 1300–1620	137	Ryan 1977
Pecos Pueblo	Large	Anasazi	A.D. 1300–1846	1254	Hooton 1930
Hawikku	Large	Anasazi	A.D. 1400–1680	188	Stodder 1990
San Cristobal Pueblo	Large	Anasazi	A.D. 1400–1680	268	Stodder 1990
TOTAL Anasazi large-site individuals				3,505	

(Continued)

TABLE 6.5. (Continued)

Site	Site Size[a]	Cultural Affiliation	Time Period	Number of Individuals[b]	Reference
Dolores Project sites	Variable	Anasazi	A.D. 600–1250	64	Wiener 1984; Stodder 1987
TOTAL Anasazi individuals				5,155	
La Ciudad	Large	Hohokam	Preclassic	183	McGuire 1992
La Ciudad	Large	Hohokam	Preclassic	24	Fink and Merbs 1991
Grand Canal Ruins	Large	Hohokam	Classic (A.D. 1100–1450)	72	Fink and Merbs 1991
Las Colinas	Large	Hohokam	Classic (A.D. 1100–1450)	16	Harrington 1981
Casa Buena	Large	Hohokam	Classic (A.D. 1100–1450)	43	Fink and Merbs 1991
TOTAL Hohokam individuals				338	
Point of Pines	Large	Mogollon	Pre-A.D. 400–1000	19	Bennett 1973
NAN Ranch	Large	Mimbres Mogollon	A.D. 700–1125	209	Patrick 1988; Marek 1990
Galaz Ruin	Large	Mimbres Mogollon	ca. A.D. 900–1150	934	Provinzano 1968
Point of Pines	Large	Mogollon	A.D. 1000–1285	282	Bennett 1973
Grasshopper Pueblo	Large	Mogollon	A.D. 1275–1400	674	Kelley 1980; Hinkes 1983; Berry 1985
Point of Pines	Large	Mogollon	A.D. 1285–1450	207	Bennett 1973
TOTAL Mogollon individuals				2,325	

Site	Size[a]	Culture	Date	Individuals[b]	Reference
Early Salado Phase	Varied	Salado	A.D. 1200–1300	129	Hohmann 1992
Besh-Ba-Gowah Pueblo	Large	Salado	A.D. 1225–1450	282	Hohmann 1992
Late Salado Phase	Varied	Salado	A.D. 1300–1450	421	Hohmann 1992
TOTAL Salado individuals				832	
Angel-Winona Phase sites	Varied	Sinagua	A.D. 1050–1100	96	Hohmann 1992
Padre Phase sites	Varied	Sinagua	A.D. 1100–1125	141	Hohmann 1992
Early Elden Phase sites	Varied	Sinagua	A.D. 1125–1150	41[e]	Hohmann 1992
Late Elden Phase sites	Varied	Sinagua	A.D. 1150–1200	167	Hohmann 1992
Oak Creek Pueblo	Small	Sinagua	ca. A.D. 1000–1300	7	Taylor 1985
Lizard Man Village	Small	Sinagua	A.D. 1050–1300	15	Kamp and Whittaker 1999
Tuzigoot	Large	Sinagua	A.D. 1000–late A.D. 1300s	429	Caywood and Spicer 1935; Forsberg 1935
Nuvakwewtaqa (Chavez Pass Ruin)	Large	Sinagua	A.D. 1200–1450	157	Iwaniec 1989
TOTAL Sinagua individuals				1,053	
GRAND TOTAL PREHISTORIC SOUTHWEST INDIVIDUALS				9,703	

[a] Site size designation as listed in reference.
[b] Largest number of analyzed individuals from that reference set.
[c] It is unknown what overlap, if any, there are between these data sets.
[d] Data potentially include individuals reported from Inscription House by El-Najjar et al. (1976).
[e] Excludes data from Lizard Man Village as originally reported in reference.

Childhood Mortality Rates

Childhood mortality rates are a direct reflection of the health of children in a population, assuming that the recovered human remains are an accurate representation of that population. However, there are several biases when using subadult burial rates to estimate childhood mortality for a population (Moore et al. 1975). In archaeological contexts, burials of children and infants (subadults) tend not to be as well preserved as burials of adults because infant and children bones are smaller and less dense. This was especially problematic with early archaeological techniques that focused on the recovery of larger and more obvious remains, usually with the aid of shovels, which is not conducive to the recovery of human remains in general and children's bones specifically. Even when recovered, early archaeologists were not typically interested in the study or curation of subadult skeletal remains. Many times they were discarded or not excavated at all. Some of the largest sample sizes used in this study are from early excavations. Therefore, the number of recorded and analyzed subadults from southwestern sites is clearly an underrepresentation of the number of subadults that actually died and were buried at a particular site.

Childhood mortality rates, as reflected in the number of subadult burials, are very high (table 6.6). The childhood mortality rate as demonstrated by the total number of subadult and adult burials for the entire Southwest is 42 percent. Today, such a high mortality rate is only approached by modern populations experiencing severe malnutrition and stress (Puffer and Serrano 1973; Stini 1985). Frequencies of subadult to adult burials in southwestern populations vary from 25 percent for Hohokam sites to 51 percent for Mogollon sites. Anasazi small sites have a 44 percent subadult/adult burial ratio and Anasazi large sites have a 35 percent subadult/adult burial ratio (table 6.7). This is a significant difference, indicating that childhood mortality rates were higher in Anasazi small sites than in large sites, contrary to the notion that as site size increases, childhood mortality rates also increase.

Moreover, significant temporal differences are also noted between ratios of subadult/adult burials in early versus later time periods at Anasazi sites (table 6.8). Childhood mortality rates are actually higher during earlier time periods than later time periods, again contrary to the idea that children's health decreases through time. Pueblo Bonito samples are both

TABLE 6.6. Number and Percentage of Subadults at Selected Southwestern Sites

Sites	Time Period[a]	No. and Percentage of Subadults/Adults[b]	Reference
Small Anasazi Sites			
Black Mesa	BM II (200 B.C.–A.D. 200)	4/7 (57%)	Martin et al. 1991
Mesa Verde region	BM III–early P II (A.D. 600–975)	53/150 (35%)	Stodder 1984
Yellowjacket sites	BM III–P III (A.D. 750–1300)	24/46 (52%)	Swedlund 1969
Puerco Valley	BM III (A.D. 750–850)	9/17 (53%)	Wade 1970
Puerco Valley	P I–early P II (A.D. 850–1000)	11/19 (58%)	Wade 1970
Black Mesa	BM III–P II (A.D. 800–1050)	24/49 (49%)	Martin et al. 1991
Glen Canyon sites	P II (A.D. 1000–1150)	14/40 (35%)	Ryan 1977
Puerco Valley	Late P II–early P III (A.D. 1000–1150)	52/96 (54%)	Wade 1970
Black Mesa	A.D. 1050–1150	55/111 (50%)	Martin et al. 1991
Chaco Canyon (Bc51, 53, 59, Kin Neole)	P III (A.D. 1050–1130)	92/218 (42%)	Palkovich 1982
Sundown	P II–P III (A.D. 1100–1200)	16/26 (62%)	Merbs and Vestergaard 1985
Mesa Verde region	Late P II–late P III (A.D. 975–1300)	76/178 (43%)	Stodder 1984
Glen Canyon sites	Early, middle P III (A.D. 1150–1250)	14/35 (40%)	Ryan 1977
Carter Ranch Pueblo	P III (A.D. 1100–1225)	9/34 (26%)	Danforth et al. 1994
Puerco Valley	P III (A.D. 1150–1250)	23/39 (59%)	Wade 1970
Mesa Verde	BM II–P III (A.D. 750–1300)	86/179 (48%)	Miles 1966
Mancos Canyon sites	P II–P III (A.D. 900–1275)	24/53 (45%)	Robinson 1976
Chaco Canyon	Wide age range	50/135 (37%)	Akins 1986
TOTAL Anasazi small-site subadults		636/1,432 (44%)	

(Continued)

TABLE 6.6. (Continued)

Sites	Time Period[a]	No. and Percentage of Subadults/Adults[b]	Reference
Large Anasazi Sites			
Mesa Verde	BM III–P III (A.D. 450–1350)	81/202 (40%)	Bennett 1975
Pueblo Bonito	P II (A.D. 1020–1120)	27/112 (24%)	Palkovich 1982
Mesa Verde, Site 34	P III (A.D. 1250–1300)	11/27 (41%)	Reed 1965
Glen Canyon Sites	P III (A.D. 1250–1300)	49/103 (48%)	Ryan 1977
Zuni Pueblo de los Muertos	P III–P IV (A.D. 1280–1320)	11/26 (42%)	Wheeler 1985
Cochiti sites	P III–P IV (A.D. 1225–1550+)	58/174 (33%)	Heglar 1974
Gran Quivira	P IV–P V (A.D. 1315–1673)	212/361 (59%)	Reed 1981
Arroyo Hondo Pueblo	P IV (A.D. 1300–1425)	67/120 (56%)	Palkovich 1980
Tijeras Pueblo	P IV (A.D. 1300–1425)	22/64 (34%)	Ferguson 1980
Paa-ko	P IV (A.D. 1300–1600s)	29/57 (51%)	Ferguson 1980
San Antonio	P IV (A.D. 1300–1600s)	8/28 (29%)	Ferguson 1980
Pecos Pueblo	P IV (A.D. 1300–1846)	270/1,254 (22%)	Hooton 1930
Hawikku	P IV (A.D. 1400–1680)	85/188 (45%)	Stodder 1990
San Cristobal Pueblo	P IV (A.D. 1400–1680)	120/268 (45%)	Stodder 1990
TOTAL Anasazi large-site subadults		1,050/2,984 (35%)	
Dolores Project Sites	BM II–P III (A.D. 600–1250)	11/64 (17%)	Stodder 1987
TOTAL Anasazi subadults		1,697/4,480 (38%)	
Hohokam Sites			
La Ciudad	Preclassic	50/183 (27%)	McGuire 1992
La Ciudad	Preclassic	8/24 (33%)	Fink and Merbs 1991

Site	Period	Subadults	Reference
Grand Canal Ruins	Classic (A.D. 1100–1450)	10/79 (13%)	Fink and Merbs 1991
Las Colinas	Classic (A.D. 1100–1450)	4/16 (25%)	Harrington 1981
Casa Buena	Classic (A.D. 1100–1450)	15/49 (31%)	Fink and Merbs 1991
TOTAL Hohokam subadults		87/351 (25%)	
Mogollon Sites			
Point of Pines	Pre-A.D. 400–1000	3/19 (16%)	Bennett 1973
NAN Ranch	A.D. 700–1125	113/209 (54%)	Marek 1990
Galaz Ruin	ca. A.D. 900–1150	449/934 (48%, original excavation [Anon and LeBlanc 1984]); 38/98 (39%, Provinzano study)	Provinzano 1968
Point of Pines	A.D. 1000–1285	109/282 (39%)	Bennett 1973
Grasshopper Pueblo	A.D. 1275–1400	456/674 (68%)	Hinkes 1983
Point of Pines	A.D. 1285–1450	63/207 (30%)	Bennett 1973
TOTAL Mogollon subadults		1,193/2,325 (51%; original Galaz excavation [Anon and LeBlanc 1984]); 782/1,489 (53%; Provinzano [1968] study)	
Salado Sites			
Early Salado sites	A.D. 1200–1300	42/129 (33%)	Hohmann 1992
Besh-Ba-Gowah Pueblo	A.D. 1225–1450	113/282 (40%)	Hohmann 1992
Late Salado sites	A.D. 1300–1450	152/421 (36%)	Hohmann 1992
TOTAL Salado subadults		307/832 (37%)	

(Continued)

TABLE 6.6. (*Continued*)

Sites	Time Period[a]	No. and Percentage of Subadults/Adults[b]	Reference
Sinagua Sites			
Angel-Winona Phase sites	A.D. 1050–1100	32/96 (33%)	Hohmann 1992
Padre Phase sites	A.D. 1100–1125	51/141 (36%)	Hohmann 1992
Early Elden Phase sites	A.D. 1125–1150	21/41 (51%)[c]	Hohmann 1992
Oak Creek Pueblo	ca. A.D. 1000–1300	6/7 (86%)	Taylor 1985
Lizard Man Village	A.D. 1050–1300	7/15 (47%)	Kamp and Whittaker 1999
Late Elden Phase sites	A.D. 1150–1200	59/167 (35%)	Hohmann 1992
Tuzigoot	A.D. 1000–late A.D. 1300s	268/429 (62%)	Caywood and Spicer 1935
TOTAL Sinagua subadults		444/896 (50%)	
GRAND TOTAL SUBADULTS		3,728/8,884 (42%)	

[a] Time period determination: BM = Basketmaker; P = Pueblo.
[b] Subadults determined at different ages by researchers; most frequent determination is less than 18 years or less than 15 years.
[c] Excludes samples from Lizard Man Village as presented in reference.

TABLE 6.7. Cultural Affiliation and Site Size Differences for Subadults at Selected Southwestern Sites

Cultural Affiliation	No. of Subadults/Adults	Percentage of Subadults
Anasazi small sites	636/1,432	44
Anasazi large sites	1,050/2,984	35
Anasazi total sites[a]	1,697/4,480	38
Hohokam sites	87/351	25
Mogollon sites[b]	1,193/2,325	51
Salado sites	307/832	37
Sinagua sites	444/896	50
TOTAL subadults in Southwest	3,728/8,884	42

[a] Data include Dolores Project sites (see table 6.6).
[b] Using data from the original Galaz excavation (Anon and LeBlanc 1984; see table 6.6).

TABLE 6.8. Temporal Differences in Anasazi Subadults

Time Period[a]	No. of Subadults/ Adults	Percentage of Subadults
P I (A.D. 750–1000)	97/235	41
P II (A.D. 1000–1150, not including Pueblo Bonito)	229/491	47
P II (A.D. 1000–1150, including Pueblo Bonito)	256/603	42
P I/II combined (not including Pueblo Bonito)	326/726	45
P I/II combined (including Pueblo Bonito)	353/838	42
P III (A.D. 1150–1300)	117/264	44
P IV (after A.D. 1300)	813/2340	35
P III/IV combined[b]	925/2640	35

[a] Data used from sites listed in table 6.6; P = Pueblo.
[b] Including data from Cochiti sites (see table 6.6).

included and removed from this analysis because of their atypical age distribution and their supposed high-ranking status (Palkovich 1984b). Removal of Pueblo Bonito samples does not affect the significant differences noted with chi-square analysis. It is unfortunate that there are no large human skeletal samples from hunter-gatherer time periods in the Southwest so that comparisons can be made between populations living on a varied subsistence base versus populations more dependent on agriculture.

Stature Estimation

Adult stature is employed by modern human biologists as a measure of overall health and is a good measure of cumulative stress throughout childhood (Huss-Ashmore et al. 1982; Falkner and Tanner 1986). Stature has a number of causative agents, including genetics, environmental stress, nutritional intake, disease rates, and psychological stress. Stature estimations are made using measurements of long bones, mainly the femur and tibia, and usually follow formulas devised by Genoves (1967) with Mesoamerican populations.

Stature seems to be similar throughout prehistoric populations in the Southwest, although some trends are apparent. The mean statures for prehistoric populations range between 147.7 centimeters for Anasazi Carter Ranch Pueblo females to 169.3 centimeters for Pueblo Bonito males (tables 6.9 and 6.10). Pueblo Bonito males and females have the highest stature range for Southwest samples, another potential indicator of their high-ranking status. The Sinagua tend to have the lowest stature range. Anasazi male stature in small sites seems to be slightly higher than for males in larger sites (if Pueblo Bonito samples are excluded) and Sinagua females seem to be slightly shorter, on average, than females from other Southwest areas. Unfortunately, these trends cannot be statistically compared because the number of individuals used to determine mean stature in each population was not provided by all researchers. Therefore, stature ranges can only be quantified and overall trends observed.

Porotic Hyperostosis and Cribra Orbitalia

The etiology of porotic hyperostosis has been discussed by a number of researchers (e.g., El-Najjar et al. 1976; Mensforth et al. 1978; Martin et al. 1985; Walker 1985). Porotic hyperostosis is exhibited by expansion of the diploe and cranial lesions and pitting on the surface of frontal, parietal, and occipital bones, as well as in the eye orbits (cribra orbitalia). The etiologies of porotic hyperostosis and cribra orbitalia are the same, so some researchers do not record these pathologies separately, although cribra orbitalia seems to be an early expression of anemia and porotic hyperostosis is a more severe form (Lallo et al. 1977). As noted in chapter 2, porotic hyperostosis is often found in populations who are

TABLE 6.9. Stature Estimation at Selected Southwestern Sites

Site	Stature Estimation (cm)[a]		Reference
	Male	Female	
Anasazi Small Sites			
Black Mesa (A.D. 800–1050)	167.0	156.5	Martin et al. 1991
Yellowjacket sites	158.75	160.52[b]	Swedlund 1969
Black Mesa (A.D. 1050–1150)	163.1	152.5	Martin et al. 1991
Sundown	166.0	155.0	Merbs and Vestergaard 1985
Mancos Canyon sites	168.5	157.5	Robinson 1976
Carter Ranch Pueblo	162.2	147.7	Danforth et al. 1994
Chaco Canyon	164.7 (U)	157.4 (U)	Akins 1986
Anasazi Large Sites			
Mesa Verde	162.0	152.0	Bennett 1975
Pueblo Bonito	169.3 (U)	162.0 (U)	Akins 1986
Mesa Verde, Site 34	161.3 (U)	148.6 (U)	Reed 1965
Gran Quivira	166.7 (TG)	153.6 (TG)	Scott 1981
Arroyo Hondo Pueblo (A.D. 1300–1370)	163.87	156.24	Palkovich 1980
Arroyo Hondo Pueblo (A.D. 1370–1425)	165.64	153.47	Palkovich 1980
Tijeras Pueblo	160.13	150.35	Ferguson 1980
Paa-ko	164.44	151.61	Ferguson 1980
San Antonio	162.63	153.00	Ferguson 1980
Cochiti Sites	164.41 (T) 163.86 (TG)	154.64 (T)	Heglar 1974
Pecos Pueblo	161.7	150.1	Hooton 1930
Dolores Project sites	162.31	155.95	Stodder 1987
Hohokam Sites			
La Ciudad	164.1	155.6	Fink and Merbs 1991
Grand Canal Ruins	165.3	160.2	Fink and Merbs 1991
Casa Buena	163	153	Fink and Merbs 1991
Mogollon Sites			
NAN Ranch	162.2	154.9	Patrick 1988
Galaz Ruin	166.88	156.57	Provinzano 1968
Point of Pines	161.3	152.85	Bennett 1973
Point of Pines	162.1	153.7	Bennett 1973

(*Continued*)

TABLE 6.9. (*Continued*)

Site	Stature Estimation (cm)[a]		Reference
	Male	Female	
Sinagua Sites			
Lizard Man Village	160.5	152.0	Kamp and Whittaker 1999
Tuzigoot	166.4	154.6	Caywood and Spicer 1935; Forsberg 1935
Nuvakwewtaqa (Chavez Pass Ruin)	147.3–172.1; mean = 158.2		Iwaniec 1989

[a] Stature estimation using formula developed by Genoves (1967) unless otherwise indicated; TG = Trotter and Gleser 1958; T = Telkkä 1950; U = unknown formula.
[b] One tall individual has increased female stature estimation.

TABLE 6.10. Stature Estimate Ranges at Selected Southwestern Sites (summarized from Table 6.9)

Sites	Male Stature Estimate Ranges (cm)	Female Stature Estimate Ranges (cm)
Anasazi small sites	158.75–168.5	147.7–160.52
Anasazi large sites	160.13–169.3 (including Pueblo Bonito)	148.6–162.0 (including Pueblo Bonito)
	160.13–166.7 (not including Pueblo Bonito)	148.66–156.24 (not including Pueblo Bonito)
Anasazi combined	158.75–169.3 (including Pueblo Bonito)	147.7–162.0 (including Pueblo Bonito)
	158.75–168.5 (not including Pueblo Bonito)	147.7–160.52 (not including Pueblo Bonito)
Hohokam	163.0–165.3	153.0–160.2
Mogollon	161.3–166.88	152.85–156.57
Sinagua	160.5–166.4	152.0–154.6

dependent on corn agriculture, leading to deficiencies in essential amino acids, which ultimately leads to dietary insufficiency, malnutrition, and iron-deficiency anemia. This is especially true in environments such as the Southwest, where fluctuations in the climate and environment (e.g., drought) are relatively common.

Evidence of porotic hyperostosis in prehistoric populations in the American Southwest is difficult to quantify because researchers have recorded their results differently. Some researchers recorded only the percentage of affected individuals without providing the number of individuals, some combined the percentage of porotic hyperostosis and cribra orbitalia into one category (making it impossible to separate the two for comparative purposes), and others recorded only the frequency of porotic hyperostosis present in infants and children.

Overall, however, it appears that a large segment of each population in this synthesis was affected with iron-deficiency anemia as exhibited by porotic hyperostosis. Rates of porotic hyperostosis at Anasazi sites in which researchers recorded the number of affected individuals indicate that frequencies of anemia were very high (table 6.11). Populations at smaller sites had significantly greater frequencies of anemia than at larger sites, and populations during earlier time periods had significantly greater rates of anemia than during later time periods. This is the case even when Hooton's (1930) data from Pecos Pueblo is removed from the calculations. Hooton did not realize the etiology of porotic hyperostosis, which he termed "symmetrical osteoporosis" and a "mysterious disease" (Hooton 1930:316), so it is unknown whether he correctly identified porotic hyperostosis in all cases. The rates of porotic hyperostosis at other sites were not statistically compared due to small sample sizes.

Much of the data used for comparing porotic hyperostosis and therefore anemia rates come from the study of El-Najjar et al. (1976). They looked at a variety of sites in the American Southwest and concluded that anemia rates were higher at sites in canyon regions where the populations were more dependent on agriculture and lower at sites in sage plains regions where they would have greater access to iron-rich animal products. Further, the data for this study indicate that site size and time period of occupation are important factors; larger sites and later time periods have a lower rate of anemia.

Linear Enamel Hypoplasias

Linear enamel hypoplasias (LEHs) are developmental growth disturbances that appear as linear depressions on the surface of tooth enamel. These depressions represent temporary cessation of enamel formation

TABLE 6.11. Evidence of Porotic Hyperostosis and Cribra Orbitalia at Selected Southwestern Sites

Site	Time Period[a]	Porotic Hyperostosis	Cribra Orbitalia	Reference
Anasazi Small Sites				
Black Mesa	P I/II	79.8%	54.3%	Martin et al. 1991
Mesa Verde region	P I	—	52/72 (72%)	Stodder 1994
Yellowjacket sites	E		4/12 young (33%)	Swedlund 1969
Mancos Canyon sites	E	5/27 (19%)[b]	4/24 (17%)	Robinson 1976
Puerco Valley	E	42/113 (37%)[b]	43/105 (41%)	Wade 1970
Chaco Canyon (Bc59)	P I/II	23/32 (72%)[b]	—	El-Najjar et al. 1976
Glen Canyon sites	P II	5/28 (18%)[b]	—	Ryan 1977
Sundown	P II	9/13 (69%)[b]	—	Merbs and Vestergaard 1985
Mesa Verde region	P II/III	—	68/93 (73%)	Stodder 1994
Glen Canyon sites	P III	3/31 (10%)[b]	—	Ryan 1977
Carter Ranch Pueblo	P III	2/5 before 2 yrs. (40%)	4/5 before 2 yrs. (80%)	Danforth et al. 1994
Mesa Verde	E	6 infants	—	Miles 1966
Chaco Canyon	E	22/36 (61%)[b]	24/31 (77%)	Akins 1986
Anasazi Large Sites				
Canyon de Chelly	Pre P I	67/136 (49%)[b]	—	El-Najjar et al. 1976
Navajo Reservoir	P I/II	12/92 (13%)[b]	—	El-Najjar et al. 1976
Canyon de Chelly	P I/III	43/78 (55%)[b]	—	El-Najjar et al. 1976
Mesa Verde, Site 34	P III	—	1 sm. child w/severe case	Reed 1965

Site	Period			Reference
Glen Canyon sites	P III	10/79 (13%)[b]	—	Ryan 1977
Inscription House	P III	13/24 (54%)[b]	—	El-Najjar et al. 1976
Zuni Pueblo de los Muertos	P III/IV	7/7 children (100%)	—	Wheeler 1985
Gran Quivira	P IV	27/177 (15%)[b]	—	El-Najjar et al. 1976
Arroyo Hondo Pueblo	P IV	14/120 (12%)[b], all children	9/120 (8%); 8 children	Palkovich 1980
Tijeras Pueblo	P IV	3/19 infants (16%)	—	Ferguson 1980
Kechipawan site	P IV	57.4%, both combined		Lahr and Bowman 1992
Paa-ko	P IV	14/18 infants (78%)	5/11 children (46%)	Ferguson 1980
San Antonio	P IV	4/7 infants (57%)	1/1 child (100%)	Ferguson 1980
Old Walpi	P IV	5/133 (4%)[b]	—	Ryan 1977
Pecos Pueblo	P IV	19/581 (3%)[b]; 9 children	—	Hooton 1930
Hawikku	P IV	127/151 (84%), both combined		Stodder 1990
San Cristobal Pueblo	P IV	188/209 (90%), both combined		Stodder 1990
Dolores Project	E	2/21 (10%)	27/33 (82%)	Stodder 1987
Hohokam Sites				
La Ciudad		7/13 (54%)	—	Fink and Merbs 1991
Grand Canal Ruins		26/61 (43%)	—	Fink and Merbs 1991
Casa Buena		12/24 (50%)	—	Fink and Merbs 1991
Mogollon Site				
Grasshopper Pueblo		15/375 (4%)	54/386 (14%)	Hinkes 1983
Grasshopper Pueblo		30/369 (8%)	27/369 (7%)	Kelley 1980

(Continued)

TABLE 6.11. (*Continued*)

Site	Time Period[a]	Porotic Hyperostosis	Cribra Orbitalia	Reference
Sinagua Sites				
Oak Creek Pueblo		7/7 (100%)	—	Taylor 1985
Lizard Man Village		3/12 (25%)	3/12 (25%)	Kamp and Whittaker 1999
Nuvakwewtaqa (Chavez Pass Ruin)		41/44 (93%), both combined		Iwaniec 1989

[a] Time period determination: P I, A.D. 750–1000; P II, A.D. 1000–1150; P III, A.D. 1150–1300; P IV, after A.D. 1300; E = excluded from temporal study.
[b] Data potentially include individuals reported from Inscription House by El-Najjar et al. (1976).

due to nutritional stress or infectious disease. The location of LEH determines how old the individual was when tooth enamel was forming and stress occurred (Goodman and Rose 1990), although LEH may not be apparent on teeth that have severe wear (Stodder 1990). Severe tooth wear is ubiquitous among Southwest populations. Most researchers analyze the buccal surface of incisors and canines for evidence of LEH. The presence of multiple LEHs per individual indicates that that individual experienced a number of stresses.

The problem in comparing LEH in Southwest populations is that, again, researchers are not consistent in how they record pathologies. Some researchers provide only the percentage of individuals with LEH and do not provide the number of individuals actually affected. Others record the percentage of teeth that are affected and do not provide the number of individuals these teeth represent. Still others record both deciduous and permanent teeth that are affected, again with no indication of the number of individuals who are represented by each sample. Thus, statistical comparisons of LEH across cultural boundaries and through time in the Southwest cannot be accomplished.

LEHs and the nutritional and disease-related problems causing them usually show up in high frequencies in human skeletal samples that have been analyzed for that particular pathology. The presence of LEH ranges from a high of 94 percent of permanent teeth in the individuals at Hawikku to a low of 7 percent in the individuals at Arroyo Hondo Pueblo. This is unusual considering the very high childhood mortality rate at Arroyo Hondo (56 percent; see table 6.6); however, LEHs represent a temporary cessation of growth and development, not a permanent condition. The children at Arroyo Hondo may not have had the chance to resume normal growth after a serious stress event.

Harris Lines

Harris lines are growth-arrest lines that occur on long bone shafts (fig. 2.4). Harris lines are actually lattice-like plates of bone that form in the metaphysis of long bones after growth resumes following an acute disruption. There is great debate, however, regarding the cause of Harris lines, although severe nutritional stress and disease most likely played significant roles. Some scholars estimate that the process of growth arrest and resumption may take place in as little as one week (Steinbock 1976; Goodman et al. 1984). Harris lines are visible only on radiographs; therefore, they are often not recognized in many skeletal analyses.

Only a few studies summarized here analyzed human skeletal material for Harris lines. Adults from Carter Ranch Pueblo were reported to have exhibited an 80 percent rate of Harris lines, whereas Grasshopper Pueblo exhibited a 20 percent rate. Other studies recorded the average number of Harris lines per individual: Grasshopper Pueblo individuals had an average of 7.4 Harris lines per individual, Hawikku individuals exhibited 4.16 lines per individual, and San Cristobal Pueblo individuals displayed 3.66 lines per individual. As relatively few researchers analyzed long bones for the presence of Harris lines, a comparison of Southwest samples cannot be provided.

Periosteal Infections

Periosteal lesions are nonspecific infections seen on the outer surface of bone, whereas osteomyelitis and osteitis are infections involving the inner cortex and marrow cavity of bone. Periosteal lesions are usually caused by treponematosis and treponemal disease, such as pinta, yaws, and syphilis, but can also be caused by tuberculosis and leprosy. There is little agreement about the actual cause of most periosteal lesions, but a diagnosis of infection and infectious disease can be made in many cases.

Only a few studies noted the presence of periosteal infections and these, of course, were recorded in different ways. Periosteal infection seems to have been a common problem for prehistoric Southwest populations. Kelley (1980) observed that infectious disease was the main factor in the death of infants and children of such populations. Wade (1970:172) reported that in Puerco Valley, "certainly the major cause of death in infants can be attributed to disease." Finding the actual source and cause of periosteal infections and infectious disease is the problem. The effects of infectious disease would have been intensified by underlying morbid conditions of dietary deficiency, malnutrition, and parasitism (Hinkes 1983), conditions that were prevalent in the prehistoric Southwest.

A few scholars have indicated that in some cases children in prehistoric populations could have died swiftly due to virulent gastrointestinal and upper respiratory infections (Hinkes 1983). Such swift deaths would not have allowed pathological evidence, such as porotic hyperostosis, enamel hypoplasias, Harris lines, or periosteal infections, to manifest itself on the skeleton. This may be the reason that these pathological markers occur with less frequency in populations from larger sites and from later time periods.

Other Potential Health Indicators

Although not identified or recorded in great quantities by Southwest researchers, there are a few other potential health indicators that could have been deleterious for children's health. These include tuberculosis, ear infections as evidenced in the mastoid, and infections resulting from cranial deformation through the use of cradleboards and as evidenced by occipital lesions.

Tuberculosis is an infection caused by *Mycobacterium tuberculosis* and can be observed on the skeleton, primarily on the spine but also in other areas such as the ribs, sternum, and knees (El-Najjar 1979). It was once thought that tuberculosis originated in the Old World and spread to the New World after contact by Columbus (Buikstra 1981). As the result of increasing evidence of tubercular lesions on prehistoric skeletons, however, it is now believed that tuberculosis was present in the New World before A.D. 1492. In the Southwest, tubercular lesions have been observed on a growing number of skeletal samples (see Hinkes 1983), although researchers continue to argue about whether specific infections can be attributed to tuberculosis or are a reflection of other infectious diseases (Fink 1985). Even if a small number of individuals from a population are observed to be infected with tuberculosis, the infection rate for the population would be much higher as only 5 percent to 7 percent of all tubercular cases are manifested on bone (Steinbock 1976). Therefore, the infrequent occurrence of tuberculosis on skeletons from the Southwest could indicate that a large portion of the population was infected. As such, this could indicate high infection rates for infants and children, leading to a high incidence of childhood mortality due to tuberculosis.

Mastoid infection leading to ear infection, called mastoiditis, is not commonly reported for prehistoric Southwest populations. Titche et al. (1981) analyzed 742 skulls from various Mogollon sites in an attempt to understand patterns of high otitis media (ear infection) in modern Indian populations. Their study revealed that 17 percent of the prehistoric individuals in their study exhibited evidence of ear infection. They considered this rate to be low compared to infection rates in modern populations. Martin et al. (1991) also indicated the presence of mastoid infections in up to 16.6 percent of the prehistoric population from Black Mesa. Only in rare and very severe cases would ear infections cause death, although chronic ear infections can lead to acute hearing loss in an individual.

Cranial deformation occurred through the use of cradleboards in newborns and infants, a common cultural practice by a number of prehistoric and protohistoric Southwest groups. It is unknown whether cranial deformation occurs intentionally or unintentionally as a result of transporting infants in cradleboards. The results are differing degrees of occipital flattening, which can be observed in subadult and adult crania. Researchers are beginning to realize the potential deleterious effects of this condition and the probable association with occipital infections and supra-inion depressions, which may result in newborn and infant death (Stewart 1976; Holliday 1993; Derrick 1994). Holliday (1993:283) stated that "the pressure and friction of an infant's head against a cradleboard may have (1) produced ischemic ulcers, (2) produced the conditions favorable for bacterial infections such as impetigo or carbuncles, or (3) complicated the treatment of other infections appearing on the back of the scalp." Derrick (1994) analyzed healed supra-inion lesions in adults and one active lesion in a cranially deformed infant from prehistoric populations in Texas and Arkansas, indicating that the infant may have died as a result of cranial infection exacerbated and/or caused by cradleboarding. Scholars in the Southwest seldom report occipital lesions as a possible result of cranial deformation. It is unknown whether this indicates that infection from this source is actually rare or researchers are not looking for this particular pathology.

Discussion

The health of children in prehistoric and protohistoric agricultural groups of the southwestern United States illustrates a pervasive pattern of high infant mortality, malnutrition, and disease. Children's malnutrition and ill health do not appear to decline through time; in fact, evidence indicates that the emergence of agricultural practices and sedentism led to the observed high rates of infant mortality, anemia, and infection. In conjunction, children at small sites seemed to suffer more ill health effects than children at larger sites. This does not mean, however, that children's health greatly improved through time and at larger sites. It seems that after the introduction of agriculture, children at all sites and at all times suffered pervasive ill health, chronic malnutrition, and highly infectious disease that seemed to function in a synergistic interaction. Even children of supposedly high-ranking lineages were not immune to the pervasive pattern of ill health. Children found in Pueblo Bonito burial rooms experienced dietary inadequacy, as evidenced by high frequencies of anemia and infections (Palkovich 1984b).

In effect, children's pervasive ill health in the prehistoric Southwest was influenced by a variety of factors that surrounded the introduction of agriculture in a marginal environment. These factors included malnutrition through the adoption of a nutritionally inadequate subsistence base; a greater incidence of infectious disease spread through an increasingly susceptible population weakened by malnutrion; and an increase in anemia due to malnutrition, infectious disease, and parasitic infections prevalent in a more sedentary, aggregated population dependent on agriculture. Children would have been particularly susceptible to these factors due to their increased nutritional needs for growth and development.

Case Study 4: Complementary Paleonutritional Data Sets: An Example from Medieval Christian Nubia

Many archaeological inferences are made using single data sets, such as a faunal analysis employed to outline the diet of the inhabitants of a site. This practice is often due to the paucity of complementary data, selective sampling, and/or failure to budget for such analyses. When multiple data sets are available, archaeologists eagerly employ them to add depth to their analyses, such as using artifact styles, obsidian hydration assessments, and radiocarbon assays to date the occupation of a site. Multiple data sets for paleonutrition studies are not commonly analyzed but, when they are, they can be used to increase the depth of such studies. Most archaeologists detail and list the foods represented in botanical and zooarchaeological data sets, but few examine the nutritional content of those foods and how nutrition impacted the population in question.

One of the first studies to examine nutrition was that of Cummings (1989), who employed multiple lines of data from a series of mummified remains recovered from two Medieval Christian cemeteries at Kulubnarti in Upper Nubia, now northern Sudan (fig. 6.3). Dietary constituent data from paleofeces were obtained and their nutritional values were determined. The results were then compared with data derived from previous studies of skeletal pathologies and hair, all of which were used to address the question of dietary stress in the Medieval Christian period (ca. A.D. 550 to 1450).

Dietary Stress

The general occurrence of cribra orbitalia (see Case Study 3) in various parts of the world has been attributed to the presence of abnormal hemoglobin, such as sickle cell anemia and thalassemia, as an adaptation to malaria (see Carlson et al. 1974). To investigate this general hypothesis, Carlson et al. (1974) examined skeletal data from a series of cemeteries in Nubia for evidence of active and healing lesions of cribra orbitalia and compared the results to archaeological and ethnographic evidence of diet. They concluded that the incidence of cribra orbitalia in Nubia was more likely the result of chronic iron-deficiency anemia due to a diet lacking in iron, complicated by weaning diarrhea and high rates of parasitic infection (Carlson et al. 1974:405).

In 1979, excavations were undertaken at two cemeteries in Kulubnarti, where a total of 406 individuals was recovered. One cemetery (21-S-46; N = 218) dated from the early Christian period (ca. A.D. 550 to 750) while the other (21-R-2; N = 188) dated from the late Christian Period (ca. A.D. 750 to 1450) (Van Gerven et al. 1981). The remains were in relatively good condition and many contained preserved tissues, hair, and paleofecal remains. An analysis of the skeletal materials suggested that there was a significant difference in juvenile (birth to fourteen years of age) mortality between the two groups, with mortality rates in the early Christian sample being substantially higher (Van Gerven et al. 1981:403).

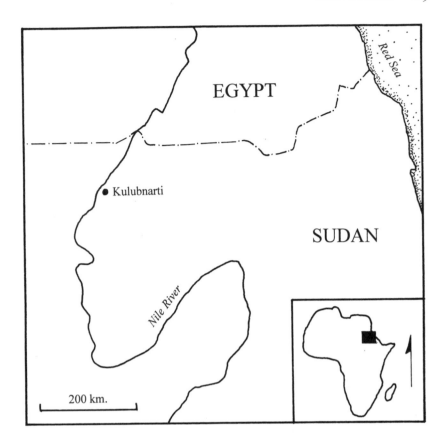

FIGURE 6.3. Location of the Kulubnarti site, northern Sudan (redrawn from Cummings 1989:fig. 1; reproduced by permission).

To measure stress between the two populations, Van Gerven et al. (1981) recorded the frequency of cribra orbitalia. It was found that there was a "high correspondence to probabilities of dying from nine months when the first signs of the lesion appear through the early adult years" (Van Gerven et al. 1981:404). A similar pattern was apparent among sub-adults and older adults, suggesting that the chronic stresses identified by Carlson et al. (1974) were acting on both populations.

To test the proposition that cribra orbitalia was associated with chronic iron-deficiency anemia, Sandford et al. (1983) and Sandford (1984) ana-lyzed hair samples for major and trace elements from 168 individuals of different ages and both sexes from the two cemeteries at Kulubnarti.

Sandford et al. (1983:839) found that those individuals with cribra orbitalia had low levels of iron and magnesium, but that iron levels were "not, in comparison to modern values, particularly low." They concluded that the anemia associated with the observed frequencies of cribra orbitalia was the result of a lack of iron and magnesium due to "reduced dietary availability combined with gastrointestinal losses and increased element demands due to parasitic infections" (Sandford et al. 1983:842). Thus, Sandford et al. (1983) generally supported the hypothesis put forth by Carlson et al. (1974) and Van Gerven et al. (1981), but suggested that the availability of magnesium was a significant factor. Additional discussions of these issues were presented in Armelagos et al. (1984) and Martin et al. (1984).

The Cummings Study

To further test the dietary stress hypothesis proposed by Carlson et al. (1974) and supported by Sandford et al. (1983), Cummings (1989) undertook to study the paleofecal remains directly associated with the skeletal materials from the two excavated cemeteries at Kulubnarti. The goal was to identify the diet and determine what influence diet may have had on the incidence of cribra orbitalia. During the excavation of the cemeteries, paleofecal specimens had been recovered from a number of the individuals, for which the analysis of pathologies (Van Gerven et al. 1981) and hair elements (Sandford et al. 1983) had been conducted, many of which were of known sex and age.

Specimens from a total of 48 individuals were analyzed for faunal and botanical macrofossils, pollen, phytoliths, and parasites. Of those 48 individuals, 33 came from the early Christian cemetery and 15 came from the late Christian cemetery. Thus, the data provided a diachronic comparison of the diet between the two periods.

The paleofecal data were used to identify a primary diet of sorghum and dates, supplemented by a number of other foods, including legumes, some greens, fish, and meat (pig and alligator). Although not identified in the paleofecal samples, it seems likely that other foods, such as milk, were also consumed. In her analysis of the nutritional content of the identified dietary constituents, Cummings (1989:191–192) noted that the diet would likely have been deficient in iron and numerous water-soluble vitamins, particularly C, B_6, B_{12}, and folacin.

Cummings (1989:128) reported that the diet of the adults in the early Christian sample appeared to have been somewhat more diverse than the diet in the late Christian sample. This same pattern was more apparent in the juvenile diet, although the sample size was smaller. In the early Christian sample, the diets of the adults and juveniles were similar (Cummings 1989:128), whereas the adults in the late Christian sample were consuming a greater variety of foods than juveniles (Cummings 1989:135). Overall, though, Cummings (1989:193) concluded that the diets were essentially the same between the early and late populations and that the high incidence of cribra orbitalia observed in the juveniles of each period was due to a series of nutritional deficiencies during childhood, along with the stress of weaning. Thus, Cummings (1989) corroborated the hypothesis originally developed by Carlson et al. (1974) and supplemented by Sandford et al. (1983) while adding detail regarding dietary and cultural factors.

Case Study 5: An Evolving Understanding of Paleodiet in the Northern Coachella Valley of California

Interior southeastern California contains a large structural depression, the Salton Sink, the bottom of which lies below sea level. This depression is bounded by the coastal mountains on the west and by a series of smaller ranges on the east. The Coachella Valley sits in the northern, and narrower, portion of the depression while the Imperial Valley lies to the south (fig. 6.4).

The Salton Sink lies within the Colorado Desert and is generally arid. At various times in the past, however, the Colorado River changed its regular course and flowed into the Salton Sink, forming a large freshwater lake called Lake Cahuilla (also known as Lake LaConte or the Blake Sea). The sink filled and the lake reached a maximum size of 185 kilometers long, 55 kilometers wide, and 97 meters deep, at which time it overflowed into the Gulf of California. When the Colorado River would reestablish its regular course, Lake Cahuilla would rapidly desiccate, perhaps in as little as sixty years (Wilke 1988:4), and the associated lake habitats would disappear.

It seems likely that most of the freshwater plants and animals would have died out due to rising salinity, even before the actual disappearance of the water (e.g., Wilke et al. 1975:49).

As the lake refilled, the associated habitats were occupied by people, who modified their economic systems to take advantage of the abundant lacustrine resources. When the lake would disappear, the settlement and subsistence systems would adjust to the drier conditions. At least three, possibly four, stands of Lake Cahuilla have been documented within the last 2,100 years (see Weide 1976; Wilke 1978; Waters 1983), with the final stand being dated between 800 and 500 B.P. (Wilke 1978:57; also see Schaefer 1994:67–74) or perhaps a bit later (e.g., Laylander 1997:68).

A considerable portion of the archaeological work conducted at ancient Lake Cahuilla has focused on its northern shore, located in the northern portion of the Coachella Valley, and much of that work has focused on the final lakestand. This is due, in part, to the easier accessibility of that area to researchers, as well as the greater pace of development, which has generated a large number of environmentally related archaeological investigations.

The Environment

The northern Coachella Valley is within the Colorado Desert. Rainfall averages about 3 inches per year and temperatures can reach about 120 degrees Fahrenheit in the summer (see Felton 1965). The valley is dominated by a creosote bush scrub biotic community that is home to a number of xeric-adapted plant and animal species (see Munz and Keck 1949, 1950). Extensive groves of mesquite (*Prosopis* sp.) are present in the lower elevations of the valley.

As Lake Cahuilla filled, a number of lacustrine habitats formed, including deep and shallow water, beaches, and marshes. As the water from the Colorado River flowed into the lake, the species present in the river colonized the lake. The major fish species included bonytail chub (*Gila elegans*), razorback sucker (*Xyrauchen texanus*), the Colorado pike minnow (*Ptychocheilus lucius*), and mullet (*Mugil cephalus*),

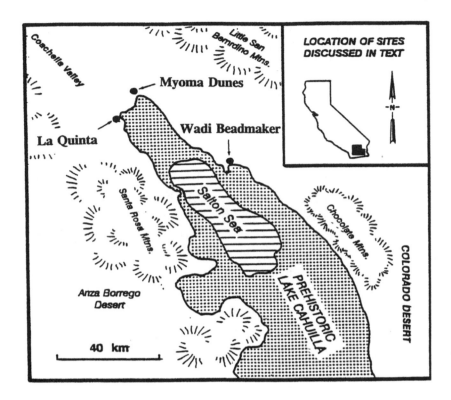

FIGURE 6.4. Map of the Salton Basin, showing the Coachella Valley, the extent of ancient Lake Cahuilla, and the locations of sites discussed in the text (from Sutton [1998:88]; reprinted by permission from *American Antiquity*, vol. 63, no. 1).

all of which were used by the native peoples of the region. Freshwater mussels (*Anodonta dejecta*) inhabited the shallow waters of the lake and were heavily exploited by the people. Various birds also resided at Lake Cahuilla, including shorebirds, waterfowl, and terrestrial species, many of which were hunted. In addition, many aquatic plants, including cattail (*Typha*) and bulrush (*Scirpus*), were present within a freshwater marsh plant community.

It is important to note that the presence or absence of the lake was due to the changing course of the Colorado River, and not to any fluctuations in the weather or climate in the Salton Sink. Even when Lake Cahuilla was full, the creosote biotic community dominated terrestrial habitats away from its shores, and the human occupants of the area had access to mountain, desert, and lacustrine biotic communities.

The Ethnographic Data Base

The Cahuilla lived (and many continue to live) in the region surrounding the Coachella Valley. Three basic divisions of the Cahuilla are recognized: the Mountain, Pass, and Desert Cahuilla. General descriptions of Cahuilla society have been provided by Barrows (1900), Hooper (1920), Kroeber (1925), Curtis (1926), Strong (1929), Drucker (1937), Bean (1972, 1978), Bean and Saubel (1972), and Bean et al. (1995).

In historical times, the Desert Cahuilla occupied the floor of the northern Coachella Valley, above and below the fossil shoreline of Lake Cahuilla. Villages consisted of loose clusters of houses covering a square kilometer or more and were located either at springs or at locations with high water tables where wells could be excavated. Wilke and Lawton (1975:fig. 6) and Wilke (1978:fig. 26) mapped the locations of the historic villages, providing the basis for an understanding of the ethnographic settlement pattern. These villages were located such that about 80 percent of resources used could be found within 5 miles; thus, no major population movement was needed for subsistence purposes (Bean and Saubel 1972:20).

Ethnographic information on the diet of the Desert Cahuilla has been obtained by a number of researchers, most notably Barrows (1900) and Bean and Saubel (1972). More than 200 species of wild plants were exploited (table 6.12) and were obtained from a variety of valley and mountain ecozones. The primary staple plants were undoubtedly mesquite (which grew on the valley floor), agave, yucca, and pinyon, with various grass seeds filling out the majority of the plant component of the diet. In addition, agricultural crops of corn, beans, and squash were grown in late prehistoric times (Wilke and Lawton 1975), with wheat, melons, barley, and fruit trees being added after European contact (Bean and Mason 1962; Lawton and Bean 1968).

A variety of animals was also utilized by the Cahuilla (see table 6.12), with small animals such as rodents and insects probably providing the majority of the calories, although lagomorphs (rabbits and hares) were important game animals. In ethnographic times, when Lake Cahuilla

TABLE 6.12. Summary of the Major Food Resources Used Ethnographically by the Cahuilla[a]

Plants		Animals	
Common Name	Scientific Name	Common Name	Scientific Name
Agave	*Agave deserti*	Chuckwalla	*Sauromalus obesus*
Spanish bayonet	*Yucca whipplei*	Mourning dove	*Zenaidura macroura*
Wild onion	*Allium validum*	Roadrunner	*Geococcyx californianus*
Barrel cactus	*Echinocactus acanthodes*	California quail	*Lophortyx californica*
Goosefoot	*Chenopodium* spp.	Various ducks	cf. *Anas* spp.
Catclaw	*Acacia Gregii* Gray	Various fish	N/A
Ocotillo	*Fourquieria splendens*	Various insects	N/A
Honey mesquite	*Prosopis juliflora*	Cottontail rabbit	*Sylvilagus audubonii*
Screwbean	*Prosopis pubescens*	Black-tailed jackrabbit	*Lepus californicus*
Manzanita	*Arctostaphylos* spp.	Various mice	cf. *Perognathus* sp.
Lily	*Hesperocallis undulata*	Various rats	cf. *Neotoma* sp.
Mormon Tea	*Ephedra nevadensis*	Various squirrels	cf. *Ammospermo philus* sp.
Sugar bush	*Rhus ovata*	Mule deer	*Odocoileus hemionus*
Tule	*Scirpus* sp.	Pronghorn	*Antilocapra americana*
Wild rose	*Rosa californica*	Mountain sheep	*Ovis canadensis*
Cattail	*Typha latifolia*		
Assorted berries	N/A		
Mohave yucca	*Yucca schidigera*		
Cactus	*Opuntia* sp.		
Assorted grass seeds	N/A		
Chia seeds	*Salvia columbariae*		
Saltbush seeds	*Atriplex* spp.		
Pinyon	*Pinus monophylla*		
Palm tree fruit	*Washintonia filifera*		
Thimbleberry	*Rubes parviflorus*		
Wild raspberry	*Rubus leucodermis*		
Wild blackberry	*Rubus vitifolius*		
Juniper berry	*Juniperus californica*		
Chokecherry	*Prunus virginiana*		

(Continued)

TABLE 6.12. (*Continued*)

Plants		Animals	
Common Name	Scientific Name	Common Name	Scientific Name
Acorns	*Quercus* sp.		
Mistletoe	*Phoradendron* spp.		
California holly	*Heteromeles arbutifolia*		

[a] Compiled from Bean and Saubel (1972:20–21) and Bean (1978:table 1).

was absent, only a few small fish were available in local waterways. Water-fowl were also uncommon.

Initial Archaeological Studies

A number of archaeological investigations had been undertaken in the northern Coachella Valley during the twentieth century, but virtually none of the results have been published (for overviews see Crabtree 1981; Schaefer 1994; Schaefer and Laylander 2007). Several radiocarbon dates on materials associated with ancient Lake Cahuilla have been reported, but only very cursory descriptions of the materials were provided (see Wilke 1978:table 3).

Among the earliest reported studies in the northern Coachella Valley was in 1972, with the survey and testing of a site within the mouth of Tahquitz Canyon, located in Desert Cahuilla territory just south of Palm Springs. Wilke et al. (1975) documented a Cahuilla presence at the site during the late Prehistoric period (ca. 300 B.P.), prior to contact and after the last stand of Lake Cahuilla. Four major seed genera were recovered from hearth features at the site: *Dicoria, Sesuvium, Chenopodium,* and *Lupinus* (Wilke et al. 1975:60). The first two genera had not previously been documented as resources that were used by the ethnographic Cahuilla, so the archaeological data from this study expanded the number of plants used by the Cahuilla (Wilke et al. 1975:61). The faunal data from the site did not add new genera. Wilke et al. (1975:69) believed that the occupation of the mouth of Tahquitz Canyon was related to a settlement shift away from Lake Cahuilla.

The Wilke Study

In the early 1970s, Philip J. Wilke began a study of the last stand of Lake Cahuilla, concentrating on a number of sites in the northeastern Coachella Valley. Wilke worked at two large sites in that region, Myoma Dunes (CA-RIV-1766) and Wadi Beadmaker (CA-RIV-881) (see fig. 6.4), where he excavated a number of units, hearths, structures, and latrines. Extensive quantities of artifactual and ecofactual materials were recovered, but only a portion of the paleofecal data were published (Wilke 1978).

Myoma Dunes is a series of habitation areas located in mesquite-anchored sand dunes along the northernmost shore of Lake Cahuilla (fig. 6.4). The site in Wilke's study is located on the floor of the northern Coachella Valley and is not directly adjacent to upland habitats. Many features, artifacts, ecofacts, and about 1,000 coprolites were recovered. The analysis of the materials recovered from the site was limited to a sample of the coprolites (N = 99) from three latrine features (Beds A, B, and D; Wilke 1978), and few of the other data were reported. Radiocarbon dates from several of the coprolites placed the general occupation of the site to the final stand of the lake (ca. 500 B.P.; Wilke 1978:table 3).

The Wadi Beadmaker site is the remnant of an extensive camp located along the northeastern shore of Lake Cahuilla and was radiocarbon dated to roughly the time of the final lakestand (ca. 500 B.P.; Wilke 1978:98). Excavations at the site resulted in the recovery of numerous artifacts, ecofacts, and approximately 70 coprolites. As with Myoma Dunes, the analysis of the materials recovered from the site was limited to a sample of the coprolites (N = 10; Wilke 1978) and some of the faunal materials.

While incomplete, Wilke's study had two results. First, a basic understanding of the resources used by the Cahuilla in late Prehistoric times was firmly established. A combination of lake, desert, and upland resources was documented and a basis of comparison with the ethnographic period was created. Second, based on ethnographic analogy and the data from the analysis of the coprolites from the two sites, Wilke (1978:103) proposed a settlement and subsistence model for the late Prehistoric period in the northern Coachella Valley. It was hypothesized that while Lake Cahuilla was full, the settlement and subsistence pattern consisted of permanent villages along the lakeshore coupled with a series of temporary upland seasonal camps to exploit upland resources. After desiccation of the lake, the environment again became dry. The pattern then shifted to one in which the villages were centered on permanent springs rather than the lakeshore. The economic focus shifted from aquatic to terrestrial resources, likely resulting in increasing utilization of the surrounding uplands, along with a population increase in those areas (Wilke 1978:113).

The La Quinta Study

In 1985, excavations were undertaken at the La Quinta site (CA-RIV-1179), located along the northwestern shore of Lake Cahuilla (fig. 6.4) in an ecotone of at least three environmental zones: lakeshore, desert, and mountain. The La Quinta site consisted of a fairly large, open camp dating from the final stand of Lake Cahuilla (ca. 500 B.P.) and contained numerous artifacts, ecofacts, cremations, and 128 coprolites. The site was interpreted as a seasonal camp (Wilke and Sutton 1988:162). A full analytical report on the recovered materials was produced (Sutton and Wilke 1988) and is the only such comprehensive report for a major site in the region.

The dietary evidence from the La Quinta site consisted of the standard botanical and faunal materials recovered from the excavations, along with materials recovered in the paleofecal specimens. The botanical remains from the site (table 6.13) included a number of genera known to have been used by the ethnographic Cahuilla, but also three genera (*Oligomeris*, *Juncus*, and *Sesuvium*) not listed among the important ethnographic Cahuilla food species (Swope 1988). Interestingly, these same three genera were not identified in the paleofecal samples from the site (see Farrell 1988).

The faunal remains recovered from the excavations (table 6.14; Sutton and Yohe 1988; Follett 1988) at the La Quinta site revealed a number of interesting results. A wide variety of animals was represented, including reptiles and birds, considerable fish, and many mammals. Several of these species, specifically bighorn sheep and waterfowl, were not identified in the paleofecal samples (Farrell 1988). In addition, razorback sucker remains were much more common in the midden than in the coprolites, suggesting that some sort of bone removal process (e.g., filleting) was involved in the preparation of razorback sucker for consumption.

TABLE 6.13. Botanical Remains from the Midden Recovered by Flotation at La Quinta (CA-RIV-1179)[a]

Context	Cat. No.	Species
Hearth 1	108-4-6A	*Chenopodium, Juncus, Oligomeris linifolia, Prosopis glandulosa* var. *torreyana, Scirpus acutus, Scirpus, Sesuvium verrucosum*, unidentified
Hearth 2	108-4-33	*Chenopodium, Scirpus acutus, Scirpus validus, Sesuvium verrucosum*
Hearth 3	108-8-9A	*Chenopodium, Juncus, Oligomeris linifolia, Prosopis glandulosa* var. *torreyana, Scirpus acutus, Scirpus validus, Sesuvium verrucosum*, unidentified
Hearth 4	108-17-56	*Chenopodium, Juncus, Scirpus acutus, Scirpus validus, Sesuvium verrucosum*, unidentified
Hearth 5	108-8-21	*Amaranthus, Juncus, Prosopis glandulosa* var. *torreyana, Scirpus acutus, Scirpus validus, Sesuvium verrucosum, Typha*
Hearth 6	108-8-29	*Scirpus acutus*, unidentified
Hearth 7	108-12-25	*Scirpus*
Hearth 8	108-12-27	*Chenopodium, Scirpus acutus, Sesuvium verrucosum*
Hearth 8	108-12-34	*Scirpus acutus*, unidentified
Hearth 9	108-14-33	*Scirpus acutus*
Soil sample	108-16-73	*Chenopodium, Juncus, Scirpus acutus, Scirpus validus, Sesuvium verrucosum*
Soil sample	108-19-21	*Chenopodium, Juncus, Scirpus acutus, Sesuvium verrucosum*

[a] From Swope (1988:table 22).

The faunal record from the La Quinta site provided insight into the availability of animal resources in the time leading up to the final stand of Lake Cahuilla. All of the reptiles, birds, and mammals identified in the faunal assemblage are found in the region today, implying that the same habitats present today were exploited during the prehistoric site occupation. Fish were important, although the fish remains suddenly decreased in the upper portion of the deposit, and the remains of other animals, primarily lagomorphs and birds (particularly quail), increased. Sutton and Yohe (1988:113) suggested that this change in taxa "might reflect the decreasing availability of fish in conjunction with the desiccation of the lake," resulting in an increasing reliance on terrestrial habitats.

TABLE 6.14. Terrestrial and Avian Faunal Remains from the Midden (by 10-cm level) at La Quinta (CA-RIV-1179)[a]

Scientific Name	0–10	10–20	20–30	30–40	40–50	50–60	60–70	70–80	80–90	Cremation	Totals
Gopherus agassizii	2	2	1	—	—	—	—	—	—	—	5
Diposaurus dorsalis	—	1	—	—	—	—	—	—	—	—	1
Sauromalus obesus	—	—	3	—	—	—	—	—	—	—	3
Order Podicipediformes	1	—	1	—	—	—	—	—	—	—	2
Pelecanus cf. *erythrorhynchos*	—	—	1	—	—	—	—	—	—	—	1
Anatidae	—	2	—	—	—	—	—	—	—	—	2
Anas sp.	—	—	—	—	—	—	—	—	1	—	1
Fulica americana	4	—	—	—	—	—	—	—	—	—	4
Unidentified bird	22	12	18	2	—	2	—	1	—	1	58
Sylvilagus audubonii	5	—	—	—	—	—	—	—	—	—	5
Lepus californicus	4	4	1	—	—	—	—	—	—	—	9
Unidentified lagomorph	31	31	10	7	1	—	—	2	—	—	82
Perognathus sp.	1	—	1	—	—	—	—	—	—	—	2
Dipodomys sp.	2	—	—	—	—	1	—	—	—	—	3
Neotoma sp.	1	—	—	—	1	—	—	—	—	—	2
Microtus californicus	—	—	—	—	1	—	—	—	—	—	1
Unidentified rodent	4	14	—	4	—	1	—	—	—	—	23
Canis latrans	5	—	—	3	—	—	—	—	—	—	8
Ovis canadensis	3	3	4	—	—	—	—	—	—	4	14
Unidentified artiodactyl	3	—	1	—	—	—	—	1	—	4	9
Unidentified mammal	100	40	31	14	2	2	—	—	—	—	189
TOTALS	188	109	72	30	5	6	—	4	1	9[b]	424

[a] From Sutton and Yohe (1988:table 19).
[b] Includes eight awls (all artiodactyl).

TABLE 6.15. Constituents of the Coprolites (N = 30) from La Quinta (CA-RIV-1179)[a]

Constituent	N[b]	Abundant	Frequent	Infrequent	Trace
Plants					
Cattail (*Typha*) anthers	21	15	2	2	2
Hardstem bulrush (*Scirpus acutus*) seed	5	—	—	—	5
Softstem bulrush (*Scirpus validus*) seed	4	—	—	—	4
Unspecified bulrush (*Scirpus* sp.) seed	14	—	—	—	14
Honey mesquite (*Prosopis glandulosa* var. *torreyana*) seed	1	—	—	—	1
Dicoria (*Dicoria canescens* var. *canescens*) seed	1	—	—	—	1
Unspecified goosefoot (*Chenopodium* sp.) seed	1	—	—	—	1
Unidentified seeds	12	—	—	—	12
Charcoal fragments	30	3	4	9	14
Animals					
Bonytail chub (*Gila elegans*)	12	—	—	—	12
Razorback sucker (*Xyrauchen texanus*)	2	—	—	—	2
Unidentified fish	30	12	6	4	8
Cottontail rabbit (*Sylvilagus* sp.)	1	—	—	—	1
Unidentified mammal	1	—	—	—	1
Desert tortoise (*Gopherus agassizi*)	1	—	—	—	1
Chuckwalla (*Sauromalus obesus*)	1	—	—	1	—
Unidentified reptile	1	—	—	—	1
Unidentified vertebrate	3	—	—	—	3
Unidentified insect	9	—	—	—	9
Mollusk (cf. *Anodonta dejecta*)	2	—	—	—	2

[a] From Farrell (1988:table 23).
[b] Number of specimens in which the item occurred.

The third major data set from La Quinta was derived from the paleo-feces: 30 of the 128 coprolites recovered from the site were analyzed (Farrell 1988). The breadth of the identified taxa (table 6.15) was less than Wilke (1978) had documented at the Myoma Dunes and Wadi Beadmaker sites. Fish was identified in all of the paleofecal specimens and several appeared to consist primarily of cattail (*Typha* sp.) pollen. Farrell (1988:139) concluded that fishing "was an extremely important activity on a day-to-day basis" and that the site was occupied primarily during the late spring and/or early summer.

The excavations at the La Quinta site revealed a great deal of information regarding the paleonutrition of the inhabitants of the northern Coachella Valley during the last stand of Lake Cahuilla. La Quinta provided the first large-scale midden-derived data set on the use of plants and animals from that time period and revealed details about the use of resources from different ecozones. The coprolite data augmented and complemented the other data and provided an important basis of comparison to other coprolite data sets from elsewhere in the valley.

Additional Excavations in the Northern Coachella Valley

A number of other excavations were conducted in the region in the 1980s and 1990s that added to an understanding of human diet. Work at CA-RIV-2827 (Sutton 1988c), a small camp near the La Quinta site, resulted in the recovery of a considerable range of ecofactual materials, including mesquite (*Prosopis* sp.) seeds and the remains of freshwater shell, fish, reptiles, birds, and mammals. Three coprolites were discovered and analyzed (see Farrell 1988:133). Each was found to contain large amounts of fish bone, some insects, and only a few plants.

Several other sites were test-excavated in the La Quinta area in 1990 (Yohe 1990a). Of these, the CA-RIV-3682 site was dated between 620 and 240 radiocarbon years B.P. (Yohe 1990a:26) and contained considerable artifactual and faunal materials but no botanical remains. In addition, 26 coprolites were recovered. Considerable fish was identified in the faunal assemblage, but nearly half of the faunal material was not fish (Yohe 1990b:57), and rodents seemed to have been an important resource. A nearby site (CA-RIV-2936), dated by diagnostic artifacts to about the same time as CA-RIV-3682, contained few fish bones but considerable mammal bone, including bighorn sheep (Yohe 1990a:table 11). Several other sites in close proximity (CA-RIV-3679 and CA-RIV-3680/3681) contained similar faunal assemblages, but dated to about 1,000 years earlier (Yohe 1990a:91, table 12).

Further Analysis of the Coprolite Constituents from La Quinta

In 1993, additional analysis of the coprolite data from the La Quinta site (from Farrell 1988) was undertaken by Sutton (1993). The objective of that

TABLE 6.16. Paleofecal Constituent Clusters from La Quinta (CA-RIV-1179)[a]

Cluster	N	Primary Constituents	Culinary Inference	Seasonality Inference
1	13	Abundant cattail, few fish	Meals of cattail	Spring, summer
2	7	Abundant unidentified fish, some mammals and reptiles, few plants	Mixed meals, fish unidentified due to processing, other resources included in meals	Late winter/early spring?
3	8	Abundant bonytail and unidentified fish (mostly charred)	Meals of bonytail	Summer?
4	2	Abundant razorback and unidentified fish (cattail is abundant in one specimen)	Meals of razorback	Summer?

[a] From Sutton (1993, 1998:table 2).

study was to conduct a cluster analysis of the various coprolite constituents to search for patterns of resource utilization. At a coarse level, although the La Quinta coprolite data might appear to be relatively homogeneous (e.g., "fish in every sample, cattail in most"), it was thought that patterns of food combinations regarding dietary preferences, habits (e.g., meals), and differences in the seasonal use of resources might be detectable. The faunal and botanical materials recovered from the general midden were then compared to the coprolite data in an attempt to delineate additional patterns between the two data sets.

The constituents from the coprolites (N = 30) fell into four distinct clusters (see table 6.16): (1) cattail and few fish; (2) abundant unidentified fish and a few other constituents; (3) abundant bonytail and unidentified fish; and (4) abundant razorback and unidentified fish. A number of patterns were apparent. First, it is clear that the diet was not uniform; rather, it was varied, likely on a seasonal basis. Second, the importance of fish and other aquatic resources appears to have changed seasonally, despite the presumed constant availability of fish.

Several specific combinations of resources were found, perhaps constituting the remains of meals. Cattail appears to have been consumed largely by itself. Terrestrial animals were apparently not consumed in meals with cattail, although some fish was included. In addition, bulrush often was identified in specimens containing bonytail. Bonytail seems to have been the preferred fish, although razorback occasionally was consumed (the same pattern existed at Myoma Dunes Bed A; Wilke 1978:82). The two fish species were not identified in the same specimen, suggesting differential use and/or preparation of these fish.

Two other observations were made by Sutton (1993). The first is that fish, which have generally been viewed as an everyday staple (e.g., Wilke 1978; Farrell 1988), did not appear to have been a staple at certain times, specifically during that portion of the year when cattail was consumed. As cattail pods ripen from late fall to early spring, presumably it is during this time that consumption is at its greatest. Terrestrial animals may have been more important at lakeside sites than previously thought. Second, it seems that cattail was very heavily exploited when available, perhaps to the exclusion of other resources.

Finally, Sutton (1993) offered an alternative to the settlement/subsistence model proposed by Wilke (1978; see above). Wilke and Sutton (1988:162) argued that the La Quinta site was a seasonal camp occupied during the spring and/or summer and that the inhabitants of La Quinta moved to another residential base camp (or camps) for the fall and winter. The location of such camps is unknown but might be situated in the uplands and/or another lakeshore location, such as Myoma Dunes where a winter occupation is indicated (Wilke 1978).

Sutton (1993) suggested that the La Quinta site was part of an intermediate settlement/subsistence system, one between the lake-focused pattern proposed by Wilke (1978) and that observed in ethnographic times. Sutton (1993) concluded that people living around Lake Cahuilla at the time of its final stand (ca. 500 B.P.) functioned within a complex system of seasonal resource use and changing settlement. There is little doubt that people camped near the lake to exploit the resources there, such as fish, cattail, and waterfowl.

A Refinement of Diet and Cuisine

Following the cluster analysis of the La Quinta coprolite constituents (Sutton 1993), a statistical study of the paleofecal data from the Myoma Dunes, Wadi Beadmaker, and La Quinta sites was conducted by Sutton

(1998). As noted above, together these three sites contained almost 1,200 coprolites (of which 139 were analyzed) and complementary botanical and faunal data sets. Analyses of the coprolites from these three sites had previously been conducted (Wilke 1978; Farrell 1988) and those specimens formed the data base for the Sutton (1993) study, with the exception of two specimens that did not contain constituent data. Each of the four data sets (Myoma Dunes Beds A, B, and D, and Wadi Beadmaker) was analyzed individually, compared to the previous La Quinta study, then combined with the La Quinta data and analyzed as a single sample (Sutton 1998).

The goal of the study was twofold (Sutton 1998): (1) to conduct a cluster analysis of the coprolite constituents from Myoma Dunes and Wadi Beadmaker (Wilke 1978), and then to compare the results to the La Quinta data in order to test the two settlement/subsistence models offered by Wilke (1978) and Sutton (1993), and (2) to determine any patterns of food preferences and combinations within the samples in an attempt to elucidate both diet and cuisine. In reference to the competing models, if Myoma Dunes and Wadi Beadmaker were permanent lakeshore villages, the coprolite clusters from those sites were expected to reflect a diet that contained resources available during all seasons, including dicoria (*Dicoria canescens*) and pinyon (*Pinus monophylla*). In addition, aquatic resources should also be emphasized at both sites.

The analysis of the Myoma Dunes Bed A sample (N = 75) identified seven clusters, each having a defining resource (table 6.17). Five clusters reflected the use of spring and/or summer resources and two clusters reflected winter resources. Sutton (1998:98) argued that this may reflect an occupation by a population that was largest in the spring and summer and smallest in the winter, along with changing and/or differing resource procurement tactics. The Myoma Dunes Bed B sample (N = 10) revealed two clusters, each with a defining resource. Most of the specimens reflected the use of spring and/or summer resources. Two clusters were identified in the Myoma Dunes Bed D sample (N = 12), each with a key resource. Cluster 1 reflected the use of spring and/or summer resources, while Cluster 2 reflected winter resources. Sutton (1998:100) suggested that this indicated a winter occupation.

The analysis of the Wadi Beadmaker sample (N = 10) resulted in the identification of three clusters, each having a key resource (table 6.18).

TABLE 6.17. Paleofecal Constituent Clusters from Myoma Dunes (CA-RIV-1766)[a]

Cluster	N	Primary Constituents	Culinary Inference	Seasonality Inference
1, Bed A	11	Abundant bonytail and unidentified fish, frequent charcoal, trace amount of plants	Meals of fish, mostly processed	Summer
2, Bed A	16	Abundant cattail, some bulrush, some fish (some bonytail, but mostly unidentified), frequent charcoal, some coot	Meals of cattail supplemented with bulrush and processed fish	Late spring, summer
3, Bed A	13	Abundant fish (bonytail, razorback, and unidentified), frequent cattail and bulrush, some mesquite	Meals of bonytail and/or razorback, supplemented with cattail and bulrush	Late spring, summer
4, Bed A	8	Frequent mammals (hare and unidentified), dicoria, mesquite and sea purslane, trace of fish	Meals of mammals supplemented with dicoria, mesquite, and purslane	Winter
5, Bed A	10	Abundant goosefoot and mesquite, some coot, trace of fish	Meals of goosefoot, usually with mesquite, some coot	Late spring, early summer
6, Bed A	12	Abundant mesquite, frequent unidentified fish, some mammals, some sea purslane	Meals of mesquite, mixed with either fish and/or mammal or sea purslane	Summer to fall
7, Bed A	5	Abundant dicoria and mesquite (a combination of dicoria, mesquite, unidentified fish, pine, and coot in one specimen)	Meals of dicoria and mesquite, supplemented with a variety of other resources	Winter
1, Bed B	2	Unidentified fish	Meals of processed fish	Undetermined
2, Bed B	8	Abundant panic grass, frequent mesquite, some unidentified fish, insects, cattail, goosefoot, amaranth, and purslane	Meals of panic grass, often supplemented with mesquite, each supplemented with another, different resource	Spring, summer

(Continued)

TABLE 6.17. (*Continued*)

Cluster	N	Primary Constituents	Culinary Inference	Seasonality Inference
1, Bed D	7	Abundant cattail anthers and pollen and unidentified fish, abundant bonytail in some specimens	Meals of cattail and fish	Spring, summer
2, Bed D	5	Frequent mesquite, abundant panic grass in two specimens, frequent dicoria in two specimens, some unidentified fish	Meals of mesquite, supplemented with dicoria, fish, and panic grass	Winter

ª Compiled from Sutton (1998:tables 4, 6, and 8).

TABLE 6.18. Paleofecal Constituent Clusters from Wadi Beadmaker (CA-RIV-881)ª

Cluster	N	Primary Constituents	Culinary Inference	Seasonality Inference
1	6	Abundant unidentified fish, some charcoal	Meals of processed fish	Late winter/ early spring?
2	2	Abundant bonytail and unidentified fish, some charcoal	Meals of fish	Summer
3	2	Abundant panic grass	Meals of panic grass	Winter

ª From Sutton (1998:table 10).

One cluster reflected the use of spring and/or summer resources and two clusters reflected winter resources. The faunal data from the site (Wilke 1978:table 13) demonstrated that a variety of terrestrial animal resources were processed and/or consumed.

Discussion

Sutton (1998) observed several patterns in the distribution and relative abundance of the resources by site (table 6.19). Mesquite was largely absent from the La Quinta and Wadi Beadmaker samples, whereas it was fairly important in the Myoma Dunes samples, suggesting a middle to late

TABLE 6.19. Resource Summary and Abundance in Paleofeces at Studied Northern Coachella Valley Sites[a]

Resource	La Quinta	MD,[b] Bed A	MD, Bed B	MD, Bed D	Wadi Beadmaker
Bonytail chub (*Gila elegans*)	14	6	Absent	11	14
Razorback sucker (*Xyrauchen texanus*)	3	2	Absent	Absent	7
Unidentified fish	33	16	12	22	55
Tortoise (*Gopherus agassizii*)	1	<1	Absent	Absent	Absent
Chuckwalla (*Sauromalus obesus*)	<1	Absent	Absent	Absent	Absent
Unidentified reptile	<1	Absent	Absent	Absent	Absent
Cottontail (*Sylvilagus audubonii*)	<1	<1	Absent	Absent	Absent
Unidentified mammal	<1	5	Absent	Absent	Absent
Unidentified vertebrate	1	<1	1	Absent	Absent
Freshwater mussel (*Anodonta*)	<1	Absent	Absent	Absent	2
Snail (*Physa*)	<1	Absent	Absent	Absent	Absent
Unidentified insect parts	3	4	11	4	2
Cattail (*Typha*)	26	11	3	19	Absent
Bulrush (*Scirpus*)	6	9	6	9	2
Dicoria (*Dicoria canescens*)	1	5	Absent	5	Absent
Mesquite (*Prosopis* spp.)	<1	13	22	9	Absent
Goosefoot (*Chenopodium* sp.)	<1	5	4	1	Absent
Unidentified plant remains	4	2	2	2	Absent
Charcoal[c]	—	—	—	—	—
Panic grass (*Panicum capillare*)	Absent	3	30	12	14
Cuscuta sp.	Absent	Absent	2	Absent	2

Taxon					
Amaranth (*Amaranthus* sp.)	Absent	<1	Absent	Absent	2
Sorrel (*Rumex* cf. *salicifolius*)	Absent	Absent	Absent	2	Absent
Pine (*Pinus monophylla*) nuts	Absent	2	Absent	2	Absent
American coot (*Fulica americana*)	Absent	3	Absent	5	Absent
Sea purslane (*Sesuvium verrucosum*)	Absent	7	2	Absent	Absent
Purslane (*Calyptridium* cf. *unbellatum*)	Absent	Absent	5	Absent	Absent
Benth (*Monardella exilis*)	Absent	<1	Absent	Absent	Absent
Striped mullet (*Mugil cephalus*)	Absent	1	Absent	Absent	Absent
Linear-leaved cambess (*Oligomeris linifolia*)	Absent	<1	Absent	Absent	Absent
Black-tailed jackrabbit (*Lepus californicus*)	Absent	1	Absent	Absent	Absent
Barrel cactus (*Ferocatus acanthodes*)	Absent	<1	Absent	Absent	Absent
Barnyard grass (*Echinochloa* sp.)	Absent	<1	Absent	Absent	Absent
Cactus (*Opuntia* sp.)	Absent	<1	Absent	Absent	Absent
Earred grebe (*Podiceps caspicus*)	Absent	<1	Absent	Absent	Absent

a From Sutton (1998:table 12); abundance is the percentages of constituents from paleofecal samples.

b MD = Myoma Dunes.

c Charcoal is considered to be a processing by-product, rather than a resource.

TABLE 6.20. Concordance of Coprolite Clusters from the Northern Coachella Valley[a]

Primary Cluster Constituents	Site/Cluster
Abundant cattail, few fish	La Quinta/1
	Myoma Dunes A/2
Abundant cattail and fish (bonytail and unidentified)	Myoma Dunes D/1
Abundant unidentified fish, some mammals and reptiles, few plants	La Quinta/2
	Wadi Beadmaker/1
Abundant bonytail and unidentified fish	La Quinta/3
	Myoma Dunes A/1
	Myoma Dunes B/1
	Wadi Beadmaker/2
Abundant razorback and unidentified fish	La Quinta/4
Abundant fish (frequent bonytail, razorback, and unidentified), frequent cattail and bulrush, some mesquite	Myoma Dunes A/3
Frequent mammals, dicoria, mesquite and sea purslane, only trace of fish	Myoma Dunes A/4
Abundant goosefoot and mesquite, some coot, only trace of fish	Myoma Dunes A/5
Abundant mesquite, frequent unidentified fish, some mammals, some sea purslane	Myoma Dunes A/6
Abundant dicoria and mesquite	Myoma Dunes A/7
	Myoma Dunes D/2
Abundant panic grass, frequent mesquite, some unidentified fish, insects, cattail, goosefoot, amaranth, and purslane	Myoma Dunes B/2
Abundant panic grass	Wadi Beadmaker/3

[a] From Sutton (1998:table 13).

summer occupation of the former two sites with little to no use of stored mesquite (Sutton 1998:101). A number of other plants showed skewed distributions, including panic grass and dicoria, and a large number of resources (see table 6.13) were absent from the La Quinta samples.

Twelve distinct resource clusters were identified in the five data sets (table 6.20; Sutton 1998). Eight clusters were unique, occurring at only one site each, while three other clusters occurred at two localities each.

One cluster, comprised of abundant bonytail and other unidentified fish, was present at four localities. While no correlation between clusters and environmental zones was made, it was apparent that a variety of resource combinations and meals were represented.

Animal protein seems to have been derived from either fish or mammals, but they were generally not identified in the same sample. Since both of these resource categories should have been available at the same time, the pattern may reflect some dietary preference, an aspect of cuisine, and/or a processing factor. For fish, razorback and bonytail appeared to occur independently of each other, suggesting a clear pattern in preference and/or processing.

One of the goals of the Sutton (1998) study was an evaluation of the merits of the several settlement/subsistence models proposed for the area during the late Prehistoric period (Wilke 1978; Sutton 1993). At issue was whether the major sites on the shoreline of Lake Cahuilla were occupied year-round, thus forming the foundation of a system centered on the lake. The key issue was the presence of a winter-related diet at those sites.

Wilke (1978:104) argued that a winter diet should have included dicoria, supplemented by stored seeds, with fish and waterfowl also being important. Dicoria was present in 22 specimens, but fish is not noticeably more important in those samples than in other specimens, and coot (a waterbird) was rarely found with dicoria. Of the 137 specimens from the five data sets, a total of 20 (14.6 percent) supports a winter diet. This suggests that there was only a limited occupation of the sites during the winter and that the majority of the population had gone elsewhere during that time. Thus, if the various sites other than La Quinta were occupied in the winter, it would have been by reduced populations. Based on these conclusions, the Wilke (1978) model of large, permanent lakeside villages was not supported (Sutton 1998). It was further argued that the ethnohistoric pattern of large, permanent springside villages must have developed from a system of large spring/summer and small winter habitation sites (Sutton 1998).

Summary

Since the late 1800s, there have been attempts to understand the ethnobiology and diet of the Cahuilla people living in the northern Coachella

Valley. Ethnographers first documented Cahuilla ethnobotany (e.g., Barrows 1900), then augmented that understanding with further study (Bean and Saubel 1972). Later, archaeologists began to investigate the Cahuilla diet just prior to contact and then in relation to the exploitation of resources associated with a large lake in the region. The presence of the lake, and its desiccation some 500 years ago, demonstrated a dynamic environment and provided a basis for detailing the evolution of Cahuilla diet in response to the changing environment.

This case study demonstrates an evolution in the understanding of diet in a particular region and among a particular people. Paleodietary data sets from sites associated with Lake Cahuilla were obtained and a model of settlement and subsistence was formed (Wilke 1978). Additional data were acquired (Sutton and Wilke 1988) and a better understanding of lacustrine adaptation was the result. These data were reanalyzed and a new settlement/subsistence model was proposed (Sutton 1993). Finally, a statistical analysis of paleofecal data from a number of sites in the region was conducted (Sutton 1998) and the Wilke (1978) model was rejected. This statistical analysis provided the most complete picture yet of trends in diet and cuisine in the northern Coachella Valley during the last 500 years.

References

Aikens, C. Melvin, and Younger T. Witherspoon

1986 Great Basin Prehistory: Linguistics, Archaeology, and Environment. In: *Anthropology of the Desert West: Papers in Honor of Jesse D. Jennings*, Carol J. Condie and Don D. Fowler, eds., pp. 7–20. Salt Lake City: University of Utah, Anthropological Papers, No. 110.

Akins, N. J.

1986 *A Biocultural Approach to Human Burials from Chaco Canyon, New Mexico.* Santa Fe: National Park Service, Reports of the Chaco Center, No. 9.

Allen, Lindsay H.

1984 Functional Indicators of Nutritional Status of the Whole Individual of the Community. *Clinical Nutrition* 3(5):169–175.

Al-Shorman, Abdulla

2004 Stable Carbon Isotope Analysis of Human Tooth Enamel from the Bronze Age Cemetery of Ya'amoun in Northern Jordan. *Journal of Archaeological Science* 31(12):1693–1698.

Alt, K. W., C. P. Adler, C. H. Buitrago-Téllez, and B. Lohrke

2002 Infant Osteosarcoma. *International Journal of Osteoarchaeology* 12(6):442–448.

Ambrose, Stanley H.

1987 Chemical and Isotopic Techniques of Diet Reconstruction in Eastern North America. In: *Emergent Horticultural Economies of the Eastern Woodlands*, William F. Keegan, ed., pp. 87–107. Carbondale: Southern Illinois University, Center for Archaeological Investigations, Occasional Paper No. 7.

1990 Preparation and Characterization of Bone and Tooth Collagen for Isotopic Analysis. *Journal of Archaeological Science* 17(4):431–451.

1991 Effects of Diet, Climate and Physiology on Nitrogen Isotope Abundances in Terrestrial Foodwebs. *Journal of Archaeological Science* 18(3):293–317.

1993 Isotopic Analysis of Paleodiets: Methodological and Interpretive Considerations. In: *Investigations of Ancient Human Tissue: Chemical Analyses in Anthropology*, Mary K. Sandford, ed., pp. 59–130. Langhorne, Penn.: Gordon and Breach.

2000 Controlled Diet and Climate Experiments on Nitrogen Isotope Ratios of Rats. In: *Biogeochemical Approaches to Paleodietary Analysis*, Stanley H. Ambrose and M. Anne Katzenberg, eds., pp. 243–259. New York: Kluwer Academic/Plenum Publishers.

Ambrose, Stanley H., and Michael J. DeNiro

1986 Reconstruction of African Human Diet Using Bone Collagen Carbon and Nitrogen Isotope Ratios. *Nature* 319:321–324.

Ambrose, Stanley H., and Michael J. DeNiro

1987   Bone Nitrogen Isotope Composition and Climate. *Nature* 325:201.

Ambrose, Stanley H., and John Krigbaum

2003   Bone Chemistry and Bioarchaeology. *Journal of Anthropological Archaeology* 22(3):193–199.

Ambrose, Stanley H., and Lynette Norr

1992   On Stable Isotopic Data and Prehistoric Subsistence in the Soconusco Region. *Current Anthropology* 33(4):401–404.

1993   Experimental Evidence for the Relationship of the Carbon Isotope Ratios of Whole Diet and Dietary Protein to Those of Bone Collagen and Carbonate. In: *Prehistoric Human Bone: Archaeology at the Molecular Level*, Joseph B. Lambert and Gisela Grupe, eds., pp. 1–37. Berlin: Springer-Verlag.

Ambrose, Stanley H., Jane Buikstra, and Harold W. Krueger

2003   Status and Gender Differences in Diet at Mound 72, Cahokia, Revealed by Isotopic Analysis of Bone. *Journal of Anthropological Archaeology* 22(3):217–226.

Ames, Kenneth M.

1994   The Northwest Coast: Complex Hunter-Gatherers, Ecology, and Social Evolution. *Annual Review of Anthropology* 23:209–229,

Ammitzbøll, T., S. Ry Andersen, H. P. Andersson, J. Bodenhoff, M. Eiken, B. Eriksen, N. Foged, M. Ghisler, A. Gotfredsen, H. E. Hansen, J. P. Hart Hansen, J. Jakobsen, J. Balslev Jøgensen, T. Kobayasi, N. Kromann, K. J. Lyberth, L. Lyneborg, F. Mikkelsen, J. Møhl, R. Møller, J. Myhre, P. O. Pedersen, J. U. Prause, O. Sebbesen, E. Svejgaard, D. D. Thompson, V. Frølund Thomsen, and L. Vanggaard

1991   The People. In: *The Greenland Mummies*, Jens Peder Hart Hansen, Jørgen Meldgaard, and Jørgen Nordqvist, eds., pp. 64–101. Washington, D.C.: Smithsonian Institution Press.

Ancibor, Elena, and Cecilia Pérez de Micou

1995   Identification of Firewood Species in the Archaeological Record of the Patagonian Steppe. *Journal of Ethnobiology* 15(2):189–200.

Andersen, John G.

1991   The Medieval Diagnosis of Leprosy. In: *Human Paleopathology: Current Syntheses and Future Options*, Donald J. Ortner and Arthur C. Aufderheide, eds., pp. 205–208. Washington, D.C.: Smithsonian Institution Press.

Anderson, R. H., and I. S. Perold

1964   Chemical and Physical Properties of South African Honeys. *South African Journal of Agricultural Science* 7:365–374.

Andrus, C. Fred T., and Douglas E. Crowe

2000   Geochemical Analysis of *Crassostrea virginica* as a Method to Determine Season of Capture. *Journal of Archaeological Science* 27(1):33–42.

Angel, J. Lawrence

1969   Paleodemography and Evolution. *American Journal of Physical Anthropology* 31(3):343–353.

Anon, Roger, and Steven A. LeBlanc

1984   *The Galaz Ruin: A Prehistoric Mimbres Village in Southwestern New Mexico.* Albuquerque: Maxwell Museum of Anthropology.

Antoine, S. E., P. Q. Dresser, A. Mark Pollard, and A.W.R. Whittle

1988   Bone Chemistry and Dietary Reconstruction in Prehistoric Britain: Examples from Wessex. In: *Science and Archaeology, Glasgow 1987*, Elizabeth A. Slater and James O. Tate, eds., pp. 369–380. Oxford: British Archaeological Reports, International Series, No. 196 (2 vols.).

Appleyard, H. M., and A. B. Wildman

1970   Fibers of Archaeological Interest: Their Examination and Identification. In: *Science in Archaeology: A Survey of Progress and Research*, Don R. Brothwell and Eric Higgs, eds., pp. 624–633. New York: Praeger.

Arabi, Asma, Rafic Baddoura, Hassane Awada, Nabil Khoury, Souha Haddad, Ghazi Ayoub, and Ghada El-Hajj Fuleihan

2007   Discriminative Ability of Dual-Energy X-Ray Absorptiometry Site Selection in Identifying Patients with Osteoporotic Fractures. *Bone* 40(4):1060–1065.

Araus, José Luis, Gustavo Ariel Slafer, Ignacio Romagosa, and Miquel Molist

2001   Estimated Wheat Yields during the Emergence of Agriculture Based on the Carbon Isotope Discrimination of Grains: Evidence from a 10th Millennium BP Site on the Euphrates. *Journal of Archaeological Science* 28(4):341–350.

Armelagos, George J.

1994   "You Are What You Eat." In: *Paleonutrition: The Diet and Health of Prehistoric Americans*, Kristin D. Sobolik, ed., pp. 235–244. Carbondale: Southern Illinois University, Center for Archaeological Investigations, Occasional Paper No. 22.

Armelagos, George J., David S. Carlson, and Dennis P. Van Gerven

1982   The Theoretical Foundations and Development of Skeletal Biology. In: *A History of American Physical Anthropology 1930–1980*, F. Spence, ed., pp. 305–328. New York: Academic Press.

Armelagos, George J., Dennis P. Van Gerven, Debra L. Martin, and Rebecca Huss-Ashmore

1984   Effects of Nutritional Change on the Skeletal Biology of Northeast African (Sudanese Nubian) Populations. In: *From Hunters to Farmers: The Causes and Consequences of Food Production in Africa*, J. Desmond Clark and Steven A. Brandt, eds., pp. 132–146. Berkeley: University of California Press.

Armelagos, George J., Barrett Brenton, Michael Alcorn, Debra Martin, and Dennis P. Van Gerven

1989   Factors Affecting Elemental and Isotopic Variation in Prehistoric Human Skeletons. In: *The Chemistry of Prehistoric Human Bone*, T. Douglas Price, ed., pp. 230–244. Cambridge: Cambridge University Press.

Arriaza, Bernardo T.

1995   *Beyond Death: The Chinchorro Mummies of Ancient Chile.* Washington, D.C.: Smithsonian Institution Press.

Arriaza, Bernardo T., Wilmar Salo, Arthur C. Aufderheide, and Todd A. Holcomb

1995   Pre-Columbian Tuberculosis in Northern Chile: Molecular and Skeletal Evidence. *American Journal of Physical Anthropology* 98(1):37–45.

Ascenzi, Antonio, A. Bellelli, M. Brunori, G. Citro, R. Ippoliti, E. Lendaro, and R. Zito

1991   Diagnosis of Thalassemia in Ancient Bones: Problems and Prospects in Pathology. In: *Human Paleopathology: Current Syntheses and Future Options*, Donald J. Ortner and Arthur C. Aufderheide, eds., pp. 73–75. Washington, D.C.: Smithsonian Institution Press.

Aschmann, Homer

1959   *The Central Desert of Baja California: Demography and Ecology. Ibero-Americana, No. 42*. Berkeley: University of California.

Aufderheide, Arthur C.

1989   Chemical Analysis of Skeletal Remains. In: *Reconstruction of Life from the Skeleton*, Mehmet Y. Işcan and Kenneth A. R. Kennedy, eds., pp. 237–260. New York: Alan R. Liss, Inc.

2003   *The Scientific Study of Mummies*. Cambridge: Cambridge University Press.

Aufderheide, Arthur C., and Marvin J. Allison

1995a   Strontium Patterns in Infancy Can Validate Retention of Biogenic Signal in Human Archaeological Bone. In: *Proceedings of the First World Congress on Mummy Studies*, Vol. 1, pp. 443–450. Museo Arqueológico y Etnográfico de Tenerife.

1995b   Chemical Dietary Reconstruction of North Chile Prehistoric Populations by Trace Mineral Analysis. In: *Proceedings of the First World Congress on Mummy Studies*, Vol. 1, pp. 451–461. Museo Arqueológico y Etnográfico de Tenerife.

Aufderheide, Arthur C., and Mary L. Aufderheide

1991   Taphonomy of Spontaneous ("Natural") Mummification with Applications to the Mummies of Venzone, Italy. In: *Human Paleopathology: Current Syntheses and Future Options*, Donald J. Ortner and Arthur C. Aufderheide, eds., pp. 79–86. Washington, D.C.: Smithsonian Institution Press.

Aufderheide, Arthur C., and Conrado Rodríguez-Martín

1998   *The Cambridge Encyclopedia of Human Paleopathology*. Cambridge: Cambridge University Press.

Aufderheide, Arthur C., A. C. Neiman, Lorentz E. Wittmers Jr., and George Rapp Jr.

1981   Lead in Bone. II: Skeletal Lead Content as an Indicator of Lifetime Lead Ingestion and the Social Correlates in an Archaeological Population. *American Journal of Physical Anthropology* 55(3):285–291.

Aufderheide, Arthur C., J. Lawrence Angel, Jennifer O. Kelley, Alain C. Outlaw, Merry A. Outlaw, George Rapp Jr., and Lorentz E. Wittmers Jr.

1985   Lead in Bone. III: Prediction of Social Correlates from Skeletal Lead Content in Four Colonial American Populations (Catoctin Furnace, College Landing, Governor's Land, and Irene Mound). *American Journal of Physical Anthropology* 66(4):353–361.

Aufderheide, Arthur C., Larry L. Tiezen, Marvin J. Allison, JoAnn Wallgren, and George Rapp Jr.

1988a   Chemical Reconstruction of Components in Complex Diets: A Pilot Study. In: *Diet and Subsistence: Current Archaeological Perspectives*, Brenda V. Kennedy and Genevieve M. LeMoine, eds., pp. 301–306. Proceedings of the Nineteenth Annual Chacmool Conference, University of Calgary.

Aufderheide, Arthur C., Lorentz E. Wittmers Jr., George Rapp Jr., and JoAnn Wallgren

1988b   Anthropological Applications of Skeletal Lead Analysis. *American Anthropologist* 90(4):931–936.

Aufderheide, Arthur C., Conrado Rodríguez-Martin, Fernando Estévez-González, and Michael Torbenson

1995   Chemical Dietary Reconstruction of Tenerife's Guanche Diet Using Skeletal Trace Element Content. In: *Proceedings of the First World Congress on Mummy Studies*, Vol. 1, pp. 33–40. Museo Arqueológico y Etnográfico de Tenerife.

Aufderheide, Arthur C., Wilmar Salo, Michael Madden, John Streitz, Jane Buikstra, Felipe Guhl, Bernardo Arriaza, Colleen Renier, Lorentz E. Wittmers Jr., Gino Fornaciari, and Marvin Allison

2004   A 9,000-Year Record of Chagas' Disease. *Proceedings of the National Academy of Sciences* 101(7):2034–2039.

Aykroyd, Robert G., David Lucy, A. Mark Pollard, and Charolette A. Roberts

1999   Nasty, Brutish, but Not Necessarily Short: A Reconsideration of the Statistical Methods Used to Calculate Age at Death from Adult Human Skeletal and Dental Age Indicators. *American Antiquity* 64(1):55–70.

Ayliffe, Linda K., and Allan R. Chivas

1990   Oxygen Isotope Composition of the Bone Phosphate of Australian Kangaroos: Potential as a Palaeoenvironmental Recorder. *Geochimica et Cosmochimica Acta* 54(9):2603–2609.

Bailey, G. N.

1975   The Role of Mollusks in Coastal Economies: The Results of Midden Analysis in Australia. *Journal of Archaeological Science* 2(1):45–62.

Baker, Brenda J., Tosha L. Dupras, and Matthew W. Tocheri

2005   *The Osteology of Infants and Children*. College Station: Texas A&M University Press.

Baker, Jack, and Osbjorn M. Pearson

2006   Statistical Methods for Bioarchaeology: Applications of Age-Adjustment and Logistic Regression to Comparisons of Skeletal Populations with Differing Age-Structures. *Journal of Archaeological Science* 33(2):218–226.

Balabanova, Svetla, Franz Parsche, and Wolfgang Pirsig

1992   First Identification of Drugs in Egyptian Mummies. *Naturwissenschafter* 79:358.

Balabanova, Svetla, Wolfgang Pirsig, Franz Parsche, and Erhard Schneider

1995   Cocaine, Xanthine Derivatives and Nicotine in Cranial Hair of a Pre-Columbian Mummy. In: *Proceedings of the First World Congress on Mummy Studies*, Vol. 2, pp. 465–470. Museo Arqueológico y Etnográfico de Tenerife.

Balasse, Marie

2002   Reconstructing Dietary and Environmental History from Enamel Isotopic Analysis: Time Resolution of Intra-tooth Sequential Sampling. *International Journal of Osteoarchaeology* 12(3):155–165.

Balasse, Marie, and Stanley H. Ambrose

2005   Distinguishing Sheep and Goats Using Dental Morphology and Stable Carbon Isotopes in C$_4$ Grassland Environments. *Journal of Archaeological Science* 32(5):691–702.

Balasse, Marie, Hervé Bocherens, and André Mariotti

1999   Intra-bone Variability of Collagen and Apatite Isotopic Composition Used as Evidence of a Change of Diet. *Journal of Archaeological Science* 26(6):593–598.

Balasse, Marie, Hervé Bocherens, André Mariotti, and Stanley H. Ambrose

2001   Detection of Dietary Changes in Intra-tooth Carbon and Nitrogen Isotopic Analysis: An Experimental Study of Dentine Collagen of Cattle (*Bos taurus*). *Journal of Archaeological Science* 28(3):235–245.

Balasse, Marie, Stanley H. Ambrose, Andrew B. Smith, and T. Douglas Price

2002   The Seasonal Mobility Model for Prehistoric Herders in the South-western Cape of South Africa Assessed by Isotopic Analysis of Sheep Tooth Enamel. *Journal of Archaeological Science* 29(9):917–932.

Ball, Terry, John S. Gardner, and Jack Brotherson

1996   Identifying Phytoliths Produced by the Inflorescence Bracts of Three Species of Wheat (*Triticum monococcum* L., *T. Dicoccon* Schrank., and *T. aestivum* L.) Using Computer-Assisted Image and Statistical Analysis. *Journal of Archaeological Science* 23(4):619–632.

Baraybar, José Pablo

1999   Diet and Death in a Fog Oasis Site in Central Coastal Peru: A Trace Element Study of Tomb 1 Malanche 22. *Journal of Archaeological Science* 26(5):471–482.

Baraybar, José Pablo, and Concepción de la Rua

1997   Reconstruction of Diet with Trace Elements of Bone at the Chalcolithic Site of Pico Ramos, Basque Country, Spain. *Journal of Archaeological Science* 24(4):355–364.

Bar-Gal, G. Kahila, H. Khalaily, O. Mader, P. Ducos, and L. Kolska Horwitz

2002   Ancient DNA Evidence for the Transition from Wild to Domestic Status in Neolithic Goats: A Case Study from the Site of Abu Gosh, Israel. *Ancient Biomolecules* 4(1):9–17.

Barnes, I., J.P.W. Young, and K. M. Dobney

2000   DNA-Based Identification of Goose Species from Two Archaeological Sites in Lincolnshire. *Journal of Archaeological Science* 27(2):91–100.

Baron, Heike, Susanne Hummel, and Bernd Herrmann

1996   *Mycobacterium tuberculosis* Complex DNA in Ancient Human Bones. *Journal of Archaeological Science* 23(5):667–671.

Barraco, Robin A.

1980   Paleobiochemistry. In: *Mummies, Disease, and Ancient Cultures* (1st ed.), Aidan Cockburn and Eve Cockburn, eds., pp. 312–326. Cambridge: Cambridge University Press.

Barrett, James, Cluny Johnstone, Jennifer Harland, Wim Van Neer, Anton Ervynck, Daniel Makowiecki, Dirk Heinrich, Anne Karin Hufthammer, Inge Bødker Enghoff, Colin Amundsen, Jørgen Schou Christiansen, Andrew K. G. Jones, Alison Locker, Sheila Hamilton-Dyer, Leif Jonsson, Lembi Lõugas, Callum Roberts, and Michael Richards

2008   Detecting the Medieval Cod Trade: A New Method and First Results. *Journal of Archaeological Science* 35(4):850–861.

Barrows, David

1900   *The Ethno-botany of the Coahuilla Indians of Southern California.* Chicago: University of Chicago Press.

Bartelink, Eric John

2006   Resource Intensification in Pre-Contact Central California: A Bioarchaeological Perspective on Diet and Health Patterns among Hunter-Gatherers from the Lower Sacramento Valley and San Francisco Bay. Ph.D. dissertation, Texas A&M University, College Station.

Barth, Frederik

1969   Introduction. In: *Ethnic Groups and Boundaries,* Frederik Barth, ed., pp. 9–38. Boston: Little, Brown and Company.

Barton, Huw, Robin Torrence, and Richard Fullagar

1998   Clues to Stone Tool Function Re-examined: Comparing Starch Grain Frequencies on Used and Unused Obsidian Artifacts. *Journal of Archaeological Science* 25(12):1231–1238.

Bass, William M.

1987   *Human Osteology: A Laboratory and Field Manual* (3d ed.). Springfield: Missouri Archaeological Society, Special Publication No. 2.

Bathurst, Rhonda R.

2005   Archaeological Evidence of Intestinal Parasites from Coastal Shell Middens. *Journal of Archaeological Science* 32(1):115–123.

Bathurst, Rhonda R., and Jodi Lynn Barta

2004   Molecular Evidence of Tuberculosis Induced Hypertrophic Osteopathy in a 16th-Century Iroquoian Dog. *Journal of Archaeological Science* 31(7):917–925.

Baud, C.-A., and Christiane Kramar

1991   Soft Tissue Calcifications in Paleopathology. In: *Human Paleopathology: Current Syntheses and Future Options,* Donald J. Ortner and Arthur C. Aufderheide, eds., pp. 87–89. Washington, D.C.: Smithsonian Institution Press.

Bean, Lowell J.

1972   *Mukat's People: The Cahuilla Indians of Southern California.* Berkeley: University of California Press.

1978   Cahuilla. In: *Handbook of North American Indians. Vol. 8: California,* Robert F. Heizer, ed., pp. 575–587. Washington, D.C.: Smithsonian Institution.

Bean, Lowell J., and William M. Mason

1962   *Diaries and Accounts of the Romero Expeditions in Arizona and California, 1823–1826.* Palm Springs: The Desert Museum.

Bean, Lowell J., and Katherine S. Saubel
1972   *Temalpakh: Cahuilla Indian Knowledge and Usage of Plants.* Banning, Calif.: Malki Museum Press.

Bean, Lowell J., Jerry Schaefer, and Sylvia Brakke Vane
1995   Archaeological, Ethnographic, and Ethnohistoric Investigations at Tahquitz Canyon, Palm Springs, California. Report on file at the Eastern Archaeological Information Center, University of California, Riverside.

Beattie, Owen
1995   The Results of Multidisciplinary Research into Preserved Human Tissues from the Franklin Arctic Expedition of 1845. In: *Proceedings of the First World Congress on Mummy Studies,* Vol. 2, pp. 579–586. Museo Arqueológico y Etnográfico de Tenerife.

Becker, Rory J.
2004   Eating Ethnicity: Examining 18th Century French Colonial Identity through Selective Consumption of Animal Resources in the North American Interior. Master's thesis, Department of Anthropology, Western Michigan University, Kalamazoo.

Begg, P. R.
1954   Stone Age Man's Dentition. *American Journal of Orthodontics* 40:298–312, 517–531.

Bell, John C., Stephen R. Palmer, and Jack M. Payne
1988   *The Zoonoses: Infections Transmitted from Animals to Man.* London: Edward Arnold.

Bell, Lynne S., Sheila J. Jones, and Alan Boyde
1991   Backscattered Electron Imaging of Diagenic Changes to Teeth and Related Alveolar Bone. In: *Archaeological Sciences 1989,* Paul Budd, Barbara Chapman, Caroline Jackson, Rob Janaway, and Barbara Ottaway, eds., pp. 345–351. Oxford: Oxbow Monograph 9.

Bello, Silvia M., Aminte Thomann, Michel Signoli, Olivier Dutour, and Peter Andrews
2005   Age and Sex Bias in the Reconstruction of Past Population Structures. *American Journal of Physical Anthropology* 129(1):24–38.

Benfer, Robert A., John T. Typpo, Vicki B. Graf, and Edward E. Pickett
1978   Mineral Analysis of Ancient Peruvian Hair. *American Journal of Physical Anthropology* 48(3):277–282.

Bennett, K. A.
1973   *Indians of Point of Pines, Arizona: A Comparative Study of Their Physical Characteristics.* Tucson: University of Arizona, Anthropological Papers, No. 23.
1975   *Skeletal Remains from Mesa Verde National Park, Colorado.* Washington, D.C.: National Park Service, Publications in Archaeology, 7F, Wetherill Mesa Studies.

Benninghoff, W. S.
1947   Use of Trisodium Phosphate with Herbarium Material and Microfossils in Peat. *Science* 183:1206–1207.

Benson, Larry, Linda Cordell, Kirk Vincent, Howard Taylor, John Stein, G. Lang Farmer, and Kiyoto Futa

2003   Ancient Maize from Chacoan Great Houses: Where Was It Grown? *Proceedings of the National Academy of Sciences* 100(22):13111–13115.

Benson, L. V., E. M. Hattori, H. E. Taylor, S. R. Poulson, and E. A. Jolie

2006   Isotope Sourcing of Prehistoric Willow and Tule Textiles Recovered from Western Great Basin Rock Shelters and Caves—Proof of Concept. *Journal of Archaeological Science* 33(11):1588–1599.

Bentley, R. Alexander, T. Douglas Price, and Elisabeth Stephan

2004   Determining the "Local" $^{87}Sr/^{86}Sr$ Range for Archaeological Skeletons: A Case Study from Neolithic Europe. *Journal of Archaeological Science* 31(4):365–375.

Berg, Gregory E.

2002   Last Meals: Recovering Abdominal Contents from Skeletonized Remains. *Journal of Archaeological Science* 29(12):1349–1365.

Berna, Francesco, Alan Matthews, and Stephen Weiner

2004   Solubilities of Bone Mineral from Archaeological Sites: The Recrystallization Window. *Journal of Archaeological Science* 31(7):867–882.

Bernard, H., L. Shoemaker, O. E. Craig, M. Rider, R. E. Parr, M. Q. Sutton, and R. M. Yohe II

2007   Introduction to the Analysis of Protein Residues in Archaeological Ceramics. In: *Theory and Practice of Archaeological Residue Analysis*, Hans Barnard and Jelmer W. Eerkens, eds., pp. 216–231. BAR International Series 1650.

Berry, D. R.

1985   Aspects of Paleodemography at Grasshopper Pueblo, Arizona. In: *Health and Disease in the Prehistoric Southwest*, C. Merbs and R. Miller, eds., pp. 43–64. Tempe: Arizona State University, Anthropological Research Papers, No. 34.

Bethell, Philip H.

1991   Inorganic Analysis of Organic Residues at Sutton Hoo. In: *Archaeological Sciences 1989*, Paul Budd, Barbara Chapman, Caroline Jackson, Rob Janaway, and Barbara Ottaway, eds. pp. 316–318. Oxford: Oxbow Monograph 9.

Bethell, Philip H., and Ian Máté

1989   The Use of Soil Phosphate Analysis in Archaeology: A Critique. In: *Scientific Analysis in Archaeology and Its Interpretation*, Julian Henderson, ed., pp. 1–29. Oxford: Oxford University Committee for Archaeology, Monograph No. 19.

Bethell, Philip H., and J. U. Smith

1989   Trace-Element Analysis of an Inhumation from Sutton Hoo, Using Inductively-Coupled Plasma Emission Spectrometry: An Evaluation of the Technique Applied to Analysis of Organic Residues. *Journal of Archaeological Science* 16(1):47–55.

Bethell, Philip H., Richard P. Evershed, and L. J. Goad

1993   The Investigation of Lipids in Organic Residues by Gas Chromatography/Mass Spectrometry: Applications to Paleodietary Studies. In: *Prehistoric Human Bone: Archaeology at the Molecular Level*, Joseph B. Lambert and Gisela Grupe, eds., pp. 229–255. Berlin: Springer-Verlag.

Bettinger, Robert L.

1975   The Surface Archaeology of Owens Valley, Eastern California: Prehistoric Man-Land Relationships in the Great Basin. Ph.D. dissertation, University of California, Riverside.

1991   *Hunter-Gatherers: Archaeological and Evolutionary Theory.* New York: Plenum Press.

Biers, William R., and Patrick E. McGovern

1990   *Organic Contents of Ancient Vessels: Materials Analysis and Archaeological Investigation.* Philadelphia: University of Pennsylvania, University Museum of Archaeology and Anthropology, MASCA Research Papers in Science and Archaeology, Vol. 7.

Binford, Lewis R.

1962   Archaeology as Anthropology. *American Antiquity* 28(2):217–225.

1968   Archaeological Perspectives. In: *New Perspectives in Archaeology,* Sally R. Binford and Lewis R. Binford, eds. pp. 5–33. Chicago: University of Chicago Press.

Blackburn, Roderic H.

1971   Honey in Okiek Personality, Culture, and Society. Ph.D. dissertation, Michigan State University, East Lansing.

1974   The Okiek and Their History. *Azania* 9:139–157.

1982a   *Okiek: Kenya's People.* London: Evans Brothers Limited.

1982b   In the Land of Milk and Honey: Okiek Adaptations to Their Forests and Neighbors. In: *Politics and History in Band Societies,* Eleanor Leacock and Richard Lee, eds., pp. 283–305. Cambridge: University of Cambridge Press.

Blackman, James, Marvin J. Allison, Arthur C. Aufderheide, Norman Oldroyd, and R. Ted Steinbock

1991   Secondary Hyperparathyroidism in an Andean Mummy. In: *Human Paleopathology: Current Syntheses and Future Options,* Donald J. Ortner and Arthur C. Aufderheide, eds., pp. 291–296. Washington, D.C.: Smithsonian Institution Press.

Blake, Michael, Brian S. Chisholm, John E. Clark, Barbara Voorhies, and Michael W. Love

1992   Prehistoric Subsistence in the Soconusco Region. *Current Anthropology* 33(1):83–94.

Blakely, Robert L.

1989   Bone Strontium in Pregnant and Lactating Females from Archaeological Samples. *American Journal of Physical Anthropology* 80(2):173–185.

Blakely, Robert L., and George J. Armelagos

1985   Deciduous Enamel Defects in Prehistoric Americans from Dickson Mounds: Prenatal and Postnatal Stress. *American Journal of Physical Anthropology* 66(4):371–380.

Bloch-Smith, Elizabeth

2003   Israelite Ethnicity in Iron I: Archaeology Preserves What Is Remembered and What Is Forgotten in Israel's History. *Journal of Biblical Literature* 122(3):401–425.

Blumenbach, Johann Friedrich

1969   *On the Natural Varieties of Mankind: De generis humani varietate nativa.* New York: Bergman (3d ed. of Goettingen, 1795).

Boas, Franz

1912   *Changes in Bodily Form of Descendants of Immigrants*. New York: Columbia University Press.

Bocek, Barbara

1986   Rodent Ecology and Burrowing Behavior: Predicted Effects on Archaeological Site Formation. *American Antiquity* 51(3):589–603.

Bocherens, Hervé

2000   Preservation of Isotopic Signals (^{13}C, ^{15}N) in Pleistocene Mammals. In: *Biogeochemical Approaches to Paleodietary Analysis*, Stanley H. Ambrose and M. Anne Katzenberg, eds., pp. 65–88. New York: Kluwer Academic/Plenum Publishers.

Bocherens, Hervé, and Dorothée G. Drucker

2003   Trophic Level Isotopic Enrichment of Carbon and Nitrogen in Bone Collagen: Case Studies from Recent and Ancient Terrestrial Ecosystems. *International Journal of Osteoarchaeology* 13(1–2):46–53.

Bocherens, Hervé, Marc Fizet, André Mariotti, Brigitt Lange-Badre, Bernard Vandermeersch, Jacques Paul Borel, and Georges Bellon

1991   Isotopic Biogeochemistry (^{13}C, ^{15}N) of Fossil Vertebrate Collagen: Application to the Study of a Past Food Web Including Neanderthal Man. *Journal of Human Evolution* 20(6):481–492.

Bocherens, Hervé, Daniel Billiou, André Mariotti, Marylène Patou-Mathis, Marcel Otte, Dominique Bonjean, and Michel Toussaint

1999   Palaeoenvironmental and Palaeodietary Implications of Isotopic Biogeochemistry of Last Interglacial Neanderthal and Mammal Bones in Scladina Cave (Belgium). *Journal of Archaeological Science* 26(6):599–607.

Bocherens, Hervé, Marjan Mashkour, Dorothée G. Drucker, Issam Moussa, and Daniel Billiou

2006   Stable Isotope Evidence for Palaeodiets in Southern Turkmenistan during the Historical Period and Iron Age. *Journal of Archaeological Science* 33(2):253–264.

Bocherens, Hervé, Caroline Polet, and Michel Toussaint

2007   Palaeodiet of Mesolithic and Neolithic Populations of Meuse Basin (Belgium): Evidence from Stable Isotopes. *Journal of Archaeological Science* 34(1):10–27.

Bocquet-Appel, J.-P., and C. Masset

1982   Farewell to Paleodemography. *Journal of Human Evolution* 11(4):321–333.

Boddington, A.

1987   From Bones to Population: The Problem of Numbers. In: *Death, Decay, and Reconstruction: Approaches to Archaeology and Forensic Science*, A. Boddington, A. N. Garland, and R. C. Janaway, eds., pp. 180–197. Manchester: Manchester University Press.

Bogaard, A., T.H.E. Heaton, P. Poulton, and I. Merbach

2007   The Impact of Manuring on Nitrogen Isotope Ratios in Cereals: Archaeological Implications for Reconstruction of Diet and Crop Management Practices. *Journal of Archaeological Science* 34(3):335–343.

Bökönyi, S.

1969   Archaeological Problems and Methods of Recognizing Animal Domestication. In: *The Domestication and Exploitation of Plants and Animals*, Peter J. Ucko and Geoffrey W. Dimbleby, eds., pp. 219–229. Chicago: Aldine Publishing Company.

Boldsen, Jesper L., George R. Milner, Lyle W. Konigsberg, and James W. Wood

2002   Transition Analysis: A New Method for Estimating Age from Skeletons. In: *Paleodemography: Age Distributions from Skeletal Samples*, Robert D. Hoppa and James W. Vaupel, eds., pp. 73–106. Cambridge: Cambridge University Press.

Bonnichsen, Robson

1996   Implications of Ancient DNA Research for First American Studies. Paper presented at the Great Basin Anthropological Conference, Kings Beach, California.

Bonnichson, Robson, Larry Hodges, Walter Ream, Katharine G. Field, Donna L. Kirner, Karen Selsor, and R. E. Taylor

2001   Methods for the Study of Ancient Hair: Radiocarbon Dates and Gene Sequences from Individual Hairs. *Journal of Archaeological Science* 28(7):775–785.

Boone, James L., and Eric Alden Smith

1998   Is It Evolution Yet? A Critique of Evolutionary Archaeology. *Current Anthropology* 39(supplement):141–173.

Boserup, Ester

1965   *Conditions of Agricultural Growth: The Economics of Agrarian Change under Population Pressure*. Chicago: Aldine Publishing Company.

Bösl, C., G. Grupe, and J. Peters

2006   A Late Neolithic Vertebrate Food Web Based on Stable Isotope Analyses. *International Journal of Osteoarchaeology* 16(4):296–315.

Bourbou, C., and M. P. Richards

2006   The Middle Byzantine Menu: Palaeodietary Information from Isotopic Analysis of Humans and Fauna from Kastella, Crete. *International Journal of Osteoarchaeology* 17(1):63–72.

Bourke, J. B.

1986   The Medical Investigation of Lindow Man. In: *Lindow Man: The Body in the Bog*, I. M. Stead, J. B. Bourke, and Don R. Brothwell, eds., pp. 46–51. Ithaca: Cornell University Press.

Bourque, Bruce J., and Harold W. Krueger

1994   Dietary Reconstruction from Human Bone Isotopes for Five Coastal New England Populations. In: *Paleonutrition: The Diet and Health of Prehistoric Americans*, Kristin D. Sobolik, ed., pp. 195–209. Carbondale: Southern Illinois University, Center for Archaeological Investigations, Occasional Paper No. 22.

Boutton, Thomas W., P. D. Klein, Mark J. Lynott, J. E. Price, and L. L. Tieszen

1984   Stable Isotope Ratios as Indicators of Prehistoric Human Diet. In: *Stable Isotopes in Nutrition*, Judith R. Turnlund and Phyllis E. Johnson, eds., pp. 191–204. Washington, D.C.: American Chemical Society.

Boutton, Thomas W., Mark J. Lynott, and M. Pamela Bumsted
1991   Stable Carbon Isotopes and the Study of Prehistoric Human Diet. *Critical Reviews in Food Science and Nutrition* 30(3):373–385.

Boyd, Donna C.
1996   Skeletal Correlates of Human Behavior in the Americas. *Journal of Archaeological Method and Theory* 3(3):189–251.

Brace, C. Loring
1982   The Roots of the Race Concept in American Physical Anthropology. In: *A History of American Physical Anthropology 1930–1980*, F. Spencer, ed., pp. 11–29. New York: Academic Press.

Braidwood, Linda, and Robert J. Braidwood (eds.)
1982   *Prehistoric Village Archaeology in South-Eastern Turkey: The Eight Millennium B.C. Site at Cayönü: Its Chipped and Ground Stone Industries and Faunal Remains*. Oxford: British Archaeological Reports, International Series 138.

Braidwood, Robert J.
1952   The Near East and the Foundations for Civilization. Condon Lectures, Oregon State System of Higher Education, University of Oregon, Eugene.

Braidwood, Robert J., and Linda Braidwood
1950   Jarmo: A Village of Early Farmers in Iraq. *Antiquity* 24(96):189–195.

Brandt, Elisabeth, Ingrid Wiechmann, and Gisela Grupe
2002   How Reliable Are Immunological Tools for the Detection of Ancient Proteins in Fossil Bones? *International Journal of Osteoarchaeology* 12(5):307–316.

Braun, Mark, Della Collins Cook, and Susan Pfeiffer
1998   DNA from *Mycobacterium tuberculosis* Complex Identified in North American, Pre-Columbian Human Skeletal Remains. *Journal of Archaeological Science* 25(3):271–277.

Bresciani, J., W. Dansgaard, B. Fredskild, M. Ghisler, P. Grandjean, J. C. Hansen, J. P. Hart Hansen, N. Haarløv, B. Lorentzen, P. Nansen, A. M. Rørdam, and H. Tauber
1991   Living Conditions. In: *The Greenland Mummies*, Jens Peder Hart Hansen, Jørgen Meldgaard, and Jørgen Nordqvist, eds., pp. 150–167. Washington, D.C.: Smithsonian Institution Press.

Brewer, Douglas J.
1992   Zooarchaeology: Method, Theory, and Goals. In: *Archaeological Method and Theory, Vol. 4*, Michael B. Schiffer, ed., pp. 195–244. Tucson: University of Arizona Press.

Brickley, Megan
2005   Rib Fractures in the Archaeological Record: A Useful Source of Sociocultural Information? *International Journal of Osteoarchaeology* 16(1):61–85.

Brickley, Megan, and Rachel Ives
2005   Skeletal Manifestations of Infantile Scurvy. *American Journal of Physical Anthropology* 129(2):163–172.

Brickley, Megan, Simon Mays, and Rachel Ives
2005   Skeletal Manifestations of Vitamin D Deficiency Osteomalacia in Documented Historical Collections. *International Journal of Osteoarchaeology* 15(6):389–403.

Brickley, Megan, Simon Mays, and Rachel Ives

2006   An Investigation of Skeletal Indicators of Vitamin D Deficiency in Adults: Effective Markers for Interpreting Past Living Conditions and Pollution Levels in 18th and 19th Century Birmingham, England. *American Journal of Physical Anthropology* 132(1):67–79.

Britton, Nathaniel Lord

1908   *North American Trees.* New York: H. Holt.

Briuer, Frederick L.

1976   New Clues to Stone Tool Function: Plant and Animal Residues. *American Antiquity* 41(4):478–484.

Broca, P.

1871   *Memoires d'anthropologie.* Paris: C. Reinwald.

1875   Instructions craniologiques et craniometriques. *Memoires de la Societe d Anthropologie de Paris, Series 2,* 2:1–203.

Brooks, Robert R., and Dieter Johannes

1990   *Phytoarchaeology.* Portland, Ore.: Dioscorides Press.

Brothwell, Don R.

1981   *Digging Up Bones* (3d ed.). Oxford: Oxford University Press.

1987   *The Bog Man and the Archaeology of People.* Cambridge: Harvard University Press.

1991   On Zoonoses and Their Relevance to Paleopathology. In: *Human Paleopathology: Current Syntheses and Future Options,* Donald J. Ortner and Arthur C. Aufderheide, eds., pp. 18–22. Washington, D.C.: Smithsonian Institution Press.

1999   Biosocial and Bio-Archaeological Aspects of Conflict and Warfare. In: *Ancient Warfare: Archaeological Perspectives,* John Carman and Anthony Harding, eds., pp. 25–38. Phoenix Mill, U.K.: Sutton Publishing.

Brothwell, Don R., and Patricia Brothwell

1998   *Food in Antiquity: A Survey of the Diet of Early Peoples* (2d ed.). Baltimore: Johns Hopkins University Press.

Brothwell, Don R., T. Holden, D. Liversage, B. Gottleib, P. Bennike, and J. Boesen

1990   Establishing a Minimum Damage Procedure for the Gut Sampling of Intact Human Bodies: The Case of the Huldremose Woman. *Antiquity* 64(245):830–835.

Broughton, Jack M.

1994   Late Holocene Resource Intensification in the Sacramento Valley, California: The Vertebrate Evidence. *Journal of Archaeological Science* 21:501–514.

1999   *Resource Depression and Intensification during the Late Holocene, San Francisco Bay: Evidence from the Emeryville Shellmound Vertebrate Fauna.* Berkeley: University of California Anthropological Records, 32.

Broughton, Jack M., and Frank E. Bayham

2003   Showing Off, Foraging Models, and the Ascendance of Large-Game Hunting in the California Middle Archaic. *American Antiquity* 68(4):783–789.

Broughton, Jack M., and James F. O'Connell

1999   On Evolutionary Ecology, Selectionist Archaeology, and Behavioral Archaeology. *American Antiquity* 64(1):153–165.

Brown, Keri A.

1998   Gender and Sex—What Can Ancient DNA Tell Us? *Ancient Biomolecules* 2(1):3–16.

2001   Identifying the Sex of Human Remains by Ancient DNA Analysis. *Ancient Biomolecules* 3(3):215–225.

Brown, Terrence A., and Keri A. Brown

1992   Ancient DNA and the Archaeologist. *Antiquity* 66(250):10–23.

Brown, Terrence A., Robin G. Allaby, Keri A. Brown, and Martin K. Jones

1993   Biomolecular Archaeology of Wheat: Past, Present and Future. *World Archaeology* 25(1):64–73.

Bryant, J. Daniel, Boas Luz, and Philip N. Froelich

1994   Oxygen Isotopic Composition of Fossil Horse Tooth Phosphate as a Record of Continental Paleoclimate. *Palaeogeography, Palaeoclimatology, Palaeoecology* 107(3–4):303–316.

Bryant, Vaughn M., Jr.

1974a   The Eric O. Callen Collection. *American Antiquity* 39(3):497–498.

1974b   Pollen Analysis of Prehistoric Human Feces from Mammoth Cave. In: *Archeology of the Mammoth Cave Area*, Patty Jo Watson, ed., pp. 203–209. New York: Academic Press.

1974c   Prehistoric Diet in Southwest Texas: The Coprolite Evidence. *American Antiquity* 39(3):407–420.

1975   Pollen as an Indicator of Prehistoric Diets in Coahuila, Mexico. *Bulletin of the Texas Archaeological Society* 46:87–106.

1994   Callen's Legacy. In: *Paleonutrition: The Diet and Health of Prehistoric Americans*, Kristin D. Sobolik, ed., pp. 151–160. Carbondale: Southern Illinois University, Center for Archaeological Investigations, Occasional Paper No. 22.

Bryant, Vaughn M., Jr., and Glenna W. Dean

2006   Archaeological Coprolite Science: The Legacy of Eric O. Callen (1912–1970). *Palaeogeography, Palaeoclimatology, Palaeoecology* 237:51–66.

Bryant, Vaughn M., Jr., and J. Philip Dering

1995   A Guide to Palaeoethnobotany. *Manitoba Archaeological Journal* 5(2):23–45.

Bryant, Vaughn M., Jr., and Richard G. Holloway

1983   The Role of Palynology in Archaeology. In: *Advances in Archaeological Method and Theory, Vol. 6*, Michael B. Schiffer, ed., pp. 191–224. New York: Academic Press.

Bryant, Vaughn M., Jr., and Glenna Williams-Dean

1975   The Coprolites of Man. *Scientific American* 232(1):100–109.

Buckland, Paul C., and Jon P. Sadler

1989   A Biogeography of the Human Flea, *Pulex irritans* L. (Siphonaptera:Pullicidae). *Journal of Biogeography* 16(2):115–120.

Buikstra, Jane E.

1977   Biocultural Dimensions of Archaeology Study: A Regional Perspective. In: *Biocultural Adaptation in Prehistoric America*, R. L. Blakely, ed., pp. 67–84. Athens: University of Georgia Press.

Buikstra, Jane E. (ed.)

1981   *Prehistoric Tuberculosis in the Americas.* Evanston: Northwestern University Archaeological Program.

Buikstra, Jane E., and Lane A. Beck

2006   *Bioarchaeology: The Contextual Analysis of Human Remains.* Amsterdam: Elsevier Academic Press.

Buikstra, Jane E., and James H. Mielke

1985   Demography, Diet, and Health. In: *The Analysis of Prehistoric Diets*, Robert I. Gilbert Jr. and James H. Mielke, eds., pp. 360–422. New York: Academic Press.

Buikstra, Jane E., and George R. Milner

1991   Isotopic and Archaeological Interpretations of Diet in the Central Mississippi Valley. *Journal of Archaeological Science* 18(3):319–329.

Buikstra, Jane E., and Douglas H. Ubelaker (eds.)

1994   *Standards for Data Collection from Human Skeletal Materials.* Fayetteville: Arkansas Archeological Survey, Research Series, No. 44.

Buikstra, Jane E., and Sloan Williams

1991   Tuberculosis in the Americas: Current Perspectives. In: *Human Paleopathology: Current Syntheses and Future Options*, Donald J. Ortner and Arthur C. Aufderheide, eds., pp. 161–172. Washington, D.C.: Smithsonian Institution Press.

Buikstra, Jane E., William Autry, Emanuel Breitburg, Leslie Eisenberg, and Nikolas van der Merwe

1988   Diet and Health in the Nashville Basin: Human Adaptation and Maize Agriculture in Middle Tennessee. In: *Diet and Subsistence: Current Archaeological Perspectives*, Brenda V. Kennedy and Genevieve M. LeMoine, eds., pp. 243–259. Proceedings of the Nineteenth Annual Chacmool Conference, University of Calgary.

Buikstra, Jane E., Susan Frankenberg, Joseph B. Lambert, and Liang Xue

1989   Multiple Elements: Multiple Expectations. In: *The Chemistry of Prehistoric Human Bone*, T. Douglas Price, ed., pp. 155–210. Cambridge: Cambridge University Press.

Bumsted, M. Pamela

1981   The Potential of Stable Carbon Isotopes in Bioarchaeological Archaeology. In: *Biocultural Adaptation: Comprehensive Approaches to Skeletal Analysis*, Debra L. Martin and M. Pamela Bumsted, eds., pp. 108–126. Amherst: University of Massachusetts, Research Reports, No. 20.

1985   Past Human Behavior from Bone Chemical Analysis—Respects and Prospects. *Journal of Human Evolution* 14(5):539–551.

Bunn, Henry T.

1991   A Taphonomic Perspective on the Archaeology of Human Origins. *Annual Review of Anthropology* 20:433–467.

Burger, J., R. Schoon, B. Zeike, S. Hummel, and B. Herrmann

2002   Species Determination Using Species-Discriminating PCR-RFLP of Ancient DNA from Prehistoric Skeletal Remains. *Ancient Biomolecules* 4(1):19–23.

Burger, Richard L., and Nikolaas van der Merwe

1990   Maize and the Origin of Highland Chavín Civilization: An Isotopic Perspective. *American Anthropologist* 92(1):85–95.

Burleigh, Richard, and Don R. Brothwell

1978   Studies on Amerindian Dogs: 1. Carbon Isotopes in Relation to Maize in the Diet of Domestic Dogs from Early Peru and Ecuador. *Journal of Archaeological Science* 5(4):355–362.

Burton, James H.

1996   Trace Elements in Bone as Paleodietary Indicators. In: *Archaeological Chemistry*, Mary Virginia Orna, ed., pp. 327–333. Washington, D.C.: American Chemical Society Symposium Series 625.

Burton, James H., and T. Douglas Price

1990   The Ratio of Barium to Strontium as a Paleodietary Indicator of the Consumption of Marine Resources. *Journal of Archaeological Science* 17(5):547–557.

1991   *Paleodietary Application of Barium Values in Bone.* In: *Archaeometry '90*, Ernst Pernicka and Günther A. Wagner, eds., pp. 787–795. Basel: Birkhäuser Verlag.

1999   Evaluation of Bone Strontium as a Measure of Seafood Consumption. *International Journal of Osteoarchaeology* 9(4):233–236.

2000   The Use and Abuse of Trace Elements for Paleodietary Research. In: *Biogeochemical Approaches to Paleodietary Analysis*, Stanley H. Ambrose and M. Anne Katzenberg, eds., pp. 159–171. New York: Kluwer Academic/Plenum Publishers.

Burton, James H., and Lori E. Wright

1995   Nonlinearity in the Relationship between Bone Sr/Ca and Diet: Paleodietary Implications. *American Journal of Physical Anthropology* 96(3):273–282.

Burton, James H., T. Douglas Price, and William D. Middleton

1999   Correlation of Bone Ba/Ca and Sr/Ca Due to Biological Purification of Calcium. *Journal of Archaeological Science* 26(6):609–616.

Burton, James H., T. Douglas Price, L. Cahue, and Lori E. Wright

2003   The Use of Barium and Strontium Abundances in Human Skeletal Tissues to Determine Their Geographic Origins. *International Journal of Osteoarchaeology* 13(1–2):88–95.

Buschan, G.

1895   *Vorgeschichtliche Botanik der Kultur-und Nutzpflanzen der alten Welt.* Breslau.

Bush, Helen, and Marek Zvelebil (eds.)

1991   *Health in Past Societies: Biocultural Interpretations of Human Skeletal Remains in Archaeological Context.* Oxford: British Archaeological Reports, International Series, No. 567.

Busvine, J. R.

1976   *Insects, Hygiene and History.* London: Athlone Press.

Butler, E. Ann

1988   The SEM and Seed Identification, with Particular Reference to the Vicieae. In: *Scanning Electron Microscopy in Archaeology*, Sandra L. Olsen, ed., pp. 215–224. Oxford: British Archaeological Reports, International Series, No. 452.

256 REFERENCES

Butler, Virginia L., and Nancy J. Bowers
1998   Ancient DNA from Salmon Bone: A Preliminary Study. *Ancient Biomolecules* 2(1):17–26.
Butler, Virginia L., and Roy A. Schroeder
1998   Do Digestive Processes Leave Diagnostic Traces on Fish Bones? *Journal of Archaeological Science* 25(10):957–971.
Cahill, G. F., Jr.
1986   The Future of Carbohydrates in Human Nutrition. *Nutritional Review* 44:40–43.
Calder, Angela M.
1977   Survival Properties of Organic Residues through the Human Digestive Tract. *Journal of Archaeological Science* 4(2):141–151.
Callen, Eric O.
1965   Food Habits of Some Pre-Columbian Mexican Indians. *Economic Botany* 19(4):335–343.
1967a   The First New World Cereal. *American Antiquity* 32(4):535–538.
1967b   Analysis of the Tehuacan Coprolites. In: *The Prehistory of the Tehuacan Valley*, Vol. 1, Douglas S. Byers, ed., pp. 261–289. Austin: University of Texas Press.
Callen, Eric O., and T.W.M. Cameron
1960   A Prehistoric Diet Revealed in Coprolites. *New Scientist* 8(190):35–40.
Callen, Eric O., and Paul S. Martin
1969   Plant Remains from Some Coprolites from Utah. *American Antiquity* 34(3):329–331.
Cannon, Aubrey, Henry P. Schwarcz, and Martin Knyf
1999   Marine-Based Subsistence Trends and the Stable Isotope Analysis of Dog Bones from Namu, British Columbia. *Journal of Archaeological Science* 26(4):399–407.
Cannon, Debbi Y.
1987   *Marine Fish Osteology: A Manual for Archaeologists.* Burnaby, British Columbia: Department of Archaeology, Simon Fraser University Publication 18.
Canti, M. G.
1997   An Investigation of Microscopic Calcareous Spherulites from Herbivore Dungs. *Journal of Archaeological Science* 24(3):219–231.
1998   The Micromorphological Identification of Faecal Spherulites from Archaeological and Modern Materials. *Journal of Archaeological Science* 25(5):435–444.
1999   The Production and Preservation of Faecal Spherulites: Animals, Environment, and Taphonomy. *Journal of Archaeological Science* 26(3):251–258.
Capasso, L., G. Di Tota, K. W. Jones, and C. Tuniz
1995   Synchrotron Radiation Microprobe Analysis of Human Dental Calculi from an Archaeological Site: A New Possible Perspective in Palaeonutritional Studies. *International Journal of Osteoarchaeology* 5(3):282–288.
Carbone, Victor, and Bennie C. Keel
1985   Preservation of Plant and Animal Remains. In: *The Analysis of Prehistoric Diets*, Robert I. Gilbert Jr. and James H. Mielke, eds., pp. 1–20. New York: Academic Press.

Carlson, Arne K.

1996   Lead Isotope Analysis of Human Bone for Addressing Cultural Affinity: A Case
Study from Rocky Mountain House, Alberta. *Journal of Archaeological Science*
23(4):557–567.

Carlson, David S., and Dennis P. Van Gerven

1979   Diffusion, Biological Determinism, and Biocultural Adaptation in the Nubian
Corridor. *American Anthropologist* 81(3):561–580.

Carlson, David S., George J. Armelagos, and Dennis P. Van Gerven

1974   Factors Influencing the Etiology of Cribra Orbitalia in Prehistoric Sudan. *Journal of Human Evolution* 3(5):405–410.

Casteel, Richard W.

1972   Some Archaeological Uses of Fish Remains. *American Antiquity* 37(3):404–419.

1974   A Method for Estimation of Live Weight of Fish from the Size of Skeletal Elements. *American Antiquity* 39(1):94–98.

1976   *Fish Remains in Archaeology and Paleo-Environmental Studies.* New York: Academic Press.

Catling, Dorothy, and John Grayson

1982   *Identification of Vegetable Fibers.* London: Chapman and Hall.

Cattaneo, C., K. Gelsthorpe, P. Phillips, and R. J. Sokol

1993   Blood Residues on Stone Tools: Indoor and Outdoor Experiments. *World Archaeology* 25(1):29–43.

Cattaneo, C., K. Gelsthorpe, R. J. Sokol, and P. Phillips

1994   Immunological Detection of Albumin in Ancient Human Cremations using
ELISA and Monoclonal Antibodies. *Journal of Archaeological Science* 21(4):565–571.

Cattaneo, C., K. Gelsthorpe, P. Phillips, and R. J. Sokol

1995   Differential Survival of Albumin in Ancient Bone. *Journal of Archaeological Science* 22(2):271–276.

Caywood, L. R., and E. H. Spicer (eds.)

1935   Tuzigoot: The Excavation and Repair of a Ruin on the Verde River near Clarkdale, Arizona. Washington, D.C.: National Park Service.

Chalfoun, David J., and Noreen Tuross

1999   Botanical Remains: Utility in Protein and DNA Research. *Ancient Biomolecules*
3(1):67–79.

Charters, S., Richard P. Evershed, A Quye, P. W. Blinkhorn, and V. Reeves

1997   Simulation Experiments for Determining the Use of Ancient Pottery Vessels: The
Behaviour of Epicticular Leaf Wax during Boiling of a Leafy Vegetable. *Journal
of Archaeological Science* 24(1):1–7.

Chase, Debra A.

1991   Evidence of Disease in Ancient Near Eastern Texts: Leprosy in the Epilogue
to the Code of Hammurapi? In: *Human Paleopathology: Current Syntheses and*

Future Options, Donald J. Ortner and Arthur C. Aufderheide, eds., pp. 200–204. Washington, D.C.: Smithsonian Institution Press.

Chatters, James C.

2001   *Ancient Encounters: Kennewick Man and the First Americans*. New York: Simon & Schuster.

Chaya, Henry J.

1996   Studies of Soils from an Aleutian Island Site. In: *Archaeological Chemistry*, Mary Virginia Orna, ed., pp. 131–138. Washington, D.C.: American Chemical Society Symposium Series 625.

Chege, Nancy, David J. Sartoris, Rose Tyson, and Donald Resnick

1996   Imaging Evaluation of Skull Trepanation Using Radiography and CT. *International Journal of Osteoarchaeology* 6(3):249–258.

Child, Angela M., and A. Mark Pollard

1992   A Review of the Applications of Immunochemistry to Archaeological Bone. *Journal of Archaeological Science* 19(1):39–47.

1995   Immunochemistry Applied to Archaeology. In: *Science in Archaeology: A Review*, by Patrick E. McGovern, pp. 132–136. *American Journal of Archaeology* 99(1):79–142.

Chisholm, Brian S.

1989   Variation in Diet Reconstructions Based on Stable Carbon Isotope Evidence. In: *The Chemistry of Prehistoric Human Bone*, T. Douglas Price, ed., pp. 10–37. Cambridge: Cambridge University Press.

Chisholm, Brian S., and R. G. Matson

1994   Carbon and Nitrogen Isotopic Evidence on Basketmaker II Diet at Cedar Mesa, Utah. *Kiva* 60(2):239–255.

Cipriani, L.

1966   *The Andaman Islanders*. London: George Weindenfeld and Nicolson.

Claassen, Cheryl

1998   *Shells*. Cambridge: Cambridge Manuals in Archaeology, Cambridge University Press.

2002   Gender and Archaeology. In: *Archaeology: Original Readings in Method and Practice*, Peter N. Peregrine, Carol R. Ember, and Melvin Ember, eds., pp. 210–224. Uppder Saddle River, N.J.: Prentice Hall.

Clarke, David L.

1968   *Analytical Archaeology*. London: Muthuen and Company.

Clayton, Fiona, Judith Sealy, and Susan Pfeiffer

2006   Weaning Age among Foragers at Matjes River Rock Shelter, South Africa, from Stable Nitrogen and Carbon Isotope Analyses. *American Journal of Physical Anthropology* 129(2):311–317.

Cleland, Charles E.

1976   The Focal-Diffuse Model: An Evolutionary Perspective on the Prehistoric Cultural Adaptations of the Eastern United States. *Mid-Continental Journal of Archaeology* 1(1):59–76.

Clementz, Mark T., Peter Holden, and Paul L. Koch
2003   Are Calcium Isotopes a Reliable Monitor of Trophic Level in Marine Settings? *International Journal of Osteoarchaeology* 13(1–2):29–36.

Cockburn, Aidan
1971   Infectious Diseases in Ancient Populations. *Current Anthropology* 12(1):45–62.

Cockburn, Aidan, and Eve Cockburn (eds.)
1980   *Mummies, Disease, and Ancient Cultures* (1st ed.). Cambridge: Cambridge University Press.

Cockburn, Aidan, Eve Cockburn, and Theodore A. Reyman (eds.)
1998   *Mummies, Disease, and Ancient Cultures* (2d ed.). Cambridge: Cambridge University Press.

Codron, Jacqui, Daryl Codron, Julia A. Lee-Thorp, Matt Sponheimer, William J. Bond, Darryl de Ruiter, and Rina Grant
2005   Taxonomic, Anatomical, and Spatio-Temporal Variations in the Stable Carbon and Nitrogen Isotopic Compositions of Plants from an African Savanna. *Journal of Archaeological Science* 32(12):1757–1772.

Cohen, Alan, and Dale Serjeantson
1986   *A Manual for the Identification of Bird Bones from Archaeological Sites.* London: Jubilee Printers.

Cohen, Mark N., and George J. Armelagos (eds.)
1984   *Paleopathology at the Origins of Agriculture.* Orlando, Fla.: Academic Press.

Colley, Sara M.
1990   The Analysis and Interpretation of Archaeological Fish Remains. In: *Archaeological Method and Theory,* Vol. 2, Michael B. Schiffer, ed., pp. 207–253. Tucson: University of Arizona Press.

Collins, Matthew J., Michael S. Riley, Angela M. Child, and Gordon Turner-Walker
1995   A Basic Mathematical Simulation of the Chemical Degradation of Ancient Collagen. *Journal of Archaeological Science* 22(2):175–183.

Colson, I. B., M. B. Richards, J. F. Bailey, and Bryan C. Sykes
1997   DNA Analysis of Seven Human Skeletons Excavated from the Terp of Wijnaldum. *Journal of Archaeological Science* 24(10):911–917.

Coltrain, Joan Brenner, M. Geoffrey Hayes, and Dennis H. O'Rourke
2004   Sealing, Whaling and Caribou: The Skeletal Isotope Chemistry of Eastern Arctic Foragers. *Journal of Archaeological Science* 31(1):39–57.

Comar, C. L., R. Scott Russell, and R. H. Wasserman
1957   Strontium-Calcium Movement from Soil to Man. *Science* 126:485–492.

Commisso, R. G., and D. E. Nelson
2007   Patterns of Plant $\delta^{15}N$ Values on a Greenland Norse Farm. *Journal of Archaeological Science* 34(3):440–450.

Committee on Dietary Allowances
1980   *Recommended Dietary Allowances.* Washington, D.C.: National Academy of Sciences.

Confalonieri, U.C.E., L. F. Ferreira, A.J.G. Araújo, M. Chame, and B. M. Ribeiro Filho

1991   Trends and Perspectives in Paleoparasitological Research. In: *Human Paleopa-thology: Current Syntheses and Future Options*, Donald J. Ortner and Arthur C. Aufderheide, eds., pp. 76–78. Washington, D.C.: Smithsonian Institution Press.

Conkey, Margaret W., and Joan M. Gero

1997   Programme to Practice: Gender and Feminism in Archaeology. *Annual Review of Anthropology* 26:411–437.

Conkey, Margaret W., and Janet D. Spector

1984   Archaeology and the Study of Gender. In: *Advances in Archaeological Method*, Vol. 7, Michael J. Schiffer, ed., pp. 1–38. New York: Academic Press.

Conlogue, Gerald

2002   More TB in Peruvian Mummies. *Archaeology* 55(2):14.

Connolly, R. C.

1986   The Anatomical Description of Lindow Man. In: *Lindow Man: The Body in the Bog*, I. M. Stead, J. B. Bourke, and Don R. Brothwell, eds., pp. 54–62. Ithaca: Cornell University Press.

Connolly, R. C., Richard P. Evershed, G. Embery, J. B. Stanbury, D. Green, P. Beahan, and J. B. Shortfall

1986   The Chemical Composition of Some Body Tissues. In: *Lindow Man: The Body in the Bog*, I. M. Stead, J. B. Bourke, and Don R. Brothwell, eds., pp. 72–76. Ithaca: Cornell University Press.

Cook, Delta Collins, and Kevin D. Hunt

1998   Sex Differences in Trace Elements: Status or Self-Selection? In: *Sex and Gender in Paleopathological Perspective*, Anne L. Grauer and Patricia Stuart-Macadam, eds., pp. 64–78. Cambridge: Cambridge University Press.

Cook, S. F., and Robert F. Heizer

1962   Chemical Analysis of the Hotchkiss Site (CCo-138). *Reports of the University of California Archaeological Survey* 57:1–25.

1965   *Studies on the Chemical Analysis of Archaeological Sites*. Berkeley: University of California Publications in Anthropology, Vol. 2.

Cordell, Linda S., Stephen R. Durand, Ronald C. Antweiler, and Howard E. Taylor

2001   Toward Linking Maize Chemistry to Archaeological Agricultural Sites in the North American Southwest. *Journal of Archaeological Science* 28(5):501–513.

Core, H., W. Core, and A. Day

1979   *Wood Structure and Identification* (2d ed.). New York: Syracuse University Press.

Corr, Lorna T., Judith C. Sealy, Mark C. Horton, and Richard P. Evershed

2005   A Novel Marine Dietary Indicator Utilising Compound-Specific Bone Collagen Amino Acid $\delta^{13}C$ Values of Ancient Humans. *Journal of Archaeological Science* 32(3):321–330.

Corruccini, Robert S., Arthur C. Aufderheide, Jerome S. Handler, and Lorentz E. Wittmers Jr.

1987   Patterning of Skeletal Lead Content in Barbados Slaves. *Archaeometry* 29(2):233–239.

Corruccini, Robert S., Elizabeth M. Brandon, and Jerome S. Handler

1989   Inferring Fertility from Relative Mortality in Historically Controlled Cemetery
        Remains from Barbados. *American Antiquity* 54(3):609–614.

Costin, Cathy L.

1996   Exploring the Relationship between Gender and Craft in Complex Societies:
        Methodological and Theoretical Issues of Gender Attribution. In: *Gender and
        Archaeology*, Rita P. Wright, ed., pp. 111–140. Philadelphia: University of Pennsyl-
        vania Press.

2002   Cloth Production and Gender Relations in the Inka Empire. In: *Archaeology:
        Original Readings in Method and Practice*, Peter N. Peregrine, Carol R. Ember,
        and Melvin Ember, eds., pp. 261–279. Upper Saddle River, N.J.: Prentice Hall.

Cox, Glenda, Judith Sealy, Carmel Schire, and Alan Morris

2001   Stable Carbon and Nitrogen Isotopic Analyses of the Underclass at the Colonial
        Cape of Good Hope in the Eighteenth and Nineteenth Centuries. *World Archae-
        ology* 33(1):73–97.

Cox, Margaret, and Simon Mays (eds.)

2000   *Human Osteology in Archaeology and Forensic Science*. Cambridge: Cambridge
        University Press.

Coyston, Shannon, Christine D. White, and Henry P. Schwarcz

1999   Dietary Carbonate Analysis of Bone and Enamel for Two Sites in Belize. In:
        Reconstructing Ancient Maya Diet, Christine D. White, ed., pp. 221–243. Salt
        Lake City: University of Utah Press.

Crabtree, Pam J.

1990   Zooarchaeology and Complex Societies: Some Uses of Faunal Analysis for the
        Study of Trade, Social Statue, and Ethnicity. In: *Archaeological Method and Theory*,
        Vol. 2, Michael B. Schiffer, ed., pp. 155–205. Tucson: University of Arizona Press.

Crabtree, Robert H.

1981   Archaeology. In: *A Cultural Resources Overview of the Colorado Desert Planning
        Units*, by Elizabeth von Till Warren, Robert H. Crabtree, Claude N. Warren,
        Martha Knack, and Richard McCarty, pp. 25–54. Riverside, Calif.: Bureau of
        Land Management, Cultural Resources Publications, Anthropology–History.

Craig, Oliver E., G. Taylor, J. Mulville, Matthew J. Collins, and M. Parker Pearson

2005   The Identification of Prehistoric Dairying Activities in the Western Isles of Scot-
        land: An Integrated Biomolecular Approach. *Journal of Archaeological Science*
        32(1):91–103.

Craig, Oliver E., R. Ross, Søren H. Andersen, Nicky Milner, and Geoff N. Bailey

2006   Focus: Sulphur Isotope Variation in Archaeological Marine Fauna from North-
        ern Europe. *Journal of Archaeological Science* 33(11):1642–1646.

Crane, Cathy J., and H. Sorayya Carr

1994   The Integration and Quantification of Economic Data from a Late Preclassic
        Maya Community in Belize. In: *Paleonutrition: The Diet and Health of Prehis-
        toric Americans*, Kristin D. Sobolik, ed., pp. 66–79. Carbondale: Southern Illinois
        University, Center for Archaeological Investigations, Occasional Paper No. 22.

Crane, Eve

1975   *Honey: A Comprehensive Survey*. London: Heinemann.

1980   *A Book of Honey*. New York: Charles Scribner's Sons.

Cronk, Lee

1989a   The Behavioral Ecology of Change among the Mukogodo of Kenya. Ph.D. dissertation, Northwestern University, Evanston/Chicago.

1989b   From Hunters to Herders: Subsistence Change as a Reproductive Strategy among the Mukogodo. *Current Anthropology* 30(2):224–234.

1989c   Low Socioeconomic Status and Female-Biased Parental Investment: The Mukogodo Example. *American Anthropologist* 91(2):414–429.

2004   *From Mukogodo to Masai: Ethnicity and Cultural Change in Kenya*. Boulder, Colo.: Westview Press.

Cross, J. F., N. W. Keer, and M. F. Morris

1986   An Evaluation of Scott's Method for Scoring Dental Wear. In: *Teeth and Anthropology*, E. Cruwys and R. A. Foley, eds., pp. 101–108. Oxford: British Archaeological Reports, International Series, No. 291.

Cruwys, E., and R. A. Foley (eds.)

1986   *Teeth and Anthropology*. Oxford: British Archaeological Reports, International Series, No. 291.

Cummings, Linda Scott

1989   Coprolites from Medieval Christian Nubia: An Interpretation of Diet and Nutritional Stress. Ph.D. dissertation, University of Colorado, Boulder.

1994   Anasazi Diet: Variety in the Hoy House and Lion House Coprolite Record and Nutritional Analysis. In: *Paleonutrition: The Diet and Health of Prehistoric Americans*, Kristin D. Sobolik, ed., pp. 134–150. Carbondale: Southern Illinois University, Center for Archaeological Investigations, Occasional Paper No. 22.

1996   Pollen Analysis of CA-SBR-1913, California. In: *Archaeological Investigations at Guapiabit, CA-SBR-1913*, by Mark Q. Sutton and Joan S. Schneider, appendix, pp. 74–76. San Bernardino County Museum Association Quarterly 43(4).

Cummings, Linda Scott, Kathryn Puseman, and Richard A. Marlar

1996   Removing Protein Residue from Artifacts: A Critical First Step. Paper presented at the annual meeting of the Society for American Archaeology, New Orleans.

Cunha, Eugénia, Marie-Laure Fily, Isabelle Clisson, Ana Luísa Santos, Ana Marie Silva, Cláudia Umbelino, Paulo César, Artur Corte-Real, Eric Crubézy, and Bertrand Ludes

2000   Children at the Convent: Comparing Historical Data, Morphology and DNA Extracted from Ancient Tissues for Sex Diagnosis at Santa Calra-a-Velha (Coimbra, Portugal). *Journal of Archaeological Science* 27(10):949–952.

Curtis, Edward S.

1926   The Cahuilla. In: *The North American Indian*, Vol. 15, pp. 21–38. Published by Edward S. Curtis (reprinted by Johnson Reprint Corporation in 1970).

Dahlberg, Albert A.

1991   Interpretations of General Problems in Amelogenesis. In: *Human Paleopathology: Current Syntheses and Future Options*, Donald J. Ortner and Arthur C.

Aufderheide, eds., pp. 269–272. Washington, D.C.: Smithsonian Institution Press.

Dailey, R. C.

1983   Osteology for the Investigator. In: *Handbook of Forensic Archaeology and Anthropology*, D. Morse, J. Duncan, and J. Stoutamire, eds., pp. 76–85. Tallahassee: Florida State University Foundation, Inc.

Daly, Patricia

1969   Approaches to Faunal Analysis in Archaeology. *American Antiquity* 34(2): 146–153.

Danforth, Marie Elaine

1999   Coming Up Short: Stature and Nutrition among the Ancient Maya of the Southern Lowlands. In: *Reconstructing Ancient Maya Diet*, Christine D. White, ed., pp. 103–117. Salt Lake City: University of Utah Press.

Danforth, Marie Elaine, Della Collins Cook, and Stanley G. Knick III

1994   The Human Remains from Carter Ranch Pueblo, Arizona: Health in Isolation. *American Antiquity* 59(1):88–101.

Danielson, Dennis R.

1993   The Role of Phytoliths in Prehistoric Diet Reconstruction and Dental Attrition. Master's thesis, University of Nebraska, Lincoln.

Davenport, Christian, and Mike Ruddell

1995   Identification of Equus Species, Based on Bone Histology (abstract). *Journal of Vertebrate Palenotology* 15:25a.

Davies, G. R., and A. Mark Pollard

1988   Organic Residues in an Anglo-Saxon Grave. In: *Science and Archaeology, Glasgow 1987*, Elizabeth A. Slater and James O. Tate, eds., pp. 391–402. Oxford: British Archaeological Reports, British Series, No. 196 (2 vols.).

Davis, Simon J. M.

1987   *The Archaeology of Animals*. New Haven: Yale University Press.

Day, S. P.

1996   Dogs, Deer and Diet at Star Carr: A Reconsideration of C-Isotope Evidence from Early Mesolithic Dog Remains from the Vale of Pickering, Yorkshire, England. *Journal of Archaeological Science* 23(5):783–787.

Dean, Glenna

1993   Use of Pollen Concentrations in Coprolite Analysis: An Archaeobotanical Viewpoint with a Comment to Reinhard et al. (1991). *Journal of Ethnobiology* 13(1):102–114.

de Candolle, Alphonse

1884   *Origin of Cultivated Plants*. London: Kegan Paul.

deFrance, Susan D., William F. Keegan, and Lee A. Newsom

1996   The Archaeobotanical, Bone Isotope, and Zooarchaeological Records from Caribbean Sites in Comparative Perspective. In: *Case Studies in Environmental Archaeology*, Elizabeth J. Reitz, Lee A. Newsom, and Sylvia J. Scudder, eds., pp. 289–304. New York: Plenum Press.

DeGusta, David, and Tim D. White

1996   On the Use of Skeletal Collections for DNA Analysis. *Ancient Biomolecules* 1(1):89–92.

DeLeon, Valerie B.

2006   Fluctuating Asymmetry and Stress in a Medieval Nubian Population. *American Journal of Physical Anthropology* 132(4):520–534.

Delgado-Darias, T., J. Velasco-Vásquez, M. Arnay-de-la-Rosa, E. Martín-Rodríquez, and E. González-Reimers

2006   Calculus, Periodontal Disease and Tooth Decay among the Prehispanic Population from Gran Canaria. *Journal of Archaeological Science* 33(5):663–670.

DeNiro, Michael J.

1985   Postmortem Preservation and Lateration of *in vivo* Bone Collagen Isotope Ratios in Relation to Paleodietary Reconstruction. *Nature* 317:806–809.

1987   Stable Isotopy and Archaeology. *American Scientist* 75(2):182–191.

1988   Marine Food Sources for Prehistoric Coastal Peruvian Camilids: Isotopic Evidence and Implications. In: *Economic Prehistory of the Central Andes*, Elizabeth S. Wing and Jane C. Wheeler, eds., pp. 119–129. Oxford: British Archaeological Reports, International Series, No. 427.

DeNiro, Michael J., and Samuel Epstein

1978   Influence of Diet on the Distribution of Carbon Isotopes in Animals. *Geochimica et Cosmochimica Acta* 42(5):495–506.

1981   Influence of Diet on the Distribution of Nitrogen Isotopes in Animals. *Geochimica et Cosmochimica Acta* 45(3):341–351.

DeNiro, Michael J., and Christine A. Hastorf

1985   Alteration of $^{15}N/^{14}N$ and $^{13}C/^{12}C$ Ratios of Plant Matter during the Initial Stages of Diagenesis: Studies Utilizing Archaeological Specimens from Peru. *Geochimica et Cosmochimica Acta* 49(1):97–115.

DeNiro, Michael J., and Margaret J. Schoeninger

1983   Stable Carbon and Nitrogen Isotope Ratios of Bone Collagen: Variations within Individuals, between Sexes, and within Populations Raised on Monotonous Diets. *Journal of Archaeological Science* 10(3):199–203.

DeNiro, Michael J., Margaret J. Schoeninger, and Christine A. Hastorf

1985   Effect of Heating on the Stable Carbon and Nitrogen Isotope Ratios of Bone Collagen. *Journal of Archaeological Science* 12(1):1–7.

Dennell, R. W.

1970   Seeds from a Medieval Sewer in Woolster Street, Plymouth. *Economic Botany* 24(2):151–154.

1979   Prehistoric Diet and Nutrition: Some Food for Thought. *World Archaeology* 11(2):121–135.

Dequeker, Jan

1991   Paleopathology of Rheumatism in Paintings. In: *Human Paleopathology: Current Syntheses and Future Options*, Donald J. Ortner and Arthur C. Aufderheide, eds., pp. 216–221. Washington, D.C.: Smithsonian Institution Press.

Derrick, S. McCormick

1994   Evidence of Association between Cranial Modeling and Supra-Inion Depressions. Paper presented at the annual meeting of the American Association of Physical Anthropologists, Denver.

DeSalle, Rob, John Gatesy, Ward Wheeler, and David Grimaldi

1992   DNA Sequences from a Fossil Termite in Oligo-Miocene Amber and Their Phylogenetic Implications. *Science* 257:1933–1936.

Dimbleby, Geoffrey W.

1978   *Plants and Archaeology.* Boulder: Paladin.

1985   *The Palynology of Archaeological Sites.* London: Academic Press.

Dinan, Elizabeth H., and Ralph M. Rowlett

1993   Vegetational Changes at the Shriver Paleo-Indian Site, N.W. Missouri: Phytolith Analysis as an Aid in Environmental Reconstruction. In: *Current Research in Phytolith Analysis: Applications in Archaeology and Paleoecology*, Deborah M. Pearsall and Dolores R. Piperno, eds., pp. 73–82. Philadelphia: University of Pennsylvania, University Museum of Archaeology and Anthropology, MASCA Research Papers in Science and Archaeology, Vol. 10.

Dittrick, Jean, and Judy Myers Suchey

1986   Sex Determination of Prehistoric Central California Skeletal Remains Using Discriminant Analysis of the Femur and Humerus. *American Journal of Physical Anthropology* 70(1):3–9.

Dixon, Ronald A., and Charlotte A. Roberts

2001   Modern and Ancient Scourges: The Application of Ancient DNA to the Analysis of Tuberculosis and Leprosy from Archaeologically Derived Human Remains. *Ancient Biomolecules* 3(3):181–193.

Dobney, Keith, and Don R. Brothwell

1986   Dental Calculus: Its Relevance to Ancient Diet and Oral Ecology. In: *Teeth and Anthropology*, E. Cruwys and R. A. Foley, eds., pp. 55–81. Oxford: British Archaeological Reports, International Series, No. 291.

Dobney, Keith, and Anton Ervynck

2000   Interpreting Developmental Stress in Archaeological Pigs: The Chronology of Linear Enamel Hypoplasia. *Journal of Archaeological Science* 27(7): 597–607.

Downs, Elinor F., and Jerold M. Lowenstein

1995   Identification of Archaeological Blood Proteins: A Cautionary Note. *Journal of Archaeological Science* 22(1):11–16.

Dowson, Thomas A. (ed.)

2000   Why Queer Archaeology? An Introduction. *World Archaeology* 32(2):161–165.

Draper, H. H.

1977   The Aboriginal Eskimo Diet in Modern Perspective. *American Anthropologist* 79(2):309–316.

1980   Nutrition. In: *The Human Biology of Circumpolar Populations*, F. A. Milan, ed., pp. 257–284. Cambridge: Cambridge University Press.

Drucker, Dorothée G., and Hervé Bocherens

2004   Carbon and Nitrogen Stable Isotopes as Tracers of Change in Diet Breadth during Middle and Upper Palaeolithic in Europe. *International Journal of Osteoarchaeology* 14(3–4):162–177.

Drucker, Philip

1937   *Culture Element Distributions: V*, Southern California. University of California
Anthropological Records 1(1).

Dudar, J. C., J. S. Waye, and S. R. Saunders

2003   Determination of a Kinship System Using Ancient DNA, Mortuary Practice, and
Historic Records in an Upper Canadian Pioneer Cemetery. *International Journal
of Osteoarchaeology* 13(4):232–246.

Dudd, Stephanie N., Richard P. Evershed, and Alex M. Gibson

1999   Evidence for Varying Patterns of Exploitation of Animal Products in Different
Prehistoric Pottery Traditions Based on Lipids Preserved in Surface and Absorbed
Residues. *Journal of Archaeological Science* 26(12):1473–1482.

Dufour, Elise, Hervé Bocherens, and André Mariotti

1999   Paleodietary Implications of Isotopic Variability in Eurasian Lacustrine Fish.
Journal of Archaeological Science 26(6):617–627.

Dufour, Elise, Chris Holmden, Wim Van Neer, Antoine Zazzo, William P. Patterson,
Patrick Degryse, and Eddy Keppens

2007   Oxygen and Strontium Isotopes and Provenance Indicators of Fish at Archaeological Sites: The Case Study of Salalassos, SW Turkey. *Journal of Archaeological
Science* 34(8):1226–1239.

Dunn, Frederick L.

1968   Epidemiological Factors: Health and Disease in Hunter-Gatherers. In: *Man the Hunter*,
Richard B. Lee and Irven DeVore, eds., pp. 221–228. Chicago: Aldine-Atherton.

Dunn, Frederick L., and R. Watkins

1970   Parasitological Examinations of Prehistoric Human Coprolites from Lovelock
Cave, Nevada. In: *Archaeology and the Prehistoric Great Basin Lacustrine Subsistence Regime as Seen from Lovelock Cave, Nevada*, by Robert F. Heizer and
Lewis K. Napton, pp. 176–185. Berkeley: Contributions of the University of California Archaeological Research Facility, No. 10.

Dupras, Tosha L., and Henry P. Schwarcz

2001   Strangers in a Strange Land: Stable Isotope Evidence for Human Migration in
the Dakhleh Oasis, Egypt. *Journal of Archaeological Science* 28(11):1199–1208.

Duray, Stephen M.

1990   Deciduous Enamel Defects and Caries Susceptibility in a Prehistoric Ohio Population. *American Journal of Physical Anthropology* 81(1):27–34.

1996   Dental Indicators of Stress and Reduced Age at Death in Prehistoric Native
Americans. *American Journal of Physical Anthropology* 99(2):275–286.

Dürrwächter, Claudia, Oliver E. Craig, Matthew J. Collins, Joachim Burger, and Kurt W. Alt

2006   Beyond the Grave: Variability in Neolithic Diets in Southern Germany? *Journal
of Archaeological Science* 33(1):39–48.

Eaton, S. B., and M. Konner

1985   Paleolithic Nutrition: A Consideration of Its Nature and Current Implications. *New England Journal of Medicine* 312:283–289.

Edward, Jeremy B., and Robert A. Benfer

1993   The Effects of Diagenesis on the Paloma Skeletal Material. In: *Investigations of Ancient Human Tissue: Chemical Analyses in Anthropology*, Mary K. Sandford, ed., pp. 183–268. Langhorne, Penn.: Gordon and Breach.

Efremov, Ivan

1940   Taphonomy: A New Branch of Paleontology. *Pan-American Geologist* 74(2):81–93.

Eglinton, Geoffrey, and Graham A. Logan

1991   Molecular Preservation. *Philosophical Transactions of the Royal Society of London* 333(1268):315–328.

Ehrenberg, Margaret

1989   *Women in Prehistory*. Norman: University of Oklahoma Press.

Eidt, Robert C.

1973   A Rapid Chemical Field Test for Archaeological Site Surveying. *American Antiquity* 38(2):206–210.

Eisele, J. A., D. D. Fowler, G. Haynes, and R. A. Lewis

1995   Survival and Detection of Blood Residues on Stone Tools. *Antiquity* 69(262):36–46.

Elias, Scott A.

1994   *Quaternary Insects and Their Environments*. Washington, D.C.: Smithsonian Institution Press.

El-Najjar, Mahmoud Y.

1979   Human Treponematosis and Tuberculosis: Evidence from the New World. *American Journal of Physical Anthropology* 51(4):599–618.

El-Najjar, Mahmoud Y., Betsy Lozoff, and Dennis J. Ryan

1975   The Paleoepidemiology of Porotic Hyperostosis in the American Southwest: Radiological and Ecological Considerations. *American Journal of Roentgenology, Radium Therapy, and Nuclear Medicine* 125(4):918–924.

El-Najjar, Mahmoud Y., Dennis J. Ryan, Christy G. Turner II, and Betsy Lozoff

1976   The Etiology of Porotic Hyperostosis among the Prehistoric and Historic Anasazi Indians of the Southwestern United States. *American Journal of Physical Anthropology* 44(3):477–488.

Emery, Kitty F., Lori E. Wright, and Henry Schwarcz

2000   Isotopic Analysis of Ancient Deer Bone: Biotic Stability in Collapse Period Maya Land-Use. *Journal of Archaeological Science* 27(6):537–550.

Eneroth, Peter, Kjell Hellström, and Ragnar Ryhage

1964   Identification and Quantification of Neutral Fecal Steroids by Gas-Liquid Chromatography and Mass Spectrometry: Studies of Human Excretion during Two Dietary Regimens. *Journal of Lipid Research* 5:245–262.

Eneroth, Peter, B. Gordon, and J. Sjövall

1966a   Characterization of Trisubstituted Cholanic Acids in Human Feces. *Journal of Lipid Research* 7:524–530.

Eneroth, Peter, B. Gordon, Ragnar Ryhage, and J. Sjövall

1966b   Identification of Mono- and Dihydroxy Bile Acids in Human Feces. *Journal of Lipid Research* 7:511–523.

Ericksen, M. F.

1997   Comparison of Two Methods of Estimatig Age at Death in a Chilean Preceramic Population. *International Journal of Osteoarchaeology* 7(1):65–70.

Ericson, Jonathon E.

1985   Strontium Isotope Characterization in the Study of Prehistoric Human Ecology. *Journal of Human Evolution* 14(5):503–514.

1989   Some Problems and Potentials of Strontium Isotope Analysis for Human and Animal Ecology. In: *Stable Isotopes in Ecological Research*, P. W. Rundel, J. R. Ehleringer, and K. A. Nagy, eds., pp. 252–259. Berlin: Springer-Verlag.

1993   Ba/Ca as a Diagenetic Indicator for Evaluating Buried Bone Tissues: Advances in Tissue Selection, Reducing Contamination, and Data Evaluation. In: *Prehistoric Human Bone: Archaeology at the Molecular Level*, Joseph B. Lambert and Gisela Grupe, eds., pp. 157–171. Berlin: Springer-Verlag.

Ericson, Jonathon E., Hiroshi Shirahata, and Clair C. Patterson

1979   Skeletal Concentrations of Lead in Ancient Peruvians. *New England Journal of Medicine* 300:946–951.

Ericson, Jonathon E., Michael West, Charles H. Sullivan, and Harold W. Krueger

1989   The Development of Maize Agriculture in the Viru Valley, Peru. In: *The Chemistry of Prehistoric Human Bone*, T. Douglas Price, ed., pp. 68–104. Cambridge: Cambridge University Press.

Ericson, Jonathon E., Donald R. Smith, and A. Russell Flegal

1991   Skeletal Concentrations of Lead, Cadmium, Zinc, and Silver in Ancient North American Pecos Indians. *Environmental Health Perspectives* 93:217–223.

Eriksson, Gunilla

2004   Part-Time Farmers or Hard-Core Sealers? Västerbjers Studied by Means of Stable Isotope Analysis. *Journal of Anthropological Archaeology* 23(2):135–162.

Eshed, Vered, Avi Gopher, and Israel Hershkovitz

2005   Tooth Wear and Dental Pathology at the Advent of Agriculture: New Evidence from the Levant. *American Journal of Physical Anthropology* 130(2):145–159.

Esper, J. E.

1774   *Ausfurliche Nachrichten von neuentdeckten Zoolithen unbekannter vierfussiger thiere*. Nuremberg.

Etspüler, H., Y. Kaup, P. Eiring, H. Werner, E. M. Bailyes, P. J. Luzio, and U. Weser

1996   Functional and Immunological Activity of an Egyptian Mummified Bone Enzyme from the Old Kingdom. *Ancient Biomolecules* 1(1):17–23.

Evans, J. G.

1972   *Land Snails in Archaeology*. London: Seminar Press.

Evershed, Richard P.

1990   Lipids from Samples of Skin from Seven Dutch Bog Bodies: Preliminary Report. *Archaeometry* 32(2):139–153.

1991   Bog Body Lipid Taphonomy. In: *Archaeological Sciences 1989*, Paul Budd, Barbara Chapman, Caroline Jackson, Rob Janaway, and Barbara Ottaway, eds., pp. 352–361. Oxford: Oxbow Monograph 9.

1993   Biomolecular Archaeology and Lipids. *World Archaeology* 25(1):74–93.

Evershed, Richard P., and Philip H. Bethell

1996   Application of Multimolecular Biomarker Techniques to the Identification of Fecal Material in Archaeological Soils and Sediments. In: *Archaeological Chemistry*, Mary Virginia Orna, ed., pp. 157–172. Washington, D.C.: American Chemical Society Symposium Series 625.

Evershed, Richard P., and Robert C. Connolly

1994   Post-Mortem Transformations of Sterols in Bog Body Tissues. *Journal of Archaeological Science* 21(5):577–583.

Evershed, Richard P., and Noreen Tuross

1996   Protenaceous Material from Potsherds and Associated Soils. *Journal of Archaeological Science* 23(3):429–436.

Evershed, Richard P., Carl Heron, and L. J. Goad

1990   Analysis of Organic Residues of Archaeological Origin by High-Temperature Gas Chromatography and Gas Chromatography Mass Spectometry. *Analyst* 115:1339–1342.

Evershed, Richard P., Carl Heron, S. Charters, and L. J. Goad

1992   The Survival of Food Residues: New Methods of Analysis, Interpretation and Application. In: *New Developments in Archaeological Science*, A. Mark Pollard, ed., pp. 187–208. Proceedings of the British Academy 77.

Evershed, Richard P., Gordon Turner-Walker, Robert E. M. Hedges, Noreen Tuross, and Ann Leyden

1995   Preliminary Results for the Analysis of Lipids in Ancient Bone. *Journal of Archaeological Science* 22(2):277–290.

Evershed, Richard P., Sarah J. Vaughan, Stephanie N. Dudd, and Jeffrey S. Soles

2000   Organic Residue, Petrographic and Typological Analyses of Late Minoan Lamps and Conical Cups from Excavations at Mochlos in East Crete, Greece. In: *Palaeodiet in the Aegean*, Sarah J. Vaughan and William D. E. Coulson, eds., pp. 37–54. Oxford: Oxbow Books.

Ezzo, Joseph A.

1992   A Test of Diet versus Diagenesis at Ventana Cave, Arizona. *Journal of Archaeological Science* 19(1):23–37.

1993   *Human Adaptation at Grasshopper Pueblo, Arizona.* Ann Arbor: International Monographs in Prehistory, Archaeological Series 4.

1994a   Putting the "Chemistry" Back into Archaeological Bone Chemistry Analysis: Modeling Potential Paleodietary Indicators. *Journal of Anthropological Archaeology* 13(1):1–34.

1994b   Zinc as a Paleodietary Indicator: An Issue of Theoretical Validity in Bone-Chemistry Analysis. *American Antiquity* 59(4):606–621.

1994c   Paleonutrition at Grasshopper Pueblo, Arizona. In: *Paleonutrition: The Diet and Health of Prehistoric Americans*, Kristin D. Sobolik, ed., pp. 265–279.

Carbondale: Southern Illinois University, Center for Archaeological Investigations, Occasional Paper No. 22.

Ezzo, Joseph A., Clark M. Johnson, and T. Douglas Price

1997   Analytical Perspectives on Prehistoric Migration: A Case Study from East-Central Arizona. *Journal of Archaeological Science* 24(5):447–466.

Facchini, F., E. Rastelli, and P. Brasili

2004   Cribra Orbitalia and Cribra Cranii in Roman Skeletal Remains from the Ravenna Area and Rimini (I–IV Century AD). *International Journal of Osteoarchaeology* 14(2):126–136.

Fægri, Knut, Peter Emil Kaland, and Knut Krzywinski

2000   *Textbook of Pollen Analysis* (4th ed.). Chichester, U.K.: John Wiley & Sons.

Faerman, Marina, Dvora Filon, Gila Kahila Bar-Gal, Charles L. Greenblatt, Patricia Smith, and Ariella Oppenheim

1995   Sex Identification of Archaeological Human Remains Based on Amplification of the X and Y Amelogenin Alleles. *Gene* 167(1–2):327–332.

Faerman, Marina, R. Jankauskas, A. Gorski, H. Bercovier, and Charles L. Greenblatt

1997   Prevalence of Human Tuberculosis in a Medieval Population of Lithuania Studied by Ancient DNA. *Ancient Biomolecules* 1(3):205–215.

Faerman, Marina, Gila Kahila Bar-Gal, Dvora Filon, Charles L. Greenblatt, Lawrence Stager, Ariella Oppenheim, and Patricia Smith

1998   Determining the Sex of Infanticide Victims from the Late Roman Era through Ancient DNA Analysis. *Journal of Archaeological Science* 25(9):861–865.

Falkner, Frank, and J. M. Tanner

1986   *Human Growth: A Comprehensive Treatise*, Vol. 3 (2d ed.). New York: Plenum Press.

Fankhauser, Barry

1994   Protein and Lipid Analysis of Food Residues. In: *Tropical Archaeobotany: Applications and New Developments*, Jon G. Hather, ed., pp. 227–250. London: Routledge.

Farnum, J. F., M. D. Glascock, Mary K. Sandford, and G. Gerritsen

1995   Trace Elements in Ancient Human Bone and Associated Soil Using NAA. *Journal of Radioanalytical and Nuclear Chemistry* 196(2):267–274.

Farrell, Nancy

1988   Analysis of Human Coprolites from CA-RIV-1179 and CA-RIV-2827. In: *Archaeological Investigations at CA-RIV-1179, CA-RIV-2823, and CA-RIV-2827, La Quinta, Riverside County, California*, Mark Q. Sutton and Philip J. Wilke, eds., pp. 129–142. Salinas: Coyote Press Archives of California Prehistory, No. 20.

Farrer, K.T.H.

1993   Lead and the Last Franklin Expedition. *Journal of Archaeological Science* 20(4):399–409.

Farris, Glenn J.

1982   Pine Nuts as an Aboriginal Food Source in California and Nevada: Some Contrasts. *Journal of Ethnobiology* 2(2):114–122.

Faulkner, Charles T.

1991   Prehistoric Diet and Parasitic Infection in Tennessee: Evidence from the Analysis of Desiccated Human Paleofeces. *American Antiquity* 56(4):687–700.

Federation Dentaire Internationale

1982   An Epidemiological Index of Developmental Defects of Dental Enamel (DDE Index). *International Dental Journal* 32:159–167.

Felton, E. L.

1965   *California's Many Climates*. Palo Alto: Pacific Books.

Fenner, Frank

1970   The Effects of Changing Social Organisation on the Infectious Diseases of Man. In: *The Impact of Civilisation on the Biology of Man*, S. V. Boyden, ed., pp. 48–76. Toronto: University of Toronto Press.

Ferguson, C.

1980   Analysis of Skeletal Remains. In: *Tijeras Canyon: Analyses of the Past*, Linda S. Cordell, ed., pp. 121–148. Albuquerque: University of New Mexico Press.

Fewkes, Jesse W.

1896   Pacific Coast Shell from Prehistoric Tusayan Pueblos. *American Anthropologist* 9(11):359–367.

Fiedel, Stuart J.

1996   Blood from Stones? Some Methodological and Interpretive Problems in Blood Residue Analysis. *Journal of Archaeological Science* 23(1):139–147.

1997   Reply to Newman et al. *Journal of Archaeological Science* 24(11):1029–1030.

Filer, Joyce

1995   *Disease*. Austin: University of Texas Press.

Fink, T. Michael

1985   Tuberculosis and Anemia in a Pueblo II–III (ca. AD 900–1300) Anasazi Child from New Mexico. In: *Health and Disease in the Prehistoric Southwest*, Charles F. Merbs and Robert J. Miller, eds., pp. 359–379. Tempe: Arizona State University, Anthropological Research Papers, No. 34.

Fink, T. Michael, and Charles E. Merbs

1991   Paleonutrition and Paleopathology of the Salt River Hohokam: A Search for Correlates. *Kiva* 56(3):293–318.

Finkelstein, Israel

1996   Ethnicity and Origin of the Iron I Settlers in the Highlands of Canaan: Can the Real Israel Stand Up? *Biblical Archaeologist* 59(4):198–212.

Finucane, Brian, Patricia Maita Agurto, and William H. Isbell

2006   Human and Animal Diet at Conchopata, Peru: Stable Isotope Evidence for Maize Agriculture and Animal Management Practices during the Middle Horizon. *Journal of Archaeological Science* 33(12):1766–1776.

Fisher, Deborah L., Mitchell M. Holland, Lloyd G. Mitchell, Paul S. Sledzik, Allison Webb Wilcox, Mark Wadhams, and Victor W. Weedn

1993   Extraction, Evaluation, and Amplification of DNA from Decalcified and Undecalcified United States Civil War Bone. *Journal of Forensic Sciences* 38(1):60–68.

FitzGerald, Charles M., and Jerome C. Rose

2000   Reading between the Lines: Dental Development and Subadult Age Assessment Using the Microstructural Growth Markers of Teeth. In: *Biological Anthropology of the Human Skeleton*, M. Anne Katzenberg and Shelley R. Saunders, eds., pp. 163–186. New York: Wiley-Liss.

Flaherty, T., and T. J. Haigh

1986   Blood Groups in Mummies. In: *Science in Egyptology*, A. R. David, ed., pp. 379–382. Manchester: Manchester University Press.

Flannery, Kent V.

1968   Archaeological Systems Theory and Early Mesoamerica. In: *Anthropological Archaeology in the Americas*, Betty J. Meggers, ed., pp. 67–78. Washington, D.C.: Anthropological Society of Washington.

2002   Prehistoric Social Evolution. In: *Archaeology: Original Readings in Method and Practice*, Peter N. Peregrine, Carol R. Ember, and Melvin Ember, eds., pp. 225–244. Upper Saddle River, N.J.: Prentice Hall.

Flenley, J. R.

1994   Pollen in Polyneasia: The Use of Palynology to Detect Human Activity in the Pacific Islands. In: *Tropical Archaeobotany: Applications and New Developments*, Jon G. Hather, ed., pp. 202–214. London: Routledge.

Fogel, Marilyn L., and Noreen Tuross

2003   Extending the Limits of Paleodietary Studies of Humans with Compound Specific Carbon Isotope Analysis of Amino Acids. *Journal of Archaeological Science* 30(5):535–545.

Follett, W. I.

1988   Analysis of Fish Remains from Two Archaeological Sites (CA-RIV-1179 and CA-RIV-2827) at La Quinta, Riverside County, California. In: *Archaeological Investigations at CA-RIV-1179, CA-RIV-2823, and CA-RIV-2827, La Quinta, Riverside County, California*, Mark Q. Sutton and Philip J. Wilke, eds., pp. 143–156. Salinas: Coyote Press Archives of California Prehistory, No. 20.

Forcella, Frank

1978   Irregularity of Pinyon Cone Production and Its Relation to Pinyon Cone Moth Predation. *Madroño* 25:170–172.

Ford, Richard I.

1968   An Ecological Analysis Involving the Population of San Juan Pueblo, New Mexico. Ph.D. dissertation, University of Michigan, Lansing.

1979   Paleoethnobotany in American Archaeology. In: *Advances in Archaeological Method and Theory*, Vol. 2, Michael B. Schiffer, ed., pp. 285–336. New York: Academic Press.

Forsberg, Helen

1935   The Skeletal Remains from Tuzigoot. In: Tuzigoot: The Excavation and Repair of a Ruin on the Verde River near Clarkdale, Arizona, L. R. Caywood and E. H. Spicer, eds., pp. 112–119. Washington, D.C.: National Park Service.

Fount, M. M.

1981 Intestinal Parasitic Disease among Pre-Columbian Indians. Master's thesis, Virginia Commonwealth University, Richmond.

Fowler, Catherine S.

1986 Subsistence. In: *Handbook of North American Indians. Vol. 11: Great Basin*, Warren L. d'Azevedo, ed., pp. 64–97. Washington, D.C.: Smithsonian Institution.

Fox, Carles Lalueza

1996 Analysis of Ancient Mitochrondrial DNA from Extinct Aborigines from Tierra del Fuego-Patagonia. *Ancient Biomolecules* 1(1):43–54.

Fox, Carles Lalueza, Jordi Juan, and Rosa M. Albert

1996 Phytolith Analysis on Dental Calculus, Enamel Surface, and Burial Soil: Information about Diet and Paleoenvironment. *American Journal of Physical Anthropology* 101(1):101–113.

Francalacci, Paolo

1989 Dietary Reconstruction at Arene Candide Cave (Liguria, Italy) by Means of Trace Element Analysis. *Journal of Archaeological Science* 16(2):109–124.

Fraser, H. M.

1951 *Beekeeping in Antiquity* (2d ed.). London: University of London Press.

Fredlund, Glen G.

1993 Paleoenvironmental Interpretations of Stable Carbon, Hydrogen, and Oxygen Isotopes from Opal Phytoliths, Eustis Ash Pit, Nebraska. In: *Current Research in Phytolith Analysis: Applications in Archaeology and Paleoecology*, Deborah M. Pearsall and Dolores R. Piperno, eds., pp. 37–46. Philadelphia: University of Pennsylvania, University Museum of Archaeology and Anthropology, MASCA Research Papers in Science and Archaeology, Vol. 10.

Freitas, Fábio O., and Paulo S. Martins

2000 Calcite Crystals Inside Archaeological Plant Tissues. *Journal of Archaeological Science* 27(11):981–985.

Frisancho, A. Roberto

1990 *Anthropometric Standards for the Assessment of Growth and Nutritional Status*. Ann Arbor: University of Michigan Press.

Fritz, Gayle J.

1994 The Value of Archaeological Plant Remains for Paleodietary Reconstruction. In: *Paleonutrition: The Diet and Health of Prehistoric Americans*, Kristin D. Sobolik, ed., pp. 21–33. Carbondale: Southern Illinois University, Center for Archaeological Investigations, Occasional Paper No. 22.

Frost, H. M.

1985 The "New Bone": Some Anthropological Potentials. *Yearbook of Physical Anthropology* 28:211–226.

Fry, Gary F.

1970a Prehistoric Human Ecology in Utah: Based on the Analysis of Coprolites. Ph.D. dissertation, University of Utah, Salt Lake City.

Fry, Gary F.

1970b   Preliminary Analysis of the Hogup Cave Coprolites. In: *Hogup Cave*, by C. Melvin Aikens, pp. 247–250. Salt Lake City: University of Utah, Anthropological Papers, No. 93.

1976   *Analysis of Prehistoric Coprolites from Utah*. Salt Lake City: University of Utah, Anthropological Papers, No. 97.

1985   Analysis of Fecal Material. In: *The Analysis of Prehistoric Diets*, Robert I. Gilbert Jr. and James H. Mielke, eds., pp. 127–154. Orlando, Fla.: Academic Press.

Fry, Gary F., and J. G. Moore

1969   *Enterobius vermicularis*: 10,000 Year Old Human Infection. *Science* 166:1620.

Fujiwara, Hiroshi

1993   Research into the History of Rice Cultivation Using Plant Opal Analysis. In: *Current Research in Phytolith Analysis: Applications in Archaeology and Paleoecology*, Deborah M. Pearsall and Dolores R. Piperno, eds., pp. 147–158. Philadelphia: University of Pennsylvania, University Museum of Archaeology and Anthropology, MASCA Research Papers in Science and Archaeology, Vol. 10.

Galvin, K.

1985   Food Procurement, Diet, Activities and Nutrition of Ngisonyoka, Turkana, Pastoralists in an Ecological and Social Context. Ph.D. dissertation, State University of New York, Binghamton.

Gandulla, Bernardo

2000   Review of The Archaeology of Israel: Constructing the Past, Interpreting the Present, by N. A. Silberman and David Small. *Journal of the American Oriental Society* 120(4):655–658.

Gardner, Jill K.

2007   *The Potential Impact of the Medieval Climatic Anomaly on Human Populations in the Western Mojave Desert*. Salinas: Coyote Press Archives of Great Basin Prehistory, No. 7.

Gardner, Paul S.

1992   Diet Optimization Models and Prehistoric Subsistence Change in the Eastern Woodlands. Ph.D. dissertation, University of North Carolina, Chapel Hill.

Garn, Stanley M.

1992   The Iron-Deficiency Anemias and Their Skeletal Manifestations. In: *Diet, Demography, and Disease: Changing Perspectives on Anemia*, Patricia Stuart-Macadam and Susan Kent, eds., pp. 33–61. New York: Aldine de Gruyter.

Garvie-Lok, Sandra J., Tamara L. Varney, and M. Anne Katzenberg

2004   Preparation of Bone Carbonate for Stable Isotope Analysis: The Effects of Treatment Time and Acid Concentration. *Journal of Archaeological Science* 31(6):763–776.

Gasser, Robert E., and E. Charles Adams

1981   Aspects of Deterioration of Plant Remains in Archaeological Sites: The Walpi Archaeological Project. *Journal of Ethnobiology* 1(1):182–192.

Gearing, Juanita Newman

1991   The Study of Diet and Trophic Relationships through Natural Abundance of
        ¹³C. In: *Carbon Isotope Techniques*, David C. Coleman and Brian Fry, eds.,
        pp. 201–218. San Diego: Academic Press.

Geib, Phil R., and Susan J. Smith

2008   Palynology and Archaeological Inference: Bridging the Gap between Pollen
        Washes and Past Behavior. *Journal of Archaeological Science* 35(8):2085–2101.

Gejvall, Nils-Gustaf

1970   Cremations. In: *Science in Archaeology*, Don R. Brothwell and Eric Higgs, eds.,
        pp. 468–479. London: Thames and Hudson.

Genoves, Santiago

1967   Proportionality of the Long Bones and Their Relation to Stature among Meso-
        americans. *American Journal of Physical Anthropology* 26(1):67–77.

Gero, Joan M., and Margaret W. Conkey (eds.)

1991   *Engendering Archaeology: Women and Prehistory*. Oxford: Blackwell.

Gerszten, Enrique, and Marvin J. Allison

1991   Human Soft Tissue Tumors in Paleopathology. In: *Human Paleopathol-
        ogy: Current Syntheses and Future Options*, Donald J. Ortner and Arthur C.
        Aufderheide, eds., pp. 257–260. Washington, D.C.: Smithsonian Institution
        Press.

Gilbert, Allan S., and Burton H. Singer

1982   Reassessing Zooarchaeological Quantification. *World Archaeology* 14(1):21–40.

Gilbert, B. Miles

1990   *Mammalian Osteology*. Columbia: Missouri Archaeological Society.

Gilbert, B. Miles, Larry D. Martin, and Howard G. Savage

1981   *Avian Osteology*. Laramie, Wyo.: Modern Printing Co.

Gilbert, Cheryl, Judith C. Sealy, and Andrew Sillen

1994   An Investigation of Barium, Calcium and Strontium as Palaeodietary Indica-
        tors in the Southwestern Cape, South Africa. *Journal of Archaeological Science*
        21(2):173–184.

Gilbert, M.T.P., A. J. Hansen, E. Willerslev, G. Turner-Walker, and M. Collins

2006   Insights into the Processes behind the Contamination of Degraded Human
        Teeth and Bone Samples with Exogenous Sources of DNA. *International Journal
        of Osteoarchaeology* 16(2):156–164.

Gilbert, Robert I., Jr.

1985   Stress, Paleonutrition, and Trace Elements. In: *The Analysis of Prehistoric Diets*,
        Robert I. Gilbert Jr. and James H. Mielke, eds., pp. 339–358. New York: Academic
        Press.

Gilbert, Robert I., Jr., and James H. Mielke (eds.)

1985   *The Analysis of Prehistoric Diets*. New York: Academic Press.

Gill, George W., and Douglas W. Owsley

1985   Electron Microscopy of Parasite Remains on the Pitchfork Mummy and Possible
        Social Implications. *Plains Anthropologist* 30(107):45–50.

Gilmore, Melvin R.

1919   Uses of Plants by the Indians of the Missouri River Region. Thirty-third Annual Report of the Bureau of American Ethnology to the Secretary of the Smithsonian Institution, 1911–1912, pp. 43–154. Washington, D.C.: Government Printing Office.

1932   *The Ethnobotanical Laboratory at the University of Michigan*. Ann Arbor: Occasional Contributions from the Museum of Anthropology of the University of Michigan, No. 1.

Glassman, David M., and James F. Garber

1999   Land Use, Diet, and Their Effects on the Biology of the Prehistoric Maya of Northern Ambergris Cay, Belize. In: *Reconstructing Ancient Maya Diet*, Christine D. White, ed., pp. 119–132. Salt Lake City: University of Utah Press.

Gobalet, Kenneth W.

1989   Remains of Tiny Fish from a Late Prehistoric Pomo Site near Clear Lake, California. *Journal of California and Great Basin Anthropology* 11(2):231–239.

Goldberg, Carol F.

1993   The Application of Stable Carbon and Nitrogen Isotope Analysis to Human Dietary Reconstruction in Prehistoric Southern California. Ph.D. dissertation, University of California, Los Angeles.

Goldfuss, A.

1810   *Die Umgebringen von muggendorf*. Erlangen.

Goloubinoff, Pierre, Svante Pääbo, and Allan C. Wilson

1993   Evolution of Maize Inferred from Sequence Diversity of an *Adh2* Gene Segment from Archaeological Specimens. *Proceedings of the National Academy of Sciences* 90(5):1997–2001.

Gonzalez-Reimers, E., J. Velasco-Vázquez, M. Arnay-de-la-Rosa, and M. Machado-Calvo

2007   Quantitative Computerized Tomography for the Diagnosis of Osteopenia in Prehistoric Skeletal Remains. *Journal of Archaeological Science* 34(4):554–561.

Goodman, Alan H.

1988   Teeth as Tools: Dental Development Defects as Records of Dietary Insufficiency. In: *Diet and Subsistence: Current Archaeological Perspectives*, Brenda V. Kennedy and Genevieve M. LeMoine, eds., pp. 260–266. Proceedings of the Nineteenth Annual Chacmool Conference, University of Calgary.

1991   Stress, Adaptation, and Enamel Developmental Defects. In: *Human Paleopathology: Current Syntheses and Future Options*, Donald J. Ortner and Arthur C. Aufderheide, eds., pp. 280–287. Washington, D.C.: Smithsonian Institution Press.

1994   Cartesian Reductionism and Vulgar Adaptationism: Issues in the Interpretation of Nutritional Status in Prehistory. In: *Paleonutrition: The Diet and Health of Prehistoric Americans*, Kristin D. Sobolik, ed., pp. 163–177. Carbondale: Southern Illinois University, Center for Archaeological Investigations, Occasional Paper No. 22.

Goodman, Alan H., and George J. Armelagos

1985   Factors Affecting the Distribution of Enamel Hypoplasias within the Human Permanent Dentition. *American Journal of Physical Anthropology* 68(4):479–493.

1988   Childhood Stress and Decreased Longevity in a Prehistoric Population. *American Anthropologist* 90(4):936–944.

Goodman, Alan H., and Debra L. Martin

2002   Reconstructing Health Profiles from Skeletal Remains. In: *The Backbone of History: Health and Nutrition in the Western Hemisphere*, Richard H. Steckel and Jerome C. Rose, eds., pp. 11–60. Cambridge: Cambridge University Press.

Goodman, Alan H., and Jerome C. Rose

1990   Assessment of Systemic and Physiological Perturbations from Dental Enamel Hypoplasias and Associated Histological Structures. *Yearbook of Physical Anthropology* 33:59–110.

1991   Dental Enamel Hypoplasias and Indicators of Nutritional Stress. In: *Advances in Dental Anthropology*, Marc A. Kelley and Clark Spencer Larsen, eds., pp. 279–293. New York: Wiley-Liss.

Goodman, Alan H., and Rhan-Ju Song

1999   Sources of Variation in Estimated Ages at Formation of Linear Enamel Hypoplasias. In: *Human Growth in the Past: Studies from Bones and Teeth*, Robert D. Hoppa and Charles M. Fitzgerald, eds., pp. 210–240. New York: Cambridge University Press.

Goodman, Alan H., Debra L. Martin, George J. Armelagos, and George Clark

1984   Indications of Stress from Bone and Teeth. In: *Paleopathology at the Origins of Agriculture*, Mark Nathan Cohen and George J. Armelagos, eds., pp. 13–49. Orlando, Fla.: Academic Press.

Gordon, Elizabeth A.

1993   Screen Size and Differential Faunal Recovery: A Hawaiian Example. *Journal of Field Archaeology* 20(4):453–460.

Götherström, A., K. Lidén, T. Ahlström, M. Källersjö, and T. A. Brown

1998   Osteology, DNA and Sex Identification: Morphological and Molecular Sex Identifications of Five Neolithic Individuals from Ajvide, Gotland. *International Journal of Osteoarchaeology* 7(1):71–81.

Grauer, Anne L., and Patricia Stuart-Macadam (eds.)

1998   *Sex and Gender in Paleopathological Perspective*. Cambridge: Cambridge University Press.

Grayson, Donald K.

1984   *Quantitative Zooarchaeology*. New York: Academic Press.

Greene, Lawrence S., and Francis E. Johnston (eds.)

1980   *Social and Biological Predictors of Nutritional Status, Physical Growth, and Neurological Development*. New York: Academic Press.

Gregg, Susan Alling

1988   *Foragers and Farmers: Population Interaction and Agricultural Expansion in Prehistoric Europe*. Chicago: University of Chicago Press.

Greig, James

1981   The Investigation of a Medieval Barrel-Latrine from Worcester. *Journal of Archaeological Science* 8(3):265–282.

Greig, James
1983   Plant Foods in the Past: A Review of Evidence from Northern Europe. *Journal of Plant Foods* 5(4):179–214.
1984   Garderobes, Sewers, Cesspits and Latrines. *Current Archaeology* 85:49–52.
Gremillion, Kristen J. (ed.)
1997   *People, Plants, and Landscapes: Studies in Paleoethnobotany.* Tuscaloosa: University of Alabama Press.
Gremillion, Kristin J., and Kristin D. Sobolik
1996   Dietary Variability among Prehistoric Forager-Farmers of Eastern North America. *Current Anthropology* 37(3):529–539.
Grupe, Gisela
1988   Impact of the Choice of Bone Samples on Trace Element Data in Excavated Human Skeletons. *Journal of Archaeological Science* 15(2):123–129.
1995   Reconstructing Migration in the Bell Beaker Period by $^{87}Sr/^{86}Sr$ Isotope Ratios in Teeth and Bones. In: *Proceedings of the 10th International Symposium on Dental Morphology*, R. J. Radlanski and H. Ranz, eds., pp. 339–342. Berlin: "M" Marketing Services.
Grupe, Gisela, and Klaus Dörner
1989   Trace Elements in Excavated Human Hair. *Zeitschrift für Morphologie und Anthropolgie* 77(3):297–308.
Grupe, Gisela, and S. Hummel
1991   Trace Element Studies on Experimentally Cremated Bone. I: Alteration of the Chemical Composition at High Temperatures. *Journal of Archaeological Science* 18(2):177–186.
Grupe, Gisela, and Hermann Piepenbrink
1989   Impact of Microbial Activity on Trace Element Concentrations in Excavated Bones. *Applied Geochemistry* 4(3):293–298.
Grupe, Gisela, Hermann Piepenbrink, and Margaret J. Schoeninger
1989   Note on Microbial Influence on Stable Carbon and Nitrogen Isotopes in Bone. *Applied Geochemistry* 4(3):299.
Grupe, Gisela, Astrid Balzer, and Susanne Turban-Just
2000   Modeling Protein Diagenesis in Ancient Bone: Toward a Validation of Stable Isotope Data. In: *Biogeochemical Approaches to Paleodietary Analysis*, Stanley H. Ambrose and M. Anne Katzenberg, eds., pp. 173–187. New York: Kluwer Academic/Plenum Publishers.
Gülaçar, Fazil O., Alberto Susini, and Max Klohn
1990   Preservation and Post-mortem Transformations of Lipids in Samples from a 4000-Year-Old Nubian Mummy. *Journal of Archaeological Science* 17(6):691–705.
Gunn, C. R., J. V. Dennis, and P. J. Paradine
1976   *World Guide to Tropical Drift Seeds and Fruits.* New York: Quadrangle/The New York Times Book Co.
Gunness-Hay, Michele
1981   Spondyloysis in the Koniag Eskimo Vertebral Column. In: *Biocultural Adaptation: Comprehensive Approaches to Skeletal Analysis*, Debra L. Martin and

M. Pamela Bumsted, eds., pp. 16–23. Amherst: University of Massachusetts, Department of Anthropology, Research Reports, No. 20.

Guthrie, H. A.

1986   *Introductory Nutrition.* St. Louis: Times Mirror/Mosby College Publishing.

Guy, Hervé, Claude Masset, and Charles-Albert Baud

1997   Infant Taphonomy. *International Journal of Osteoarchaeology* 7(3):221–229.

Haberle, Simon

1994   Anthropogenic Indicators in Pollen Diagrams: Problems and Prospects for Late Quaternary Palynology in New Guinea. In: *Tropical Archaeobotany: Applications and New Developments,* Jon G. Hather, ed., pp. 172–201. London: Routledge.

Hagelberg, Erika

1994a   Ancient DNA Studies. *Evolutionary Anthropology* 2(6):199–207.

1994b   Mitochondrial DNA from Ancient Bones. In: *Ancient DNA: Recovery and Analysis of Genetic Material from Paleontological, Archaeological, Museum, Medical, and Forensic Specimens,* Bernd Herrmann and Susanne Hummel, eds., pp. 195–204. Berlin: Springer-Verlag.

Hagelberg, Erika, Bryan C. Sykes, and Robert E. M. Hedges

1989   Ancient Bone DNA Amplified. *Nature* 342:485.

Hall, Henry J.

1972   Diet and Disease at Clyde's Cavern, Utah: As Revealed via Paleoscatology. Master's thesis, University of Utah, Salt Lake City.

1977   A Paleoscatological Study of Diet and Disease at Dirty Shame Rockshelter, Southeastern Oregon. *Tebiwa* 8:1–15.

Hancock, R.G.V., M. D. Grynpas, and K.P.H. Pritzker

1989   The Abuse of Bone Analyses for Archaeological Dietary Studies. *Archaeometry* 31(2):169–179.

Hancock, R.G.V., M. D. Grynpas, K. Åkesson, K. B. Obrant, J. Turnquist, and M. J. Kessler

1993   Baselines and Variabilities of Major Trace Elements in Bone. In: *Prehistoric Human Bone: Archaeology at the Molecular Level,* Joseph B. Lambert and Gisela Grupe, eds., pp. 189–201. Berlin: Springer-Verlag.

Handt, Oliva, Matthias Krings, R. H. Ward, and Svante Pääbo

1996   The Retrieval of Ancient Human DNA Sequences. *American Journal of Human Genetics* 59:368–376.

Hannerz, Ulf

1992   *Cultural Complexity: Studies in the Social Organization of Meaning.* New York: Columbia University.

Hard, Robert J., Raymond P. Mauldin, and Gerry R. Raymond

1996   Mano Size, Stable Carbon Isotope Ratios, and Macrobotanical Remains as Multiple Lines of Evidence of Maize Dependence in the American Southwest. *Journal of Archaeological Method and Theory* 3(4):243–318.

Hardy, Bruce L., and Gary T. Garufi

1998   Identification of Woodworking on Stone Tools through Residue and Use-Wear Analyses: Experimental Results. *Journal of Archaeological Science* 25(2):177–184.

Hardy, Bruce L., Rudolf A. Raff, and Venu Raman

1997   Recovery of Mammalian DNA from Middle Paleolithic Stone Tools. *Journal of Archaeological Science* 24(7):601–611.

Hare, P. Edgar, Marilyn L. Fogel, Thomas W. Stafford Jr., Alva D. Mitchell, and Thomas C. Hoering

1991   The Isotopic Composition of Carbon and Nitrogen in Individual Amino Acids Isolated from Modern and Fossil Proteins. *Journal of Archaeological Science* 18(3):277–292.

Harmon, Anna M., and Jerome C. Rose

1988   The Role of Dental Microwear Analysis in the Reconstruction of Prehistoric Diet. In: *Diet and Subsistence: Current Archaeological Perspectives*, Brenda V. Kennedy and Genevieve M. LeMoine, eds., pp. 267–272. Proceedings of the Nineteenth Annual Chacmool Conference, University of Calgary.

Harrington, R. J.

1981   Analysis of the Human Skeletal Remains from Las Colinas. In: *The 1968 Excavations at Mound 8, Las Colinas Ruins Group, Phoenix, Arizona*, L. D. Hammack and Alan P. Sullivan, eds., pp. 251–256. Tucson: University of Arizona, Arizona State Museum, Cultural Resources Management Section, Archaeological Series, No. 154.

Harrison, Roman G., and M. Anne Katzenberg

2003   Paleodiet Studies Using Stable Carbon Isotopes from Bone Apatite and Collagen: Examples from Southern Ontario and San Nicolas Island, California. *Journal of Anthropological Archaeology* 22(3):227–244.

Harritt, R. K., and S. C. Radosevich

1992   Results of Instrument Neutron-Activation Trace-Element Analysis of Human Remains from the Naknek Region, Southwest Alaska. *American Antiquity* 57(2):288–299.

Harshberger, J. W.

1896   The Purpose of Ethnobotany. *American Antiquarian* 17(2).

Hart, John P., William A. Lovis, Janet K. Schulenberg, and Gerald R. Urquhart

2007   Paleodietary Implications from Stable Carbon Isotope Analysis of Experimental Cooking Residues. *Journal of Archaeological Science* 34(5):804–813.

Harvey, Emma L., and Dorian Q. Fuller

2005   Investigating Crop Processing Using Phytolith Analysis: The Example of Rice and Millets. *Journal of Archaeological Science* 32(5):739–752.

Haslam, Michael

2004   The Decomposition of Starch Grains in Soils: Implications for Archaeological Residue Analysis. *Journal of Archaeological Science* 31(12):1715–1734.

Hastorf, Christine A.

1999   Recent Research in Paleoethnobotany. *Journal of Archaeological Research* 7(1):55–103.

Hastorf, Christine A., and Michael J. DeNiro

1985   Reconstruction of Prehistoric Plant Production and Cooking Practices by a New Isotopic Method. *Nature* 315:489–491.

Hastorf, Christine A., and Virginia S. Popper (eds.)

1988   *Current Paleoethnobotany*. Chicago: University of Chicago Press.

Hastorf, Christine A., and Melanie F. Wright

1998   Interpreting Wild Seeds from Archaeological Sites: A Dung Charring Experiment from the Andes. *Journal of Ethnobiology* 18(2):211–227.

Hather, Jon G.

1991   The Identification of Charred Archaeological Remains of Vegetative Parenchymous Tissue. *Journal of Archaeological Science* 18(6):661–675.

1993   *An Archaeological Guide to Root and Tuber Identification. Vol. 1: Europe and South West Asia*. Oxford: Oxbow Monograph 28.

1994   The Identification of Charred Root and Tuber Crops from Archaeological Sites in the Pacific. In: *Tropical Archaeobotany: Applications and New Developments*, Jon G. Hather, ed., pp. 51–64. London: Routledge.

Hauswirth, William H., Cynthia D. Dickel, Glen H. Doran, Philip J. Laipis, and David N. Dickel

1991   8000-Year-Old Brain Tissue from the Windover Site: Anatomical, Cellular, and Molecular Analysis. In: *Human Paleopathology: Current Syntheses and Future Options*, Donald J. Ortner and Arthur C. Aufderheide, eds., pp. 60–72. Washington, D.C.: Smithsonian Institution Press.

Hauswirth, William H., Cynthia D. Dickel, and David A. Lawlor

1994   DNA Analysis of the Windover Population. In: *Ancient DNA: Recovery and Analysis of Genetic Material from Paleontological, Archaeological, Museum, Medical, and Forensic Specimens*, Bernd Herrmann and Susanne Hummel, eds., pp. 104–121. Berlin: Springer-Verlag.

Haverkort, Caroline M., Andrzej Weber, M. Anne Katzenberg, Olga I. Goriunova, Antonio Simonetti, and Robert A. Creaser

2008   Hunter-Gatherer Mobility Strategies and Resource Use Based on Strontium Isotope (^{87}Sr/^{86}Sr) Analysis: A Case Study from Middle Holocene Lake Baikal, Siberia. *Journal of Archaeological Science* 35(5):1265–1280.

Hayden, Brian, Brian Chisholm, and Henry P. Schwarcz

1987   Fishing and Foraging: Marine Resources in the Upper Paleolithic of France. In: *The Pleistocene Old World: Regional Perspectives*, Ogla Soffer, ed., pp. 279–291. New York: Plenum Press.

Hayes, I. M.

1982   Fractionation: An Introduction to Isotope Measurements and Terminology. *Spectra* 8:3–8.

Heaton, Tim H. E.

1999   Spatial, Species, and Temporal Variations in the ^{13}C/^{12}C Ratios of C$_3$ Plants: Implications for Paleodiet Studies. *Journal of Archaeological Science* 26(6): 637–649.

Heaton, Tim H. E., John C. Vogel, Gertrud von la Chevallarie, and Gill Collett

1986   Climatic Influence on the Isotopic Composition of Bone Nitrogen. *Nature* 322:822–823.

Hedges, Robert E. M.

2003   On Bone Collagen-Apatite-Carbonate Isotopic Relationships. *International Journal of Osteoarchaeology* 13(1–2):66–79.

Hedges, Robert E. M., and Linda M. Reynard

2007   Nitrogen Isotopes and the Trophic Level of Humans in Archaeology. *Journal of Archaeological Science* 34(8):1240–1251.

Hedges, Robert E. M., and Bryan C. Sykes

1992   Biomolecular Archaeology: Past, Present and Future. In: *New Developments in Archaeological Science*, A. Mark Pollard, ed., pp. 267–283. Proceedings of the British Academy 77, Oxford University Press, Oxford.

Hedges, Robert E. M., and Gert J. van Klinken

2000   "Consider a Spherical Cow . . ." — on Modeling and Diet. In: *Biogeochemical Approaches to Paleodietary Analysis*, Stanley H. Ambrose and M. Anne Katzenberg, eds., pp. 211–241. New York: Kluwer Academic/Plenum Publishers.

Heer, Oswald

1872   *Le monde primitif de la Suisse*. Geneve et Bale: H. Georg, Libraire-Editeur.

Heglar, R.

1974   The Prehistoric Population of Cochiti Pueblo and Selected Inter-Population Biological Comparisons. Ph.D. dissertation, Department of Anthropology, University of Michigan, Ann Arbor.

Hegsted, D. M.

1978   Protein-Calorie Malnutrition. *American Scientist* 66:61–65.

Heizer, Robert F.

1970   The Anthropology of Prehistoric Great Basin Coprolites. In: *Science in Archaeology: A Survey of Progress and Research*, Don R. Brothwell and Eric Higgs, eds., pp. 244–250. New York: Praeger.

Heizer, Robert F., and Lewis K. Napton

1969   Biological and Cultural Evidence from Prehistoric Human Coprolites. *Science* 165:563–568.

Helbaek, Hans

1960   The Paleoethnobotany of the Near East and Europe. In: *Prehistoric Investigations in Iraqi Kurdistan*, Robert J. Braidwood and B. Howe, eds., pp. 99–118. Chicago: University of Chicago Press.

1969   Plant Collecting, Dry-Farming, and Irrigation Agriculture in Prehistoric Deh Luran. In: *Prehistory and Human Ecology of the Deh Luran Plain*, Frank Hole, Kent V. Flannery, and James A. Neely, eds., pp. 383–426. Ann Arbor: Museum of Anthropology.

Hemphill, Brian E.

1999   Wear and Tear: Osteoarthritis as an Indicator of Mobility among Great Basin Hunter-Gatherers. In: *Prehistoric Lifeways in the Great Basin Wetlands: Bioarchaeological Reconstruction and Interpretation*, Brian E. Hemphill and Clark Spencer Larsen, eds., pp. 241–289. Salt Lake City: University of Utah Press.

Henderson, Julian

2000   *The Science and Archaeology of Materials: An Investigation of Inorganic Materials*. London: Routledge.

Henderson, Julian, John A. Evans, Hilary J. Sloane, Melanie J. Leng, and Chris Doherty

2005   The Use of Oxygen, Strontium and Lead Isotopes to Provenance Ancient Glasses in the Middle East. *Journal of Archaeological Science* 32(5):665–673.

Henry, Raymond L.

1980   Paleoserology. In: *Mummies, Disease, and Ancient Cultures* (1st ed.), Aidan Cockburn and Eve Cockburn, eds., pp. 327–334. Cambridge: Cambridge University Press.

Heron, Carl, and Richard P. Evershed

1993   The Analysis of Organic Residues and the Study of Pottery Use. In: *Archaeological Method and Theory, Vol. 5*, Michael B. Schiffer, ed., pp. 247–286. Tucson: University of Arizona Press.

Heron, Carl, Richard P. Evershed, and L. J. Goad

1991a   Effects of Migration of Soil Lipids on Organic Residues Associated with Buried Potsherds. *Journal of Archaeological Science* 18(6):641–659.

Heron, Carl, Richard P. Evershed, L. J. Goad, and V. Denham

1991b   New Approaches to the Analysis of Organic Residues from Archaeological Remains. In: *Archaeological Sciences 1989*, Paul Budd, Barbara Chapman, Caroline Jackson, Rob Janaway, and Barbara Ottaway, eds., pp. 332–339. Oxford: Oxbow Monograph 9.

Herring, D. Ann, Shelley R. Saunders, and M. Anne Katzenberg

1998   Investigating the Weaning Process in Past Populations. *American Journal of Physical Anthropology* 105(4):425–439.

Herrmann, Bernd

1993   Indicators for Seasonality in Trace Element Studies. In: *Prehistoric Human Bone: Archaeology at the Molecular Level*, Joseph B. Lambert and Gisela Grupe, eds., pp. 203–215. Berlin: Springer-Verlag.

Herrmann, Bernd, and Susanne Hummel (eds.)

1994   *Ancient DNA: Recovery and Analysis of Genetic Material from Paleontological, Archaeological, Museum, Medical, and Forensic Specimens*. Berlin: Springer-Verlag.

Hershkovitz, I., B. M. Rothschild, O. Dutour, and C. Greenwald

1998   Clues to Recognition of Fungal Origin of Lytic Skeletal Lesions. *American Journal of Physical Anthropology* 106(1):47–60.

Hesse, Brian, and Paula Wapnish

1997   Can Pig Remains Be Used for Ethnic Diagnosis in the Ancient Near East? In: *The Archaeology of Israel: Constructing the Past, Interpreting the Present*, Neil A. Silberman and David Small, eds., pp. 238–270. Sheffield: Sheffield Academic Press.

Higham, T.F.G., and P. L. Horn

2000   Seasonal Dating Using Fish Otoliths: Results from the Shag River Mouth Site, New Zealand. *Journal of Archaeological Science* 27(5):439–448.

Hildebolt, Charles F., Stephen Molnar, Memory Elvin-Lewis, and Jeffrey K. McKee

1988   The Effect of Geochemical Factors on Prevalences of Dental Diseases for Prehistoric Inhabitants of the State of Missouri. *American Journal of Physical Anthropology* 75(1):1–14.

Hildebrandt, William R., and Kelly R. McGuire

2002   The Ascendance of Hunting during the California Middle Archaic: An Evolutionary Perspective. *American Antiquity* 67(2):231–256.

2003   Large-Game Hunting, Gender-Differentiated Work Organization, and the Role of Evolutionary Ecology in California and Great Basin Prehistory: A Reply to Broughton and Bayham. *American Antiquity* 68(4):790–792.

Hill, Erica

1998   Gender-Informed Archaeology: The Priority of Definition, the Use of Analogy, and the Multivariate Approach. *Journal of Archaeological Method and Theory* 5(1):99–128.

Hill, H. Edward, and John Evans

1988   Vegeculture in Solomon Islands Prehistory from Pottery Residues. In: *Science and Archaeology, Glasgow 1987*, Elizabeth A. Slater and James O. Tate, eds., pp. 449–458. Oxford: British Archaeological Reports, International Series, No. 196 (2 vols.).

1989   Crops of the Pacific: New Evidence from the Chemical Analysis of Organic Residues in Pottery. In: *Foraging and Farming: The Evolution of Plant Exploitation*, David R. Harris and Gordon C. Hillman, eds., pp. 418–425. London: Unwin Hyman.

Hill, James N., and Richard H. Hevly

1968   Pollen at Broken K Pueblo: Some New Interpretations. *American Antiquity* 33(2):200–210.

Hill, Kim

1988   Macronutrient Modifications of Optimal Foraging Theory: An Approach Using Indifference Curves Applied to Some Modern Foragers. *Human Ecology* 16(2):157–197.

Hillman, Gordon C.

1986   Plant Foods in Ancient Diet: The Archaeological Role of Palaeofaeces in General and Lindow Man's Gut Contents in Particular. In: *Lindow Man: The Body in the Bog*, I. M. Stead, J. B. Bourke, and Don R. Brothwell, eds., pp. 99–115. Ithaca: Cornell University Press.

1989   Late Palaeolithic Plant Foods from Wadi Kubbaniya in Upper Egypt: Dietary Diversity, Infant Weaning, and Seasonality in a Riverine Environment. In: *Foraging and Farming: The Evolution of Plant Exploitation*, David R. Harris and Gordon C. Hillman, eds., pp. 207–239. London: Unwin Hyman.

Hillman, Gordon C., and M. Stuart Davies

1990   Measured Domestication Rates in Wild Wheats and Barley under Primitive Cultivation, and Their Archaeological Implications. *Journal of World Prehistory* 4(2):157–322.

Hillman, Gordon C., Ewa Madeyska, and Jonathan Hather

1989   Wild Plant Foods and Diet at Late Paleolithic Wadi Kubbaniya: The Evidence from Charred Remains. In: *The Prehistory of Wadi Kubbaniya. Vol. 2: Stratigraphy, Paleoeconomy, and Environment*, Fred Wendorf, Romuald Schild, and Angela E. Close, eds., pp. 162–242. Dallas: Southern Methodist University.

Hillman, Gordon C., Sue Wales, Francis McLaren, John Evans, and Ann Butler

1993   Identifying Problematic Remains of Ancient Plant Foods: A Comparison of the Role of Chemical, Histological and Morphological Criteria. *World Archaeology* 25(1):94–121.

Hillson, Simon W.

1979   Diet and Dental Disease. *World Archaeology* 11(2):147–162.

1986   *Teeth*. Cambridge: Cambridge Manuals in Archaeology, Cambridge University Press.

1996   *Dental Anthropology*. Cambridge: Cambridge University Press.

2001   Recording Dental Caries in Archaeological Human Remains. *International Journal of Osteoarchaeology* 11(4):249–289.

Hinkes, M. J.

1983   Skeletal Evidence of Stress in Subadults: Trying to Come of Age at Grasshopper Pueblo. Ph.D. dissertation, Department of Anthropology, University of Arizona, Tucson.

Ho, K.-J., K. Biss, B. Mikkelson, L. A. Lewis, and C. B. Taylor

1971   The Masai of East Africa: Some Unique Biological Characteristics. *Archives of Pathology* 91(5):387–410.

Hodell, David A., Rhonda L. Quinn, Mark Brenner, and George Kamenov

2004   Spatial Variation of Strontium Isotopes ($^{87}Sr/^{86}Sr$) in the Maya Region: A Tool for Tracking Ancient Human Migration. *Journal of Archaeological Science* 31(5):585–601.

Hoffman, R., and C. Hays

1987   The Eastern Wood Rat (*Neotoma floridana*) as a Taphonomic Factor in Archaeological Sites. *Journal of Archaeological Science* 14:325–337.

Hohmann, J. W.

1992   Through the Mirror of Death: A View of Prehistoric Social Complexity in Central Arizona. Ph.D. dissertation, Department of Anthropology, Arizona State University, Tempe.

Holden, Timothy G.

1986   Preliminary Report on the Detailed Analyses of the Macroscopic Remains from the Gut of Lindow Man. In: *Lindow Man: The Body in the Bog*, I. M. Stead, J. B. Bourke, and Don R. Brothwell, eds., pp. 116–125. Ithaca: Cornell University Press.

1990   The Rehydration of Coprolites Using Trisodium Phosphate Solution: Colour Reaction and Smell. *Paleopathology Newsletter* 71:9–12.

1991   Evidence of Prehistoric Diet from Northern Chile: Coprolites, Gut Contents and Flotation Samples from the Tulán Quebrada. *World Archaeology* 22(3):320–331.

Holden, Timothy G.

1994   Dietary Evidence from the Intestinal Contents of Ancient Humans with Particular Reference to Desiccated Remains from Northern Chile. In: *Tropical Archaeobotany: Applications and New Developments*, Jon G. Hather, ed., pp. 65–85. London: Routledge.

Holland, Mitchell M., Deborah L. Fisher, Lloyd G. Mitchell, William C. Rodriquez,
James J. Canik, Carl R. Merril, and Victor W. Weedn

1993   Mitrochondrial DNA Sequence Analysis of Human Skeletal Remains: Identification of Remains from the Vietnam War. *Journal of Forensic Sciences*
38(3):542–553.

Holland, Thomas D.

1989   Fertility in the Prehistoric Midwest: A Critique of Unifactoral Models. *American
Antiquity* 54(3):614–625.

Holland, Thomas D., and Michael J. O'Brien

1997   Parasites, Porotic Hyperostosis, and the Implications of Changing Perspectives.
American Antiquity 62(2):183–193.

Holliday, D. Y.

1993   Occipital Lesions: A Possible Cost of Cradleboards. *American Journal of Physical
Anthropology* 90:283–290.

Holloway, Richard G., and Vaughn M. Bryant Jr.

1986   New Directions in Palynology in Ethnobiology. *Journal of Ethnobiology*
6(1):47–65.

Honch, Noah V., T.F.G. Higham, J. Chapman, B. Gaydarska, and Robert E. M. Hedges

2006   A Palaeodietary Investigation of Carbon ($^{13}C/^{12}C$) and Nitrogen ($^{15}N/^{14}N$) in
Human and Faunal Bones from the Copper Age Cemeteries of Varna I and
Durankulak, Bulgaria. *Journal of Archaeological Science* 33(11):1493–1504.

Hoogewerff, Jurian, Wolfgang Papesch, Martin Kralik, Margit Berner, Pieter Vroon, Hermann Miesbauer, Othmar Gaber, Karl-Heinz Künzel, and Jos Kleinjans

2001   The Last Domicile of the Iceman from Hauslabjoch: A Geochemical Approach
Using Sr, C and O Isotopes and Trace Element Signatures. *Journal of Archaeological Science* 28(9):983–989.

Hooper, Lucile

1920   *The Cahuilla Indians*. Berkeley: University of California Publications in American Archaeology and Ethnology 16(6).

Hooton, E. A.

1930   *The Indians of Pecos Pueblo: A Study of Their Skeletal Remains*. New Haven: Yale
University Press.

Hoppa, Robert D., and Charles M. FitzGerald (eds.)

1999   *Human Growth in the Past: Studies from Bones and Teeth*. Cambridge: Cambridge University Press.

Hoppa, Robert D., and James W. Vaupel (eds.)

2002   *Paleodemography: Age Distributions from Skeletal Samples*. Cambridge: Cambridge University Press.

Hoppe, Kathryn A., Paul L. Koch, and T. T. Furutani

2003   Assessing the Preservation of Biogenic Strontium in Fossil Bones and Tooth Enamel. *International Journal of Osteoarchaeology* 13(1–2):20–28.

Hopps, Howard C.

1974   The Biologic Bases for Using Hair and Nail for Analysis of Trace Elements. In: *Trace Elements in Environmental Health, Vol. 8*, Delbert D. Hemphill. ed., pp. 59–73. Columbia: University of Missouri Press.

Horne, Patrick D.

1985   A Review of the Evidence of Human Endoparasitism in the Pre-Columbian New World through the Study of Coprolites. *Journal of Archaeological Science* 12(4):299–310.

Horrocks, M.

2005   A Combined Procedure for Recovering Phytoliths and Starch Residues from Soils, Sedimentary Deposits and Similar Materials. *Journal of Archaeological Science* 32(8):1169–1175.

Hortolà, Policarp

2002   Red Blood Cell Haemotaphonomy of Experimental Human Bloodstains on Techno-Prehistoric Lithic Raw Materials. *Journal of Archaeological Science* 29(7):733–739.

Howland, Michael R., Lorna T. Corr, Suzanne M. M. Young, V. Jones, S. Jim, Nikolaas J. van der Merwe, Alva D. Mitchell, and Richard P. Evershed

2003   Expression of the Dietary Isotope Signal in the Compound-Specific $\delta^{13}C$ Values of Pig Bone Lipids and Amino Acids. *International Journal of Osteoarchaeology* 13(1–2):54–65.

Hrdlička, Aleš

1910   Report on Skeletal Material from Missouri Mounds, Collected in 1906–1907 by Mr. Gerand Fowke. *Bureau of American Ethnology Bulletin* 37:103–319.

1927   Anthropology and Medicine. *American Journal of Physical Anthropology* 10(1):1–9.

1941   Diseases of and Artifacts on Skulls and Bones from Kodiak Island. *Smithsonian Miscellaneous Collections* 101(4).

Hu, Yaowu, Stanley H. Ambrose, and Changsui Wang

2006   Stable Isotopic Analysis of Human Bones from the Jiahu Site, Henan, China: Implications for the Transition to Agriculture. *Journal of Archaeological Science* 33(9):1319–1330.

Hudson, Jean

1993   The Impacts of Domestic Dogs on Bone in Forager Camps. In: *From Bones to Behavior: Ethnoarchaeological and Experimental Contributions to the Interpretation of Faunal Remains*, Jean Hudson, ed., pp. 301–323. Carbondale: Center for Archaeological Investigations, Southern Illinois University, Occasional Paper No. 21.

Hummel, Susanne, and Bernd Herrmann

1994   Y-Chromosomal DNA from Ancient Bones. In: *Ancient DNA: Recovery and Analysis of Genetic Material from Paleontological, Archaeological, Museum,*

Medical, and Forensic Specimens, Bernd Herrmann and Susanne Hummel, eds., pp. 205–210. Berlin: Springer-Verlag.

Hunt, C. O., G. Rushworth, D. D. Gilbertson, and D. J. Mattingly

2001   Romano-Lybian Dryland Animal Husbandry and Landscape: Pollen and Paly-nofacies Analysis of Coprolites from a Farm in the Wadi el-Amud, Tripolitania. *Journal of Archaeological Science* 28(4):351–363.

Huntingford, G.W.B.

1953   The Southern Nilo-Hamites. *Ethnographic Survey of Africa* 2(8), International African Institute, London.

1955   The Economic Life of the Dorobo. *Anthropos* 50:602–634.

Hurlbut, Sharon A.

2000   The Taphonomy of Cannibalism: A Review of Anthropogenic Bone Modification in the American Southwest. *International Journal of Osteoarchaeology* 10(1):4–26.

Huss-Ashmore, Rebecca, Alan H. Goodman, and George J. Armelagos

1982   Nutritional Inference from Paleopathology. In: *Advances in Archaeological Method and Theory, Vol. 5*, Michael B. Schiffer, ed., pp. 395–474. New York: Academic Press.

Hutchinson, Dale L., and Clark Spencer Larsen

1995   Physiological Stress in the Prehistoric Stillwater Marsh: Evidence of Enamel Defects. In: *Bioarchaeology of the Stillwater Marsh: Prehistoric Human Adaptation in the Western Great Basin*, Clark Spencer Larsen and Robert L. Kelly, eds., pp. 81–95. New York: American Museum of Natural History, Anthropological Papers 77.

2001   Enamel Hypoplasia and Stress in La Florida. In: *Bioarchaeology of Spanish Florida: The Impact of Colonialism*, Clark Spencer Larsen, ed., pp. 181–206. Gainesville: University of Florida Press.

Hyland, D. C., J. M. Tersak, J. M. Adovasio, and M. I. Siegel

1990   Identification of the Species of Origin of Residual Blood on Lithic Material. *American Antiquity* 55(1):104–113.

Hylander, W. C.

1975   The Adaptive Significance of Eskimo Craniofacial Morphology. In: *Oro-facial Growth and Development*, A. A. Dahlberg and T. M. Graber, eds., pp. 129–169. The Hague: Mouton.

Iacumin, P., H. Bocherens, L. Chaix, and A. Marioth

1998   Stable Carbon and Nitrogen Isotopes as Dietary Indicators of Ancient Nubian Populations (Northern Sudan). *Journal of Archaeological Science* 25(4):293–301.

Ingold, Tim

1987   *The Appropriation of Nature: Essays on Human Ecology and Social Relations.* Iowa City: University of Iowa Press.

Işcan, Mehmet Y., and Kenneth A. R. Kennedy (eds.)

1989   *Reconstruction of Life from the Skeleton.* New York: Alan R. Liss, Inc.

Ivanhoe, Francis

1985   Elevated Orthograde Skeletal Plasticity of Some Archaeological Populations from Mexico and the American Southwest: Direct Relation to Maize Phytate

Nutritional Load. In: *Health and Disease in the Prehistoric Southwest*, Charles F. Merbs and Robert J. Miller, eds., pp. 165–175. Tempe: Arizona State University, Anthropological Research Papers, No. 34.

Ives, Rachel, and Megan Brickley

2005   Metacarpal Radiogrammetry: A Useful Indicator of Bone Loss throughout the Skeleton? *Journal of Archaeological Science* 32(10):1552–1559.

Iwaniec, U.T.

1989   Nuvakwewtaqa: An Analysis of Pathology in a Sinagua Population. Master's thesis, Arizona State University, Tempe.

Izumi, S., and T. Sono

1963   *Andes 2: Excavations at Kotosh, Peru, 1960*. Tokyo: Kadokawa Publishing Company.

Izumi, S., and K. Terada

1972   *Andes 4: Excavations at Kotosh, Peru, 1963–1966*. Tokyo: University of Tokyo Press.

Jackes, Mary

1992   Paleodemography: Problems and Techniques. In: *The Skeletal Biology of Past People: Research Methods*, Shelley R. Saunders and M. Anne Katzenberg, eds., pp. 189–224. New York: John Wiley & Sons.

Jahren, A. H., L. C. Todd, and R. G. Amundson

1998   Stable Isotope Dietary Analysis of Bison Bone Samples from the Hudson-Meng Bonebed: Effects on Paleotopography. *Journal of Archaeological Science* 25(5):465–475.

Jay, Mandy, and Michael P. Richards

2006   Diet in the Iron Age Cemetery Population at Wetwang Slack, East Yorkshire, U.K.: Carbon and Nitrogen Stable Isotope Evidence. *Journal of Archaeological Science* 33(5):653–662.

Jenkins, Dennis L.

2007   Distribution and Dating of Cultural and Paleontological Remains at the Paisley Five Mile Point Caves in the Northern Great Basin. In: *Paleoindian or Paleoarchaic: Great Basin Human Ecology at the Pleistocene-Holocene Transition*, Kelly E. Graf and Dave N. Schmitt, eds., pp. 57–81. Salt Lake City: University of Utah Press.

Jennings, Jesse D.

1957   *Danger Cave*. Salt Lake City: University of Utah, Anthropological Papers, No. 27.

Jin, Ye, and Hak-Kong Yip

2002   Supragingival Calculus: Formation and Control. *Critical Reviews in Oral Biology and Medicine* 13(5):426–441.

Jochim, Michael A.

1983   Optimization Models in Context. In: *Archaeological Hammers and Theories*, James A. Moore and Authur S. Keene, eds., pp. 157–172. New York: Academic Press.

1998   *A Hunter-Gatherer Landscape: Southwest Germany in the Late Paleolithic and Mesolithic*. New York: Plenum Press.

Jones, Andrew K. G.

1986a   Fish Bone Survival in the Digestive System of the Pig, Dog, and Man: Some Experiments. In: *Fish and Archaeology: Studies in Osteometry, Taphonomy, Seasonality and Fishing Methods*, D. C. Brinkhuizen and A. T. Claseneds, eds., pp. 53–61. Oxford: British Archaeological Reports, International Series, No. 294.

1986b   Parasitological Investigations on Lindow Man. In: *Lindow Man: The Body in the Bog*, I. M. Stead, J. B. Bourke, and Don R. Brothwell, eds., pp. 136–139. Ithaca: Cornell University Press.

Jones, C. E. Roland

1989   Archaeochemistry: Fact or Fancy? In: *The Prehistory of Wadi Kubbaniya. Vol. 2: Stratigraphy, Paleoeconomy, and Environment*, Fred Wendorf, Romuald Schild, and Angela E. Close, eds., pp. 260–266. Dallas: Southern Methodist University.

Jones, Joseph

1876   Explorations of the Aboriginal Remains of Tennessee. *Smithsonian Contributions to Knowledge* 22(259).

Jones, John G.

1988   Middle to Late Preceramic (6000–3000 BP) Subsistence Patterns on the Central Coast of Peru: The Coprolite Evidence. Master's thesis, Texas A&M University, College Station.

1993   Analysis of Pollen and Phytoliths in Residue from a Colonial Period Ceramic Vessel. In: *Current Research in Phytolith Analysis: Applications in Archaeology and Paleoecology*, Deborah M. Pearsall and Dolores R. Piperno, eds., pp. 31–35. Philadelphia: University of Pennsylvania, University Museum of Archaeology and Anthropology, MASCA Research Papers in Science and Archaeology, Vol. 10.

Jones, Volney H.

1936   The Vegetable Remains of Newt Kash Hollow. In: *Rockshelters in Menefee County, Kentucky*, W. S. Webb and W. D. Funkhouser, eds., pp. 147–165. Lexington: University of Kentucky Reports in Archaeology and Anthropology 3.

Jouy-Avantin, Françoise, André Debenath, Anne-Marie Moigne, and Hélène Moné

2003   A Standardized Method for the Description and the Study of Coprolites. *Journal of Archaeological Science* 30(3):367–372.

Kaestle, Frederika A.

1995   Mitochondrial DNA Evidence for the Identity of the Descendants of the Prehistoric Stillwater Marsh Population. In: *Bioarchaeology of the Stillwater Marsh: Prehistoric Human Adaptation in the Western Great Basin*, Clark Spencer Larsen and Robert L. Kelly, eds., pp. 73–80. New York: American Museum of Natural History, Anthropological Papers 77.

Kaestle, Frederika A., and David Glenn Smith

2001   Ancient Mitochondrial DNA Evidence for Prehistoric Population Movement: The Numic Expansion. *American Journal of Physical Anthropology* 115(1):1–12.

Kamp, Kathryn A., and John C. Whittaker

1999   *Surviving Adversity: The Sinagua of Lizard Man Village*. Salt Lake City: University of Utah, Anthropological Papers, No. 120.

Katzenberg, M. Anne

1988   Stable Isotope Analysis of Animal Bone and the Reconstruction of Human Paleo-
diet. In: *Diet and Subsistence: Current Archaeological Perspectives*, Brenda V.
Kennedy and Genevieve M. LeMoine, eds., pp. 307–314. Proceedings of the
Nineteenth Annual Chacmool Conference, University of Calgary.

1992   Advances in Stable Isotope Analysis of Prehistoric Bones. In: *The Skeletal Biology
of Past People: Research Methods*, Shelley R. Saunders and M. Anne Katzenberg,
eds., pp. 105–120. New York: John Wiley & Sons.

1993   Age Differences and Population Variation in Stable Isotope Values from
Ontario, Canada. In: *Prehistoric Human Bone: Archaeology at the Molecu-
lar Level*, Joseph B. Lambert and Gisela Grupe, eds., pp. 39–62. Berlin:
Springer-Verlag.

Katzenberg, M. Anne, and Roman G. Harrison

1997   What's in a Bone? Recent Advances in Archaeological Bone Chemistry. *Journal
of Archaeological Research* 5(3):265–293.

Katzenberg, M. Anne, and H. Roy Krouse

1989   Application of Stable Isotope Variation in Human Tissues to Problems in Identification. *Canadian Journal of Forensic Science* 22(1):7–19.

Katzenberg, M. Anne, and Mary K. Sandford

1995   Applications of Trace Mineral Analysis of Archaeological Tissue. In: *Proceedings of the First World Congress on Mummy Studies*, Vol. 2, pp. 543–548. Museo
Arqueológico y Etnográfico de Tenerife.

Katzenberg, M. Anne, and Andrzej Weber

1999   Stable Isotope Ecology and Palaeodiet in the Lake Baikal Region of Siberia. *Journal of Archaeological Science* 26(6):651–659.

Katzenberg, M. Anne, Shelley R. Saunders, and William R. Fitzgerald

1993   Age Differences in Stable Carbon and Nitrogen Isotope Ratios in a Population
of Prehistoric Maize Horticulturalists. *American Journal of Physical Anthropology*
90(3):267–281.

Katzenberg, M. Anne, Henry P. Schwarcz, Martin Knyf, and F. Jerome Melbye

1995   Stable Isotope Evidence for Maize Horticulture and Paleodiet in Southern
Ontario, Canada. *American Antiquity* 60(2):335–350.

Katzenberg, M. Anne, D. A. Herring, and Shelley R. Saunders

1996   Weaning and Infant Mortality: Evaluating the Skeletal Evidence. *Yearbook of
Physical Anthropology* 39:177–199.

Katzenberg, M. Anne, Shelley R. Saunders, and Sylvia Abonyi

2000   Bone Chemistry, Food and History: A Case Study from 19th Century Upper Canada. In: *Biogeochemical Approaches to Paleodietary Analysis*, Stanley H. Ambrose
and Anne M. Katzenberg, eds., pp. 1–22. New York: Kluwer Academic/Plenum
Publishers.

Kealhofer, Lisa, Robin Torrence, and Richard Fullagar

1999   Integrating Phytoliths within Use-Wear/Residue Studies of Stone Tools. *Journal
of Archaeological Science* 26(5):527–546.

Keegan, William F.

1989   Stable Isotope Analysis of Prehistoric Diet. In: *Reconstruction of Life from the Skeleton*, Mehmet Y. Işcan and Kenneth A. R. Kennedy, eds., pp. 223–236. New York: Alan R. Liss, Inc.

Keegan, William F., and Michael J. DeNiro

1988   Stable Carbon- and Nitrogen-Isotope Ratios of Bone Collegen Used to Study Coral-Reef and Terrestrial Components of Prehistoric Bahamian Diet. *American Antiquity* 53(2):320–336.

Keenleyside, Anne, X. Song, D. R. Chettle, and C. E. Weber

1996   The Lead Content of Human Bones from the 1845 Franklin Expedition. *Journal of Archaeological Science* 23(3):461–465.

Keenleyside, Anne, Henry Schwarcz, and Kristina Panayotova

2006   Stable Isotope Evidence of Diet in a Greek Colonial Population from the Black Sea. *Journal of Archaeological Science* 33(9):1205–1215.

Kelley, J. Charles

1980   Discussion of Papers by Plog, Doyel and Riley. In: *Current Issues in Hohokam Prehistory, Proceedings of a Symposium*, David Doyel and Fred Plog, eds., pp. 23–48. Tempe: Arizona State University, Anthropological Research Papers, No. 23.

Kelley, Marc A.

1989   Infectious Disease. In: *Reconstruction of Life from the Skeleton*, Mehmet Y. Işcan and Kenneth A. R. Kennedy, eds., pp. 191–199. New York: Alan R. Liss, Inc.

1991   Ethnohistorical Accounts as a Method of Assessing Health, Disease, and Population Decline among Native Americans. In: *Human Paleopathology: Current Syntheses and Future Options*, Donald J. Ortner and Arthur C. Aufderheide, eds., pp. 111–118. Washington, D.C.: Smithsonian Institution Press.

Kelley, Marc A., and Clark Spencer Larsen (eds.)

1991   *Advances in Dental Anthropology*. New York: Wiley-Liss.

Kelso, Gerald K.

1976   Absolute Pollen Frequencies Applied to the Interpretation of Human Activities in Northern Arizona. Ph.D. dissertation, University of Arizona, Tucson.

1994   Palynology in Historical Rural-Landscape Studies: Great Meadows, Pennsylvania. *American Antiquity* 59(2):359–372.

Kennedy, Kenneth A. R.

1989   Skeletal Markers of Occupational Stress. In: *Reconstruction of Life from the Skeleton*, Mehmet Y. Işcan and Kenneth A. R. Kennedy, eds., pp. 129–160. New York: Alan R. Liss, Inc.

Kennett, Douglas J., and Barbara Voorhies

1996   Oxygen Isotopic Analysis of Archaeological Shells to Detect Seasonal Use of Wetlands on the Southern Pacific Coast of Mexico. *Journal of Archaeological Science* 23(5):689–704.

Kent, Susan

1992   Anemia through the Ages: Changing Perspectives and Their Implications. In: *Diet, Demography, and Disease: Changing Perspectives on Anemia*, Patricia Stuart-Macadam and Susan Kent, eds., pp. 1–30. New York: Aldine de Gruyter.

Kenward, Harry, and John Carrott

2001   *Technical Report: Invertebrate Remains from Two Samples from Excavations at Broadgate, London (Sitecode: BGA90)*. London: Museum of London Specialist Services, Reports from the Environmental Archaeology Unit, York 2001/32.

Kimura, Birgitta, Steven A. Brandt, Bruce L. Hardy, and William W. Hauswirth

2001   Analysis of DNA from Ethnoarchaeological Stone Scrapers. *Journal of Archaeological Science* 28(1):45–53.

Kjellström, A.

2004   Evaluations of Sex Assessment Using Weighted Traits on Incomplete Skeletal Remains. *International Journal of Osteoarchaeology* 14(5):360–373.

Klein, Richard G., and Kathryn Cruz-Uribe

1984   *The Analysis of Animal Bones from Archaeological Sites*. Chicago: University of Chicago Press.

Klepinger, Linda L.

1984   Nutritional Assessment from Bone. *Annual Review of Anthropology* 13:75–96.

1994   Can Elemental Analysis of Archaeological Skeletons Determine Past Diet and Health? In: *Ancient Technologies and Archaeological Materials*, Sarah U. Wisseman and Wendell S. Williams, eds., pp. 87–97. Amsterdam: Gordon and Breach.

Kliks, M. M.

1990   Helminths as Heirlooms and Souvenirs: A Review of New World Paleoparasitology. *Parasitology Today* 6(4):93–100.

Klippel, W. E.

2001   Sugar Monoculture, Bovid Skeletal Part Frequencies, and Stable Carbon Isotopes: Interpreting Enslaved African Diet at Brimstone Hill, St. Kitts, West Indies. *Journal of Archaeological Science* 28(11):1191–1198.

Knights, B. A., Camilla A. Dickson, J. H. Dickson, and D. J. Breeze

1983   Evidence Concerning the Roman Military Diet at Bearsden, Scotland, in the 2nd Century AD. *Journal of Archaeological Science* 10(2):139–152.

Knörzer, K.-H.

1984   Aussagemöglichkeiten von Paläoethnobotanischen Latrinenuntersuchungen (The Prospects of the Palaeoethnobotanical Examination of Cesspits). In: *Plants and Ancient Man: Studies in Paleoethnobotany*, W. Van Zeist and W. A. Casparie, eds., pp. 331–338. Rotterdam: A. A. Balkema.

Knudson, Kelly J., Tiffiny A. Tung, Kenneth C. Nystrom, T. Douglas Price, and Paul D. Fullagar

2005   The Origin of the Juch'uypampa Cave Mummies: Strontium Isotope Analysis of Archaeological Human Remains from Bolivia. *Journal of Archaeological Science* 32(6):903–913.

Knudson, Kelly J., Arthur E. Aufderheide, and Jane E. Buikstra
2007   Seasonality and Paleodiet in the Chiribaya Polity of Southern Peru. *Journal of Archaeological Science* 34(3):451–462.

Kobori, Larry S.
1979   Differential Bone Recovery Experiment. In: *Ezra's Retreat: A Rockshelter/Cave Occupation Site in the North Central Great Basin*, James C. Bard, Colin I. Busby, and Larry S. Kobori, eds., pp. 228–229. Davis: University of California, Davis, Center for Archaeological Research at Davis, Publication No. 6.

Koch, Paul L., Noreen Tuross, and Marilyn L. Fogel
1997   The Effects of Sample Treatment and Diagenesis on the Isotopic Integrity of Carbonate in Biogenic Hydroxylapatite. *Journal of Archaeological Science* 24(5):417–429.

Koch, Paul L., Anna K. Behrensmeyer, Andrew W. Stott, Noreen Tuross, Richard P. Evershed, and Marilyn L. Fogel
2001   The Effects of Weathering on the Stable Isotope Composition of Bone. *Ancient Biomolecules* 3(2):117–134.

Kolman, Connie J., and Noreen Tuross
2000   Ancient DNA Analysis of Human Populations. *American Journal of Physical Anthropology* 111(1):5–23.

Kolman, Connie J., Eldredge Bermingham, Richard Cooke, R. H. Ward, Tomas D. Arias, and Francoise Guionneau-Sinclair
1995   Reduced mDNA Diversity in the Ngäbé Amerinds of Panama. *Genetics* 140:275–283.

Konigsberg, Lyle W., Jane Buikstra, and Jill Bullington
1989   Paleodemographic Correlates of Fertility: A Reply to Corruccini, Brandon, and Handler and to Holland. *American Antiquity* 54(3):626–636.

Kooyman, Brian, Margaret E. Newman, and Howard Ceri
1992   Verifying the Reliability of Blood Residue Analysis of Archaeological Tools. *Journal of Archaeological Science* 19(3):265–269.

Kooyman, Brian, Margaret E. Newman, Christine Cluney, Murray Lobb, Shayne Tolman, Paul McNeil, and L. V. Hills
2001   Identification of Horse Exploitation by Clovis Hunters Based on Protein Analysis. *American Antiquity* 66(4):686–691.

Körber-Grohne, Udelgard
1981   Distinguishing Prehistoric Cereal Grains of *Triticum* and *Sacale* on the Basis of Their Surface Patterns Using the Scanning Electron Microscope. *Journal of Archaeological Science* 8(2):197–204.

Körber-Grohne, Udelgard, and Ulrike Piening
1980   Microstructure of the Surfaces of Carbonized and Non-Carbonized Grains of Cereals as Observed in Scanning Electron and Light Microscopes as an Additional Aid in Determining Prehistoric Findings. *Flora* 170:189–228.

Kowal, Walter, Owen B. Beattie, Halfdan Baadsgaard, and Peter M. Krahn
1991   Source Identification of Lead Found in Tissues of Sailors from the Franklin Arctic Expedition of 1845. *Journal of Archaeological Science* 18(2):193–203.

Krantz, G. S.

1968   A New Method of Counting Mammal Bones. *American Journal of Archaeology* 72:285–288.

Kroeber, Albert L.

1925   *Handbook of the Indians of California*. Washington, D.C.: Bureau of American Ethnology Bulletin 78.

Krouse, H. R., and M. K. Herbert

1988   Sulphur and Carbon Isotope Studies of Food Webs. In: *Diet and Subsistence: Current Archaeological Perspectives*, Brenda V. Kennedy and Genevieve M. LeMoine, eds., pp. 315–322. Proceedings of the Nineteenth Annual Chacmool Conference, University of Calgary.

Krueger, Harold W.

1991   Exchange of Carbon with Biological Apatites. *Journal of Archaeological Science* 18(3):355–361.

Krueger, Harold W., and Charles H. Sullivan

1984   Models for Carbon Isotope Fractionation between Diet and Bone. In: *Stable Isotopes in Nutrition*, Judith R. Turnlund and Phyllis E. Johnson, eds., pp. 205–220. Washington, D.C.: American Chemical Society Symposium Series 258.

Kuckelman, Kristin A., Ricky R. Lightfoot, and Debra L. Martin

2002   The Bioarchaeology and Taphonomy of Violence at Castle Rock and Sand Canyon Pueblos, Southwestern Colorado. *American Antiquity* 67(3):486–513.

Kuhnlein, Harriet V., Alvin C. Chan, J. Neville Thompson, and Shuryo Nakai

1982   *Ooligan* Grease: A Nutritious Fat Used by Native People of Coastal British Columbia. *Journal of Ethnobiology* 2(2):154–161.

Kukis, A., P. Child, J. J. Myher, L. Marai, I. M. Yousef, and P. K. Lewin

1978   Bile Acids of a 3200-Year-Old Egyptian Mummy. *Canadian Journal of Biochemistry* 56:1141–1148.

Kunth, C.

1826   Examen Botanique. In: *Catalogue Raisonné et Historique des Antiquités Découvertes en Egypte*, Joseph Passalacqua, ed., pp. 227–229. Paris: Galerie d'Antiquités Égyptiennes.

Kyle, James H.

1986   Effect of Post-burial Contamination on the Concentrations of Major and Minor Elements in Human Bones and Teeth — The Implications for Paleodietary Research. *Journal of Archaeological Science* 13(5):403–416.

Lahr, M. M., and J. E. Bowman

1992   Paleopathology of the Kechipawan Site: Health and Disease in a Southwestern Pueblo. *Journal of Archaeological Science* 19(6):639–654.

Lallo, John W., George J. Armelagos, and Robert C. Mensforth

1977   The Role of Diet, Disease and Physiology in the Origin of Porotic Hyperostosis. *Human Biology* 49(3):471–483.

Lam, Y. M.

1994   Isotopic Evidence for Change in Dietary Patterns during the Baikal Neolithic. *Current Anthropology* 35(2):185–190.

Lambert, Joseph B.

1997   *Traces of the Past: Unraveling the Secrets of Archaeology through Chemistry.* Reading, Mass.: Helix Books.

Lambert, Joseph B., and Gisela Grupe (eds.)

1993   *Prehistoric Human Bone: Archaeology at the Molecular Level.* Berlin: Springer-Verlag.

Lambert, Joseph B., and Jane M. Weydert-Homeyer

1993a   Dietary Inferences from Elemental Analyses of Bone. In: *Prehistoric Human Bone: Archaeology at the Molecular Level*, Joseph B. Lambert and Gisela Grupe, eds., pp. 217–228. Berlin: Springer-Verlag.

1993b   The Fundamental Relationship between Ancient Diet and the Inorganic Constituents of Bone as Derived from Feeding Experiments. *Archaeometry* 35(2):279–294.

Lambert, Joseph B., Carole Bryda Szpunar, and Jane E. Buikstra

1979   Chemical Analysis of Excavated Human Bone from Middle and Late Woodland Sites. *Archaeometry* 21(2):115–129.

Lambert, Joseph B., Sharon Vlasak Simpson, Carole Bryda Szpunar, and Jane E. Buikstra

1984   Ancient Human Diet from Inorganic Analysis of Bone. *Accounts of Chemical Research* 17(9):298–305.

Lambert, Joseph B., Liang Xue, and Jane E. Buikstra

1989   Physical Removal of Contaminative Inorganic Material from Buried Human Bone. *Journal of Archaeological Science* 16(4):427–436.

Lambert, Joseph B., Jane M. Weydert, Sloan R. Williams, and Jane E. Buikstra

1990   Comparison of Methods for the Removal of Diagenetic Material in Buried Bone. *Journal of Archaeological Science* 17(4):453–468.

Lambert, Joseph B., Liang Xue, and Jane E. Buikstra

1991   Inorganic Analysis of Excavated Human Bone after Surface Removal. *Journal of Archaeological Science* 18(3):363–383.

Lambert, Patricia M.

1993   Health in Prehistoric Populations of the Santa Barbara Channel Islands. *American Antiquity* 58(3):509–522.

Lambert, Patricia M., Brian R. Billman, and Banks L. Leonard

2000   Explaining Variability in Mutilated Human Bone Assemblages from the American Southwest: A Case Study from the Southern Piedmont of Sleeping Ute Mountain, Colorado. *International Journal of Osteoarchaeology* 10(1):49–64.

Langdon, F. W.

1881   The Madisonville Prehistoric Cemetery: Anthropological Notes. *Journal of the Cincinnati Society of Natural History* 4:237–257.

Langsjoen, Odin

1998   Diseases of the Dentition. In: *The Cambridge Encyclopedia of Human Paleopathology*, by Authur C. Aufderheide and Conrado Rodríguez-Martín, pp. 393–412. Cambridge: Cambridge University Press.

Lanner, Ronald M.

1981   *The Piñon Pine*. Reno: University of Nevada Press.

1983   *Trees of the Great Basin*. Reno: University of Nevada Press.

Larsen, Clark Spencer

1983   Behavioral Implications of Temporal Changes in Cariogenesis. *Journal of Archaeological Science* 10(1):1–8.

1985   Dental Modifications and Tool Use in the Western Great Basin. *American Journal of Physical Anthropology* 67(4):393–402.

1987   Bioarchaeological Interpretations of Subsistence Economy and Behavior from Human Skeletal Remains. In: *Advances in Archaeological Method and Theory*, Vol. 10, Michael B. Schiffer, ed., pp. 339–445. New York: Academic Press.

1994   Health in Transition: Disease and Nutrition in the Georgia Bight. In: *Paleonutrition: The Diet and Health of Prehistoric Americans*, Kristin D. Sobolik, ed., pp. 222–234. Carbondale: Southern Illinois University, Center for Archaeological Investigations, Occasional Paper No. 22.

1997   *Bioarchaeology: Interpreting Behavior from the Human Skeleton*. Cambridge: Cambridge Studies in Biological Anthropology 21.

1998   Gender, Health, and Activity in Foragers and Farmers in the American Southeast: Implications for Social Organization in the Georgia Bight. In: *Sex and Gender in Paleopathological Perspective*, Anne L. Grauer and Patricia Stuart-Macadam, eds., pp. 165–187. Cambridge: Cambridge University Press.

2000   *Skeletons in Our Closet: Revealing Our Past through Bioarchaeology*. Princeton: Princeton University Press.

2002   Bioarchaeology: The Lives and Lifestyles of Past People. *Journal of Archaeological Research* 10(2):119–166.

2006   The Agricultural Revolution as Environmental Catastrophe: Implications for Health and Lifestyle in the Holocene. *Quaternary International* 150(1):12–20.

Larsen, Clark Spencer, Rebecca Shavit, and Mark C. Griffin

1991   Dental Caries Evidence for Dietary Change: An Archeological Context. In: *Advances in Dental Anthropology*, Marc A. Kelley and Clark Spencer Larsen, eds., pp. 179–202. New York: Wiley-Liss.

Larsen, Clark Spencer, Margaret J. Schoeninger, Nikolass J. van der Merwe, Katherine M. Moore, and Julia A. Lee-Thorp

1992   Carbon and Nitrogen Stable Isotopic Signatures of Human Dietary Change in the Georgia Bight. *American Journal of Physical Anthropology* 89(2):197–214.

Larsen, Clark Spencer, Dale L. Hutchenson, Margaret J. Schoeninger, and Lynette Norr

2001   Food and Stable Isotopes in La Florida. In: *Bioarchaeology of Spanish Florida: The Impact of Colonialism*, Clark Spencer Larsen, ed., pp. 52–81. Gainesville: University of Florida Press.

Lassen, Cadja, Susanne Hummel, and Bernd Herrmann

1996   PCR Based Sex Identification of Ancient Human Bones by Amplification of X- and Y-Chromosomal Sequences: A Comparison. *Ancient Biomolecules* 1(1):25–33.

Lawlor, Elizabeth J.

1992   Effects of Mojave Desert Rodents and Harvester Ants on Carbonized Seeds: Pre-
        liminary Results. Paper presented at the Great Basin Anthropological Confer-
        ence, Boise, Idaho.

1995   Archaeological Site-Formation Processes Affecting Plant Remains in the Mojave
        Desert. Ph.D. dissertation, University of California, Riverside.

Lawrence, Barbara

1957   Zoology. In: *The Identification of Non-artifactual Archaeological Materials*, Wal-
        ter W. Taylor, ed., pp. 41–42. Washington, D.C.: National Academy of Sciences–
        Natural Resource Council Publication 565.

Lawton, Harry W., and Lowell J. Bean

1968   A Preliminary Reconstruction of Aboriginal Agricultural Technology among the
        Cahuilla. *Indian Historian* 1(5):18–24, 29.

Laylander, Don

1997   The Last Days of Lake Cahuilla: The Elmore Site. *Pacific Coast Archaeological
        Society Quarterly* 33(1–2).

Leach, Jeff D.

1998   A Brief Comment on the Immunological Identification of Plant Residues on
        Prehistoric Stone Tools and Ceramics: Results of a Blind Test. *Journal of Archaeo-
        logical Science* 25(2):171–175.

Lee, Richard B.

1979   *The !Kung San: Men, Women, and Work in a Foraging Society.* Cambridge: Cam-
        bridge University Press.

1984   *The Dobe !Kung.* New York: Holt, Rinehart and Winston.

Lee-Thorp, Julia A.

2000   Preservation of Biogenic Carbon Isotopic Signals in Plio-Pleistocene Bone and
        Tooth Mineral. In: *Biogeochemical Approaches to Paleodietary Analysis*, Stanley H.
        Ambrose and Anne M. Katzenberg, eds., pp. 89–115. New York: Kluwer Academic/
        Plenum Publishers.

Lee-Thorp, Julia A., and Matt Sponheimer

2003   Three Case Studies Used to Assess the Reliability of Fossil Bone and Enamel Isotope
        Signals for Paleodietary Suudies. *Journal of Anthropological Archaeology* 22(3):208–216.

2006   Contributions of Biogeochemistry to Understanding Hominin Dietary Ecology.
        Yearbook of Physical Anthropology 49:131–148.

Lee-Thorp, Julia A., and Nikolaas J. van der Merwe

1987   Carbon Isotope Analysis of Fossil Bone Apatite. *South African Journal of Science*
        83(6):712–715.

1991   Aspects of the Chemistry of Modern and Fossil Biological Apatites. *Journal of
        Archaeological Science* 18(3):343–354.

Lee-Thorp, Julia A., Judith C. Sealy, and Nikolaas J. van der Merwe

1989   Stable Carbon Isotope Ratio Differences between Bone Collagen and Bone Apatite,
        and Their Relationship to Diet. *Journal of Archaeological Science* 16(6):585–599.

Lee-Thorp, Julia A., Judith C. Sealy, and Alan G. Morris

1993   Isotopic Evidence for Diets of Prehistoric Farmers in South Africa. In: *Prehistoric Human Bone: Archaeology at the Molecular Level*, Joseph B. Lambert and Gisela Grupe, eds., pp. 99–120. Berlin: Springer-Verlag.

Lee-Thorp, Julia A., Nikolaas J. van der Merwe, and C. K. Brain

1994   Diet of *Australopithecus robustus* at Swartkrans from Stable Carbon Isotope Analysis. *Journal of Human Evolution* 27(5):361–372.

Le Huray, Jonathan D., and Holger Schutkowski

2005   Diet and Social Status during the La Tène Period in Bohemia: Carbon and Nitrogen Stable Isotope Analysis of Bone Collagen from Kutná Hora-Karlov and Radovesice. *Journal of Anthropological Archaeology* 24(2):135–147.

Leney, Lawrence, and Richard W. Casteel

1975   Simplified Procedure for Examining Charcoal Specimens for Identification. *Journal of Archaeological Science* 2:153–159.

Leonard, Robert D.

2001   Evolutionary Archaeology. In: *Archaeological Theory Today*, Ian Hodder, ed., pp. 65–97. Cambridge, U.K.: Polity Press.

Leonardi, Giovanni, Mara Miglavacca, and Serenella Nardi

1999   Soil Phosphorus Analysis as an Integrative Tool for Recognizing Burial Ancient Ploughsoils. *Journal of Archaeological Science* 26(4):343–352.

Lewin, Peter K.

1991   Technological Innovations and Discoveries in the Investigation of Ancient Preserved Man. In: *Human Paleopathology: Current Syntheses and Future Options*, Donald J. Ortner and Arthur C. Aufderheide, eds., pp. 90–91. Washington, D.C.: Smithsonian Institution Press.

Lewis, Henry T.

1982   Fire Technology and Resource Management in Aboriginal North America and Australia. In: *Resource Managers: North American and Australian Hunter-Gatherers*, Nancy M. Williams and Eugene S. Hunn, eds., pp. 45–67. Boulder: Westview Press.

Lewis, M. E.

2004   Endocranial Lesions in Non-adult Skeletons: Understanding Their Aetiology. *International Journal of Osteoarchaeology* 14(2):82–97.

Lewis, Rhoda Owen

1981   Use of Opal Phytoliths in Paleoenvironmental Reconstruction. *Journal of Ethnobiology* 1(1):175–181.

Lieberman L. S.

2003   Dietary, Evolutionary, and Modernizing Influences on the Prevalence of Type-2 Diabetes. *Annual Review of Nutrition* 23:345–377.

Lieverse, Angela R.

1999   Diet and the Aetiology of Dental Calculus. *International Journal of Osteoarchaeology* 9(4):219–232.

Lieverse, Angela R., Andrzej W. Weber, Vladimir Ivanovich Bazaliiskiy, Olga Ivanovna
    Goriunova, and Nikolai Aleksandrovich Savel'ev
2006   Osteoarthritis in Siberia's Cis-Baikal: Skeletal Indicators of Hunter-Gatherer
        Adaptation and Cultural Change. *American Journal of Physical Anthropology*
        132(1):1–16.

Ligon, J. D.
1978   Reproductive Interdependence of Piñon Jays and Piñon Pines. *Ecological Mono-
        graphs* 48:111–126.

Likovsky, Jakub, Markéta Urbanova, Martin Hájek, Viktor Černý, and Petr Čech
2006   Two Cases of Leprosy from Žatec (Bohemia), Dated to the Turn of the 12th
        Century and Confirmed by DNA Analysis for *Mycobacterium leprae*. *Journal of
        Archaeological Science* 33(9):1276–1283.

Lillie, Malcolm C.
1996   Mesolithic and Neolithic Populations of Ukraine: Indications of Diet from Den-
        tal Pathology. *Current Anthropology* 37(1):135–142.

Lillie, Malcolm C., and Kenneth Jacobs
2006   Stable Isotope Analysis of 14 Individuals from the Mesolithic Cemetery of Vasi-
        lyevka II, Dnieper Rapids Region, Ukraine. *Journal of Archaeological Science*
        33(6):880–886.

Lillie, Malcolm C., and Mike Richards
2000   Stable Isotopic Analysis and Dental Evidence of Diet at the Mesolithic-
        Neolithic Transition in Ukraine. *Journal of Archaeological Science* 27(10):
        965–972.

Lin, D. S., W. E. Conner, Lewis K. Napton, and Robert F. Heizer
1978   The Steroids of 2,000-Year-Old Coprolites. *Journal of Lipid Research* 19(2):
        215–221.

Little, Barbara J.
1994   Consider the Hermaphroditic Mind: Comment on "The Interplay of Evidential
        Constraints and Political Interests: Recent Archaeological Research on Gender."
        American Antiquity 59(3):539–544.

Little, Elbert L., Jr.
1938   *Food Analysis of Piñon Nuts*. Tucson: Southwestern Forest and Range Experi-
        ment Station, Research Notes, No. 48.
1941   Managing Woodlands for Piñon Nuts. *Chronica Botanica* 6(15):348–349.

Little, Elizabeth A., and Margaret J. Schoeninger
1995   The Late Woodland Diet on Nantucket Island and the Problem of Maize in
        Coastal New England. *American Antiquity* 60(2):351–368.

Little, John D. C., and Elizabeth A. Little
1997   Analysing Prehistoric Diets by Linear Programming. *Journal of Archaeological
        Science* 24(8):741–747.

Lloyd, L. E., B. E. McDonald, and E. W. Crampton
1978   *Fundamentals of Nutrition* (2d ed.). San Francisco: W. H. Freeman and
        Company.

Loomis, F. B., and D. B. Young

1912   Shell Heaps of Maine. *The American Journal of Science* 34(199):17–42.

Loreille, Odile, Jean-Denis Vigne, Chris Hardy, Cecille Callou, Françoise Treinen-Claustre, Nicole Dennebouy, and Monique Monnerot

1997   First Distinction of Sheep and Goat Archaeological Bones by the Means of Their Fossil mtDNA. *Journal of Archaeological Science* 24(1):33–37.

Losey, Robert J., Sylvia Behrens Yamanda, and Leah Largaespada

2004   Late-Holocene Dungeness Crab (*Cancer magister*) Harvest at an Oregon Coast Estuary. *Journal of Archaeological Science* 31(11):1603–1612.

Loud, Llewellyn L., and Mark R. Harrington

1929   *Lovelock Cave*. University of California Publications in American Archeology and Ethnology 25(1).

Lovejoy, C. Owen, Richard S. Meindl, Thomas R. Pryzbeck, and Robert P. Mensforth

1985a   Chronological Metamorphosis of the Auricular Surface of the Ilium: A New Method for the Determination of Adult Skeletal Age at Death. *American Journal of Physical Anthropology* 68(1):15–28.

Lovejoy, C. Owen, Richard S. Meindl, Robert P. Mensforth, and Thomas J. Barton

1985b   Multifactorial Determination of Skeletal Age at Death: A Method and Blind Tests of Its Accuracy. *American Journal of Physical Anthropology* 68(1):1–14.

Lovell, Nancy C.

2000   Paleopathological Description and Diagnosis. In: *Biological Anthropology of the Human Skeleton*, M. Anne Katzenberg and Shelley R. Saunders, eds., pp. 211–242. New York: John Wiley & Sons.

Loy, Thomas H.

1983   Prehistoric Blood Residues: Detection on Tool Surfaces and Identification of Species of Origin. *Science* 220:1269–1271.

1991   Prehistoric Organic Residues: Recent Advances in Identification, Dating, and Their Antiquity. In: *Archaeometry '90*, Ernst Pernicka and Günther A. Wagner, eds., pp. 645–655. Basel: Birkhäuser Verlag.

1993   The Artifact as Site: An Example of the Biomolecular Analysis of Organic Residues on Prehistoric Tools. *World Archaeology* 25(1):44–63.

1994   Methods in the Analysis of Starch Residues on Prehistoric Stone Tools. In: *Tropical Archaeobotany: Applications and New Developments*, Jon G. Hather, ed., pp. 86–114. London: Routledge.

1996   Species-of-Origin Identification of Prehistoric Blood Residues Using Ancient DNA. Paper presented at the annual meeting of the Society for American Archaeology, New Orleans.

Loy, Thomas H., and E. James Dixon

1998   Blood Residues on Fluted Points from Eastern Beringia. *American Antiquity* 63(1):21–46.

Loy, Thomas H., and Andrée R. Wood

1989   Blood Residue Analysis at Çayönü Tepesi, Turkey. *Journal of Field Archaeology* 16(4):451–460.

Lubell, David, Mary Jackes, Henry P. Schwarcz, Martin Knyf, and Christopher Meiklejohn

1994   The Mesolithic-Neolithic Transition in Portugal: Isotopic and Dental Evidence of Diet. *Journal of Archaeological Science* 21(2):201–216.

Lukacs, John R.

1989   Dental Paleopathology: Methods for Reconstructing Dietary Patterns. In: *Reconstruction of Life from the Skeleton*, Mehmet Y. Işcan and Kenneth A. R. Kennedy, eds., pp. 261–286. New York: Alan R. Liss, Inc.

1996   Sex Differences in Dental Caries Rates with the Origin of Agriculture in South Asia. *Current Anthropology* 37(1):147–153.

Lukacs, John R., and Robert F. Pastor

1988   Activity-Induced Patterns of Dental Abrasion in Prehistoric Pakistan: Evidence from Mehrgarh and Harappa. *American Journal of Physical Anthropology* 76(3): 377–398.

Lukacs, John R., and Subhash R. Walimbe

1998   Physiological Stress in Prehistoric India: New Data on Localized Hypoplasia of Primary Canines Linked to Climate and Subsistence Change. *Journal of Archaeological Science* 25(6):571–585.

Lukacs, John R., Greg C. Nelson, and Subhash R. Walimbe

2001   Enamel Hypoplasia and Childhood Stress in Prehistory: New Data from India and Southwest Asia. *Journal of Archaeological Science* 28(11):1159–1169.

Luna, Leandro H.

2006   Evaluation of Uniradicular Teeth for Age-at-Death Estimations in a Sample from a Pampean Hunter-Gatherer Cemetery (Argentina). *Journal of Archaeological Science* 33(12):1706–1717.

Lyman, R. Lee

1979   Available Meat from Faunal Remains: A Consideration of Techniques. *American Antiquity* 44(3):536–546.

1982   Archaeofaunas and Subsistence Studies. In: *Advances in Archaeological Method and Theory, Vol. 5*, Michael B. Schiffer, ed., pp. 331–393. New York: Academic Press.

1987a   Archaeofaunas and Butchery Studies: An Archaeological Perspective. In: *Advances in Archaeological Method and Theory, Vol. 10*, Michael B. Schiffer, ed., pp. 249–337. New York: Academic Press.

1987b   Zooarchaeology and Taphonomy: A General Consideration. *Journal of Ethnobiology* 7(1):93–117.

1994a   *Vertebrate Taphonomy*. Cambridge: Cambridge University Press.

1994b   Quantitative Units and Terminology in Zooarchaeology. *American Antiquity* 59(1):36–71.

2008   *Quantitative Paleozoology*. Cambridge: Cambridge Manuals in Archaeology, Cambridge University Press.

Lyman, R. Lee, and Michael J. O'Brien

1998   The Goals of Evolutionary Archaeology: History and Explanation. *Current Anthropology* 39(5):615–652.

Lynn, George E., and Jaime T. Benitez

1974   Temporal Bone Preservation in a 2600-Year-Old Egyptian Mummy. *Science* 183:200–202.

Lynnerup, Niels, Henrik Hjalgrim, Lene Rindal Nielsen, Henrik Gregersen, and Ingolf Thuesen

1997   Non-invasive Archaeology of Skeletal Material by CT Scanning and Three-Dimensional Reconstruction. *International Journal of Osteoarchaeology* 7(1):91–94.

Macho, G. A., R. L. Abel, and H. Schutkowski

2005   Age Changes in Bone Microstructure: Do They Occur Uniformly? *International Journal of Osteoarchaeology* 15(6):421–430.

MacHugh, David E., Ceiridwen J. Edwards, Jillian F. Bailey, David R. Bancroft, and Daniel G. Bradley

2000   The Extraction and Analysis of Ancient DNA from Bone and Teeth: A Survey of Current Methodologies. *Ancient Biomolecules* 3(2):81–102.

Mack, Richard N., and Vaughn M. Bryant Jr.

1974   Modern Pollen Spectra from the Columbia Basin, Washington. *Northwest Science* 48:183–194.

MacNeish, Richard S.

1958   Preliminary Archaeological Investigations in the Sierra de Tamaulipas, Mexico. *Transactions of the American Philosophical Society* 48(6).

1964   Ancient Mesoamerican Civilization. *Science* 143:531–537.

1967   An Interdisciplinary Approach to an Archaeological Problem. In: *The Prehistory of the Tehuacan Valley. Vol. I: Environment and Subsistence*, Douglas S. Byers, ed., pp. 14–24. Austin: University of Texas Press.

Madsen, David B.

1986   Great Basin Nuts: A Short Treatise on the Distribution, Productivity, and Prehistoric Use of Pinyon. In: *Anthropology in the Desert West: Essays in Honor of Jesse D. Jennings*, Carol J. Condie and Don D. Fowler, eds., pp. 21–41. Salt Lake City: University of Utah, Anthropological Papers, No. 110.

Madsen, David B., and David Rhode (eds.)

1994   *Across the West: Human Population Movement and the Expansion of the Numa.* Salt Lake City: University of Utah Press.

Magennis, Ann L., and Linda Scott Cummings

1986   A Record of Food and Grit in Human Dental Calculus at Kichpanha, Belize. *American Journal of Physical Anthropology, Supplement* 22:155 (abstract).

Maguire, David J.

1983   The Identification of Agricultural Activity Using Pollen Analysis. In: *Integrating the Subsistence Economy*, Martin Jones, ed., pp. 5–18. Oxford: British Archaeological Reports, International Series, No. 181.

Mainland, Ingrid L.

1998   Dental Microwear and Diet in Domestic Sheep (*Ovis aries*) and Goats (*Capra hircus*): Distinguishing Grazing and Fodder-Fed Ovicaprids Using a Quantitative Analytical Approach. *Journal of Archaeological Science* 25(12):1259–1271.

Makarewicz, Cheryl, and Noreen Tuross

2006   Foddering by Mongolian Pastoralists Is Recorded in the Stable Carbon ($\delta^{13}C$) and Nitrogen ($\delta^{15}N$) Isotopes of Caprine Dentinal Collagen. *Journal of Archaeological Science* 33(6):862–870.

Malainey, M. E., R. Przybylski, and B. L. Sherriff

1999a   Identifying the Former Contents of Late Precontact Period Pottery Vessels from Western Canada Using Gas Chromatography. *Journal of Archaeological Science* 26(4):425–438.

1999b   The Effects of Thermal and Oxidative Degradation on the Fatty Acid Composition of Food Plants and Animals of Western Canada: Implications for the Identification of Archaeological Vessel Residues. *Journal of Archaeological Science* 26(1):95–103.

Maloney, Bernard K.

1994   The Prospects and Problems of Using Palynology to Trace the Origins of Tropical Agriculture: The Case of Southeast Asia. In: *Tropical Archaeobotany: Applications and New Developments*, Jon G. Hather, ed., pp. 139–171. London: Routledge.

Manchester, Keith

1981   A Leprous Skeleton of the 7th Century from Eccles, Kent, and the Present Evidence of Leprosy in Great Britain. *Journal of Archaeological Science* 8(2):205–209.

1991   Tuberculosis and Leprosy: Evidence for Interaction of Disease. In: *Human Paleopathology: Current Syntheses and Future Options*, Donald J. Ortner and Arthur C. Aufderheide, eds., pp. 23–35. Washington, D.C.: Smithsonian Institution Press.

Mangafa, Maria, and Kostas Kotsakis

1996   A New Method for the Identification of Wild and Cultivated Charred Grape Seeds. *Journal of Archaeological Science* 23(3):409–418.

Manning, Andrew P.

1994   A Cautionary Note on the Use of Hemastix and Dot-Blot Assays for the Detection and Confirmation of Archaeological Blood Residues. *Journal of Archaeological Science* 21(2):159–162.

Marchbanks, Michael Lee

1989   Lipid Analysis in Archaeology: An Initial Study of Ceramics and Subsistence at the George C. Davis Site. Master's thesis, University of Texas, Austin.

Marchi, Damiano, Vitale S. Sparacello, Brigitte M. Holt, and Vincenzo Formicola

2006   Biomechanical Approach to the Reconstruction of Activity Patterns in Neolithic Western Liguria, Italy. *American Journal of Physical Anthropology* 131(4): 447–455.

Marek, M.

1990   Long Bone Growth of Mimbres Subadults from the NAN Ranch (LA15049), New Mexico. Master's thesis, Texas A&M University, College Station.

Marlar, Richard A., Kathryn Puseman, and Linda Scott Cummings

1995   Protein Residue Analysis of Archaeological Materials: Comments on Criticisms and Methods. *Southwestern Lore* 61(2):27–37.

Marlar, Richard A., Banks L. Leonard, Brian R. Billman, Patricia M. Lambert, and Jennifer E. Marlar

2000   Biochemical Evidence of Cannibalism at a Prehistoric Puebloan Site in Southwestern Colorado. *Nature* 407:74–78.

Marquardt, William H.

1974   A Statistical Analysis of Constituents in Human Paleofecal Specimens from Mammoth Cave. In: *Archeology of the Mammoth Cave Area*, Patty J. Watson, ed., pp. 193–202. New York: Academic Press.

Martin, A. C., and W. D. Barkley

1961   *Seed Identification Manual.* Berkeley: University of California Press.

Martin, Debra L.

1981   Microstructural Examination: Possibilities for Skeletal Analysis. In: *Biocultural Adaptation: Comprehensive Approaches to Skeletal Analysis*, Debra L. Martin and M. Pamela Bumsted, eds., pp. 96–107. Amherst: University of Massachusetts, Department of Anthropology, Research Reports, No. 20.

1991   Bone Histology and Paleopathology: Methodological Considerations. In: *Human Paleopathology: Current Syntheses and Future Options*, Donald J. Ortner and Arthur C. Aufderheide, eds., pp. 55–59. Washington, D.C.: Smithsonian Institution Press.

Martin, Debra L., and George J. Armelagos

1986   Histological Analysis of Bone Remodeling in Prehistoric Sudanese Nubian Specimens (350 BC–AD 1100). In: *Science in Egyptology*, R. A. David, ed., pp. 389–397. Manchester: Manchester University Press.

Martin, Debra L., George J. Armelagos, Alan H. Goodman, and Dennis P. Van Gerven

1984   The Effects of Socioeconomic Change in Prehistoric Africa: Sudanese Nubia as a Case Study. In: *Paleopathology at the Origins of Agriculture*, Mark Nathan Cohen and George J. Armelagos, eds., pp. 193–214. Orlando, Fla.: Academic Press.

Martin, Debra L., Alan H. Goodman, and George J. Armelagos

1985   Skeletal Pathologies as Indicators of Quality and Quantity of Diet. In: *The Analysis of Prehistoric Diets*, Robert I. Gilbert Jr. and James H. Mielke, eds., pp. 227–280. New York: Academic Press.

Martin, Debra L., Alan H. Goodman, George J. Armelagos, and Ann L. Magennis

1991   *Black Mesa Anasazi Health: Reconstructing Life from Patterns of Death and Disease.* Carbondale: Southern Illinois University, Center for Archaeological Investigations, Occasional Paper No. 14.

Martin, Paul S., and F. W. Sharrock

1964   Pollen Analysis of Prehistoric Human Feces: A New Approach to Ethnobotany. *American Antiquity* 30(2):168–180.

Martin, W. J., M. T. Ravi Subbiah, B. A. Kottke, C. C. Birk, and M. C. Naylor

1973   Nature of Fecal Sterols and Intestinal Bacterial Flora. *Lipids* 8(4):208–215.

Martiniaková, M., B. Grosskopf, R. Omelka, K. Dammers, M. Vondráková, and M. Bauerová

2006   Histological Study of Compact Bone Tissue in Some Mammals: A Method for Species Determination. *International Journal of Osteoarchaeology* 17(1):82–90.

Maschner, Herbert D. G (ed.)

1996   *Darwinian Archaeologies*. New York: Plenum Press.

Matheson, D. Carney, and Thomas H. Loy

2001   Genetic Sex Identification for 9400-Year-Old Human Skull Samples from Çayönü Tepesi, Turkey. *Journal of Archaeological Science* 28(5):569–575.

Matos, Vitor, and Ana Luisa Santos

2005   On the Trail of Pulmonary Tuberculosis Based on Rib Lesions: Results from the Human Identified Skeletal Collection from the Museu Bocage (Lisbon, Portugal). *American Journal of Physical Anthropology* 130(2):190–200.

Matson, R. G., and Brian Chisholm

1991   Basketmaker II Subsistence: Carbon Isotopes and Other Dietary Indicators from Cedar Mesa, Utah. *American Antiquity* 56(3):444–459.

Maxwell, Timothy D.

1995   The Use of Comparative and Engineering Analyses in the Study of Prehistoric Agriculture. In: *Evolutionary Archaeology: Methodological Issues*, Patrice A. Teltser, ed., pp. 113–128. Tucson: University of Arizona Press.

Mayer, D.

1854   Ueber Krankhafter Knochen Vorweltlicher Thiere. *Nova Acta Leopoldina* 24(2):673–689.

Maynard Smith, J.

1978   Optimization Theory in Evolution. *Annual Review of Ecology and Systematics* 9:31–56.

Mays, Simon

1995   The Relationship between Harris Lines and Other Aspects of Skeletal Development in Adults and Juveniles. *Journal of Archaeological Science* 22(4):511–520.

1997   Carbon Stable Isotope Ratios in Mediaeval and Later Human Skeletons from Northern England. *Journal of Archaeological Science* 24(6):561–567.

1998   *The Archaeology of Human Bones*. London: Routledge.

2000   Stable Isotope Analysis in Ancient Human Skeletal Remains. In: *Human Osteology in Archaeology and Forensic Science*, M. Cox and S. Mays, eds., pp. 425–438. London: Greenwich Medical Media.

2002   The Relationship between Molar Wear and Age in an Early 19th Century AD Archaeological Human Skeletal Series of Documented Age at Death. *Journal of Archaeological Science* 29(8):861–871.

Mays, Simon, and Marina Faerman

2001   Sex Identification in Some Putative Infanticide Victims from Roman Britain Using Ancient DNA. *Journal of Archaeological Science* 28(5):555–559.

Mays, Simon, and G. Michael Taylor

2002   Osteological and Biomolecular Study of Two Possible Cases of Hypertrophic Osteoarthropathy from Mediaeval England. *Journal of Archaeological Science* 29(11):1267–1276.

2003   A First Prehistoric Case of Tuberculosis from England. *International Journal of Osteoarchaeology* 13:189–196.

Mays, Simon, Megan Brickley, and Rachel Ives

2005   Skeletal Manifestations of Rickets in Infants and Young Children in a Historic Population from England. *American Journal of Physical Anthropology* 129(3): 362–374.

Mbida, Ch., E. De Langhe, L. Vrydaghs, H. Doutrelepont, Ro. Swennen, W. Van Neer, and P. de Maret

2006   Phytolith Evidence for the Early Presence of Domesticated Banana (*Musa*) in Africa. In: *Documenting Domestication: New Genetic and Archaeological Paradigms*, Melinda A. Zeder, Daniel G. Bradley, Eve Emshwiller, and Bruce D. Smith, eds., pp. 68–81. Berkeley: University of California Press.

McArdle, W. D., F. I. Katch, and V. L. Katch

1986   *Exercise Physiology: Energy, Nutrition, and Human Performance.* Philadelphia: Lea & Febiger.

McCobb, Lucy M. E., Derek E. G. Briggs, Richard P. Evershed, Allan R. Hall, and Richard A. Hall

2001   Preservation of Fossil Seeds from a 10th Century AD Cess Pit at Coppergate, York. *Journal of Archaeological Science* 28(9):929–940.

McEwan, J. M., S. Mays, and G. M. Blake

2005   The Relationship of Bone Mineral Density and Other Growth Parameters to Stress Indicators in a Medieval Juvenile Population. *International Journal of Osteoarchaeology* 15(3):155–163.

McGinnis, Samuel M.

1984   *Freshwater Fishes of California.* Berkeley: University of California Press.

McGovern-Wilson, Richard, and Carol Quinn

1996   Stable Isotope Analysis of Ten Individuals from Afetna, Saipan, Northern Mariana Islands. *Journal of Archaeological Science* 23(1):59–65.

McGuire, Randall H.

1992   *Death, Society, and Ideology in a Hohokam Community.* Boulder: Westview Press.

McHenry, Henry M.

1968   Transverse Lines in Long Bones of Prehistoric California Indians. *American Journal of Physical Anthropology* 29(1):1–29.

McHenry, Henry M., and Peter D. Schulz

1976   The Association between Harris Lines and Enamel Hypoplasia in Prehistoric California Indians. *American Journal of Physical Anthropology* 44(3):507–512.

McKinley, J.

2000   Phoenix Rising: Aspects of Cremation in Roman Britain. In: *Burial, Society and Context in the Roman World*, J. Pearce, M. Millett, and M. Struck, eds., pp. 38–44. Oxford: Oxford Journal of Archaeology, Oxbow Books.

McLaren, F. S., J. Evans, and Gordon C. Hillman

1991   Identification of Charred Seeds from Epipalaeolithic Sites of S.W. Asia. In: *Arcaeometry '90*, Ernst Pernicka and Günther A. Wagner, eds., pp. 797–806. Basel: Birkhäuser Verlag.

Meade, Timothy M.

1994   A Dietary Analysis of Coprolites from a Prehistoric Mexican Cave Site. Master's thesis, University of Nebraska, Lincoln.

Meeks, Nigel

1988   Backscattered Electron Imaging of Archaeological Materials. In: *Scanning Electron Microscopy in Archaeology*, Sandra L. Olsen, ed., pp. 23–44. Oxford: British Archaeological Reports, International Series, No. 452.

Meighan, Clement W.

1970   Mollusks as Food Remains in Archaeological Sites. In: *Science in Archaeology: A Survey of Progress and Research* (2d ed.), Don R. Brothwell and Eric Higgs, eds., pp. 415–422. New York: Praeger.

Meigs, J. A.

1857   *Catalogue of Human Crania from the Collection of the Academy of Natural Sciences of Philadelphia.* Philadelphia: Merrihew and Thompson.

Meiklejohn, Christopher, Jan H. Baldwin, and Catherine T. Schentag

1988   Caries as a Probable Dietary Marker in the Western European Mesolithic. In: *Diet and Subsistence: Current Archaeological Perspectives*, Brenda V. Kennedy and Genevieve M. LeMoine, eds., pp. 273–279. Proceedings of the Nineteenth Annual Chacmool Conference, University of Calgary.

Meindl, Richard S., and C. Owen Lovejoy

1985   Ectocranial Suture Closure: A Revised Method for the Determination of Skeletal Age at Death Based on the Lateral-Anterior Sutures. *American Journal of Physical Anthropology* 68(1):57–66.

Meindl, Richard S., and Katherine F. Russell

1998   Recent Advances in Method and Theory in Paleodemography. *Annual Review of Anthropology* 27:375–399.

Mensforth, Robert C., C. Owen Lovejoy, John W. Lallo, and George J. Armelagos

1978   The Role of Constitutional Factors, Diet, and Infectious Disease in the Etiology of Porotic Hyperostosis and Periosteal Reactions in Prehistoric Infants and Children. *Medical Anthropology* 2(1):1–59.

Merbs, Charles F.

1967   Cremated Human Remains from Point of Pines, Arizona: A New Approach. *American Antiquity* 32(4):498–506.

1989   Trauma. In: *Reconstruction of Life from the Skeleton*, Mehmet Y. İşcan and Kenneth A. R. Kennedy, eds., pp. 161–189. New York: Alan R. Liss, Inc.

2002   Spondylolysis in Inuit Skeletons from Arctic Canada. *International Journal of Osteoarchaeology* 12(4):279–290.

Merbs, Charles F., and E. M. Vestergaard

1985   The Paleopathology of Sundown, a Prehistoric Site Near Prescott, Arizona. In: *Health and Disease in the Prehistoric Southwest*, C. Merbs and R. Miller, eds., pp. 85–103. Tempe: Arizona State University, Anthropological Research Papers, No. 34.

Messer, E.

1986   The "Small but Healthy" Hypothesis: Historical, Political, and Ecological Influences on Nutritional Standards. *Human Ecology* 14(1):57–75.

Metcalfe, Duncan, and Kevin T. Jones

1988   A Reconsideration of Animal Body-Part Utility Indices. *American Antiquity*
53(3):486–504.

Meyers, Carol

2003   Engendering Syro-Palestinian Archaeology: Reasons and Resources. *Near Eastern Archaeology* 66(4):185–197.

Micozzi, Marc S., and Marc A. Kelley

1985   Evidence for Pre-Columbian Tuberculosis at the Point of Pines Site, Arizona:
Skeletal Pathology in the Sacro-Iliac Region. In: *Health and Disease in the Pre-
historic Southwest,* Charles F. Merbs and Robert J. Miller, eds., pp. 347–358.
Tempe: Arizona State University, Anthropological Research Papers, No. 34.

Miettinen, Tatu A., E. H. Ahrens Jr., and Scott M. Grundy

1965   Quantitative Isolation and Gas-Liquid Chromatographic Analysis of Total
Dietary and Fecal Neutral Steroids. *Journal of Lipid Research* 6:411–424.

Miksicek, Charles H.

1987   Formation Processes of the Archaeobotanical Record. In: *Advances in Archaeological Method and Theory, Vol. 10,* Michael B. Schiffer, ed., pp. 211–247. New
York: Academic Press.

Miles, A.E.W.

2000   The Miles Method of Assessing Age from Tooth Wear Revisited. *Journal of
Archaeological Science* 28(9):973–982.

Miles, J. S.

1966   Diseases Encountered at Mesa Verde, Colorado. II: Evidence of Disease. In:
Human Paleopathology, S. Jarcho, ed., pp. 91–98. New Haven: Yale University
Press.

Miller, Elizabeth, Bruce D. Ragsdale, and Donald J. Ortner

1996   Accuracy in Dry Bone Diagnosis: A Comment on Palaeopathological Methods.
International Journal of Osteoarchaeology 6(3):221–229.

Miller, Naomi F.

1995   Archaeobotany: Macroremains. *American Journal of Archaeology* 99:91–93.

2002   The Analysis of Archaeological Plant Remains. In: *Archaeology: Original Readings in Method and Practice,* Peter N. Peregrine, Carol R. Ember, and Melvin
Ember, eds., pp. 81–91. Upper Saddle River, N.J.: Prentice Hall.

Miller, Naomi F., and Tristine Lee Smart

1984   Intentional Burning of Dung as Fuel: A Mechanism for the Incorporation of Charred
Seeds into the Archaeological Record. *Journal of Ethnobiology* 4(1):15–28.

Miller, Robert D., II

2004   Identifying Earliest Israel. *Bulletin of the American Schools of Oriental Research*
333:55–68.

Miller, S. A., and G. V. Mitchell
1982   Optimization of Human Protein Requirements. In: *Food Proteins*, P. F. Fox and
J. J. Condon, eds., pp. 105–120. London: Applied Science Publishers.

Milner, George R., and Clark Spencer Larsen
1991   Teeth as Artifacts of Human Behavior: Intentional Mutilation and Accidental
Modification. In: *Advances in Dental Anthropology*, Marc A. Kelley and Clark
Spencer Larsen, eds., pp. 357–378. New York: Wiley-Liss.

Milner, George R., J. W. Wood, and J. L. Boldsen
2000   Paleodemography. In: *Biological Anthropology of the Human Skeleton*. Shelley R.
Saunders and M. Anne Katzenberg, eds., pp. 467–497. New York: Wiley-Liss.

Milner, Nicky, James Barrett, and Jon Welsh
2007   Marine Resource Intensification in Viking Age Europe: The Molluscan Evidence
from Quoygrew, Orkney. *Journal of Archaeological Science* 34(9):1461–1472.

Minagawa, Masao, and Eitaro Wada
1984   Stepwise Enrichment of ^{15}N along Food Chains: Further Evidence and the Relation
between δ^{15}N and Animal Age. *Geochimica et Cosmochimica Acta* 48(5):1135–1140.

Minnis, Paul E.
1981   Seeds in Archaeological Sites: Sources and Some Interpretive Problems. *American Antiquity* 46(1):143–152.

Mirov, N. T.
1967   *The Genus* Pinus. New York: Ronald Press Company.

Moffat, Brian
1988   Field Tests for Medieval Dumps of Blood at Soutra, Midlothian. In: *Science and
Archaeology, Glasgow 1987*, Elizabeth A. Slater and James O. Tate, eds., pp. 381–
390. Oxford: British Archaeological Reports, International Series, No. 196 (2 vols.).

Molnar, Stephen
1971   Human Tooth Wear, Tooth Function, and Cultural Variability. *American Journal
of Physical Anthropology* 34(2):175–190.
1972   Tooth Wear and Culture: A Survey of Tooth Function among Some Prehistoric
Populations. *Current Anthropology* 13(5):511–526.

Montgomery, F. H.
1977   *Seeds and Fruits of Eastern Canada and Northeastern United States*. Toronto:
University of Toronto Press.

Moodie, R. L.
1931   *Roentgenologic Studies of Egyptian and Peruvian Mummies*. Chicago: Field
Museum of Natural History, Anthropological Memoirs, No. 3.

Moore, J. A., Alan C. Swedlund, and George J. Armelagos
1975   The Use of Life Tables in Paleodemography. In: *Population Studies in Archaeology and Biological Anthropology: A Symposium*, Alan C. Swedlund, ed. Washington, D.C.: Memoirs of the Society for American Archaeology, No. 30.

Moore, J. G., B. K. Krotoszynski, and H. J. O'Neill
1984   Fecal Odorgrams: A Method for Partial Reconstruction of Ancient and Modern
Diets. *Digestive Diseases and Sciences* 29(10):907–911.

Moore, J. G., R. C. Straight, D. N. Osborne, and A. W. Wayne

1985   Olfactory, Gas Chromatographic and Mass-Spectral Analyses of Fecal Volatiles Traced to Ingested Licorice and Apple. *Biochemical and Biophysical Research Communications* 131(1):339–346.

Moore, P. D., J. A. Webb, and M. E. Collinson

1991   *Pollen Analysis* (2d ed.). Oxford: Blackwell Scientific Publications.

Moratto, Michael J.

1984   *California Archaeology*. Orlando, Fla.: Academic Press.

Morgan, E. D., L. Titus, R. J. Small, and C. Edwards

1984   Gas Chromatographic Analysis of Fatty Material from a Thule Midden. *Archaeometry* 26(1):43–48.

Morse, Dan

1978   *Ancient Disease in the Midwest*. Springfield: Illinois State Museum, Reports of Special Investigations, No. 15.

Morton, June D., and Henry P. Schwarcz

2004   Palaeodietary Implications from Stable Isotopic Analysis of Residues on Prehistoric Ontario Ceramics. *Journal of Archaeological Science* 31(5):503–517.

Morton, June D., R. B. Lammers, and Henry P. Schwarcz

1991   Estimation of Palaeodiet: A Model from Stable Isotope Analysis. In: *Archaeometry '90*, Ernst Pernicka and Günther A. Wagner, eds., pp. 807–820. Basel: Birkhäuser Verlag.

Moss, Melvin O.

1972   Twenty Years of Functional Cranial Analysis. *American Journal of Orthodontics* 61:479–485.

Moss, Melvin O., and Richard W. Young

1960   A Functional Approach to Craniology. *American Journal of Physical Anthropology* 18(4):281–292.

Müldner, Gundula, and Michael P. Richards

2005   Fast or Feast: Reconstructing Diet in Later Medieval England by Stable Isotope Analysis. *Journal of Archaeological Science* 32(1):39–48.

Mulligan, Connie J.

2006   Anthropological Applications of Ancient DNA: Problems and Prospects. *American Antiquity* 71(2):365–380.

Mulville, Jacqui, and Alan K. Outram (eds.)

2005   *The Zooarchaeology of Fats, Oils, Milk, and Dairying*. Oxford: Oxbow Books.

Munz, P. A., and D. D. Keck

1949   California Plant Communities. *El Aliso* 2:87–105.

1950   California Plant Communities—A Supplement. *El Aliso* 2:199–202.

Nagaoka, Lisa

2005   Differential Recovery of Pacific Island Fish Remains. *Journal of Archaeological Science* 32(6):941–955.

Napton, Lewis K.

1969   The Lacustrine Subsistence Pattern in the Desert West. In: *Archaeological and Paleobiological Investigations in Lovelock Cave, Nevada*, Robert F. Heizer and

Lewis K. Napton, eds. pp. 28–97. Berkeley: Kroeber Anthropological Society, Special Publication No. 2.

1970   Archaeological Investigation in Lovelock Cave, Nevada. Ph.D. dissertation, University of California, Berkeley.

Needham, Stuart, and John Evans

1987   Honey and Dripping: Neolithic Food Residues from Runnymede Bridge. *Cambridge Journal of Archaeology* 6(1):21–28.

Neff, Hector

2000   On Evolutionary Ecology and Evolutionary Archaeology: Some Common Ground? *Current Anthropology* 41(3):427–429.

Neiburger, E. J.

1990   Enamel Hypoplasias: Poor Indicators of Dietary Stress. *American Journal of Physical Anthropology* 82(2):231–232.

Nelson, Bruce K., Michael J. DeNiro, Margaret J. Schoeninger, and Donald J. De Paolo

1986   Effects of Diagenesis on Strontium, Carbon, Nitrogen and Oxygen Concentration and Isotopic Composition of Bone. *Geochimica et Cosmochimica Acta* 50(9):1941–1949.

Nelson, D. E., Thomas H. Loy, J. S. Vogel, and J. R. Southon

1986   Radiocarbon Dating Blood Residues on Prehistoric Stone Tools. *Radiocarbon* 28(1):170–174.

Nelson, G. S.

1967   Human Behavior in the Transmission of Parasitic Diseases. In: *Behavioural Aspects of Parasite Transmission*, Elizabeth U. Canning and C. A. Wright, eds. London: Linnaean Society of London.

Nelson, Sarah Milledge

1997   *Gender in Archaeology: Analyzing Power and Prestige.* Walnut Creek, Calif.: AltaMira Press.

Neumann, Alan, Richard Holloway, and Colin Busby

1989   Determination of Prehistoric Use of Arrowhead (*Sagittaria*, Alismataceae) in the Great Basin of North America by Scanning Electron Microscopy. *Economic Botany* 43(3):287–296.

Neuweiler, E.

1905   Die prähistorischen Pflanzenreste Mitteleuropas mit besonderer Berücksichtigung der schweizerischen Funde. *Vierteljahrsschrift der Naturforschenden Gesellschaft in Zürich* 50:23–134.

Newesely, Heinrich

1993   Abrasion as an Intrinsic Factor in Paleodiet. In: *Prehistoric Human Bone: Archaeology at the Molecular Level*, Joseph B. Lambert and Gisela Grupe, eds., pp. 293–308. Berlin: Springer-Verlag.

Newman, Margaret E.

1990   The Hidden Evidence from Hidden Cave, Nevada. Ph.D. dissertation, University of Toronto.

1993   Immunological Residue Analysis of Samples from CA-SBR-6580. In: *The Siphon Site (CA-SBR-6580): A Millingstone Horizon Site in the Summit Valley, California,* by Mark Q. Sutton, Joan S. Schneider, and Robert M. Yohe II, Appendix 3, pp. 79–83. San Bernardino County Museum Association Quarterly 40(3).

Newman, Margaret E., and P. Julig

1989   The Identification of Protein Residues on Lithic Artifacts from a Stratified Boreal Forest Site. *Canadian Journal of Archaeology* 13:119–132.

Newman, Margaret E., Robert M. Yohe II, Howard Ceri, and Mark Q. Sutton

1993   Immunological Protein Residue Analysis of Non-lithic Archaeological Materials. *Journal of Archaeological Science* 20(1):93–100.

Newman, Margaret E., Howard Ceri, and Brian Kooyman

1996   The Use of Immunological Techniques in the Analysis of Archaeological Materials—A Response to Eisele; with Report of Studies at Head-Smashed-In Buffalo Jump. *Antiquity* 70(269):677–682.

Newman, Margaret E., Robert M. Yohe II, B. Cooyman, and Howard Ceri

1997   "Blood" from Stones? Probably: A Response to Fiedel. *Journal of Archaeological Science* 24(11):1023–1027.

Newman, Margaret E., Greg Byrne, Howard Ceri, Leo S. Dimnik, and Peter J. Bridge

1998   Immunological and DNA Analysis for Blood Residues from a Surgeon's Kit Used in the American Civil War. *Journal of Archaeological Science* 25(6):553–557.

Newman, Margaret E., Jullian S. Parboosingh, Peter J. Bridge, and Howard Ceri

2002   Identification of Archaeological Animal Bone by PCR/DNA Analysis. *Journal of Archaeological Science* 29(1):77–84.

Newsome, Seth D., Donald L. Phillips, Brendan J. Culleton, Tom P. Guilderson, and Paul L. Koch

2004   Dietary Reconstruction of an Early to Middle Holocene Human Population from the Central California Coast: Insights from Advanced Stable Isotope Mixing Models. *Journal of Archaeological Science* 31(8):1101–1115.

Nielsen, Henrik, Jan Engberg, and Ingolf Thuesen

1994   DNA from Arctic Human Burials. In: *Ancient DNA: Recovery and Analysis of Genetic Material from Paleontological, Archaeological, Museum, Medical, and Forensic Specimens*, Bernd Herrmann and Susanne Hummel, eds., pp. 122–140. Berlin: Springer-Verlag.

Nielsen-Marsh, Christina M., and Robert E. M. Hedges

2000a   Patterns of Diagenesis in Bone. I: The Effects of Site Environment. *Journal of Archaeological Science* 27(12):1139–1150.

2000b   Patterns of Diagenesis in Bone. II: Effects of Acetic Acid Treatment and the Removal of Diagenetic CO_3^{2-}. *Journal of Archaeological Science* 27(12):1151–1159.

Nissenbaum, Arie

1992   Molecular Archaeology: Organic Geochemistry of Egyptian Mummies. *Journal of Archaeological Science* 19(1):1–6.

Niven, Laura B., Charles P. Egeland, and Lawrence C. Todd

2004   An Inter-site Comparison of Enamel Hypoplasia in Bison: Implications for Paleo-ecology and Modeling Late Plains Archaic Subsistence. *Journal of Archaeological Science* 31(12):1783–1794.

Noe-Nygaard, Nanna, T. Douglas Price, and S. U. Hede
2005   Diet of Aurochs and Early Cattle in Southern Scandinavia: Evidence from ^{15}N and ^{13}C Stable Isotopes. *Journal of Archaeological Science* 32(6):855–871.

Noli, D., and G. Avery
1988   Protein Poisoning and Coastal Subsistence. *Journal of Archaeological Science* 15(4):395–401.

Nolin, Luc, John K. G. Kramer, and Margaret E. Newman
1994   Detection of Animal Residues in Humus Samples from a Prehistoric Site in the Lower Mackenzie River Valley, Northwest Territories. *Journal of Archaeological Science* 21(3):403–412.

Norr, Lynette
1995   Interpreting Dietary Maize from Bone Stable Isotopes in the American Tropics: The State of the Art. In: *Archaeology in the Lowland American Tropics*, Peter W. Stahl, ed., pp. 198–223. Cambridge: Cambridge University Press.

Notman, Derek N. H.
1986   Ancient Scannings: Computed Tomography of Egyptian Mummies. In: *Science in Egyptology*, R. A. David, ed., pp. 251–320. Manchester: Manchester University Press.
1995   Paleoradiology and Human Mummies: A Basic Guide to Imaging the Past. In: *Proceedings of the First World Congress on Mummy Studies, Vol. 2*, pp. 587–590. Museo Arqueológico y Etnográfico de Tenerife.
1998   Paleoimaging. In: *Mummies, Disease, and Ancient Cultures* (2d ed.), Aidan Cockburn, Eve Cockburn, and Theodore A. Reyman, eds., pp. 363–372. Cambridge: Cambridge University Press.

Notman, Derek N. H., and Carter L. Lupton
1995   Three-Dimensional Computed Tomography and Densitometry of Human Mummies and Associated Materials. In: *Proceedings of the First World Congress on Mummy Studies, Vol. 2*, pp. 479–484. Museo Arqueológico y Etnográfico de Tenerife.

Novak, Shannon A., and Dana D. Kollmann
2000   Perimortem Processing of Human Remains among the Great Basin Fremont. *International Journal of Osteoarchaeology* 10(1):65–75.

O'Brien, Michael J. (ed.)
1996   *Evolutionary Archaeology: Theory and Application*. Salt Lake City: University of Utah Press.

O'Brien, Michael J., and R. Lee Lyman
2000   *Applying Evolutionary Archaeology: A Systematic Approach*. New York: Kluwer Academic/Plenum Publishers.

O'Connell, James F.
1995   Ethnoarchaeology Needs a General Theory of Behavior. *Journal of Archaeological Research* 3(3):205–255.

O'Connell, T. C., and Robert E. M. Hedges
1999   Isotopic Comparison of Hair and Bone: Archaeological Analyses. *Journal of Archaeological Science* 26(6):661–665.

O'Connell, T. C., Robert E. M. Hedges, M. A. Healey, and A.H.R.W. Simpson

2001   Isotopic Comparison of Hair, Nail and Bone: Modern Analyses. *Journal of Archaeological Science* 28(11):1247–1255.

O'Connor, Terry

2000   *The Archaeology of Animal Bones.* College Station: Texas A&M University Press.

O'Donoghue, Alan Clapham, Richard P. Evershed, and Terrence A. Brown

1996   Remarkable Preservation of Biomolecules in Ancient Radish Seeds. *Proceedings of the Royal Society of London* 263:541–547.

O'Leary, M. H.

1981   Carbon Isotope Fractionation in Plants. *Phytochemistry* 20(4):553–567.

Oliveira, R. N., S.F.S.M. Silva, A. Kawano, and J.L.F. Antunes

2006   Estimating Age by Tooth Wear of Prehistoric Human Remains in Brazilian Archaeological Sites. *International Journal of Osteoarchaeology* 16(5):407–414.

Olsen, Sandra L.

1988   Introduction: Applications of Scanning Electron Microscopy to Archaeology. In: *Scanning Electron Microscopy in Archaeology*, Sandra L. Olsen, ed., pp. 3–7. Oxford: British Archaeological Reports, International Series, No. 452.

Olsen, Stanley J.

1968   *Fish, Amphibian and Reptile Remains from Archaeological Sites. Part 1: Southeastern and Southwestern United States.* Papers of the Peabody Museum of Archaeology and Ethnology 56(2).

1979   *Osteology for the Archaeologist.* Papers of the Peabody Museum of Archaeology and Ethnology 56(3, 4, 5).

Orchard, T. J.

2005   The Use of Statistical Size Estimations in Minimum Number Calculations. *International Journal of Osteoarchaeology* 15(5):351–359.

O'Rourke, Dennis H., Shawn W. Carlyle, and Ryan L. Parr

1996   Ancient DNA: Methods, Progress, and Perspectives. *American Journal of Human Biology* 8(5):557–571.

O'Rourke, Dennis H., M. Geoffrey Hayes, and Shawn W. Carlyle

2000   Ancient DNA Studies in Physical Anthropology. *Annual Review of Anthropology* 29:217–242.

Ortner, Donald J.

1991   Theoretical and Methodological Issues in Paleopathology. In: *Human Paleopathology: Current Syntheses and Future Options*, Donald J. Ortner and Arthur C. Aufderheide, eds., pp. 5–11. Washington, D.C.: Smithsonian Institution Press.

1994   Descriptive Methodology in Paleopathology. In: *Skeletal Biology in the Great Plains: Migration, Warfare, Health, and Subsistence*, Douglas W. Owsley and Richard L. Jantz, eds., pp. 73–80. Washington, D.C.: Smithsonian Institution Press.

Ortner, Donald J., and Simon Mays

1998   Dry-Bone Manifestations of Rickets in Infancy and Early Childhood. *International Journal of Osteoarchaeology* 8(1):45–55.

Ortner, Donald J., and Walter G. J. Putschar
1981   *Identification of Pathological Conditions in Human Skeletal Remains*. Washington, D.C.: Smithsonian Contributions to Anthropology, No. 28.

Oshima, Minako, Tokuji Inoue, and Mitsuwo Hara
1982   Identification of Species Specific Hemoglobin by Isoelectric Focusing. *Forensic Science International* 20:277–286.

Outram, Alan K., Christopher J. Knüsel, Stephanie Knight, and Anthony F. Harding
2005   Understanding Complex Fragmented Assemblages of Human and Animal Remains: A Fully Integrated Approach. *Journal of Archaeological Science* 32(12):1699–1710.

Owsley, D. W., M. K. Marks, and M. H. Manhein
1989   Human Skeletal Samples in the Southern Great Plains. In: *From Clovis to Comanchero: Archeological Overview of the Southern Great Plains*, J. L. Hofman, R. L. Brooks, J. S. Hays, D. W. Owsley, R. L. Jantz, M. K. Marks, and M. H. Manhein, eds., pp. 111–122. Fayetteville: University of Arkansas Study Unit 5, Southwestern Division Archeological Overview, U.S. Army Corps of Engineers, Southwestern Division.

Oxenham, Marc F., Nguyen Lan Cuong, and Nguyen Kim Thuy
2002   Identification of *Areca catechu* (Betel Nut) Residues on the Dentitions of Bronze Age Inhabitants of Nui Nap, Northern Vietnam. *Journal of Archaeological Science* 29(9):909–915.

Pääbo, Svante
1985a   Preservation of DNA in Ancient Egyptian Mummies. *Journal of Archaeological Science* 12(6):411–417.

1985b   Molecular Cloning of Ancient Egyptian Mummy DNA. *Nature* 314:644–645.

1990   Amplifying Ancient DNA. In: *PCR Protocols: A Guide to Methods and Applications*, Michael A. Innis, David H. Gelfand, John J. Sninsky, and Thomas J. White, eds., pp. 159–166. San Diego: Academic Press.

1993   Ancient DNA. *Scientific American* 269(5):86–92.

Pääbo, Svante, John A. Gifford, and Allan C. Wilson
1988   Mitochondrial DNA Sequences from a 7000-Year-Old Brain. *Nucleic Acids Research* 16(20):9775–9787.

Pääbo, Svante, Hendrik Poinar, David Serre, Viviane Jaenicke-Després, Juliane Hebler, Nadin Rohland, Melanie Kuch, Johannes Krause, Linda Vigilant, and Michael Hofreiter
2004   Genetic Analyses from Ancient DNA. *Annual Review of Genetics* 38:645–679.

Paap, N. A.
1984   Palaeobotanical Investigations in Amsterdam. In: *Plants and Ancient Man: Studies in Palaeoethnobotany*, W. Van Zeist and W. A. Casparie, eds., pp. 339–344. Rotterdam: A. A. Balkema.

Pager, H.
1973   Rock Paintings in Southern Africa Showing Bees and Honey Hunting. *Bee World* 54(2):61–68.

Pahl, Wolfgang M.

1986   Possibilities, Limitations and Prospects of Computed Tomography as a Non-
        Invasive Method of Mummy Studies. In: *Science in Egyptology*, R. A. David, ed.,
        pp. 13–24. Manchester: Manchester University Press.

Pahl, Wolfgang M., and W. Undeutsch

1991   Noma–Cancer Aquaticus: First Indication of the Skin Involving Disease in
        Ancient Egypt? In: *Human Paleopathology: Current Syntheses and Future
        Options*, Donald J. Ortner and Arthur C. Aufderheide, eds., pp. 297–304. Wash-
        ington, D.C.: Smithsonian Institution Press.

Palkovich, Ann M.

1980   *Pueblo Population and Society: The Arroyo Hondo Skeletal and Mortuary Remains.*
        Santa Fe: School of American Research, Arroyo Hondo Archaeological Series, Vol. 3.

1982   Disease and Mortality Patterns in the Burial Rooms of Pueblo Bonito: Prelimi-
        nary Considerations. In: *Recent Advances on Chacoan Prehistory*, W. J. Judge and
        J. D. Schelberg, eds., pp. 103–114. Albuquerque: National Park Service, Division
        of Cultural Research.

1984a   Agriculture, Marginal Environments, and Nutritional Stress in the Prehistoric
        Southwest. In: *Paleopathology at the Origins of Agriculture*, Mark Nathan Cohen
        and George J. Armelagos, eds., pp. 425–438. Orlando, Fla.: Academic Press.

1984b   Disease and Mortality Patterns in the Burial Rooms of Pueblo Bonito: Prelimi-
        nary Considerations. In: *Recent Research in Chaco Prehistory*, No. 8, W. James
        Judge and John D. Schelberg, eds., pp. 103–113. Albuquerque, N.M.: Division of
        Cultural Research, U.S. Department of the Interior, National Park Service.

Palmer, Patricia G.

1976   Grass Cuticles: A New Paleoecological Tool for East African Lake Sediments.
        Canadian Journal of Botany 54(15):1725–1734.

Panagiotakopulu, Eva

1999   An Examination of Biological Materials from Coprolites from XVIII Dynasty
        Amarna, Egypt. *Journal of Archaeological Science* 26(5):547–551.

Papathanasiou, Anastasia

2003   Stable Isotope Analysis in Neolithic Greece and Possible Implications on Human
        Health. *International Journal of Osteoarchaeology* 13(5):314–324.

Parkes, P. A.

1986   *Current Scientific Techniques in Archaeology.* New York: St. Martin's Press.

Parkington, John

1987   On Stable Carbon Isotopes and Dietary Reconstruction. *Current Anthropology*
        28(1):91–93.

1991   Approaches to Dietary Reconstruction in the Western Cape: Are You What You
        Have Eaten? *Journal of Archaeological Science* 18(3):331–342.

Parmalee, Paul W.

1985   Identification and Interpretation of Archaeologically Derived Animal Remains.
        In: *The Analysis of Prehistoric Diets*, Robert I. Gilbert Jr. and James H. Mielke,
        eds., pp. 61–96. New York: Academic Press.

318   REFERENCES

Parr, Ryan L., Shawn W. Carlyle, and Dennis H. O'Rourke
1996   Ancient DNA Analysis of Fremont Amerindians of the Great Salt Lake Wetlands. *American Journal of Physical Anthropology* 99(4):507–518.

Parsche, Franz, and Andreas G. Nerlich
1997   Suitability of Immunohistochemistry for the Determination of Collagen Stability in Historic Bone Tissue. *Journal of Archaeological Science* 24(3):275–281.

Pate, F. Donald
1994   Bone Chemistry and Paleodiet. *Journal of Archaeological Method and Theory* 1(2):161–207.

1997   Bone Chemistry and Paleodiet: Reconstructing Prehistoric Subsistence-Settlement Systems in Australia. *Journal of Anthropological Archaeology* 16(2):103–120.

Pate, F. Donald, and John T. Hutton
1988   The Use of Soil Chemistry Data to Address Post-mortem Diagenesis in Bone Material. *Journal of Archaeological Science* 15(6):729–739.

Patrick, S. S.
1988   Description and Demographic Analysis of a Mimbres Mogollon Population from LA15049 (NAN Ruin). Master's thesis, Texas A&M University, College Station.

Patrucco, Raul, Raul Tello, and Duccio Bonavia
1983   Parasitological Studies in Coprolites of Pre-Hispanic Peruvian Populations. *Current Anthropology* 24(3):393–394.

Pearsall, Deborah M.
1988   Interpreting the Meaning of Macroremain Abundance: The Impact of Source and Context. In: *Current Paleoethnobotany*, Christine A. Hastorf and Virginia S. Popper, eds., pp. 97–118. Chicago: University of Chicago Press.

1993   Contributions of Phytolith Analysis for Reconstructing Subsistence: Examples from Research in Ecuador. In: *Current Research in Phytolith Analysis: Applications in Archaeology and Paleoecology*, Deborah M. Pearsall and Dolores R. Piperno, eds., pp. 108–122. Philadelphia: University of Pennsylvania, University Museum of Archaeology and Anthropology, MASCA Research Papers in Science and Archaeology, Vol. 10.

1994   Investigating New World Tropical Agriculture: Contributions from Phytolith Analysis. In: *Tropical Archaeobotany: Applications and New Developments*, Jon G. Hather, ed., pp. 115–138. London: Routledge.

2000   *Paleoethnobotany: A Handbook of Procedures* (2d ed.). San Diego: Academic Press.

Pearsall, Deborah M., Karol Chandler-Ezell, and Alex Chandler-Ezell
2003   Identifying Maize in Neotropical Sediments and Soils Using Cob Phytoliths. *Journal of Archaeological Science* 30(5):611–627.

Pechenkina, Ekaterina A., Stanley H. Ambrose, Ma Xiaolin, and Robert A. Benfer Jr.
2005   Reconstructing Northern Chinese Neolithic Subsistence Practices by Isotopic Analysis. *Journal of Archaeological Science* 32(8):1176–1189.

Perlman, Dorothy
1974   *The Magic of Honey*. New York: Avon Publishers.

Perry, Linda

2004   Starch Analyses Reveal the Relationship between Tool Type and Function: An Example from the Orinoco Valley of Venezuela. *Journal of Archaeological Science* 31(8):1069–1081.

Persson, Per

1992   A Method to Recover DNA from Ancient Bones. *Ancient DNA Newsletter* 1(1):25–27.

Peterson, James B., and Nancy Asch Sidell

1996   Mid-Holocene Evidence of *Cucurbita* sp. from Central Maine. *American Antiquity* 61(4):685–698.

Pfeiffer, Susan, and Tamara L. Varney

2000   Quantifying Histological and Chemical Preservation of Archaeological Bone. In: *Biogeochemical Approaches to Paleodietary Analysis*, Stanley H. Ambrose and Anne M. Katzenberg, eds., pp. 141–158. New York: Kluwer Academic/Plenum Publishers.

Pfeiffer, Susan, Christian Crowder, Lesley Harrington, and Michael Brown

2006   Secondary Osteon and Haversian Canal Dimensions as Behavioral Indicators. *American Journal of Physical Anthropology* 131(4):460–468.

Phenice, T. W.

1969   A Newly Developed Visual Method of Sexing the Os Pubis. *American Journal of Physical Anthropology* 30(2):297–302.

Pike, Alan W.

1967   The Recovery of Parasite Eggs from Ancient Cesspit and Latrine Deposits: An Approach to the Study of Early Parasite Infections. In: *Diseases in Antiquity: A Survey of Diseases, Injuries and Surgery of Early Populations*, Don R. Brothwell and A. T. Sanderson, eds., pp. 184–188. Springfield, Ill.: Charles C. Thomas.

1968   Recovery of Helminth Eggs from Archaeological Excavations, and Their Possible Usefulness in Providing Evidence for the Purpose of an Occupation. *Nature* 219:303–304.

1975   Parasite Eggs. In: *Excavations in Medieval Southampton 1953–1969*, Colin Platt and Richard Coleman-Smith, eds., pp. 347–348. London: Leicester University Press.

Pike, Alan W., and Martin Biddle

1966   Parasite Eggs in Medieval Winchester. *Antiquity* 40(160):293–296.

Piperno, Dolores R.

1988   *Phytolith Analysis: An Archaeological and Geological Perspective*. San Diego: Academic Press.

1991   The Status of Phytolith Analysis in the American Tropics. *Journal of World Prehistory* 5(2):155–191.

2006a   *Phytoliths: A Comprehensive Guide for Archaeologists and Paleoecologists*. Walnut Creek, Calif.: AltaMira Press.

2006b   Identifying Manioc (*Manihot esculenta* Crantz) and Other Crops in Pre-Columbian Tropical America through Starch Grain Analysis: A Case Study from Central Panama. In: *Documenting Domestication: New Genetic and Archaeological Paradigms*, Melinda A. Zeder, Daniel G. Bradley, Eve Emshwiller, and Bruce D. Smith, eds., pp. 46–67. Berkeley: University of California Press.

Piperno, Dolores R., and Irene Holst
1998   The Presence of Starch Grains on Prehistoric Stone Tools from the Humid Neo-
        tropics: Indications of Early Tuber Use and Agriculture in Panama. *Journal of
        Archaeological Science* 25(8):765–776.
Piperno, Dolores R., and Deborah M. Pearsall
1993   The Nature and Status of Phytolith Analysis. In: *Current Research in Phytolith
        Analysis: Applications in Archaeology and Paleoecology*, Deborah M. Pearsall and
        Dolores R. Piperno, eds., pp. 9–18. Philadelphia: University of Pennsylvania, Uni-
        versity Museum of Archaeology and Anthropology, MASCA Research Papers in
        Science and Archaeology, Vol. 10.
Piperno, Dolores R., Thomas C. Andres, and Karen E. Stothert
2000   Phytoliths in *Cucurbita* and Other Neotropical Cucurbitaceae and Their Occur-
        rence in Early Archaeological Sites from the Lowland American Tropics. *Journal
        of Archaeological Science* 27(3):193–208.
Poduch, C. C., R. Silverstein, K. Paul, and M. Green
1988   Normal Diet and Desirable Intake. In: *Current Therapy in Nutrition*, K. H.
        Jeejeebhoy, ed., pp. 10–23. Hamilton, Ontario: BC Decker Inc.
Poinar, Hendrik N., and Artur B. Stankiewicz
1999   Protein Preservation and DNA Retrieval from Ancient Tissues. *Proceedings of the
        National Academy of Sciences* 96(15):8426–8431.
Poinar, Hendrik N., Melanie Kuch, Kristin D. Sobolik, Ian Barnes, Artur B. Stankiewicz,
        Thomas Kuder, W. Geoffrey Spaulding, Vaughan M. Bryant, Alan Cooper, and
        Svante Pääbo
2001   A Molecular Analysis of Dietary Diversity for Three Archaic Native Americans.
        Proceedings of the National Academy of Sciences 98(8):4317–4322.
Polet, C., and M. Anne Katzenberg
2003   Reconstruction of the Diet in a Mediaeval Monastic Community from the Coast
        of Belgium. *Journal of Archaeological Science* 30(5):525–533.
Pollard, A. Mark, and Carl Heron
1996   *Archaeological Chemistry*. Cambridge: Royal Society of Chemistry.
Pollard, A. Mark, S. E. Antoine, P. Q. Dresser, and A.W.R. Whittle
1991   Methodological Study of the Analysis of Bone. In: *Archaeological Sciences 1989*,
        Paul Budd, Barbara Chapman, Caroline Jackson, Rob Janaway, and Barbara Ott-
        away, eds., pp. 363–372. Oxford: Oxbow Monograph 9.
Powell, Mary Lucas
1985   The Analysis of Dental Wear and Caries for Dietary Reconstruction. In: *The
        Analysis of Prehistoric Diets*, Robert I. Gilbert Jr. and James H. Mielke, eds., pp.
        307–338. New York: Academic Press.
Powers, Alix
1988   Phytoliths: Animal, Vegetable *and* Mineral. In: *Science and Archaeology, Glasgow
        1987*, Elizabeth A. Slater and James O. Tate, eds., pp. 459–472. Oxford: British
        Archaeological Reports, International Series, No. 196 (2 vols.).

Price, Mary F.

1999   All in the Family: The Impact of Gender and Family Constructs on the Study of Prehistoric Settlement. In: *Making Places in the Prehistoric World: Themes in Settlement Archaeology*, Joanna Brück and Melissa Goodman, eds., pp. 30–51. London: UCL Press.

Price, T. Douglas

1989a   Multi-Element Studies of Diagenesis in Prehistoric Bone. In: *The Chemistry of Prehistoric Human Bone*, T. Douglas Price, ed., pp. 126–154. Cambridge: Cambridge University Press.

Price, T. Douglas (ed.)

1989b   *The Chemistry of Prehistoric Human Bone*. Cambridge: Cambridge University Press.

Price, T. Douglas, Margaret J. Schoeninger, and George J. Armelagos

1985   Bone Chemistry and Past Behavior: An Overview. *Journal of Human Evolution* 14(5):419–447.

Price, T. Douglas, Jennifer Blitz, James Burton, and Joseph A. Ezzo

1992   Diagenesis in Prehistoric Bone: Problems and Solutions. *Journal of Archaeological Science* 19(5):513–529.

Price, T. Douglas, Gisela Grupe, and Peter Schröter

1994a   Reconstruction of Migration Patterns in the Bell Beaker Period by Stable Strontium Isotope Analysis. *Applied Geochemistry* 9(4):413–417.

Price, T. Douglas, Clark M. Johnson, Joseph A. Ezzo, Jonathan Ericson, and James H. Burton

1994b   Residential Mobility in the Prehistoric Southwest United States: A Preliminary Study Using Strontium Isotope Analysis. *Journal of Archaeological Science* 21(3):315–330.

Price, T. Douglas, Linda Manzanilla, and William D. Middleton

2000   Immigration and the Ancient City of Teotihuacan in Mexico: A Study Using Strontium Isotope Ratios in Human Bone and Teeth. *Journal of Archaeological Science* 27(10):903–913.

Prior, Juliet

1988   Methods Used in Charcoal Analysis and the Relationship between Woods Used in Archaeological Times and the Present Fuelwood Crisis. In: *Scanning Electron Microscopy in Archaeology*, Sandra L. Olsen, ed., pp. 187–202. Oxford: British Archaeological Reports, International Series, No. 452.

Privat, Karen L., Tamsin C. O'Connell, and Robert E. M. Hedges

2007   The Distinction between Freshwater- and Terrestrial-Based Diets: Methodological Concerns and Archaeological Applications of Sulphur Stable Isotope Analysis. *Journal of Archaeological Science* 34(8):1197–1204.

Provinzano, J.

1968   The Osteological Remains of the Galaz Mimbres Amerinds. Master's thesis, Department of Anthropology, University of Minnesota, Minneapolis.

Prowse, Tracy, Henry P. Schwarcz, Shelley Saunders, Roberto Macchiarelli, and Luca
   Bondioli
2004   Isotopic Paleodiet Studies of Skeletons from the Imperial Roman-Age Cemetery
   of Isola Sacra, Rome, Italy. *Journal of Archaeological Science* 31(3):259–272.
Prowse, Tracy L., Henry P. Schwarcz, Peter Garnsey, Martin Knyf, Roberto Macchiarelli,
   and Luca Bondioli
2007   Isotopic Evidence for Age-Related Immigration to Imperial Rome. *American
   Journal of Physical Anthropology* 132(4):510–519.
Puech, Pierre-Francois, and F. Filce Leek
1986   Dental Microwear as an Indication of Plant Food in Early Man. In: *Science in
   Egyptology*, R. David, ed., pp. 239–241. Manchester: Manchester University Press.
Puffer, R. R., and C. V. Serrano
1973   *Patterns of Mortality in Childhood.* Washington, D.C.: Pan American Health
   Organization.
Pumpelly, Rafael
1908   *Explorations in Turkestan, Expedition of 1904. Prehistoric Civilizations of Anau:
   Origins, Growth, and Influence of Environment* (2 vols.). Washington, D.C.:
   Carnegie Institution of Washington.
Putnam, F. W.
1884   Abnormal Human Skull from Stone Graves in Tennessee. *Proceedings of the
   American Association for the Advancement of Science* 32:390–392.
Pyatt, F. B., G. Gilmore, J. P. Grattan, C. O. Hunt, and S. McLaren
2000   An Imperial Legacy? An Exploration of the Environmental Impact of Ancient
   Metal Mining and Smelting in Southern Jordan. *Journal of Archaeological Science* 27(9):771–778.
Raab, L. Mark
1996   Debating Prehistory in Coastal Southern California: Resource Intensification
   versus Political Economy. *Journal of California and Great Basin Anthropology*
   18(1):64–80.
Radosavljevich, Paul R.
1911   Professor Boas' New Theory of the Head—A Critical Contribution to School
   Anthropology. *American Anthropologist* 13(3):394–436.
Radosevich, Stefan C.
1993   The Six Deadly Sins of Trace Element Analysis: A Case of Wishful Thinking
   in Science. In: *Investigations of Ancient Human Tissue: Chemical Analyses in
   Anthropology*, Mary K. Sandford, ed., pp. 269–332. Langhorne, Penn.: Gordon and
   Breach.
Radovsky, Frank J.
1970   Mites Associated with Coprolites and Mummified Human Remains in Nevada.
   In: *Archaeology and the Prehistoric Great Basin Lacustrine Subsistence Regime
   as Seen from Lovelock Cave, Nevada*, by Robert F. Heizer and Lewis K. Napton,
   pp. 186–190. Berkeley: Contributions of the University of California Archaeological Research Facility, No. 10.

Ramos-Elorduy de Conconi, Julieta, Jose Manuel Pino Moreno, Carlos Marquez May-
    audon, Fernando Rincon Valdez, Manuel Alvarado Perez, Esteban Escamilla
    Prado, and Hector Bourges Rodriguez

1984   Protein Content of Some Edible Insects in Mexico. *Journal of Ethnobiology*
        4(1):61–72.

Rapp, George, Jr., and Susan C. Mulholland (eds.)

1992   *Phytolith Systematics: Emerging Issues.* New York: Plenum Press.

Raxter, Michelle H., Benjamin M. Auerbach, and Christopher B. Ruff

2006   Revision of the Fully Technique for Estimating Statures. *American Journal of
        Physical Anthropology* 130(3):374–384.

Redding, Richard W.

2002   The Study of Human Subsistence Behavior Using Faunal Evidence from Archaeo-
        logical Sites. In: *Archaeology: Original Readings in Method and Practice*, Peter N.
        Peregrine, Carol R. Ember, and Melvin Ember, eds., pp. 92–110. Upper Saddle
        River, N.J.: Prentice Hall.

Reddy, Seetha N.

1991   Complementary Approaches to Late Harappan Subsistence: An Example from
        Oriyo Timbo. In: *Harappa Excavations 1986–1990: A Multidisciplinary Approach
        to Third Millennium Urbanism*, Richard H. Meadow, ed., pp. 127–135. Madison,
        Wis.: Prehistory Press Monographs in World Archaeology, No. 3.

Reed, David M.

1994   Ancient Maya Diet at Copán, Honduras, as Determined through the Analysis of
        Stable Carbon and Nitrogen Isotopes. In: *Paleonutrition: The Diet and Health of Pre-
        historic Americans*, Kristin D. Sobolik, ed., pp. 210–221. Carbondale: Southern Illinois
        University, Center for Archaeological Investigations, Occasional Paper No. 22.

Reed, E. K.

1965   Human Skeletal Material from Site 34, Mesa Verde National Park. *El Palacio*
        72:31–45.

1981   Human Skeletal Material from the Gran Quivira District. In: *Contributions to
        Gran Quivira Archaeology: Gran Quivira National Monument, New Mexico*,
        Alden C. Hayes, ed., pp. 75–118. Washington, D.C.: National Park Service, Pub-
        lications in Archaeology, No. 17.

Reinhard, Karl J.

1985   Recovery of Helminths from Prehistoric Feces: The Cultural Ecology of Ancient
        Parasitism. Master's thesis, Northern Arizona University, Flagstaff.

1988   Cultural Ecology of Prehistoric Parasitism on the Colorado Plateau as Evidenced
        by Coprology. *American Journal of Physical Anthropology* 77(3):355–366.

1992a   Patterns of Diet, Parasitism, and Anemia in Prehistoric West North America. In:
        Diet, Demography, and Disease: Changing Perspectives on Anemia, Patricia Stu-
        art-Macadam and Susan Kent, eds., pp. 219–258. New York: Aldine de Gruyter.

1992b   Parasitology as an Interpretive Tool in Archaeology. *American Antiquity* 57(2):231–245.

1993   The Utility of Pollen Concentrations in Coprolite Analysis: Expanding upon
        Dean's Comments. *Journal of Ethnobiology* 13(1):114–128.

Reinhard, Karl J.

1998a   Mummy Studies and Paleonutrition. In: *Mummies, Disease, and Ancient Cultures* (2d ed.), Aidan Cockburn, Eve Cockburn, and Theodore A. Reyman, eds., pp. 372–377. Cambridge: Cambridge University Press.

1998b   Mummy Studies and Archaeoparasitology. In: *Mummies, Disease, and Ancient Cultures* (2d ed.), Aidan Cockburn, Eve Cockburn, and Theodore A. Reyman, eds., pp. 377–380. Cambridge: Cambridge University Press.

2006   A Coprological View of Ancestral Pueblo Cannibalism. *American Scientist* 94(3):254–261.

Reinhard, Karl J., and Vaughn M. Bryant Jr.

1992   Coprolite Analysis: A Biological Perspective on Archaeology. In: *Archaeological Method and Theory, Vol. 4*, Michael B. Schiffer, ed., pp. 245–288. Tucson: University of Arizona Press.

1995   Investigating Mummified Intestinal Contents: Reconstructing Diet and Parasitic Disease. In: *Proceedings of the First World Congress on Mummy Studies, Vol. 1*, pp. 403–408. Museo Arqueológico y Etnográfico de Tenerife.

Reinhard, Karl J., and Dennis R. Danielson

2005   Pervasiveness of Phytoliths in Prehistoric Southwestern Diet and Implications for Regional and Temporal Trends for Dental Microwear. *Journal of Archaeological Science* 32(7):981–988.

Reinhard, Karl J., J. Richard Ambler, and Magdalene McGuffie

1985   Diet and Parasitism at Dust Devil Cave. *American Antiquity* 50(4):819–824.

Reinhard, Karl J., Richard H. Hevly, and Glenn A. Anderson

1987   Helminth Remains from Prehistoric Indian Coprolites on the Colorado Plateau. *Journal of Parasitology* 73(3):630–639.

Reinhard, Karl J., Don L. Hamilton, and Richard H. Hevly

1991   Use of Pollen Concentration in Paleopharmacology: Coprolite Evidence of Medicinal Plants. *Journal of Ethnobiology* 11(1):117–134.

Reinhard, Karl J., Phil R. Geib, Martha M. Callahan, and Richard H. Hevly

1992   Discovery of Colon Contents in a Skeletonized Burial: Soil Sampling for Dietary Remains. *Journal of Archaeological Science* 19(6):697–705.

Reinhard, Karl J., S.M.F. de Souza, C. D. Rodrigues, E. Kimmerle, and S. Dorsey-Vinton

2001   Microfossils in Dental Calculus: A New Perspective on Diet and Dental Disease. In: *Human Remains: Conservation, Retrieval, and Analysis*, Emily Williams, ed., pp. 113–118. Oxford: Archaeopress.

Reitz, Elizabeth J., and Elizabeth S. Wing

1999   *Zooarchaeology*. Cambridge: Cambridge Manuals in Archaeology, Cambridge University Press.

Reitz, Elizabeth J., Lee A. Newsom, and Sylvia J. Scudder

1996   Issues in Environmental Archaeology. In: *Case Studies in Environmental Archaeology*, Elizabeth J. Reitz, Lee A. Newsom, and Sylvia J. Scudder, eds., pp. 3–16. New York: Plenum Press.

Remington, S. James

1994   Identifying Species of Origin from Prehistoric Blood Residues. *Science* 266:298–299.

Renfrew, Colin

1998   Applications of DNA in Archaeology: A Review of the DNA Studies of the Ancient Biomolecules Initiative. *Ancient Biomolecules* 2(2/3):107–117.

Renfrew, Jane M.

1969   The Archaeological Evidence for the Domestication of Plants: Methods and Problems. In: *The Domestication and Exploitation of Plants and Animals*, George W. Dimbleby and Peter Ucko, eds., pp. 149–172. Chicago: Aldine Publishing Company.

1973   *Palaeoethnobotany: The Prehistoric Food Plants of the Near East and Europe.* New York: Columbia University Press.

Reuther, Joshua D., Jerold M. Lowenstein, S. Craig Gerlach, Darden Hood, Gary Scheuenstuhl, and Douglas H. Ubelaker

2006   The Use of an Improved pRIA Technique in the Identification of Protein Residues. *Journal of Archaeological Science* 33(4):531–537.

Reynolds, Amanda C., Julio L. Betancourt, Jay Quade, P. Jonathan Patchett, Jeffrey S. Dean, and John Stein

2005 $^{87}Sr/^{86}Sr$ Sourcing of Ponderosa Pine Used in Anasazi Great House Construction at Chaco Canyon, New Mexico. *Journal of Archaeological Science* 32(7):1061–1075.

Reznek, R. H., M. G. Hallett, and M. Charlesworth

1986   Computed Tomography of Lindow Man. In: *Lindow Man: The Body in the Bog*, I. M. Stead, J. B. Bourke, and Don R. Brothwell, eds., pp. 63–65. Ithaca: Cornell University Press.

Rhode, David

2003   Coprolites from Hidden Cave, Revisited: Evidence for Site Occupation History, Diet and Sex of Occupants. *Journal of Archaeological Science* 30(7):909–922.

Ribot, Isabelle, and Charlotte A. Roberts

1996   A Study of Non-specific Stress Indicators and Skeletal Growth in Two Mediaeval Subadult Populations. *Journal of Archaeological Science* 23(1):67–79.

Richards, M. B., Kate Smalley, Bryan C. Sykes, and Robert E. M. Hedges

1993   Archaeology and Genetics: Analyzing DNA from Skeletal Remains. *World Archaeology* 25(1):18–28.

Richards, M. B., Bryan C. Sykes, and Robert E. M. Hedges

1995   Authenticating DNA Extracted from Ancient Skeletal Remains. *Journal of Archaeological Science* 22(2):291–299.

Richards, M. B., Helena Côrte-Real, Peter Forster, Vincent Macaulay, Hilde Wilkinson-Herbots, Andrew Demaine, Surinda Papiha, Robert Hedges, Hans-Jürgen Bandelt, and Bryan C. Sykes

1996   Paleolithic and Neolithic Lineages in the European Mitochondrial Gene Pool. *American Journal of Human Genetics* 59:185–203.

Richards, M. P., and Robert E. M. Hedges

1999   Stable Isotope Evidence for Similarities in the Types of Marine Foods Used by Late Mesolithic Humans at Sites along the Atlantic Coast of Europe. *Journal of Archaeological Science* 26(6):717–722.

Richards, M. P., Robert E. M. Hedges, T. I. Molleson, and J. C. Vogel

1998   Stable Isotope Analysis Reveals Variations in Human Diet at the Poundbury Camp Cemetery Site. *Journal of Archaeological Science* 25(12):1247–1252.

Richards, M. P., Robert E. M. Hedges, R. Jacobi, A. Current, and C. Stinger

2000   FOCUS: Gough's Cave and Sun Hole Cave Human Stable Isotope Values Indicate a High Animal Protein Diet in the British Upper Palaeolithic. *Journal of Archaeological Science* 27(1):1–3.

Richards, M. P., Simon Mays, and B. T. Fuller

2002   Stable Carbon and Nitrogen Isotope Values of Bone and Teeth Reflect Weaning Age at the Medieval Wharram Percy Site, Yorkshire, U.K. *American Journal of Physical Anthropology* 119(3):205–210.

Richards, M. P., B. T. Fuller, Matt Sponheimer, Todd Robinson, and Linda Ayliffe

2003a   Sulphur Isotopes in Palaeodietary Studies: A Review and Results from a Controlled Feeding Experiment. *International Journal of Osteoarchaeology* 13(1–2):37–45.

Richards, M. P., Rick J. Schulting, and Robert E. M. Hedges

2003b   Archaeology: Sharp Shift in Diet at Onset of Neolithic. *Nature* 425:366.

Richards, M. P., J. A. Pearson, T. I. Molleson, N. Russell, and L. Martin

2003c   Stable Isotope Evidence of Diet at Neolithic Çatalhöyük, Turkey. *Journal of Archaeological Science* 30(1):67–76.

Richards, M. P., B. T. Fuller, and T. I. Molleson

2006   Stable Isotope Palaeodietary Study of Humans and Fauna from the Multi-Period (Iron Age, Viking and Late Medieval) Site of Newark Bay, Orkney. *Journal of Archaeological Science* 33(1):122–131.

Richerson, Peter J., and Robert Boyd

1992   Cultural Inheritance and Evolutionary Ecology. In: *Evolutionary Ecology and Human Behavior*, Eric Alden Smith and Bruce Winterhalder, eds., pp. 61–92. New York: Aldine de Gruyter.

Rink, W. Jack, and Henry P. Schwarcz

1995   Tests for Diagenesis in Tooth Enamel: ESR Dating Signals and Carbonate Contents. *Journal of Archaeological Science* 22(2):251–255.

Rivals, Florent, and Brigitte Deniaux

2005   Investigation of Human Hunting Seasonality through Dental Microwear Analysis of Two Caprinae in Late Pleistocene Localities in Southern France. *Journal of Archaeological Science* 32(11):1603–1612.

Robbins, Gwen, V. Mushrif Tripathy, V. N. Misra, R. K. Mohanty, V. S. Shinde, Kelsey M. Gray, and Malcolm D. Schug

2009   Ancient Skeletal Evidence for Leprosy in India (2000 BC). *PLoS ONE* 4(5):1–8.

Roberts, Charlotte A.
1991   Scientific Methods in Palaeopathology: Past, Present and Future. In: *Archaeo-logical Sciences 1989*, Paul Budd, Barbara Chapman, Caroline Jackson, Rob Jan-away, and Barbara Ottaway, eds., pp. 373–385. Oxford: Oxbow Monograph 9.

Roberts, Charlotte A., and Keith Manchester
2007   *The Archaeology of Disease* (3d ed.). Ithaca: Cornell University Press.

Robins, Don, Keith Sales, Duro Oduwole, Timothy G. Holden, and Gordon Hillman
1986   Postscript: Last Minute Results from ESR Spectroscopy concerning the Cooking of Lindow Man's Last Meal. In: *Lindow Man: The Body in the Bog*, I. M. Stead, J. B. Bourke, and Don R. Brothwell, eds., pp. 140–142. Ithaca: Cornell University Press.

Robinson, C. K.
1976   Human Skeletal Remains from 1975 Archaeological Excavations in Mancos Canyon, Colorado. Master's thesis, Department of Anthropology, University of Colorado, Boulder.

Robinson, David, and Peter Rasmussen
1989   Botanical Investigations at the Neolithic Lake Village at Weier, North East Swit-zerland: Leaf Hay and Cereals as Animal Fodder. In: *The Beginnings of Agri-culture*, Annie Milles, Diane Williams, and Neville Gardner, eds., pp. 149–163. Oxford: British Archaeological Reports, International Series, No. 496.

Robison, N. D.
1978   *Zooarchaeology: Its History and Development*. Knoxville: Tennessee Anthropo-logical Association Miscellaneous Paper 2:1–22.

Robson, J.R.K., and G. R. Wadsworth
1977   The Health and Nutritional Status of Primitive Populations. *Ecology of Food and Nutrition* 6:187–202.

Rochow, Theodore George, and Paul Arthur Tucker
1994   *Introduction to Microscopy by Means of Light, Electrons, X-Rays, or Acoustics.* New York: Plenum Press.

Roehrig, K. L.
1984   *Carbohydrate Biochemistry and Metabolism*. Westport, Conn.: Avi Publishing Co.

Rogan, Peter K., and Joseph J. Salvo
1995   High-Fidelity Polymerase Chain Reaction Amplification Products from Mummified South American Human Remains. In: *Proceedings of the First World Congress on Mummy Studies*, Vol. 2, pp. 485–494. Museo Arqueológico y Etnográfico de Tenerife.

Rogers, S. L.
1984   *The Human Skull: Its Mechanics, Measurements, and Variations*. Springfield, Ill.: Charles C. Thomas.

Rollo, Franco, Franco Maria Venanzi, and Augusto Amici
1994   DNA and RNA from Ancient Plant Seeds. In: *Ancient DNA: Recovery and Analy-sis of Genetic Material from Paleontological, Archaeological, Museum, Medical, and Forensic Specimens*, Bernd Herrmann and Susanne Hummel, eds., pp. 218–236. Berlin: Springer-Verlag.

Rollo, Franco, Massimo Ubaldi, Isolina Marota, Stefania Luciani, and Luca Ermini
2002   DNA Diagenesis: Effect of Environment and Time on Human Bone. *Ancient Biomolecules* 4(1):1–7.

Rose, Jerome C., Keith W. Condon, and Alan H. Goodman
1985   Diet and Dentition: Developmental Disturbances. In: *The Analysis of Prehistoric Diets*, Robert I. Gilbert Jr. and James H. Mielke, eds., pp. 281–306. New York: Academic Press.

Rose, M. R., J. S. Dean, and W. J. Robinson
1981   *The Past Climate of Arroyo Hondo, New Mexico, Reconstructed from Tree Rings*. Santa Fe: School of American Research Press.

Rosen, Arlene Miller
1993   Phytolith Evidence for Early Cereal Exploitation in the Levant. In: *Current Research in Phytolith Analysis: Applications in Archaeology and Paleoecology*, Deborah M. Pearsall and Dolores R. Piperno, eds., pp. 160–171. Philadelphia: University of Pennsylvania, University Museum of Archaeology and Anthropology, MASCA Research Papers in Science and Archaeology, Vol. 10.

Roth, Eric Abella
1992   Applications of Demographic Models to Paleodemography. In: *The Skeletal Biology of Past People: Research Methods*, Shelley R. Saunders and M. Anne Katzenberg, eds., pp. 175–188. New York: John Wiley & Sons.

Rothhammer, Francisco, Marvin J. Allison, Lautaro Núñez, Vivien Standen, and Bernardo Arriaza
1985   Chagas' Disease in Pre-Columbian South America. *American Journal of Physical Anthropology* 68(4):495–498.

Rothschild, Bruce M., and Christine Rothschild
1996   Treponemal Disease in the New World. *Current Anthropology* 37(3):555–561.
1997   Congenital Syphilis in the Archaeological Record: Diagnostic Insensitivity of Osseous Lesions. *International Journal of Osteoarchaeology* 7(1):39–42.

Rovner, Irwin
1983   Plant Opal Phytolith Analysis: Major Advances in Archaeobotanical Research. In: *Advances in Archaeological Method and Theory*, Michael B. Schiffer, ed., pp. 225–266. New York: Academic Press.

Runia, Lex T.
1987   Strontium and Calcium Distribution in Plants: Effect on Palaeodietary Studies. *Journal of Archaeological Science* 14(6):599–608.

Ryan, Dennis John
1977   The Paleopathology and Paleoepidemiology of the Kayenta Anasazi Indians in Northeastern Arizona. Ph.D. dissertation, Department of Anthropology, Arizona State University, Tempe.

Ryan, Jack
1995   Brief Review of Research into the Photographic Recovery of Diagnostic Silica Phytoliths from Prehistoric Groundstone Artifacts and Human Dentition Using

Scanning Electron Microscopy. Paper presented at the annual meetings of the Society for American Archaeology, Minneapolis.

Rylander, Kate Aasen

1994   Corn Preparation among the Basketmaker Anasazi: A Scanning Electron Microscope Study of *Zea mays* Remains from Coprolites. In: *Paleonutrition: The Diet and Health of Prehistoric Americans*, Kristin D. Sobolik, ed., pp. 115–133. Carbondale: Southern Illinois University, Center for Archaeological Investigations, Occasional Paper No. 22.

Saffray, D. R.

1876   Les antiquites peruviennes a l'exposition de Philadelphia. *La Nature* 4:401–407, Paris.

Safont, S., A. Malgosa, M. E. Subirà, and J. Gibert

1998   Can Trace Elements in Fossils Provide Information about Palaeodiet? *International Journal of Osteoarchaeology* 8(1):23–37.

Sallares, Robert, and Susan Gomzi

2001   Biomolecular Archaeology of Malaria. *Ancient Biomolecules* 3(3):195–213.

Salo, Wilmar L., Ivy Foo, Kyle Wahlstrom, and Arthur C. Aufderheide

1995a   Searching for Tuberculosis in Residual DNA from Mummified Human, New World Remains. In: *Proceedings of the First World Congress on Mummy Studies*, Vol. 2, pp. 495–503. Museo Arqueológico y Etnográfico de Tenerife.

Salo, Wilmar L., Ivy Foo, and Arthur C. Aufderheide

1995b   Determining Relatedness among the Aboriginal People of the Canary Islands by Analysis of Their DNA. In: *Proceedings of the First World Congress on Mummy Studies*, Vol. 1, pp. 105–112. Museo Arqueológico y Etnográfico de Tenerife.

Samuels, Robert

1965   Parasitological Study of Long-Dried Fecal Samples. In: *Contributions of the Wetherill Mesa Archaeological Project*, Douglas Osborne, assembler, pp. 175–179. Washington, D.C.: Society for American Archaeology, Memoirs, No. 19.

Sandford, Mary K.

1984   Diet, Disease, and Nutritional Stress: An Elemental Analysis of Human Hair from Kulubnarti, a Medieval Sudanese Nubian Population. Ph.D. dissertation, University of Colorado, Boulder.

1992   A Reconsideration of Trace Element Analysis in Prehistoric Bone. In: *Skeletal Biology of Past Peoples: Research Methods*, Shelley R. Saunders and M. Anne Katzenberg, eds., pp. 79–103. New York: Wiley-Liss.

1993a   Understanding the Biogenic-Diagenic Continuum: Interpreting Elemental Concentrations of Archaeological Bone. In: *Investigations of Ancient Human Tissue: Chemical Analyses in Anthropology*, Mary K. Sandford, ed., pp. 3–57. Langhorne, Penn.: Gordon and Breach.

Sandford, Mary K. (ed.)

1993b   *Investigations of Ancient Human Tissue: Chemical Analyses in Anthropology*. Langhorne, Penn.: Gordon and Breach.

Sandford, Mary K., and M. Anne Katzenberg

1995   Current Status of and Methods for Trace Mineral Analysis of Archaeological Tissue. In: *Proceedings of the First World Congress on Mummy Studies*, Vol. 2, pp. 535–542. Museo Arqueológico y Etnográfico de Tenerife.

Sandford, Mary K., and Grace E. Kissling

1993   Chemical Analyses of Human Hair: Anthropological Applications. In: *Investigations of Ancient Human Tissue: Chemical Analyses in Anthropology*, Mary K. Sandford, ed., pp. 131–166. Langhorne, Penn.: Gordon and Breach.

Sandford, Mary K., and David S. Weaver

2000   Trace Element Research in Anthropology: New Perspectives and Challenges. In: *Biological Anthropology of the Human Skeleton*, M. Anne Katzenberg and Shelley R. Saunders, eds., pp. 329–350. New York: Wiley-Liss.

Sandford, Mary K., Dennis P. Van Gerven, and Robert R. Meglen

1983   Elemental Hair Analysis: New Evidence on the Etiology of Cribra Orbitalia in Sudanese Nubia. *Human Biology* 55(4):831–844.

Sanson, Gordon D., Stuart A. Kerr, and Karlis A. Gross

2007   Do Silica Phytoliths Really Wear Mammalian Teeth? *Journal of Archaeological Science* 34(4):526–531.

Sargent, Charles Sprague

1922   *Manual of the Trees of North America*. Boston: Houghton Mifflin.

Scaife, Robert G.

1986   Pollen in Human Palaeofaeces; and a Preliminary Investigation of the Stomach and Gut Contents of Lindow Man. In: *Lindow Man: The Body in the Bog*, I. M. Stead, J. B. Bourke, and Don R. Brothwell, eds., pp. 126–135. Ithaca: Cornell University Press.

Schaefer, Jerry

1994   The Challenge of Archaeological Research in the Colorado Desert: New Approaches and Discoveries. *Journal of California and Great Basin Anthropology* 16(1):60–80.

Schaefer, Jerry, and Don Laylander

2007   The Colorado Desert: Ancient Adaptations to Wetlands and Wastelands. In: *California Prehistory: Colonization, Culture, and Complexity*, Terry L. Jones and Kathryn A. Klar, eds., pp. 247–257. Lanham, Md.: AltaMira Press.

Schaefer, O.

1977   Changing Dietary Patterns in the Canadian North: Health, Social and Economic Consequences. *Journal of Canada Dietary Association* 38:17–25.

Schäfer, Jürgen, Woldgang Pirsig Wolfgang, and Franz Parsche

1995   Strontium Patterns in Infancy Can Validate Retention of Biogenic Signal in Human Archaeological Bone. In: *Proceedings of the First World Congress on Mummy Studies*, Vol. 1, pp. 443–450. Museo Arqueológico y Etnográfico de Tenerife.

Scheuer, Louise, and Sue Black

2004   *The Juvenile Skeleton*. Amsterdam: Elsevier Academic Press.

Schiemann, E.

1951   New Results on the History of Cultivated Cereals. *Heredity* 5(3):305–318.

Schlezinger, David R., and Brian L. Howes

2000   Organic Phosphorus and Elemental Ratios as Indicators of Prehistoric Human Occupation. *Journal of Archaeological Science* 27(6):479–492.

Schlumbaum, Angela, and Stefanie Jacomet

1998   Coexistence of Tetraploid and Hexaploid Naked Wheat in a Neolithic Lake Dwelling of Central Europe: Evidence from Morphology and Ancient DNA. *Journal of Archaeological Science* 25(11):1111–1118.

Schmerling, P. C.

1835   Description des Ossemens Fossiles, a l'etat Pathologique, Provenant des Cavernes de la Province de Liege. *Bulletin de la Societe Geologique de France* 7:51–61.

Schmidt, Robert A., and Barbara L. Voss

2000   *Archaeologies of Sexuality*. New York: Routledge.

Schmitt, A.

2004   Age at Death Assessment Using the Os Pubis and the Auricular Surface of the Ilium: A Test on an Identified Asian Sample. *International Journal of Osteoarchaeology* 14(1):1–6.

Schmucker, Betty J.

1985   Dental Attrition: A Correlative Study of Dietary and Subsistence Patterns in California and New Mexico Indians. In: *Health and Disease in the Prehistoric Southwest*, Charles F. Merbs and Robert J. Miller, eds., pp. 275–323. Tempe: Arizona State University, Anthropological Research Papers, No. 34.

Schneider, Kim N.

1986   Dental Caries, Enamel Composition, and Subsistence among Prehistoric Amerindians of Ohio. *American Journal of Physical Anthropology* 71(1):95–102.

Schoeller, Dale A.

1999   Isotope Fractionation: Why Aren't We What We Eat? *Journal of Archaeological Science* 26(6):667–673.

Schoeninger, Margaret J.

1979   Diet and Status at Chalcatzingo: Some Empirical and Technical Aspects of Strontium Analysis. *American Journal of Physical Anthropology* 51(3):295–310.

1989   Reconstructing Prehistoric Human Diet. In: *The Chemistry of Prehistoric Human Bone*, T. Douglas Price, ed., pp. 38–67. Cambridge: Cambridge University Press.

1995   Dietary Reconstruction in the Prehistoric Carson Desert: Stable Carbon and Nitrogen Isotopic Analysis. In: *Bioarchaeology of the Stillwater Marsh: Prehistoric Human Adaptation in the Western Great Basin*, Clark Spencer Larsen and Robert L. Kelly, eds., pp. 96–106. New York: American Museum of Natural History, Anthropological Papers 77.

Schoeninger, Margaret J., and Michael J. DeNiro

1982   Carbon Isotope Ratios for Apatite from Fossil Bone Cannot Be Used to Reconstruct Diets of Animals. *Nature* 297:577–578.

Schoeninger, Margaret J., and Michael J. DeNiro

1984   Nitrogen and Carbon Isotopic Composition of Bone Collagen from Marine and Terrestrial Animals. *Geochimica et Cosmochimica Acta* 48(4):625–639.

Schoeninger, Margaret J., and Katherine M. Moore

1992   Bone Stable Isotope Studies in Archaeology. *Journal of World Prehistory* 6(2):247–296.

Schoeninger, Margaret J., Katherine M. Moore, Matthew L. Murray, and John D. Kingston

1989   Detection of Bone Preservation in Archaeological and Fossil Samples. *Applied Geochemistry* 4(3):281–292.

Schoeninger, Margaret J., Matthew J. Kohn, and John W. Valley

2000   Tooth Oxygen Isotope Ratios as Paleoclimate Monitors in Arid Ecosystems. In: *Biogeochemical Approaches to Paleodietary Analysis*, Stanley H. Ambrose and M. Anne Katzenberg, eds., pp. 117–140. New York: Kluwer Academic/Plenum Publishers.

Schoeninger, Margaret J., Holly Reeser, and Kris Hallin

2003a   Paleoenvironment of *Australopithecus anamensis* at Allia Bay, East Turkana, Kenya: Evidence from Mammalian Herbivore Enamel Stable Isotopes. *Journal of Anthropological Archaeology* 22(3):200–207.

Schoeninger, Margaret J., Kris Hallin, Holly Reeser, John W. Valley, and John Fournelle

2003b   Isotopic Alteration of Mammalian Tooth Enamel. *International Journal of Osteoarchaeology* 13(1–2):11–19.

Schopmeyer, C. S.

1974   Seeds of Woody Plants in the United States. Washington, D.C.: U.S. Department of Agriculture, Forest Service Agricultural Handbook No. 450.

Schulting, Rick J., and Michael P. Richards

2001   Dating Women and Becoming Farmers: New Paleodietary and AMS Dating Evidence from the Breton Mesolithic Cemeteries of Téviec and Hoëdic. *Journal of Anthropological Archaeology* 20(3):314–344.

Schulting, Rick J., Stella M. Blockley, Hervé Bocherens, Dorothée Drucker, and Mike Richards

2008   Stable Carbon and Nitrogen Isotope Analysis on Human Remains from the Early Mesolithic Site of La Vergne (Charente-Maritime, France). *Journal of Archaeological Science* 35(3):763–772.

Schultz, Michael, Clark Spencer Larsen, and Kerstin Kreutz

2001   Disease in Spanish Florida: Microscopy of Porotic Hyperstosis and Cribra Orbitalia. In: *Bioarchaeology of Spanish Florida: The Impact of Colonialism*, Clark Spencer Larsen, ed., pp. 207–225. Gainesville: University of Florida Press.

Schulz, Peter D.

1977   Task Activity and Anterior Tooth Grooving in Prehistoric California Indians. *American Journal of Physical Anthropology* 46(1):87–91.

Schurr, Mark R.

1992   Isotopic and Mortuary Variability in a Middle Mississippian Population. *American Antiquity* 57(2):300–320.

1997   Stable Nitrogen Isotopes as Evidence for the Age of Weaning at the Angel Site: A Comparison of Isotopic and Demographic Measures of Weaning Age. *Journal of Archaeological Science* 25(10):919–927.

1998   Using Stable Nitrogen-Isotopes to Study Weaning Behavior in Past Populations. *World Archaeology* 30(2):327–342.

Schurr, Mark R., and Brian G. Redmond

1991   Stable Isotope Analysis of Incipient Maize Horticulturalists from Gard Island 2 Site. *Midcontinental Journal of Archaeology* 16(1):69–84.

Schutkowski, Holger, Bernd Herrmann, Felicitas Wiedemann, Hervé Bocherens, and Gisela Grupe

1999   Diet, Status and Decomposition at Weingarten: Trace Element and Isotope Analyses on Early Mediaeval Skeletal Material. *Journal of Archaeological Science* 26(6):675–685.

Schwarcz, Henry P.

1991   Some Theoretical Aspects of Isotope Paleodiet Studies. *Journal of Archaeological Science* 18(2):261–275.

2000   Some Biochemical Aspects of Carbon Isotopic Paleodiet Studies. In: *Biogeochemical Approaches to Paleodietary Analysis*, Stanley H. Ambrose and M. Anne Katzenberg, eds., pp. 189–209. New York: Kluwer Academic/Plenum Publishers.

Schwarcz, Henry P., and Margaret J. Schoeninger

1991   Stable Isotope Analysis in Human Nutritional Ecology. *Yearbook of Physical Anthropology* 34:283–321.

Schwarcz, Henry P., and Christine D. White

2004   The Grasshopper or the Ant? Cultigen-Use Strategies in Ancient Nubia from C-13 Analyses of Human Hair. *Journal of Archaeological Science* 31(6):753–762.

Schweissing, Mike M., and Gisela Grupe

2003   Tracing Migration Events in Man and Cattle by Stable Strontium Isotope Analysis of Appositionally Grown Mineralized Tissue. *International Journal of Osteoarchaeology* 13(1–2):96–103.

Scott, A. W., Richard P. Evershed, S. Jim, V. Jones, J. M. Rogers, Noreen Tuross, and Stanley Ambrose

1999   Cholesterol as a New Source of Palaeodietary Information: Experimental Approaches and Archaeological Implications. *Journal of Archaeological Science* 26(6):705–716.

Scott, Elizabeth M.

2001   Food and Social Relations at Nina Plantation. *American Anthropologist* 103(3):671–691.

Scott, G. R.

1981   A Stature Reconstruction of the Gran Quivira Skeletal Population. In: *Contributions to Gran Quivira Archaeology: Gran Quivira National Monument, New Mexico*, Alden C. Hayes, ed., pp. 129–138. Washington, D.C.: National Park Service, Publications in Archaeology, No. 17.

Scott, Linda J.
1979   Dietary Inferences from Hoy House Coprolites: A Palynological Interpretation. *Kiva* 44(2–3):257–281.

Sealy, Judith C.
1986   *Stable Carbon Isotopes and Prehistoric Diets in the South-Western Cape Province, South Africa*. Oxford: British Archaeological Reports, International Series, No. 293.

Sealy, Judith C., and Andrew Sillen
1988   Sr and Sr/Ca in Marine and Terrestrial Foodwebs in the Southwestern Cape, South Africa. *Journal of Archaeological Science* 15(4):425–438.

Sealy, Judith C., and Nikolaas J. van der Merwe
1985   Isotope Assessment of Holocene Human Diets in the Southwestern Cape, South Africa. *Nature* 315:138–140.

1986   Isotope Assessment and the Seasonal-Mobility Hypothesis in the Southwestern Cape of South Africa. *Current Anthropology* 27(2):135–150.

1988   Social, Spatial and Chronological Patterning in Marine Food Use as Determined by $\delta^{13}C$ Measurements of Holocene Human Skeletons from the South-Western Cape, South Africa. *World Archaeology* 20(1):87–102.

Sealy, Judith C., Nikolaas J. van der Merwe, Andrew Sillen, F. J. Kruger, and Harold W. Krueger
1991 $^{87}Sr/^{86}Sr$ as a Dietary Indicator in Modern and Archaeological Bone. *Journal of Archaeological Science* 18(3):399–416.

Sealy, Judith C., Richard Armstrong, and Carmel Schrire
1995   Beyond Lifetime Averages: Tracing Life Histories through Isotopic Analysis of Different Calcified Tissues from Archaeological Human Skeletons. *Antiquity* 69(263):290–300.

Seckler, D.
1982   Small but Healthy: A Basic Hypothesis in the Theory, Measurement and Policy of Malnutrition. In: *Newer Concepts in Nutrition and Their Implications for Policy*, P. V. Sukhatme, ed., pp. 127–137. Pune, India: Maharashtra Association for the Cultivation of Science.

Semal, Patrick, and Rosine Orban
1995   Collagen Extraction from Recent and Fossil Bones: Quantitative and Qualitative Aspects. *Journal of Archaeological Science* 22(4):463–467.

Sept, Jeanne
1992   Archaeological Evidence and Ecological Perspectives for Reconstructing Early Hominid Subsistence Behavior. In: *Archaeological Method and Theory*, Vol. 4, Michael B. Schiffer, ed., pp. 1–56. Tucson: University of Arizona Press.

Serjeantson, Dale
2009   *Birds*. Cambridge: Cambridge Manuals in Archaeology, Cambridge University Press.

Shafer, Harry J., Marianne Marek, and Karl J. Reinhard
1989   A Mimbres Burial with Associated Colon Remains from the NAN Ranch Ruin, New Mexico. *Journal of Field Archaeology* 16(1):17–30.

Shaffer, Brian S.

1992   Quarter-Inch-Screening: Understanding Biases in Recovery of Vertebrate Faunal Remains. *American Antiquity* 57(1):129–136.

Shaffer, Brian S., and Julia L. J. Sanchez

1994   Comparison of 1/8″- and 1/4″-Mesh Recovery of Controlled Samples of Small- to Medium-Sized Mammals. *American Antiquity* 59(3):525–530.

Shahied, I. I.

1977   *Biochemistry of Foods and the Biocatalysts.* New York: Vantage Press.

Shanks, Orin C., Marcel Kornfeld, and Dee Dee Hawk

1999   Protein Analysis of Bugas-Holding Tools: New Trends in Immunological Studies. *Journal of Archaeological Science* 26(9):1183–1191.

Shanks, Orin C., Robson Bonnichsen, Anthony T. Vella, and Walt Ream

2001   Recovery of Protein and DNA Trapped in Stone Tool Microcracks. *Journal of Archaeological Science* 28(9):965–972.

Shanks, Orin C., Larry Hodges, Lucas Tilley, Marcel Kornfeld, Mary Lou Larson, and Walt Ream

2005   DNA from Ancient Stone Tools and Bones Excavated at Bugas-Holding, Wyoming. *Journal of Archaeological Science* 32(1):27–38.

Shapiro, H. L.

1959   The History and Development of Physical Anthropology. *American Anthropologist* 61(3):371–379.

Shaw, Leslie C.

1999   Social and Ecological Aspects of Preclassic Maya Meat Consumption at Colha, Belize. In: *Reconstructing Ancient Maya Diet*, Christine D. White, ed., pp. 83–100. Salt Lake City: University of Utah Press.

Shearer, Gretchen L.

1988   Characterization of Organic Archaeological Residues Using Diffuse Reflectance Fourier Transform Infra-red Spectroscopy. In: *Science and Archaeology, Glasgow 1987*, Elizabeth A. Slater and James O. Tate, eds., pp. 413–427. Oxford: British Archaeological Reports, International Series, No. 196 (2 vols.).

Sherman, H. C.

1941   *Chemistry of Food and Nutrition.* New York: Macmillan.

Shipman, Pat

1986   Scavenging or Hunting in Early Hominids: Theoretical Framework and Tests. *American Anthropologist* 88(1):27–43.

Sillen, Andrew

1989   Diagenesis of the Inorganic Phase of Cortical Bone. In: *The Chemistry of Prehistoric Human Bone*, T. Douglas Price, ed., pp. 211–229. Cambridge: Cambridge University Press.

1992   Strontium-Calcium Ratios (Sr/Ca) of *Australopithecus robustus* and Associated Fauna from Swartkrans. *Journal of Human Evolution* 23(6):495–516.

Sillen, Andrew, and Maureen Kavanagh

1982   Strontium and Paleodietary Research: A Review. *Yearbook of Physical Anthropology* 25:67–90.

Sillen, Andrew, and Raquel LeGeros

1991   Solubility Profiles of Synthetic Apatites and of Modern and Fossil Bones. *Journal of Archaeological Science* 18(3):385–397.

Sillen, Andrew, and Judith C. Sealy

1995   Diagenesis of Strontium in Fossil Bone: A Reconsideration of Nelson et al. (1986). *Journal of Archaeological Science* 22(2):313–320.

Sillen, Andrew, and Patricia Smith

1984   Weaning Patterns Are Reflected in Strontium-Calcium Ratios of Juvenile Skeletons. *Journal of Archaeological Science* 11(3):237–245.

Sillen, Andrew, Judith C. Sealy, and Nikolass J. van der Merwe

1989   Chemistry and Paleodietary Research: No More Easy Answers. *American Antiquity* 54(3):504–512.

Sillen, Andrew, Grant Hall, and Richard Armstrong

1995   Strontium Calcium Ratios (Sr/Ca) and Strontium Isotopic Ratios ($^{87}Sr/^{86}Sr$) of *Australopithecus robustus* and *Homo* sp. from Swartkrans. *Journal of Human Evolution* 28(3):277–285.

Simms, Steven R.

1984   Aboriginal Great Basin Foraging Strategies: An Evolutionary Analysis. Ph.D. dissertation, University of Utah, Salt Lake City.

1985   Acquisition Cost and Nutritional Data on Great Basin Resources. *Journal of California and Great Basin Anthropology* 7(1):117–126.

Simpson, Scott W.

1999   Reconstructing Patterns of Growth Disruption from Enamel Microstructure. In: *Human Growth in the Past: Studies from Bones and Teeth*, Robert D. Hoppa and Charles M. Fitzgerald, eds., pp. 241–263. Cambridge: Cambridge University Press.

2001   Patterns of Growth Disruption in La Florida: Evidence from Enamel Microstructure. In: *Bioarchaeology of Spanish Florida: The Impact of Colonialism*, Clark Spencer Larsen, ed., pp. 145–180. Gainesville: University of Florida Press.

Sinclair, H. M.

1953   The Diet of Canadian Indians and Eskimos. *Proceedings of the Nutritional Society* 12:69–82.

Sjøvold, Torstein

1992   The Stone Age Iceman from the Alps: The Find and the Current Status of Investigation. *Evolutionary Anthropology* 1(4):117–124.

Skinner, Mark

1996   Developmental Stress in Immature Hominines from Late Pleistocene Eurasia: Evidence from Enamel Hypoplasia. *Journal of Archaeological Science* 23(6):833–852.

1997   Dental Wear in Immature Late Pleistocene European Hominines. *Journal of Archaeological Science* 24(8):677–700.

Skinner, Mark, and Alan H. Goodman

1992   Anthropological Uses of Developmental Defects of Enamel. In: *The Skeletal Biology of Past People: Research Methods*, Shelley R. Saunders and M. Anne Katzenberg, eds., pp. 153–174. New York: John Wiley & Sons.

Smart, Tristine Lee, and Ellen S. Hoffman

1988   Environmental Interpretation of Archaeological Charcoal. In: *Current Paleoethnobotany*, Christine A. Hastorf and Virginia S. Popper, eds., pp. 167–205. Chicago: University of Chicago Press.

Smith, B. Holly

1984   Patterns in Molar Wear in Hunter-Gatherers and Agriculturalists. *American Journal of Physical Anthropology* 63(1):39–56.

Smith, Bruce D.

1975   *Middle Mississippi Exploitation of Animal Populations*. Ann Arbor: University of Michigan Museum of Anthropology, Anthropological Papers, No. 57.

1988   SEM and the Identification of Micro-Morphological Indicators of Domestication in Seed Plants. In: *Scanning Electron Microscopy in Archaeology*, Sandra L. Olsen, ed., pp. 203–214. Oxford: British Archaeological Reports, International Series, No. 452.

Smith, C. Earle, Jr.

1985   Recovery and Processing of Botanical Remains. In: *The Analysis of Prehistoric Diets*, Robert I. Gilbert Jr. and James H. Mielke, eds., pp. 97–126. New York: Academic Press.

Smith, David Glenn, Robert L. Bettinger, and Becky K. Rolfs

1995   Serum Albumin Phenotypes at Stillwater: Implications for Population History in the Great Basin. In: *Bioarchaeology of the Stillwater Marsh: Prehistoric Human Adaptation in the Western Great Basin*, Clark Spencer Larsen and Robert L. Kelly, eds., pp. 68–72. New York: American Museum of Natural History, Anthropological Papers 77.

Smith, Eric Alden

1983   Anthropological Applications of Optimal Foraging Theory: A Critical Review. *Current Anthropology* 24(5):625–651.

Smith, Eric Alden, and Bruce Winterhalder (eds.)

1992   *Evolutionary Ecology and Human Behavior*. New York: Aldine de Gruyter.

Smith, G. Elliot, and Frederick W. Jones

1910a   *Archeological Survey of Nubia 1907–1908* (2 vols.). Cairo: National Print Department.

1910b   *Report on the Human Remains. Archeological Survey of Nubia, Vol. II.* Cairo: National Print Department.

Smith, Patricia, and Gal Avishai

2005   The Use of Dental Criteria for Estimating Postnatal Survival in Skeletal Remains of Infants. *Journal of Archaeological Science* 32(1):83–89.

Smith, Patricia R., and Michael T. Wilson

1990   Detection of Haemoglobin in Human Skeletal Remains by ELISA. *Journal of Archaeological Science* 17(3):255–268.

1992   Blood Residue on Ancient Tool Surfaces: A Cautionary Note. *Journal of Archaeological Science* 19(3):237–241.

Sneath, Peter H. A.

1962   Longevity of Micro-organisms. *Nature* 4842:643–646.

Sobolik, Kristin D.

1988a   The Importance of Pollen Concentration Values from Coprolites: An Analysis of Southwest Texas Samples. *Palynology* 12:201–214.

1988b   Diet Change in the Lower Pecos: Analysis of Baker Cave Coprolites. *Bulletin of the Texas Archaeological Society* 59:111–127.

1990   A Nutritional Analysis of Diet as Revealed in Prehistoric Human Coprolites. *Texas Journal of Science* 42(1):23–36.

1991   *Prehistoric Diet and Subsistence in the Lower Pecos as Reflected in Coprolites from Baker Cave, Val Verde County, Texas.* Austin: University of Texas, Texas Archeological Research Laboratory, Studies in Archeology 7.

1992   Microscopic Epidermal Identification of *Yucca* and *Agave* for Archaeological Use. *Texas Journal of Science* 44(2):187–199.

1993   Direct Evidence for the Importance of Small Animals to Prehistoric Diets: A Review of Coprolite Studies. *North American Archaeologist* 14(3):227–244.

1994a   Introduction. In: *Paleonutrition: The Diet and Health of Prehistoric Americans*, Kristin D. Sobolik, ed., pp. 1–18. Carbondale: Southern Illinois University, Center for Archaeological Investigations, Occasional Paper No. 22.

1994b   Paleonutrition of the Lower Pecos Region of the Chihuahuan Desert. In: *Paleonutrition: The Diet and Health of Prehistoric Americans*, Kristin D. Sobolik, ed., pp. 247–264. Carbondale: Southern Illinois University, Center for Archaeological Investigations, Occasional Paper No. 22.

1996   Lithic Organic Residue Analysis: An Example from the Southwestern Archaic. *Journal of Field Archaeology* 23(4):461–469.

2002   Children's Health in the Prehistoric Southwest. In: *Children in the Prehistoric Puebloan Southwest*, Kathryn A. Kamp, ed., pp. 125–151. Salt Lake City: University of Utah Press.

2003   *Archaeobiology.* Walnut Creek, Calif.: AltaMira Press.

Sobolik, Kristin D. (ed.)

1994c   *Paleonutrition: The Diet and Health of Prehistoric Americans.* Carbondale: Southern Illinois University, Center for Archaeological Investigations, Occasional Paper No. 22.

Sobolik, Kristin D., and Deborah J. Gerick

1992   Prehistoric Medicinal Plant Usage: A Case Study from Coprolites. *Journal of Ethnobiology* 12(2):203–211.

Sobolik, Kristin D., and D. Gentry Steele

1996   *An Atlas of Turtles to Facilitate Archaeological Identifications.* Hot Springs, S.D.: Mammoth Site.

Sobolik, Kristin D., and Richard T. Will

2000   Calcined Turtle Bones from the Little Ossipee North Site in Southwestern Maine. *Archaeology of Eastern North America* 28:15–28.

Sobolik, Kristin D., Kristen J. Gremillion, Patricia L. Whitten, and Patty Jo Watson

1996   Technical Note: Sex Determination of Prehistoric Human Paleofeces. *American Journal of Physical Anthropology* 101(2):283–290.

Sobolik, Kristin D., L. S. Zimmerman, and B. M. Guilfoyl

1997   Indoor versus Outdoor Firepit Usage: A Case Study from the Mimbres. *Kiva* 62(3):283–300.

Soren, David

2003   Can Archaeologists Excavate Evidence of Malaria? *World Archaeology* 35(2):193–209.

Spencer, Charles S.

1997   Evolutionary Approaches in Archaeology. *Journal of Archaeological Research* 5(3):209–264.

Speth, John D.

1987   Early Hominid Subsistence Strategies in Seasonal Habitats. *Journal of Archaeological Science* 14(1):13–29.

1989   Early Hominid Hunting and Scavenging: The Role of Meat as an Energy Source. *Journal of Human Evolution* 18(4):329–343.

1990   Seasonality, Resource Stress, and Food Sharing in So-Called "Egalitarian" Foraging Societies. *Journal of Anthropological Archaeology* 9(2):148–188.

Speth, John D., and Katherine A. Spielmann

1983   Energy Source, Protein Metabolism and Hunter-Gatherer Subsistence Strategies. *Journal of Anthropological Archaeology* 2(1):1–31.

Spielmann, Katherine A., Margaret J. Schoeninger, and Katherine M. Moore

1990   Plains-Pueblo Interdependence and Human Diet at Pecos Pueblo, New Mexico. *American Antiquity* 55(4):745–765.

Spigelman, Mark, Carney Matheson, Galit Lev, Charles Greenblatt, and Helen D. Donoghue

2002   Confirmation of the Presence of *Mycobacterium tuberculosis* Complex-Specific DNA in Three Archaeological Specimens. *International Journal of Osteoarchaeology* 12(6):393–401.

Sponheimer, Matt, and Julia A. Lee-Thorp

1999   Oxygen Isotopes in Enamel Carbonate and Their Ecological Significance. *Journal of Archaeological Science* 26(6):723–728.

Sponheimer, Matt, Todd Robinson, Linda Ayliffe, Beverly Roeder, Jordan Hammer, Ben Passey, Adam West, Thure Cerling, Denise Dearing, and Jim Ehleringer

2003   Nitrogen Isotopes in Mammalian Herbivores: Hair $\delta^{15}N$ Values from a Controlled Feeding Study. *International Journal of Osteoarchaeology* 13(1–2):80–87.

Srinivasan, T. N.

1981   Malnutrition: Some Measurement and Policy Issues. *Journal of Development Economics* 8:3–19.

Stahl, Peter W.

1982   On Small Mammal Remains in Archaeological Contexts. *American Antiquity* 47(4):822–829.

Stead, I. M., John B. Bourke, and Don R. Brothwell (eds.)

1986   *Lindow Man: The Body in the Bog*. Ithaca: Cornell University Press.

Steinbock, R. Ted

1976   *Paleopathological Diagnosis and Interpretation: Bone Diseases in Ancient Human Populations*. Springfield, Ill.: Charles C. Thomas.

1985   The History, Epidemiology, and Paleopathology of Kidney and Bladder Stone Disease. In: *Health and Disease in the Prehistoric Southwest*, Charles F. Merbs and Robert J. Miller, eds., pp. 177–209. Tempe: Arizona State University, Anthropological Research Papers, No. 34.

Stephan, E.

2000   Oxygen Isotope Analysis of Animal Bone Phosphate: Method Refinement, Influence of Consolidants, and Reconstruction of Palaeotemperatures for Holocene Sites. *Journal of Archaeological Science* 27(6):523–535.

Stephens, David W., and John R. Krebs

1986   *Foraging Theory*. Princeton: Princeton University Press.

Steward, Julian H.

1937   Ethnological Reconnaissance among the Desert Shoshoni. In: *Exploration and Field Work of the Smithsonian Institution in 1936*, pp. 87–92. Washington, D.C.: Smithsonian Institution.

1938   *Basin-Plateau Aboriginal Sociopolitical Groups*. Washington, D.C.: Bureau of American Ethnology Bulletin, No. 120.

1955   *Theory of Culture Change*. Urbana: University of Illinois Press.

Stewart, Francis L., and Peter W. Stahl

1977   Cautionary Note on Edible Meat Poundage Figures. *American Antiquity* 42(2):267–270.

Stewart, T. D.

1947   *Hrdlička's Practical Anthropometry*. Philadelphia: Wistar Press.

1976   Are Supra-Inion Depressions Evidence of Prophylactic Trephination? *Bulletin of the History of Medicine* 50:414–434.

Stiger, Mark A.

1977   Anasazi Diet: The Coprolite Evidence. Master's thesis, University of Colorado, Boulder.

Stini, W. A.

1975   Adaptive Strategies of Human Populations under Nutritional Stress. In: *Biosocial Interrelations in Population Adaptation*, Elizabeth S. Watts, Francis E. Johnston, and Gabriel W. Lasker, eds., pp. 19–42. The Hague: Mouton.

1985   Growth Rates and Sexual Dimorphism in Evolutionary Perspective. In: *The Analysis of Prehistoric Diets*, R. I. Gilbert and J. H. Mielke, eds., pp. 191–226. Orlando, Fla.: Academic Press.

Stodder, Ann L. W.

1984   Paleoepidemiology of the Mesa Verde Region Anasazi: Demography, Stress, Migration. Master's thesis, Department of Anthropology, University of Colorado, Boulder.

1987   The Physical Anthropology and Mortuary Practice of the Delores Anasazi: An Early Pueblo Population in Local and Regional Context. In: *Delores Archaeological Program: Supporting Studies: Settlement and Environment*, K. L. Petersen and J. D. Orcutt, compilers, pp. 339–504. Denver: U.S. Department of the Interior, Bureau of Reclamation, Engineering and Research Center.

1990   Paleoepidemiology of Eastern and Western Pueblo Communities in Protohistoric New Mexico. Ph.D. dissertation, Department of Anthropology, University of Colorado, Boulder.

1994   Bioarchaeological Investigations of Protohistoric Pueblo Health and Demography. In: *In the Wake of Contact: Biological Responses to Conquest*, Clark S. Larsen and George R. Milner, eds., pp. 97–107. New York: Wiley-Liss.

Stojanowski, Christopher M., and Ryan M. Seidemann

1999   A Reevaluation of the Sex Prediction Accuracy of the Minimum Supero-Interior Femoral Neck Diameter for Modern Individuals. *Journal of Forensic Sciences* 44(6):1215–1218.

Stone, Anne C.

2000   Ancient DNA from Skeletal Remains. In: *Biological Anthropology of the Human Skeleton*, M. Anne Katzenberg and Shelley R. Saunders, eds., pp. 351–371. New York: Wiley-Liss.

Stone, Anne C., and Mark Stoneking   •

1993   Ancient DNA from a Pre-Columbian Amerindian Population. *American Journal of Physical Anthropology* 92(4):463–471.

1996   Genetic Analysis of an 8000-Year-Old Native American Skeleton. *Ancient Biomolecules* 1(1):83–87.

Stone, Anne C., George R. Milner, Svante Pääbo, and Mark Stoneking

1996   Sex Determination of Ancient Human Skeletons Using DNA. *American Journal of Physical Anthropology* 99(2):231–238.

Storey, Rebecca

1992   The Children of Copan: Issues in Paleopathology and Paleodemography. *Ancient Mesoamerica* 3:161–167.

1999   Late Classic Nutrition and Skeletal Indicators at Copán, Honduras. In: *Reconstructing Ancient Maya Diet*, Christine D. White, ed., pp. 169–179. Salt Lake City: University of Utah Press.

2006   An Elusive Paleodemography? A Comparison of Two Methods for Estimating the Adult Age Distribution of Deaths at Late Classic Copan, Honduras. *American Journal of Physical Anthropology* 132(1):40–47.

Stout, Sam D.

1989   Histomorphometric Analysis of Human Skeletal Remains. In: *Reconstruction of Life from the Skeleton*, Mehmet Y. Işcan and Kenneth A. R. Kennedy, eds., pp. 41–52. New York: Alan R. Liss, Inc.

1992   Methods of Determining Age at Death Using Bone Microstructure. In: *The Skeletal Biology of Past People: Research Methods*, Shelley R. Saunders and M. Anne Katzenberg, eds., pp. 21–35. New York: John Wiley & Sons.

St. Pierre, Christian Gates

2006   Faunal Remains as Markers of Ethnicity: A Case Study from the St. Lawrence Estuary, Quebec, Canada. Paper presented at the Tenth Conference of the International Council for Archaeozoology (ICAZ), Mexico City. Electronic document accessed on March 9, 2008, at http://www.alexandriaarchive.org/icaz/icazForum/viewtopic.php?p=237&sid=851e72d4ae99c804099158e2d7d40889.

Strong, William D.

1929   *Aboriginal Society in Southern California*. University of California Publications in American Archaeology and Ethnology 26(1).

Struever, Stuart

1968   Flotation Techniques for the Recovery of Small-Scale Archaeological Remains. *American Antiquity* 33(3):353–362.

Stuart-Macadam, Patricia L.

1985   Porotic Hyperostosis: Representative of a Childhood Condition. *American Journal of Physical Anthropology* 66(4):391–398.

1988   Nutrition and Anaemia in Past Human Populations. In: *Diet and Subsistence: Current Archaeological Perspectives*, Brenda V. Kennedy and Genevieve M. LeMoine, eds., pp. 284–287. Proceedings of the Nineteenth Annual Chacmool Conference, University of Calgary.

1989   Nutritional Deficiency Diseases: A Survey of Scurvy, Rickets, and Iron-Deficiency Anemia. In: *Reconstruction of Life from the Skeleton*, Mehmet Y. Işcan and Kenneth A. R. Kennedy, eds., pp. 201–222. New York: Alan R. Liss, Inc.

1992a   Porotic Hyperostosis: A New Perspective. *American Journal of Physical Anthropology* 87(1):39–47.

1992b   Anemia in Past Human Populations. In: *Diet, Demography, and Disease: Changing Perspectives on Anemia*, Patricia Stuart-Macadam and Susan Kent, eds., pp. 151–170. New York: Aldine de Gruyter.

1998   Iron Deficiency Anemia: Exploring the Difference. In: *Sex and Gender in Paleopathological Perspective*, Anne L. Grauer and Patricia Stuart-Macadam, eds., pp. 45–63. Cambridge: Cambridge University Press.

Suchey, Judy M., and Sheilagh T. Brooks

1986a   *Instruction for Use of Suchey-Brooks System for Age Determination of the Male Os Pubis (instructional materials accompanying male pubic symphyseal models of the Suchey-Brooks System)*. Distributed by France Casting: Diane France, 2190 West Drake Road, Suite 259, Fort Collins, Colo. 80526.

1986b   *Instruction for Use of Suchey-Brooks System for Age Determination of the Female Os Pubis (instructional materials accompanying female pubic symphyseal models of the Suchey-Brooks System)*. Distributed by France Casting: Diane France, 2190 West Drake Road, Suite 259, Fort Collins, Colo. 80526.

Sullivan, Charles H., and Harold W. Krueger

1981   Carbon Isotope Analysis of Separate Chemical Phases in Modern and Fossil Bone. *Nature* 292:332–333.

Sumner, D. R.

1985   A Probable Case of Prehistoric Tuberculosis from Northeastern Arizona. In: *Health and Disease in the Prehistoric Southwest*, Charles F. Merbs and Robert J. Miller, eds., pp. 340–346. Tempe: Arizona State University, Anthropological Research Papers, No. 34.

Sutton, David

1980   *A Textbook of Radiology and Imaging* (2 vols.). London: Churchill Livingstone.

Sutton, Mark Q.

1984   The Productivity of *Pinus monophylla* and Modeling Great Basin Subsistence Strategies. *Journal of California and Great Basin Anthropology* 6(2):240–246.

1988a   Dental Modification in a Burial from the Southern San Joaquin Valley, California. In: *Human Skeletal Biology: Contributions to the Understanding of California's Prehistoric Populations*, Gary D. Richards, ed., pp. 91–96. Salinas: Coyote Press Archives of California Prehistory, No. 24.

1988b   *Insects as Food: Aboriginal Entomophagy in the Great Basin*. Menlo Park, Calif.: Ballena Press Anthropological Papers, No. 33.

1988c   Test Excavations at CA-RIV-2827. In: *Archaeological Investigations at CA-RIV-1179, CA-RIV-2823, and CA-RIV-2827, La Quinta, Riverside County, California*, Mark Q. Sutton and Philip J. Wilke, eds., pp. 21–35. Salinas: Coyote Press Archives of California Prehistory, No. 20.

1990   Insect Resources and Plio-Pleistocene Hominid Evolution. In: *Ethnobiology: Implications and Applications, Proceedings of the First International Congress of Ethnobiology (Belém, 1988), Vol. 1*, Darrell A. Posey, William Leslie Overal, Charles R. Clement, Mark J. Plotkin, Elaine Elisabetsky, Clarice Novaes de Mota, and José Flàvio Pessôa de Barros, eds., pp. 195–207. Belém, Brazil: Museu Paraense Emílio Goeldi.

1993   Midden and Coprolite Derived Subsistence Evidence: An Analysis of Data from the La Quinta Site, Salton Basin, California. *Journal of Ethnobiology* 13(1):1–15.

1994   Indirect Evidence in Paleonutrition Studies. In: *Paleonutrition: The Diet and Health of Prehistoric Americans*, Kristin D. Sobolik, ed., pp. 98–111. Carbondale: Southern Illinois University, Center for Archaeological Investigations, Occasional Paper No. 22.

1995   Archaeological Aspects of Insect Use. *Journal of Archaeological Method and Theory* 2(3):253–298.

1998   Cluster Analysis of Paleofecal Data Sets: A Test of Late Prehistoric Settlement and Subsistence Patterns in the Northern Coachella Valley, California. *American Antiquity* 63(1):86–107.

Sutton, Mark Q., and E. N. Anderson
2010   *Introduction to Cultural Ecology* (2nd ed.). Walnut Creek, Calif.: AltaMira Press.

Sutton, Mark Q., and Karl J. Reinhard
1995   Cluster Analysis of the Coprolites from Antelope House: Implications for Anasazi Diet and Cuisine. *Journal of Archaeological Science* 22(6):741–750.

Sutton, Mark Q., and Philip J. Wilke (eds.)
1988   *Archaeological Investigations at CA-RIV-1179, CA-RIV-2823, and CA-RIV-2827, La Quinta, Riverside County, California.* Salinas: Coyote Press Archives of California Prehistory, No. 20.

Sutton, Mark Q., and Robert M. Yohe II
1988   Terrestrial and Avian Faunal Remains from CA-RIV-1179. In: *Archaeological Investigations at CA-RIV-1179, CA-RIV-2823, and CA-RIV-2827, La Quinta, Riverside County, California,* Mark Q. Sutton and Philip J. Wilke, eds., pp. 103–117. Salinas: Coyote Press Archives of California Prehistory, No. 20.

Sutton, Mark Q., Joan S. Schneider, and Robert M. Yohe II
1993   *The Siphon Site (CA-SBR-6580): A Millingstone Horizon Site in the Summit Valley, California.* San Bernardino County Museum Association Quarterly 40(3).

Sutton, Mark Q., Minnie Malik, and Andrew Ogram
1996   Experiments on the Determination of Gender from Coprolites by DNA Analysis. *Journal of Archaeological Science* 23(2):263–267.

Sutton, Mark Q., Rebecca S. Orfila, Bruno Huerta, and Patricia Martz
2006   Analysis of Possible Paleofecal Samples from Pellejo Chico Alto, Peru: Results and Lessons. *Journal of Archaeological Science* 33(11):1600–1604.

Swedlund, A. C.
1969   Human Skeletal Material from the Yellowjacket Canyon Area, Southwestern Colorado. Master's thesis, Department of Anthropology, University of Colorado, Boulder.

Swope, Karen K.
1988   Plant Remains Recovered by Flotation from CA-RIV-1179. In: *Archaeological Investigations at CA-RIV-1179, CA-RIV-2823, and CA-RIV-2827, La Quinta, Riverside County, California,* Mark Q. Sutton and Philip J. Wilke, eds., pp. 37–52. Salinas: Coyote Press Archives of California Prehistory, No. 20.

Symmons, Robert
2004   Digital Photodensitometry: A Reliable and Accessible Method for Measuring Bone Density. *Journal of Archaeological Science* 31(6):711–719.

Tafuri, Mary Anne, R. Alexander Bentley, Giorgio Manzi, and Savino di Lernia
2006   Mobility and Kinship in the Prehistoric Sahara: Strontium Isotope Analysis of Holocene Human Skeletons from the Acacus Mts. (Southwestern Libya). *Journal of Anthropological Archaeology* 25(3):390–402.

Tapp, E., P. Stansworth, and K. Wildsmith
1984   The Endoscope in Mummy Research. In: *Evidence Embalmed: Modern Medicine and the Mummies of Ancient Egypt,* Rosalie David and Eddie Tapp, eds., pp. 65–77. Manchester: Manchester University Press.

Tauber, Henrik

1981   ¹³C Evidence for Dietary Habits of Prehistoric Man in Denmark. *Nature* 292:332–333.

Tayles, N., K. Domett, and K. Nelsen

2000   Agriculture and Dental Caries? The Case of Rice in Prehistoric Southeast Asia. *World Archaeology* 32(1):68–83.

Taylor, C. B., and K.-J. Ho

1971   Studies on the Masai. *American Journal of Clinical Nutrition* 24:1291–1293.

Taylor, E. L.

1955   Parasitic Helminths in Medieval Remains. *Veterinary Record* 67:216–218.

Taylor, G. Michael, Mary Crossey, John Saldanha, and Tony Waldron

1996   DNA from *Mycobacterium tuberculosis* Identified in Mediaeval Human Skeletal Remains Using Polymerase Chain Reaction. *Journal of Archaeological Science* 23(5):789–798.

Taylor, G. Michael, Stephanie Widdison, Ivor N. Brown, and Douglas B. Young

2000   A Mediaeval Case of Lepromatous Leprosy from 13–14th Century Orkney, Scotland. *Journal of Archaeological Science* 27(12):1133–1138.

Taylor, G. Michael, Simon Mays, A. J. Legge, T.B.L. Ho, and Douglas B. Young

2001   Genetic Analysis of Tuberculosis in Human Remains. *Ancient Biomolecules* 3(4):267–280.

Taylor, M. G.

1985   The Paleopathology of a Southern Sinagua Population from Oak Creek Pueblo, Arizona. In: *Health and Disease in the Prehistoric Southwest*, Charles F. Merbs and R. Miller, eds., pp. 115–118. Tempe: Arizona State University, Anthropological Research Papers, No. 34.

Taylor, T. G., and N. K. Jenkins (eds.)

1986   *Proceedings of the Thirteenth International Congress of Nutrition: 1985*. London: John Libbey & Company.

Taylor, Walter W., Jr.

1948   *A Study of Archaeology*. Arlington, Va.: American Anthropological Association, Memoir No. 69.

Teaford, Mark F.

1991   Dental Microwear: What Can It Tell Us about Diet and Dental Function? In: *Advances in Dental Anthropology*, Marc A. Kelley and Clark Spencer Larsen, eds., pp. 341–356. New York: Wiley-Liss.

Teaford, Mark F., Clark Spencer Larsen, Robert F. Pastor, and Vivian E. Noble

2001   Pits and Scratches: Microscopic Evidence of Tooth Use and Masticatory Behavior in La Florida. In: *Bioarchaeology of Spanish Florida: The Impact of Colonialism*, Clark Spencer Larsen, ed., pp. 82–112. Gainesville: University of Florida Press.

Telkkä, A.

1950   On the Prediction of Human Stature from the Long Bones. *Acta Anatomica* 9:103–117.

Tenney, James M.

1991   Identification and Study of Carcinoma in Paleopathological Material: Present Status and Future Directions. In: *Human Paleopathology: Current Syntheses and*

Future Options, Donald J. Ortner and Arthur C. Aufderheide, eds., pp. 261–265. Washington, D.C.: Smithsonian Institution Press.

Thomas, David Hurst

1969   Great Basin Hunting Patterns: A Quantitative Method for Treating Faunal Remains. *American Antiquity* 34(4):392–401.

1971   Prehistoric Subsistence-Settlement Patterns of the Reese River Valley, Central Nevada. Ph.D. dissertation, University of California, Davis.

1972   A Computer Simulation Model of Great Basin Shoshonean Subsistence and Settlement Patterns. In: *Models in Archaeology*, David L. Clarke, ed., pp. 671–704. London: Methuen.

1973   An Empirical Test for Steward's Model of Great Basin Settlement Patterns. *American Antiquity* 38(2):155–176.

1983   *The Archaeology of Monitor Valley. 2: Gatecliff Shelter*. New York: American Museum of Natural History, Anthropological Papers 59(1).

Thomas, Kenneth D.

1993   Molecular Biology and Archaeology: A Prospectus for Inter-Disciplinary Research. *World Archaeology* 25(1):1–17.

Thompson, Alexandra H., Michael P. Richards, Andrew Shortland, and Sonia R. Zakrzewski

2005   Isotopic Palaeodiet Studies of Ancient Egyptian Fauna and Humans. *Journal of Archaeological Science* 32(3):451–463.

Thompson, G. B.

1994   Wood Charcoals from Tropical Sites: A Contribution to Methodology and Interpretation. In: *Tropical Archaeobotany: Applications and New Developments*, Jon G. Hather, ed., pp. 9–33. London: Routledge.

Thompson, Robert G.

2006   Documenting the Presence of Maize in Central and South America through Phytolith Analysis of Food Residues. In: *Documenting Domestication: New Genetic and Archaeological Paradigms*, Melinda A. Zeder, Daniel G. Bradley, Eve Emshwiller, and Bruce D. Smith, eds., pp. 82–95. Berkeley: University of California Press.

Thuesen, Ingolf

1995   Paleogenetics: DNA for the Archaeologist. In: *Science in Archaeology: A Review*, by Patrick E. McGovern, pp. 136–139. American Journal of Archaeology 99(1):79–142.

Thuesen, Ingolf, and Jan Engberg

1990   Recovery and Analysis of Human Genetic Material from Mummified Tissue and Bone. *Journal of Archaeological Science* 17(6):679–689.

Thuesen, Ingolf, Jan Engberg, and Henrik Nielson

1995   Ancient DNA from a Very Cold and a Very Hot Place. In: *Proceedings of the First World Congress on Mummy Studies*, Vol. 2, pp. 561–568. Museo Arqueológico y Etnográfico de Tenerife.

Tieszen, Larry L.

1991 Natural Variations in the Carbon Isotope Values of Plants: Implications for Archaeology, Ecology, and Paleoecology. *Journal of Archaeological Science* 18(3):227–248.

1994 Stable Isotopes on the Plains: Vegetation Analysis and Diet Determinations. In: *Skeletal Biology in the Great Plains: Migration, Warfare, Health, and Subsistence,* Douglas W. Owsley and Richard L. Jantz, eds., pp. 261–282. Washington, D.C.: Smithsonian Institution Press.

Tieszen, Larry L., and T. W. Boutton

1989 Stable Carbon Isotopes in Terrestrial Ecosystem Research. In: *Stable Isotopes in Ecological Research,* P. W. Rundel, J. R. Ehleringer, and K. A. Nagy, eds., pp. 167–195. Berlin: Springer-Verlag.

Tieszen, Larry L., and Michael Chapman

1995 Carbon and Nitrogen Isotopic Status of the Major Marine and Terrestrial Resources in the Atacama Desert of Northern Chile. In: *Proceedings of the First World Congress on Mummy Studies,* Vol. 1, pp. 409–425. Museo Arqueológico y Etnográfico de Tenerife.

Tieszen, Larry L., and Tim Fagre

1993a Effect of Diet Quality and Composition on the Isotopic Composition of Respiratory CO_2, Bone Collagen, Bioapatite, and Soft Tissues. In: *Prehistoric Human Bone: Archaeology at the Molecular Level,* Joseph B. Lambert and Gisela Grupe, eds., pp. 121–155. Berlin: Springer-Verlag.

1993b Carbon Isotopic Variability in Modern and Archaeological Maize. *Journal of Archaeological Science* 20(1):25–40.

Tieszen, Larry L., Steven Matzner, and Sandra K. Buseman

1995a Dietary Reconstruction Based on Stable Isotopes (¹³C, ¹⁵N) of the Guanche, Pre-Hispanic Tenerife, Canary Islands. In: *Proceedings of the First World Congress on Mummy Studies,* Vol. 1, pp. 41–57. Museo Arqueológico y Etnográfico de Tenerife.

Tieszen, Larry L., Elusha Iverson, and Steven Matzner

1995b Dietary Reconstruction Based on Carbon, Nitrogen, and Sulfur Stable Isotopes in the Atacama Desert, Northern Chile. In: *Proceedings of the First World Congress on Mummy Studies,* Vol. 1, pp. 427–441. Museo Arqueológico y Etnográfico de Tenerife.

Titche, Leon L., Stanley W. Coulthard, Richard D. Wachter, A. Cole Thies, and Lucy L. Harries

1981 Prevalence of Mastoid Infection in Prehistoric Arizona Indians. *American Journal of Physical Anthropology* 56(3):269–273.

Tocheri, Matthew W., and J. Eldon Molto

2002 Aging Fetal and Juvenile Skeletons from Roman Period Egypt Using Basiocciput Osteometrics. *International Journal of Osteoarchaeology* 12(5):356–363.

Tomczak, Paula D.

2003 Prehistoric Diet and Socioeconomic Relationships within the Osmore Valley of Southern Peru. *Journal of Anthropological Archaeology* 22(3):262–278.

Tomczýnska, Zofia

1989   Identification of Charcoal Fragments from Late Paleolithic Sites in Wadi Kub-
        baniya. In: *The Prehistory of Wadi Kubbaniya. Vol. 2: Stratigraphy, Paleoeconomy,
        and Environment*, Fred Wendorf, Romuald Schild, and Angela E. Close, eds.,
        pp. 252–259. Dallas: Southern Methodist University.

Tomlinson, Philippa

1985   Use of Vegetative Remains in the Identification of Dyeplants from Water-
        logged 9th–10th Century AD Deposits at York. *Journal of Archaeological Science*
        12(4):269–283.

Toots, Heinrich, and M. R. Voorhies

1965   Strontium in Fossil Bones and the Reconstruction of Food Chains. *Science*
        149:854–855.

Torroni, Antonio, Theodore G. Schurr, Chi-Chuan Yang, Emöke J. E. Szathmary,
        Robert C. Williams, Moses S. Schanfield, Gary A. Troup, William C. Knowler,
        Dale N. Lawrence, Kenneth M. Weiss, and Douglas C. Wallace

1992   Native American Mitochondrial DNA Analysis Indicates that the Amerind and
        the Nadene Populations Were Founded by Two Independent Migrations. *Genet-
        ics* 130(1):153–162.

Torroni, Antonio, Marie T. Lott, Margaret F. Cabell, Yu-Sheng Chen, Leo Lavergne, and
        Douglas C. Wallace

1994   mtDNA and the Origin of Caucasians: Identification of Ancient Caucasian-
        Specific Haplogroups, One of Which Is Prone to a Recurrent Somatic Duplication
        in the D-Loop Region. *American Journal of Human Genetics* 55(4):760–776.

Trigg, Heather B., Richard I. Ford, John G. Moore, and Louise D. Jessop

1994   Coprolite Evidence for Prehistoric Foodstuffs, Condiments, and Medicines. In: *Eat-
        ing on the Wild Side: The Pharmacologic, Ecological, and Social Implications of Using
        Noncultigens*, Nina L. Etkin, ed., pp. 210–223. Tuscon: University of Arizona Press.

Trombold, Charles D., and Isabel Israde-Alcantara

2005   Paleoenvironment and Plant Cultivation on Terraces at La Quemada, Zacatecas,
        Mexico: The Pollen, Phytolith and Diatom Evidence. *Journal of Archaeological
        Science* 32(3):341–353.

Trotter, Mildred

1970   Estimation of Stature from Intact Limb Bones. In: *Personal Identification in Mass
        Disasters*, T. D. Stewart, ed., pp. 79–125. Washington, D.C.: Smithsonian Institution.

Trotter, Mildred, and G. C. Gleser

1958   A Re-evaluation of Estimation of Stature Based on Measurements of Stature
        Taken during Life and of Long Bones after Death. *American Journal of Physical
        Anthropology* 16:79–123.

Tsartsidou, Georgia, Simcha Lev-Yadun, Rosa-Maria Albert, Arlene Miller-Rosen, Nikos
        Efstratiou, and Steve Weiner

2007   The Phytolith Archaeological Record: Strengths and Weaknesses Evaluated
        Based on a Quantitative Modern Reference Collection from Greece. *Journal of
        Archaeological Science* 34(8):1262–1275.

Tubbs, Deborah Y., and Rainer Berger

1967   The Viability of Pathogens in Ancient Human Coprolites. *Reports of the University of California Archaeological Survey* 70:89–92.

Turkel, Spencer Jay

1989   Congenital Abnormalities in Skeletal Populations. In: *Reconstruction of Life from the Skeleton*, Mehmet Y. Işcan and Kenneth A. R. Kennedy, eds., pp. 109–127. New York: Alan R. Liss, Inc.

Turnbull, Colin M.

1966   *Wayward Servants: The Two Worlds of the African Pygmies.* London: Eyre and Spottiswoode.

Turner, B. L., J. L. Edwards, E. A. Quinn, J. D. Kingston, and D. P. Van Gerven

2006   Age-Related Variation in Isotopic Indicators of Diet at Medieval Kulubnarti, Sudanese Nubia. *International Journal of Osteoarchaeology* 17(1):1–25.

Turner, Christy G., II

1979   Dental Anthropological Indications of Agriculture among the Jomon People of Central Japan. *American Journal of Physical Anthropology* 51(4):619–636.

Turner, Christy G., II, and Jacqueline A. Turner

1999   *Man Corn: Cannibalism and Violence in the Prehistoric American Southwest.* Salt Lake City: University of Utah Press.

Turnlund, Judith R., and Phyllis E. Johnson (eds.)

1984   *Stable Isotopes in Nutrition.* Washington, D.C.: American Chemical Society Symposium Series 258.

Tuross, Noreen

1991   Recovery of Bone and Serum Proteins from Human Skeletal Tissue: IgG, Osteonectin, and Albumin. In: *Human Paleopathology: Current Syntheses and Future Options*, Donald J. Ortner and Arthur C. Aufderheide, eds., pp. 51–54. Washington, D.C.: Smithsonian Institution Press.

1993   The Other Molecules in Ancient Bone: Noncollagenous Proteins and DNA. In: *Prehistoric Human Bone: Archaeology at the Molecular Level*, Joseph B. Lambert and Gisela Grupe, eds., pp. 275–292. Berlin: Springer-Verlag.

Tuross, Noreen, and Tom D. Dillehay

1995   The Mechanism of Organic Preservation at Monte Verde, Chile, and One Use of Biomolecules in Archaeological Interpretation. *Journal of Field Archaeology* 22(1):97–110.

Tuross, Noreen, Anna K. Behrensmeyer, and E. D. Evans

1989   Strontium Increases and Crystallinity Changes in Taphonomic and Archaeological Bone. *Journal of Archaeological Science* 16(6):661–672.

Tuross, Noreen, Marilyn L. Fogel, Lee Newsom, and Glen H. Doran

1994   Subsistence in the Florida Archaic: The Stable-Isotope and Archaeobotanical Evidence from the Windover Site. *American Antiquity* 59(2):288–303.

Tuross, Noreen, Ian Barnes, and Richard Potts

1996   Protein Identification of Blood Residues on Experimental Stone Tools. *Journal of Archaeological Science* 23(2):289–296.

Tykot, Richard H., Nikolaas J. van der Merwe, and Norman Hammond
1996   Stable Isotope Analysis of Bone Collagen, Bone Apatite, and Tooth Enamel in the Reconstruction of Human Diet. In: *Archaeological Chemistry*, Mary Virginia Orna, ed., pp. 355–365. Washington, D.C.: American Chemical Society Symposium Series 625.

Tyree, E. Loeta
2000   Using Phytoliths to Identify Plant Remains from Archaeological Sites: A Phytolith Analysis of Modern Olive Oil and Wine Sediment. In: *Palaeodiet in the Aegean*, Sarah J. Vaughan and William D. E. Coulson, eds., pp. 29–36. Oxford: Oxbow Books.

Ubelaker, Douglas H.
1974   *Reconstruction of Demographic Profiles from Ossuary Skeletal Samples: A Case Study from the Tidewater Potomac.* Washington, D.C.: Smithsonian Contributions to Anthropology, No. 18.
1982   The Development of American Paleopathology. In: *A History of American Physical Anthropology 1930–1980*, F. Spencer, ed., pp. 337–356. New York: Academic Press.

Ubelaker, Douglas H., and Douglas W. Owsley
2003   Isotopic Evidence for Diet in the Seventeenth-Century Colonial Chesapeake. *American Antiquity* 68(1):129–139.

Ubelaker, Douglas H., M. Anne Katzenberg, and L. G. Doyon
1995   Status and Diet in Precontact Highland Ecuador. *American Journal of Physical Anthropology* 97(4):403–411.

Ugent, Donald
1994   Chemosystematics in Archaeology: A Preliminary Study of the Use of Chromatography and Spectrophotometry in the Identification of Four Prehistoric Root Crop Species from the Desert Coast of Peru. In: *Tropical Archaeobotany: Applications and New Developments*, Jon G. Hather, ed., pp. 215–226. London: Routledge.

Umlauf, Marcelle
1993   Phytolith Evidence for Initial Period Maize at Cardal, Central Coast of Peru. In: *Current Research in Phytolith Analysis: Applications in Archaeology and Paleoecology*, Deborah M. Pearsall and Dolores R. Piperno, eds., pp. 125–129. Philadelphia: University of Pennsylvania, University Museum of Archaeology and Anthropology, MASCA Research Papers in Science and Archaeology, Vol. 10.

U.S. Department of Agriculture
1974   Seeds of Woody Plants in the United States. Washington, D.C.: U.S. Department of Agriculture, Forest Service Agricultural Handbook No. 450.

Vahey, Thomas, and David Brown
1984   Comely Wenuhotep: Computed Tomography of an Egyptian Mummy. *Journal of Computer Assisted Tomography* 8(5):992–997.

Valentin, F., Hervé Bocherens, B. Gratuze, and C. Sand
2006   Dietary Patterns during the Late Prehistoric/Historic Period in Cikobia Island (Fiji): Insights from Stable Isotopes and Dental Pathologies. *Journal of Archaeological Science* 33(10):1396–1410.

van Cleave, Harley J., and Jean A. Ross

1947   A Method for Reclaiming Dried Zoological Specimens. *Science* 105:318.

van de Guchte, Margaret, and Richard Edging

1994   Plants and People: An Introduction to Paleoethnobotany. In: *Ancient Technolo-gies and Archaeological Materials*, Sarah U. Wisseman and Wendell S. Williams, eds., pp. 99–119. Amsterdam: Gordon and Breach.

van der Merwe, Nikolaas J.

1982   Carbon Isotopes, Photosynthesis, and Archaeology. *American Scientist* 70(6): 596–606.

1989   Natural Variation in ¹³C Concentration and Its Effect on Environmental Reconstruc-tion Using ¹³C/¹⁴C Ratios in Animal Bones. In: *The Chemistry of Prehistoric Human Bone*, T. Douglas Price, ed., pp. 105–125. Cambridge: Cambridge University Press.

van der Merwe, Nikolaas J., and J. C. Vogel

1978   ¹³C Content of Human Collagen as a Measure of Prehistoric Diet in Woodland North America. *Nature* 276:815–816.

van der Merwe, Nikolaas J., Anna Curtenius Roosevelt, and J. C. Vogel

1981   Isotopic Evidence for Prehistoric Subsistence Change at Parmana, Venezuela. *Nature* 292:536–538.

van der Merwe, Nikolaas J., Julia A. Lee-Thorp, and J. Scott Raymond

1993   Light, Stable Isotopes and the Subsistence Base of Formative Cultures at Valdivia, Ecuador. In: *Prehistoric Human Bone: Archaeology at the Molecular Level*, Joseph B. Lambert and Gisela Grupe, eds., pp. 63–97. Berlin: Springer-Verlag.

van der Merwe, Nikolaas J., Robert H. Tykot, Norman Hammond, and Kim Oakberg

2000   Diet and Animal Husbandry of the Preclassic Maya at Cuello, Belize: Isotopic and Zooarchaeological Evidence. In: *Biogeochemical Approaches to Paleodietary Analysis*, Stanley H. Ambrose and M. Anne Katzenberg, eds., pp. 23–38. New York: Kluwer Academic/Plenum Publishers.

van der Merwe, Nikolaas J., Ronald F. Williamson, Susan Pfeiffer, Stephen Cox Thomas, and Kim Oakberg Allegretto

2003   The Moatfield Ossuary: Isotopic Dietary Analysis of an Iroquoian Community, Using Dental Tissue. *Journal of Anthropological Archaeology* 22(3):245–261.

Van Gerven, Dennis P., Mary K. Sandford, and James R. Hummert

1981   Mortality and Culture Change in Nubia's Batn el Hajar. *Journal of Human Evo-lution* 10(5):395–408.

Vanhaeren, Marian, Francesco d'Errico, Isabelle Billy, and Francis Grousset

2004   Tracing the Source of Upper Palaeolithic Shell Beads by Strontium Isotope Dat-ing. *Journal of Archaeological Science* 31(10):1481–1488.

van Klinken, Gert J.

1999   Bone Collagen Quality Indicators for Palaeodietary and Radiocarbon Measure-ments. *Journal of Archaeological Science* 26(6):687–695.

van Klinken, Gert J., Michael P. Richards, and Robert E. M. Hedges

2000   An Overview of Causes for Stable Isotopic Variations in Past European Human Pop-ulations: Environmental, Ecophysiological, and Cultural Effects. In: *Biogeochemical*

Approaches to Paleodietary Analysis, Stanley H. Ambrose and M. Anne Katzenberg, eds., pp. 39–63. New York: Kluwer Academic/Plenum Publishers.

van Zeist, W.

1988   Some Aspects of Early Neolithic Plant Husbandry in the Near East. *Anatolia* 15:49–67.

van Zeist, W., K. Wasylikowa, and K. E. Behre

1991   *Progress in Old World Palaeoethnobotany*. Rotterdam: A. A. Balkema.

van Zwanenberg, R. M.

1976   Dorobo Hunting and Gathering: A Way of Life or a Mode of Production? *African Economic History* 2:12–21.

Vargas-Sanders, R., Z. Salazar, and M. C. Enriquez

1996   Ancient Nucleic Acids in Prehispanic Mexican Populations. In: *Archaeological Chemistry: Organic, Inorganic, and Biochemical Analysis*, Mary Virginia Orna, ed., pp. 391–400. Washington, D.C.: American Chemical Society Symposium Series 625.

Verano, John W., and Michael J. DeNiro

1993   Locals or Foreigners? Morphological, Biometric, and Isotopic Approaches to the Question of Group Affinity in Human Skeletal Remains Recovered from Unusual Archaeological Contexts. In: *Investigations of Ancient Human Tissue: Chemical Analyses in Anthropology*, Mary K. Sandford, ed., pp. 361–386. Langhorne, Penn.: Gordon and Breach.

Verano, John W., and Douglas H. Ubelaker (eds.)

1992   *Disease and Demography in the Americas*. Washington, D.C.: Smithsonian Institution Press.

Virchow, R.

1896   Heredity and the Formation of Race. Translated and reprinted in *This Is Race* (1950), E. W. Count, ed., pp. 178–193. New York: Schuman.

Vogel, J. C., and Nikolaas J. van der Merwe

1977   Isotopic Evidence for Early Maize Cultivation in New York State. *American Antiquity* 42(2):238–242.

Von Endt, David W., and Donald J. Ortner

1982   Amino Acid Analysis of Bone from a Suspected Case of Prehistoric Iron Deficiency Anemia. *American Journal of Physical Anthropology* 59(4):377–385.

von Hunnius, Tanya E., Charlotte A. Roberts, Anthea Boylston, and Shelley R. Saunders

2005   Histological Identification of Syphilis in Pre-Columbian England. *American Journal of Physical Anthropology* 129(4):559–566.

Voorhies, M. R.

1969   *Taphonomy and Population Dynamics of an Early Pliocene Vertebrate Fauna, Krox County, Nebraska*. Contributions to Geology, Special Paper 1:69.

Vuorinen, Heikki S., Unto Tapper, and Helena Mussalo-Rauhamaa

1990   Trace and Heavy Metals in Infants: Analysis of Long Bones from Ficana, Italy, 8–6th Century BC. *Journal of Archaeological Science* 17(3):237–254.

Vyhnanek, Lubos, and Milan Stoukal

1991   Harris Lines in Adults: An Open Problem. In: *Human Paleopathology: Current Syntheses and Future Options*, Donald J. Ortner and Arthur C. Aufderheide, eds., pp. 92–94. Washington, D.C.: Smithsonian Institution Press.

Wade, William Dexter

1970   *Skeletal Remains of a Prehistoric Population from the Puerco Valley, Eastern Arizona*. Denver: University of Colorado Press.

Wadsworth, G. R.

1992   Physiological, Pathological, and Dietary Influences on the Hemoglobin Level. In: *Diet, Demography, and Disease: Changing Perspectives on Anemia*, Patricia Stuart-Macadam and Susan Kent, eds., pp. 63–104. New York: Aldine de Gruyter.

Wakefield, E. F., and Samuel C. Dellinger

1936   Diet of the Bluff Dwellers of the Ozark Mountains and Its Skeletal Effects. *Annals of Internal Medicine* 9(10):1412–1418.

Waldron, Tony

2007   *Paleoepidemiology of Human Remains*. Walnut Creek, Calif.: Left Coast Press.

Wales, S., and J. Evans

1988   New Possibilities of Obtaining Archaeological Information from Coprolites. In: *Science and Archaeology, Glasgow 1987*, Elizabeth A. Slater and James O. Tate, eds., pp. 403–412. Oxford: British Archaeological Reports, International Series, No. 196 (2 vols.).

Wales, S., J. Evans, and A. R. Leeds

1991   The Survival of Waxes in Coprolites: The Archaeological Potential. In: *Archaeological Sciences 1989*, Paul Budd, Barbara Chapman, Caroline Jackson, Rob Janaway, and Barbara Ottaway, eds., pp. 340–344. Oxford: Oxbow Monograph 9.

Walker, A.

1981   Diet and Teeth: Dietary Hypotheses and Human Evolution. *Philosophical Transactions of the Royal Society of London* 292:57–64.

Walker, Phillip L.

1978   A Quantitative Analysis of Dental Attrition Rates in the Santa Barbara Channel Area. *American Journal of Physical Anthropology* 48(1):101–106.

1985   Anemia among Prehistoric Indians of the American Southwest. In: *Health and Disease in the Prehistoric Southwest*, Charles F. Merbs and Robert J. Miller, eds., pp. 139–164. Tempe: Arizona State University, Anthropological Research Papers, No. 34.

2001   A Bioarchaeological Perspective on the History of Violence. *Annual Review of Anthropology* 30:573–596.

Walker, Phillip L., and Michael J. DeNiro

1986   Stable Carbon and Nitrogen Isotope Ratios in Bone Collagen as Indices of Prehistoric Dietary Dependence on Marine and Terrestrial Resources in Southern California. *American Journal of Physical Anthropology* 71(1):51–61.

Walker, Phillip L., and Jon M. Erlandson

1986   Dental Evidence for Prehistoric Dietary Change on the Northern Channel Islands, California. *American Antiquity* 51(2):375–383.

Walker, Phillip L., Gregory Dean, and Perry Shapiro

1991   Estimating Age from Tooth Wear in Archaeological Populations. In: *Advances in Dental Anthropology*, Marc A. Kelley and Clark Spencer Larsen, eds., pp. 169–178. New York: Wiley-Liss.

Wall, Diana diZerega

1994   *The Archaeology of Gender: Separating the Spheres in Urban America*. New York: Plenum Press.

Wallgren, J. E., R. Caple, and Arthur C. Aufderheide

1986   Contributions of Nuclear Magnetic Resonance Studies to the Question of Alkaptonuria (Ochronosis) in an Egyptian Mummy. In: *Science in Egyptology*, R. A. David, ed., pp. 321–327. Manchester: Manchester University Press.

Waselkov, Gregory A.

1987   Shellfish Gathering and Shell Midden Archaeology. In: *Advances in Archaeological Method and Theory, Vol. 10*, Michael B. Schiffer, ed., pp. 93–210. New York: Academic Press.

Waters, Michael R.

1983   Late Holocene Lacustrine Chronology and Archaeology of Ancient Lake Cahuilla, California. *Quaternary Research* 19:373–387.

Watson, Patty Jo

1974   Theoretical and Methodological Difficulties in Dealing with Paleofecal Material. In: *Archaeology of the Mammoth Cave Area*, Patty Jo Watson, ed., pp. 239–241. New York: Academic Press.

1976   In Pursuit of Prehistoric Subsistence: A Comparative Account of Some Contemporary Flotation Techniques. *Midcontinental Journal of Archaeology* 1:77–100.

Watt, B. K., and A. L. Merrill

1963   Composition of Foods. Washington, D.C.: U.S. Department of Agriculture, Agricultural Handbook 8.

Webb, Elizabeth A., Henry P. Schwarcz, and Paul F. Healy

2004   Detection of Ancient Maize in Lowland Maya Soils Using Stable Carbon Isotopes: Evidence from Caracol, Belize. *Journal of Archaeological Science* 31(8):1039–1052.

Webb, William S., and Raymond S. Baby

1957   *The Adena People*. Columbus: Ohio State University Press.

Weide, David L.

1976   Summary of Radiometric Dates for the Salton Sink Region. In: *Background to Prehistory of the Yuha Desert Region*, Philip J. Wilke, ed., appendix, pp. 95–97. Ramona, Calif.: Ballena Press Anthropological Papers, No. 5.

Weiss, Elizabeth

2006   Osteoarthritis and Body Mass. *Journal of Archaeological Science* 33(5):690–695.

Wells, Calvin

1960   A Study of Cremations. *Antiquity* 34(133):29–37.

1964   *Bones, Bodies, and Disease: Evidence of Disease and Abnormality in Early Man.* New York: Frederick A. Praeger.

Wendorf, Michael, and Ira D. Goldfine

1991   Perspectives in Diabetes: Archaeology of NIDDM—Excavation of the "Thrifty" Genotype. *Diabetes* 40:161–165.

West, I. E.

1986   Forensic Aspects of Lindow Man. In: *Lindow Man: The Body in the Bog*, I. M. Stead, J. B. Bourke, and Don R. Brothwell, eds., pp. 77–80. Ithaca: Cornell University Press.

Westbroek, Peter, Matthew J. Collins, J. H. Fred Jansen, and Lee M. Talbot

1993   World Archaeology and Global Change: Did Our Ancestors Ignite the Ice Age? *World Archaeology* 25(1):122–133.

Western, A. Cecilia

1970   Wood and Charcoal in Archaeology. In: *Science in Archaeology: A Survey of Progress and Research*, Don R. Brothwell and Eric Higgs, eds., pp. 178–187. New York: Praeger.

Wetterstrom, Wilma

1986   *Food, Diet, and Population at Prehistoric Arroyo Hondo Pueblo, New Mexico.* Arroyo Hondo Archaeological Series, Vol. 6. Santa Fe: School of American Research Press.

Weymouth, John W., and William I. Woods

1984   Combined Magnetic and Chemical Surveys of Forts Kaskaskia and de Chartres Number 1, Illinois. *Historical Archaeology* 18(2):20–37.

Wheat, Joe Ben

1967   A Paleo-Indian Bison Kill. *Scientific American* 216:44–52.

Wheeler, Alwyne, and Andrew K. G. Jones

1989   *Fishes.* Cambridge: Cambridge University Press.

Wheeler, R. L.

1985   Pathology in Late Thirteenth Century Zuni from the El Morro Valley, New Mexico. In: *Health and Disease in the Prehistoric Southwest*, C. Merbs and R. Miller, eds., pp. 79–84. Tempe: Arizona State University, Anthropological Research Papers, No. 34.

White, Christine D.

1988   Diet and Health in the Ancient Maya at Lamanai, Belize. In: *Diet and Subsistence: Current Archaeological Perspectives*, Brenda V. Kennedy and Genevieve M. LeMoine, eds., pp. 288–296. Proceedings of the Nineteenth Annual Chacmool Conference, University of Calgary.

1995   Diet Reconstruction from Nubian Mummy Tissues: Evidence from Stable Carbon and Nitrogen Isotopes. In: *Proceedings of the First World Congress on Mummy Studies*, Vol. 2, pp. 571–578. Museo Arqueológico y Etnográfico de Tenerife.

1999   Introduction. In: *Reconstructing Ancient Maya Diet*, Christine D. White, ed., pp. ix–xxvii. Salt Lake City: University of Utah Press.

White, Christine D., and Henry P. Schwarcz

1989   Ancient Maya Diet: As Inferred from Isotopic and Elemental Analysis of Human Bone. *Journal of Archaeological Science* 16(5):451–474.

1994   Temporal Trends in Stable Isotopes for Nubian Mummy Tissues. *American Journal of Physical Anthropology* 93(2):165–187.

White, Christine D., Michael W. Spence, Fred J. Longstaffe, and Kimberly R. Law

2000   Testing the Nature of Teotihuacán Imperialism at Kaminaljuyú Using Phosphate Oxygen-Isotope Ratios. *Journal of Anthropological Research* 56(4): 535–558.

White, Christine D., Mary E. D. Pohl, Henry P. Schwartz, and Fred J. Longstaffe

2001a   Isotopic Evidence for Maya Patterns of Deer and Dog Use at Preclassic Colha. *Journal of Archaeological Science* 28(1):89–107.

White, Christine D., David M. Pendergast, Fred J. Longstaffe, and Kimberley R. Law

2001b   Social Complexity and Food Systems at Altun Ha, Belize: The Isotopic Evidence. *Latin American Antiquity* 12(4):371–393.

White, Christine D., Fred J. Longstaffe, and Kimberley R. Law

2004a   Exploring the Effects of Environment, Physiology and Diet on Oxygen Isotope Ratios in Ancient Nubian Bones and Teeth. *Journal of Archaeological Science* 31(2):233–250.

White, Christine D., Michael W. Spence, Fred J. Longstaffe, and Kimberly R. Law

2004b   Demography and Ethnic Continuity in the Tlailotlacan Enclave of Teotihuacan: The Evidence from Stable Oxygen Isotopes. *Journal of Anthropological Archaeology* 23(4):385–403.

White, J. W., and N. Hoban

1959   Composition of Honey. IV: Identification of the Disaccharides. *Archives of Biochemistry and Biophysics* 80(2):386–392.

White, J. W., M. L. Riethof, M. H. Subers, and I. Kushnir

1962   Composition of American Honeys. Washington, D.C.: U.S. Department of Agriculture, Technical Bulletin 126.

White, Theodore E.

1953   A Method of Calculating the Dietary Percentage of Various Food Animals Utilized by Aboriginal Peoples. *American Antiquity* 18(4):396–398.

White, Tim D.

1992   *Prehistoric Cannibalism at Mancos 5MUMR-2346*. Princeton: Princeton University Press.

2000   *Human Osteology* (2d ed.). San Diego: Academic Press.

White, Tim D., and Pieter A. Folkens

2005   *The Human Bone Manual*. Amsterdam: Elsevier Academic Press.

Whitehouse, Walter M.

1980   Radiologic Findings in the Royal Mummies. In: *An X-Ray Atlas of the Royal Mummies*, James E. Harris and Edward F. Wente, eds, pp. 286–327. Chicago: University of Chicago Press.

Whitney, W. F.

1886   *Notes on the Anomalies, Injuries, and Diseases of the Bones of the Native People of North America Contained in the Osteological Collection of the Museum.* Cambridge, Mass.: Annual Report of the Peabody Museum 3:433–448.

Whittington, Stephen L.

1999   Caries and Antemortem Tooth Loss at Copán: Implications for Commoner Diet. In: *Reconstructing Ancient Maya Diet*, Christine D. White, ed., pp. 151–167. Salt Lake City: University of Utah Press.

Wiedemann, Felicitas, Hervé Bocherens, André Mariotti, Angela von den Driesch, and Gisela Grupe

1999   Methodological and Archaeological Implications of Intra-tooth Isotopic Variations ($\delta^{13}C$, $\delta^{18}O$) in Herbivores from Ain Ghazal (Jordan, Neolithic). *Journal of Archaeological Science* 26(6):697–704.

Wiener, A. L.

1984   Human Skeletal Remains. In: Delores Archaeological Program, Synthetic Report, David A. Breternitz, ed., pp. 239–248. Denver: U.S. Department of the Interior, Bureau of Reclamation, Engineering and Research Center.

Wilbur, Alicia K.

1998   The Utility of Hand and Foot Bones for the Determination of Sex and the Estimation of Stature in a Prehistoric Population from West-Central Illinois. *International Journal of Osteoarchaeology* 8(3):180–191.

Wilke, Philip J.

1978   *Late Prehistoric Human Ecology at Lake Cahuilla, Coachella Valley, California.* Berkeley: University of California Archaeological Research Facility Contributions, No. 38.

1988   The Natural and Cultural Environment. In: *Archaeological Investigations at CA-RIV-1179, CA-RIV-2823, and CA-RIV-2827, La Quinta, Riverside County, California*, Mark Q. Sutton and Philip J. Wilke, eds., pp. 1–14. Salinas: Coyote Press Archives of California Prehistory, No. 20.

Wilke, Philip J., and Harry W. Lawton

1975   Early Observations on the Cultural Geography of Coachella Valley. In: *The Cahuilla Indians of the Colorado Desert: Ethnohistory and Prehistory*, Lowell J. Bean, ed., pp. 9–43. Ramona, Calif.: Ballena Press Anthropological Papers, No. 3.

Wilke, Philip J., and Mark Q. Sutton

1988   Summary and Inferences. In: *Archaeological Investigations at CA-RIV-1179, CA-RIV-2823, and CA-RIV-2827, La Quinta, Riverside County, California*, Mark Q. Sutton and Philip J. Wilke, eds., pp. 157–164. Salinas: Coyote Press Archives of California Prehistory, No. 20.

Wilke, Philip J., Thomas F. King, and Stephen Hammond

1975   Aboriginal Occupation at Tahquitz Canyon: Ethnohistory and Archaeology. In: *The Cahuilla Indians of the Colorado Desert: Ethnohistory and Prehistory*, Lowell J. Bean, ed., pp. 45–73. Ramona, Calif.: Ballena Press Anthropological Papers, No. 3.

Will, Richard T., and James A. Clark

1996   Stone Artifact Movement on Impoundment Shorelines: A Case Study from Maine. *American Antiquity* 61(3):499–519.

Will, Richard T., James Clark, and Edward Moore

1996   Phase III Archaeological Data Recovery at the Little Ossipee North Site (7.7), Bonny Eagle Project (FERC #2529), Cumberland County, Maine. Augusta, Maine: Report on file at Central Main Power Company.

Williams, D. G., J. B. Coltrain, M. Lott, N. B. English, and J. R. Ehleringer

2005   Oxygen Isotopes in Cellulose Identify Source Water for Archaeological Maize in the American Southwest. *Journal of Archaeological Science* 32(6):931–939.

Williams, D. R., and C. M. Woodhead

1986   "Attrition"—A Contemporary Dental Viewpoint. In: *Teeth and Anthropology*, E. Cruwys and R. A. Foley, eds., pp. 109–121. Oxford: British Archaeological Reports, International Series, No. 291.

Williams, H. U.

1929   Human Paleopathology, with Some Original Observations on Symmetrical Osteoporosis of the Skull. *Archives of Pathology* 7:839–902.

Williams, John A.

1985   Evidence of Hydatid Disease in a Plains Woodland Burial. *Plains Anthropologist* 30(107):25–28.

Williams-Dean, Glenna J.

1978   Ethnobotany and Cultural Ecology of Prehistoric Man in Southwest Texas. Ph.D. dissertation, Texas A&M University, College Station.

1986   Pollen Analysis in Human Coprolites. In: *Archaeological Investigations at Antelope House*, Don P. Morris, ed., pp. 189–205. Washington, D.C.: National Park Service Publications in Archaeology, No. 19.

Williams-Dean, Glenna J., and Vaughn M. Bryant Jr.

1975   Pollen Analysis of Human Coprolites from Antelope House. *Kiva* 41(1):97–111.

Wilson, D. G.

1979   Horse Dung from Roman Lancaster: A Botanical Report. *Archaeo-Physika* 8:331–349.

Wing, Elizabeth S.

1994   The Past, Present, and Future of Paleonutritional Research. In: *Paleonutrition: The Diet and Health of Prehistoric Americans*, Kristin D. Sobolik, ed., pp. 309–317. Carbondale: Southern Illinois University, Center for Archaeological Investigations, Occasional Paper No. 22.

Wing, Elizabeth S., and Antoinette B. Brown

1979   *Paleonutrition: Method and Theory in Prehistoric Foodways*. New York: Academic Press.

Winter, L. C., and C. A. Marlow

1991   Kitchen Chemistry? The Use of Microwaves in the Analysis of Human Bone. In: *Archaeological Sciences 1989*, Paul Budd, Barbara Chapman, Caroline Jackson, Rob Janaway, and Barbara Ottaway, eds., pp. 386–390. Oxford: Oxbow Monograph 9.

Winterhalder, Bruce

1981   Optimal Foraging Strategies and Hunter-Gatherer Research in Anthropology: Theory and Models. In: *Hunter-Gatherer Foraging Strategies: Ethnographic and Archaeological Analyses*, Bruce Winterhalder and Eric Alden Smith, eds., pp. 13–35. Chicago: University of Chicago Press.

Winterhalder, Bruce, and Eric Alden Smith

1992   Evolutionary Ecology and the Social Sciences. In: *Evolutionary Ecology and Human Behavior*, Eric Alden Smith and Bruce Winterhalder, eds., pp. 3–23. New York: Aldine de Gruyter.

Winterhalder, Bruce, and Eric Alden Smith (eds.)

1981   *Hunter-Gatherer Foraging Strategies: Ethnographic and Archaeological Analyses.* Chicago: University of Chicago Press.

Winters, H. D.

1969   *The Riverton Culture: A Second Millennium Occupation in the Central Wabash Valley.* Springfield: Illinois State Museum, Reports of Investigations, No. 13.

Wisseman, Sarah U.

1994   Imaging the Past: Interdisciplinary Analysis of an Egyptian Mummy. In: *Ancient Technologies and Archaeological Materials*, Sarah U. Wisseman and Wendell S. Williams, eds., pp. 217–233. Amsterdam: Gordon and Breach.

Witt, G. Bradd, and Linda K. Ayliffe

2001   Carbon Isotope Variability in the Bone Collagen of Red Kangaroos (*Macropus rufus*) Is Age Dependent: Implications for Paleodietary Studies. *Journal of Archaeological Science* 28(3):247–252.

Wohlgemuth, Eric

1996   Resource Intensification in Prehistoric Central California: Evidence from Archaeobotanical Data. *Journal of California and Great Basin Anthropology* 18(1):81–103.

Wolfe, Susan I., and Mark Q. Sutton

2006   Acorns and Dental Wear in Aboriginal California. *Society for California Archaeology Newsletter* 40(4):31–34.

Wood, James W., George R. Milner, Henry C. Harpending, and Kenneth M. Weiss

1992   The Osteological Paradox: Problems in Inferring Prehistoric Health from Skeletal Samples. *Current Anthropology* 33(4):343–358.

Woods, William I.

1977   The Quantitative Analysis of Soil Phosphate. *American Antiquity* 42(2):248–252.

Wright, Lori E.

1990   Stresses of Conquest: A Study of Wilson Bands and Enamel Hypoplasias in the Maya of Lamanai, Belize. *American Journal of Human Biology* 2(1): 25–35.

2005   Identifying Immigrants to Tikal, Guatemala: Defining Local Variability in Strontium Isotope Ratios of Human Tooth Enamel. *Journal of Archaeological Science* 32(4):555–566.

Wright, Lori E., and Henry P. Schwarcz

1996   Infrared and Isotopic Evidence for Diagenesis of Bone Apatite at Dos Pilas, Guatemala: Paleodietary Implications. *Journal of Archaeological Science* 23(6): 933–944.

1998   Stable Carbon and Oxygen Isotopes in Human Tooth Enamel: Identifying Breastfeeding and Weaning in Prehistory. *American Journal of Physical Anthropology* 106(1):1–18.

1999   Correspondence between Stable Carbon, Oxygen and Nitrogen Isotopes in Human Tooth Enamel and Dentine: Infant Diets at Kaminaljuyú. *Journal of Archaeological Science* 26(9):1159–1170.

Wright, Lori E., and Christine D. White

1996   Human Biology in the Classic Maya Collapse: Evidence from Paleopathology and Paleodiet. *Journal of World Prehistory* 10(2):147–198.

Wright, Lori E., and Cassady J. Yoder

2003   Recent Progress in Bioarchaeology: Approaches to the Osteological Paradox. *Journal of Archaeological Research* 11(1):43–70.

Wright, Patti J.

2003   Preservation or Destruction of Plant Remains by Carbonization? *Journal of Archaeological Science* 30(5):577–583.

2005   Flotation Samples and Some Paleoethnobotanical Implications. *Journal of Archaeological Science* 32(1):19–26.

Wright, Rita P. (ed.)

1996   *Gender and Archaeology*. Philadelphia: University of Pennsylvania Press.

Wylie, Alison

1992   The Interplay of Evidential Constraints and Political Interests: Recent Archaeological Research on Gender. *American Antiquity* 57(1):15–35.

Wyman, J.

1868   *Observations on Crania*. Boston: A. A. Kingman.

Yang, Dongya Y., and Kathy Watt

2005   Contamination Controls When Preparing Archaeological Remains for Ancient DNA Analysis. *Journal of Archaeological Science* 32(3):331–336.

Yarnell, Richard A.

1969   Contents of Human Paleofeces. In: *The Prehistory of Salts Cave, Kentucky*, Patty Jo Watson, ed., pp. 41–54. Springfield: Illinois State Museum, Reports of Investigations, No. 16.

Yesner, David R., Maris Jose Figuerero Torres, Richard A. Guichon, and Luis A. Borrero

2003   Stable Isotope Analysis of Human Bone and Ethnohistoric Subsistence Patterns in Tierra del Fuego. *Journal of Anthropological Archaeology* 22(3): 279–291.

Yoder, Cassady J., Douglas H. Ubelaker, and Joseph F. Powell

2001   Examination of Variation in Sternal Rib End Morphology Relevant to Age Assessment. *Journal of Forensic Sciences* 46(2):223–227.

Yohe, Robert M., II

1990a   Archaeological Investigations at Five Sites Located at One Eleven La Quinta Center in the City of La Quinta, Central Riverside County, California. Report on file at the Eastern Information Center, University of California, Riverside.

1990b   An Analysis of Human Coprolite Remains from Site CA-RIV-3682. In: *Archaeological Investigations at Five Sites Located at One Eleven La Quinta Center in the City of La Quinta, Central Riverside County, California*, Appendix B. Report on file at the Eastern Information Center, University of California, Riverside.

Yohe, Robert M., II, and Linda Scott Cummings

2001   Dental Calculus and Dietary Variability: A Comparison of Multiregional Prehistoric and Historic Samples. Paper presented at the annual meeting of the Society for American Archaeology, New Orleans.

Yohe, Robert M., II, and Jill K. Gardner

2004   Preliminary Report on the Results of Salvage Excavations of Burial Chamber 1 and the North Gate Looter Pit at Tell El-Hibeh, Egypt, 2004 Field Season. Cairo, Egypt: Report on file at the Archaeological Research Center.

Yohe, Robert M., II, Margaret E. Newman, and Joan S. Schneider

1991   Immunological Identification of Small-Mammal Proteins on Aboriginal Milling Equipment. *American Antiquity* 56(4):659–666.

Yoneda, Minoru, Ryo Suzuki, Yasuyuki Shibata, Masatoshi Morita, Tomohiro Sukegawa, Nobuo Shigehara, and Takeru Akazawa

2004   Isotopic Evidence of Inland-Water Fishing by a Jomon Population Excavated from the Boji Site, Nagano, Japan. *Journal of Archaeological Science* 31(1):97–107.

Yoshimura, K., T. Nakahashi, and K. Saito

2006   Why Did the Ancient Inhabitants of Palmyra Suffer Fluorosis? *Journal of Archaeological Science* 33(10):1411–1418.

Young, B. H.

1910   *The Prehistoric Men of Kentucky*. Louisville: Filson Club Publications 25.

Young, Suzanne M. M., and A. Mark Pollard

1997   Spectroscopy in Archaeometry. *Spectroscopy* 12(6):14–21.

Zeder, Melinda A., Daniel G. Bradley, Eve Emshwiller, and Bruce D. Smith (eds.)

2006   *Documenting Domestication: New Genetic and Archaeological Paradigms*. Berkeley: University of California Press.

Zimmerman, Michael R.

1973   Blood Cells Preserved in a Mummy 2000 Years Old. *Science* 180:303–304.

1980   Aleutian and Alaskan Mummies. In: *Mummies, Disease, and Ancient Cultures* (1st ed.), Aidan Cockburn and Eve Cockburn, eds., pp. 118–134. Cambridge: Cambridge University Press.

1998   Aleutian and Alaskan Mummies. In: *Mummies, Disease, and Ancient Cultures* (2d ed.), Aidan Cockburn, Eve Cockburn, and Theodore A. Reyman, eds., pp. 138–153. Cambridge: Cambridge University Press.

Zimmerman, Michael R., Theodore A. Reyman, and William S. Laughlin
1981   The Paleopathology of an Aleutian Mummy. *Archives of Pathology and Laboratory Medicine* 105:638–641.
Zink, A. R., C. Sola, U. Reischl, W. Grabner, N. Rastogi, H. Wolf, and A. G. Nerlich
2004   Molecular Identification and Characterization of *Mycobacterium tuberculosis* Complex in Ancient Egyptian Mummies. *International Journal of Osteoarchaeology* 14(5):404–413.

Index

About the Authors

Mark Q. Sutton began his career in anthropology in 1968. While still in high school, he took advantage of the opportunity to participate in archaeological excavations conducted by the local community college. He went on to earn a B.A. (1972), an M.A. (1977), and a Ph.D. (1987) in anthropology. He has worked as an archaeologist for the U.S. Air Force, the U.S. Bureau of Land Management, and various private consulting firms and taught at a number of community colleges and universities. He taught at California State University, Bakersfield, from 1987 to 2007, where he retired as Emeritus Professor of Anthropology. He now works for Statistical Research, Inc., in San Diego. Dr. Sutton works on understanding hunter-gatherer adaptations to arid environments but has also investigated entomophagy, prehistoric diet and technology, and optimal foraging theory. Dr. Sutton has worked at more than 120 sites in western North America and has published over 160 books, monographs, and papers on archaeology and anthropology.

Kristin D. Sobolik is a Ph.D. from Texas A&M University in College Station, Texas. Her current position is Professor of Anthropology and Climate Change, Chair of the Department of Anthropology, and Associate Director of the Climate Change Institute at the University of Maine in Orono. Dr. Sobolik's main research interests include the analysis of biological remains from archaeological sites. She is currently working in the southern North American deserts and the northeastern United States. Dr. Sobolik has published articles in *Proceedings of the National Academy of Sciences, British Journal of Nutrition, American Journal of Physical Anthropology, Current Anthropology, Quaternary Research,* and *Journal of Field Archaeology,* among others.

Jill K. Gardner is a Ph.D. from the University of Nevada, Las Vegas. Her current position is Principal Investigator for ASM Affiliates, Inc., in Carlsbad, California. Her previous two appointments were Principal Investigator for Statistical Research, Inc., and Associate Director at the Center for Archaeological Research, California State University, Bakersfield. Dr. Gardner's main research areas have included the Mojave Desert, the Great Basin, the southern Sierra Nevada, the southern San Joaquin Valley, and the southern California coast. She has also conducted excavations and analysis of Late Roman/Coptic mummies at Tell El-Hibeh in Egypt and participated in excavations at a Neolithic site in southern Jordan. Her research interests are primarily concerned with hunter-gatherer cultural development, including settlement and subsistence practices, migration patterns, and the role of the environment in social complexity. She has also conducted studies in bioarchaeological techniques and forensic anthropological analysis. Dr. Gardner has published articles in the *Journal of California and Great Basin*

Anthropology, Quaternary Science Reviews, British Archaeological Reports, Pacific Coast Archaeological Society Quarterly, Coyote Press Archives of Great Basin Prehistory, Proceedings of the Society for California Archaeology, and *Nevada State Museum Anthropological Papers,* as well as co-authored books published by the University of Arizona Press and AltaMira Press.